Travel and Trade
in the Middle Ages

ALSO BY PAUL B. NEWMAN
AND FROM MCFARLAND

Growing Up in the Middle Ages (2007)

Daily Life in the Middle Ages (2001)

Travel and Trade
in the Middle Ages

PAUL B. NEWMAN

McFarland & Company, Inc., Publishers

Jefferson, North Carolina, and London

LIBRARY OF CONGRESS CATALOGUING-IN-PUBLICATION DATA

Newman, Paul B.
Travel and trade in the Middle Ages /
Paul B. Newman.
p.   cm.
Includes bibliographical references and index.

ISBN 978-0-7864-4535-6
softcover : 50# alkaline paper ∞

1. Travel, Medieval.   2. Travel — History — 711–1516.
3. Europe — Commerce — History — To 1500.
4. Europe — History — 476–1492.
5. Travelers — Europe — History — To 1500.
6. Pilgrims and pilgrimages — History — To 1500.
I. Title.
GT5240.N48 2011   910.9'02—dc22   2011008409

BRITISH LIBRARY CATALOGUING DATA ARE AVAILABLE

Front cover: *River Transport in Paris* (French manuscript
illumination, c1317 Granger Collection)

Manufactured in the United States of America

*McFarland & Company, Inc., Publishers
Box 611, Jefferson, North Carolina 28640
www.mcfarlandpub.com*

For Mom and Dad

ACKNOWLEDGMENTS

I would like to thank the following institutions which allowed me to use images from their collections: The Burgerbibliothek Bern, the Bibliothèque Nationale de France, the British Library, the Walters Art Museum, and the Courtauld Institute of Art. I am particularly grateful for the assistance of Louisa Dare of the Courtauld Institute for her help in locating the image I needed.

I must also thank the Anne Arundel County Library, especially the Severna Park branch, for obtaining the many books I needed through inter-library loans. I also thank all the libraries and other institutions who shared their collections.

I also thank John Price for his help in deciphering the meaning of "Twärrenbrücke" and for the information he provided on Russian transportation.

Finally and most importantly, I thank my wife Alice for her endless patience and tireless support. Without her, this book would never have been written.

CONTENTS

INTRODUCTION

Apart from a few exceptions such as armies going off on the crusades and hardy merchants seeking out exotic spices, medieval people are often thought of as immobile and root-bound. Admittedly, many people did live out most or all of their lives without ever venturing more than twenty miles or so from their homes. However, throughout the Middle Ages, large numbers of people, from peasants to kings, did travel. Their travel ranged from distances of a few miles to hundreds or even thousands of miles. They traveled by foot, horse, river boat, and ocean-going ships. They experienced great hardships such as severe weather or attacks by bandits or pirates. Still, travel was an essential part of life for many people and was undertaken despite the risks.

As with people, goods, too, had to be moved from one place to another. Merchandise ranging from spices and silks to ordinary foodstuffs and wool had to be carried from producers to consumers. Some were brought to Europe from the distant reaches of Asia while others were shipped just a few miles from farms to nearby cities, but all were a vital part of trade. Again, a variety of means of transportation were used to accomplish this. Europeans used roads, rivers, and seas together to create a transportation network. Admittedly, this network was not the man-made transportation systems of high-speed highways, railroads, and air routes in use today. Still, it served to tie Europe together.

Bringing goods to market was an indispensable part of trade but trade was more in-volved than this might seem. At the simplest level, there was bartering; a farmer could trade his produce directly with a consumer who would give him something of value in exchange. However, even seemingly basic goods, such as grindstones for hand-powered grain mills and grains, were often part of international trade. To bring these goods to the consumer, merchants often engaged in complex transactions, even in the early centuries of the Middle Ages. Purchases from suppliers had to be financed. Safe shipment to markets had to be arranged. Debts had to be collected from customers and from other merchants. Tariffs and taxes had to be paid. Successful merchants in the Middle Ages coped with all these problems and were every bit as shrewd and knowledgeable of market conditions as their modern counterparts.

This book is divided into five sections. The first section addresses the various reasons that medieval Europeans traveled. Some of these motives, such as the pursuit of trade, are still found today while others, such as pilgrimages to shrines, have nearly or completely disappeared. The second section covers land transportation. This involved more than just walking or riding a horse. Bridges, inns, and roads were all vital parts of the transportation network that spanned Europe. In the third section, water transportation is presented in all its forms. From small river barges to the great galleys and sailing ships, these were all used extensively to move cargo and passengers. In the fourth section, the elements of trade are discussed. While it is discussed in passing in the other sections, trade merits a separate examination because it was an essential part of life. Finally, in the fifth section, trade goods and their sources are examined in more detail.

The geographical scope of this book is primarily western Europe, although parts of eastern Europe are included for some topics. I have also used the modern names for the various regions of medieval Europe. For example, I refer to "France" but the land within the boundaries of France today was comprised of a number of different jurisdictions that exercised varying degrees of independence from the French crown over the course of the Middle Ages. Some were even completely independent states for much of the period. Similarly, Italy was a patchwork of completely independent states along with lands under the rule of the popes and other areas under the Angevin rulers of Sicily. Germany was also a mosaic of separate states. Some other names which require clarification are "Bohemia," "the Low Countries," and "Flanders." The land of Bohemia was in the modern Czech Republic. The Low Countries included modern Belgium, the Netherlands, Luxembourg, and some adjoining lands which are now parts of France and Germany. Flanders included Belgium and neighboring lands in France.

I would also like to clarify my use of the word "Church." The word "Church" refers to the Christian religion as a whole, with the pope as its leader, while "church" means the building in which Christians worshipped. This use of "Church" is not intended as a slight to any other Christian denominations. It is simply recognizing that this form of Christianity was the dominant religion throughout western Europe for most of the Middle Ages.

Finally, this book is only a survey of transportation and trade. As the bibliography reflects, far more information exists about the topics covered in this book than space permits. This is particularly true of ships and trade. For those interested in more in-depth treatments of any of the topics covered in this book, please consult the books listed in the bibliography. Additionally, while I have included some images to illustrate various aspects of transportation and trade, I recommend that anyone who wishes to see more medieval images of these activities consult the on-line resources available from some major libraries. In particular, the medieval manuscript databases of the Bibliothèque Nationale de France, the Morgan Library and Museum, and the British Library are very accessible and extensive.

I

REASONS FOR TRAVEL

As today, medieval people traveled for a number of reasons. Most commonly, they traveled on business. Peasants carted produce to the nearest market. Royalty, nobility, and members of the higher clergy were often on the move as they traveled around their lands and abroad to attend to business. Merchants, too, often traveled widely, with some ranging across Europe and beyond in pursuit of trade. And people of all classes traveled for personal religious reasons and undertook pilgrimages which could be day trips to local minor shrines or journeys taking many months to reach Rome or Jerusalem.

There was no vacation travel in the modern sense but some medieval Europeans did combine some time for relaxation with other travel. For example, royalty and nobility often stopped at hunting lodges when traveling around their lands. And pilgrimages provided a break from routine for all classes of society. Records left by some pilgrims clearly show that, while traveling for the benefit of their souls, they were sightseeing and enjoying new experiences, both at their destinations and along the way.

The majority of medieval Europeans did not venture far from their homes. The men and women who were engaged in agriculture and constituted at least 80 percent of the population had little reason to travel far as part of their jobs. Craftsmen and merchants were more mobile but even many of these people spent most of their lives residing in their home towns and cities. There were exceptions such as masons and other building craftsmen who journeyed from one construction project to the next and merchants engaged in long-distance trade. But it is estimated that most people spent the majority of their lives within approximately 20 miles of their homes, with some spending their entire lives within this limit. Only exceptional activities, such as going on a pilgrimage, being a party in a law suit in a high court, or serving in an army, would take them outside of their home areas. Still, as outlined in this section, there were many people traveling along the roads and on the rivers and seas of Europe in the Middle Ages.

Business Travel

By far, business was the primary reason for travel in the Middle Ages and covered a wide variety of activities.

COMMERCE

Travel was an integral part of commerce. Goods had to be brought from producers to consumers. This could be as simple and direct as a peasant bringing baskets full of vegetables from a farm to a nearby market or as complex as merchants shipping spices halfway around the world. Merchants could be found everywhere in Europe and their travel is discussed in more detail later in the section on trade.

Further, while merchants or their agents typically traveled with their merchandise, carters, wagoneers, muleteers, and packmen were often employed to perform the actual task of moving the goods overland. When the merchandise was transported by water, whether across the seas or down rivers, vessels and their crews had to be hired. Thus, trade accounted for the movement of many thousands of people across Europe and in the surrounding seas.

CONSTRUCTION

As today, the construction of buildings in medieval Europe required a number of different specialists. Masons and others involved in the construction of buildings, especially large works such as castles and cathedrals, had to travel from one project to the next. The most noted of these itinerant builders were the masons. Master masons were experts in the design and construction of buildings. The best ones were highly sought after and were well paid. There were also the ordinary masons who did the actual work of cutting the stones and putting them into place. These men, along with other specialists, such as the glass painters who created stained glass windows, sculptors, and carpenters capable of large-scale work, also had to move from one major construction project to the next. Even some of the more common workers, including mortar mixers and plasterers, may have followed the masons around from one job to another.

MEDICINE

Various medical practitioners traveled around medieval Europe. These included tooth-pullers. As dentistry was primitive in the Middle Ages, extraction was the most common treatment for cavities or any other dental problems. There were also men who specialized in surgery. The two most common were those who "cut for the stone" and others who "couched for cataracts." The first were specialists in surgically removing bladder stones. The others excised the clouded lenses

from the eyes of patients with cataracts. Some of these men may have been proficient and traveled so they could reach a wide number of patients, but one must wonder if one of the reasons that they traveled was to move on before the patient realized that the treatment had failed.

ENTERTAINMENT

There were many different kinds of itinerant entertainers in the Middle Ages. Perhaps the most exclusive were the poets who composed and read or sang their works in noble courts around Europe from the late 12th through the 13th centuries. In Germany, they were called minnesingers. In northern France, they were known as trouvères and, in southern France, troubadours. Their poems were primarily about courtly love. These poets included nobility as well as talented commoners. Many of them traveled among different courts and, in their works, highly praised those lords who were the most generous.

Other traveling entertainers included acrobats, jugglers, animal trainers, and minstrels. Like the troubadours, they traveled from one engagement to the next and were often part of entertainment at royal and noble courts, as well as a common feature at fairs and festivals. The minstrels and other musicians performed at wedding celebrations as well. They also turn up among the ranks of personnel employed by kings on campaign. For example, Edward III of England had musicians aboard his ship on its voyage to the Continent in the opening stages of the Hundred Years' War, while Henry V brought along 18 minstrels on his invasion of France later in the war.

COURIERS

Unlike the Roman Empire, medieval European governments, except for the Byzantine Empire, did not operate official courier systems that provided regular service between points within their jurisdictions. Instead, kings, queens, and popes employed couriers as part of their households. When they needed to send a letter, they dispatched it with a courier who then carried it directly to its destination. It is unclear how they carried messages rapidly over long distances. Galloping at high speeds would quickly exhaust a horse and so it would have been necessary to maintain relay stations where a courier could get a fresh horse. However, no jurisdiction appears to have possessed an established network of such stations. Given the ad hoc nature of this service, messengers likely hired or requisitioned fresh horses at livery stables along the way. On the other hand, merchants in the late Middle Ages regularly needed to send messages and created and operated their own courier services despite the expense. As international trade grew, merchants needed a means of sending orders for goods and guidance to business agents at commercial centers around Europe. They equally needed to receive orders as well as information about distant market and political conditions.

Travel of the Nobility

Royalty and other nobility traveled for many reasons and were often on the move. They and their retinues often made circuits of their own lands to maintain order and oversee their management. Accompanied by their supporters, they also traveled abroad to conduct foreign policy and wage war.

Nobles frequently traveled around the lands under their dominion. One traditional explanation of this practice is based on the payment of taxes and rents in kind (that is, in the form of various foodstuffs) and that nobles traveled between their various estates so that they could consume the taxes and rents paid by their vassals. This was likely done to some degree but it is doubtful that it was the primary reason for their travel. Over the course of the Middle Ages, taxes and rents were increasingly paid in cash and not in food. Fur-

ther, some records show that the food collected was sometimes shipped out to the noble, saving him the inconvenience of having to travel to the food. In other instances, the foods were sold, yielding cash which was usually more desirable to the nobility.

Some travel within a noble's own lands was performed so that he could exercise his authority over his vassals and tenants. This typically involved hearing any legal matters, civil or criminal, worthy of his attention and then adjudicating them. By traveling, he could observe firsthand how well his subordinates were administering the lands entrusted to them and meet with them face to face. These subordinates might be as low ranking as a reeve or steward employed by a minor lord or as high ranking as a duke who was the vassal of a king.

Nobles also traveled to attend the courts of their overlords. Their lords summoned them for many reasons, such as to provide advice on important matters or to attend festivities such as weddings. Appearing at court gave the nobility an opportunity to display their wealth and importance. Some traveled with as many of their vassals and servants as they could muster, but such displays were not always appreciated by their lords. As early as the 7th century, some kings took steps to curb this behavior. The kings of Wessex in England limited the number of servants a noble could bring to court to his reeve, his smith, and the wet nurse for his children, if he had any.

Nobles sometimes traveled for pleasure or, at least, combined business and pleasure. The progresses of kings around their lands often include references to stopovers at hunting lodges along the way. Many rulers also appear to have simply had favorite places to stay. Whether for hunting or just relaxing, it appears that routes were sometimes chosen because they included such spots.

DIPLOMACY

Another reason that the nobility and royalty traveled was to conduct foreign policy. There were many occasions when the rulers of

Europe met with each other to discuss international affairs and to seal alliances, but they far more often communicated with each other through envoys. These representatives, who were selected from among the rulers' most trusted officials, performed a variety of tasks. Minor envoys would deliver messages and carry back responses and were not empowered to do anything else. More senior officials journeyed between kingdoms to negotiate peace treaties and alliances. They helped to arranged marriages between royal houses, some of which were part of peace settlements and alliances. High-ranking clergymen were often selected to serve as part of important diplomatic missions because of their education and political skills. Some ambassadors were spies as well. In fact, diplomats were expected to gather intelligence about their hosts.

War

When diplomacy failed, war was often the result. Wars in the Middle Ages ranged from skirmishes between minor lords to massive conflicts between kings. During the Hundred Years' War, thousands of knights and other men-at-arms took to the field. There were also the Crusades fought in the Middle East and Asia Minor as well as in the Iberian Peninsula and along the northeastern frontiers of Europe. These wars, too, attracted thousands of nobles and their men-at-arms from across Europe to fight in the name of the Christian faith.

Tournaments

Another reason that nobles traveled was to participate in tournaments. These were contests of martial skill and strength. The earliest tournaments were held in France in the 12th century and were conducted like war games. These early games were played over a large area and the players used the same weapons and armor they used for real combat. Knights who were captured forfeited their horse and armor, just as they would have if captured in a real war. Over time, tournaments became more formalized and safety measures were implemented, but participating was still a dangerous sport.

To attract participants, the noble or royal court holding the tournament would send out messengers or heralds to announce the event at courts around the country or even across Europe. Knights were sometimes granted safe conduct so that they could travel to attend tournaments.

Logistics

No member of the nobility traveled alone. A minor lord traveling between his estates would be accompanied by his family, his immediate servants, and as many men-at-arms as he thought prudent. They would travel on horseback with perhaps a wagon or two to carry bedding and other household goods, including indispensable items such as silver dishes which served both as tableware and as a cash reserve. He would also bring his account records to register the income of his various manors and other important information. The size of entourage increased in proportion to the noble's rank. For kings, retinues numbered in the hundreds. For example, the personal retinue for King Henry V of England when he invaded France in 1415 included:

- The master of the king's horses, 60 grooms, a clerk of the stable, 12 purveyors of oats for the horses, 12 smiths, and nine saddlers to care for 223 horses.
- Six bowyers, six fletchers, a helmet maker, and 12 armorers.
- A sergeant in charge of the tents and pavilions with four painters and 28 servants.
- Three cooks and three yeoman, a clerk of the king's poultry and eight yeoman, a clerk of the bakehouse, three clerks of spicery, a clerk of table linens, and a clerk of the king's hall.
- 156 miscellaneous yeomen, servants, carpenters, and laborers.
- Three pages, a clerk of marshalcy, a clerk

of wardrobe, two almoners (overseers of the king's daily charity), the treasurer of the royal household, the dean of the king's chapel, three clerks, 15 chaplains, and 14 monks.

• Eighteen minstrels and other musicians and singers.

Admittedly, some of these persons, particularly the armorers and bowyers, were specially brought along to serve the needs of the entire army and were not normally a part of the king's immediate servants. Still, this example provides a general sense of the huge number of personnel considered essential to care for the needs of the king and to display his status. Did the king really need all those chaplains and monks to perform masses for him? No, but they served to show that he could afford, and deserved, to have so many to attend to him.

In addition to all of the servants he required, a king was frequently accompanied by all of his officials because, while each nation had its capital city, the true seat of government was wherever the king was. These officials were all either noblemen or clerics and each of them usually traveled with their own personal retinues as well.

The wives of the nobility also had their retinues. Again, the sizes of these groups varied according to rank and they were typically smaller than those of their husbands. But, again, royal entourages were quite large and the queen and every other member of the royal family usually had their own independent retinues, even when traveling together with the king.

All these entourages also required suitable numbers of horses, pack animals, and carts and wagons to move all their bedding, clothing, cooking gear, and provisions. Additionally, many government records and, at times, portions of the king's treasury were transported as well so that the chancellor and exchequer (treasurer) could perform their duties as they traveled with the king. Eventually, these officials and their functions stopped trav-

eling and operated out of permanent offices in the capital.

Besides the number of people involved, the number of moves must have been a constant headache for those officials and servants who were responsible for the smooth transition of the king and his government from one place to the next. For example, records for the households of the kings of France in the early 14th century reveal that they moved from 60 to 80 times every year. Even if all these moves did not entail the king's entire retinue, seeing to the packing and unpacking of all the king's valuables on an average of once every five to six days had to have been taxing. Still, the officials and servants must have developed routines that enabled them to cope with the stresses of being almost constantly on the move.

Logistics for wartime travel were even more nightmarish. For example, in the Hundred Years' War, thousands of nobles, knights, and men-at-arms crossed the Channel from England to the Continent. All these men required horses for transporting their equipment as well as for use in combat, so thousands of horses were shipped over from England to meet these needs. Wagons and carts were also needed by the hundreds or even, according to some records, by the thousands to carry arms, armor, bedding, food, and other essential goods. After a successful campaign, these carts and wagons served to carry back the plunder gathered by the victors. While most of their names have been lost over the years, there must have been a large number of skilled men on the king's staff who arranged for the transportation and coordinated the movement of all these men, animals, and material so that the king could fight effectively.

Religious Travel

Clerics, like laymen, traveled on business. While an ordinary priest or monk had little need to travel, the lords of the Church, like secular lords, frequently traveled. Bishops, archbishops, and cardinals all traveled in the course of performing business for the Church. They, too, had retinues that accompanied them. Like the courts of the nobility, the courts of bishops and archbishops frequently moved around their jurisdictions and traveled to Church councils as well as to attend to matters at the papal court. One 13th century French archbishop, Eudes Rigaud, left extensive records about his activities which reveal how much travel was involved during the career of a successful cleric. Archbishop Rigaud was very conscientious in the performance of his duties and spent nearly half of each year traveling around his archdiocese to review the activities of the bishops, abbots, and abbesses under his charge. He was also an advisor to the king of France. His diligent performance of all these duties is estimated to have entailed 2,500 miles of travel every year. In one exceptional year, he had to travel to the papal court in Rome from his archdiocese in northern France. Allowing for the indirect route he followed, he traveled nearly 2,000 miles and spent over 130 days on the road on his round-trip. He would have also traveled at least once to Rome for his elevation to archbishop. In all, he is estimated to have journeyed over 54,000 miles over the course of his life. And the archbishop would not have been alone in his travels. He would have had his retinue of clerks with him, some of whom diligently recorded the details of his travel. While it is difficult to tell how typical Archbishop Rigaud's tenure and travels were, other records indicate that higher clergy traveled very frequently.

MENDICANTS

While most members of the clergy were assigned to particular locations such as monasteries, churches, or cathedrals, there were a few groups which were authorized in the 13th century to travel across Europe, preach to the peo-ple, and beg for their upkeep. These were the mendicant orders. The two primary orders were the Franciscan and Dominican friars. Both these orders had strict vows of poverty that were originally interpreted as barring them from even owning buildings for their use. Most of the laity viewed them as being more truly devoted to God than the ordinary clergy, who were frequently seen as being too worldly and obsessed with taking in donations.

MISSIONARIES

Missionaries had existed from the very beginning of Christianity and the Church continued to send out missionaries to preach the Gospel and convert non–Christians throughout the Middle Ages. From the very beginning of the period, missionaries from Rome traveled to preach to the pagans, especially the leaders of the various tribes that had conquered and were occupying the lands of the former Roman Empire. While there were setbacks and some missionaries became martyrs, the Church succeeded in bringing western Europe into its fold.

The Church also sent missionaries outside of Europe to Asia and India. The most noted of these missions were the ones made to China in the 13th century by two Franciscan friars. One was sent by the pope in 1245 while the other was sent by King Louis IX of France in 1253. In addition to converting the Mongols to Christianity, their goals included enlisting the help of the Mongols in combating the Moslems. They had no success in either pursuit. A third Franciscan arrived in China in 1294 and succeeded in establishing a church in the capital at what is now Beijing. He is recorded as having converted thousands of Chinese and Mongols to Christianity and the mission he established survived until 1369. In 1368, the Chinese overthrew the Mongols and established the Ming Dynasty. As part of eradicating the symbols of Mongol rule, the Christians who had been tolerated by the Mongol khans were expelled.

MORTUARY ROLLS

Beginning in the 9th century, monks who served as a *breviators* or *rotularius* were authorized to leave their cloisters to circulate mortuary rolls. The rolls contained lists of the names of the souls that were prayed for at a monastery along with a brief biography of each of the deceased. These people had usually been patrons of that monastery. The breviator would take the roll to another monastery. There, the monks would copy down the names to add to their list of souls to be prayed for and then add the names of the souls for whom they prayed to the roll. The breviator then continued on from one monastery to the next, with his list growing at every stop. In one instance, a monk spent nine months on the road circulating a roll before returning home. Some of the rolls were several yards long by the time they returned to their original monasteries.

The purpose of circulating mortuary rolls was to maximize the number of prayers and masses said for a soul. Monks prayed frequently and monasteries had masses said daily for the benefit of the souls of those on their mortuary rolls. Having prayers and masses said for the souls of the dead was believed to shorten their time in Purgatory and so help them be admitted to Heaven more quickly. (Under Church doctrine, Christians who had lived lives that were sinful enough to deny them direct admission to Heaven but not so sinful as to merit an eternity of torment in Hell would go to Purgatory when they died. Once there, they would expiate their sins through suffering and eventually win entry to Heaven. The Church held that there were some activities that could be performed on behalf of a person's soul, such as having a mass said for them, that would shorten their time in Purgatory.)

PARDONERS

Pardoners were officials authorized by the Church to travel around Europe and collect funds on behalf of religious institutions such as hospitals. The funds were also used to finance construction of Church buildings, including some at the papal court. To persuade people to make donations, pardoners offered indulgences that benefited their souls in the afterlife. While having masses said would help a soul who was already in Purgatory, indulgences helped a living person accumulate a reserve of blessings that would help their souls reach Heaven sooner after their death. To obtain the benefit of the indulgences from the pardoner, a person was to confess his sins to his local priest, perform the penance imposed by the priest, and then make a donation to the pardoner and receive the indulgence. Unfortunately, pardoners' activities reveal the seamier side of medieval Christianity. Pardoners frequently overstated the power of their indulgences and exaggerated their authority by claiming that they could forgive all of a person's sins, even sins so severe that they would otherwise condemn them to Hell, in exchange for a donation. To make matters worse, some appear to have pocketed some of the donations. Some may have even paid "kick-backs" to the local priests who encouraged their parishioners to buy indulgences. As early as 1212, the Church recognized the abuses committed by the pardoners, but they were not abolished until 1562.

UNIVERSITY STUDENTS AND WANDERING CLERGY

Most university students in the Middle Ages were clergymen, including friars, monks, and priests. Some of the students, once freed from the institutions and routines of the clerical life, found they did not want to return to their old vocations. Some stayed at the universities for as long as they could to avoid having to return to their proper positions. Some wandered between universities and others simply dropped out. Many of them made their living by begging, while some found occasional employment as singers and entertainers in noble households.

There were also some clergymen who were not students who simply slipped away from their assigned duties and roamed abroad. Most were friars or monks. In addition to begging, these men were sometimes able to impose on the hospitality of monasteries and other religious institutions. Wayward clerics, whether students or not, were an embarrassment to the Church. Monasteries and orders of friars were strongly advised to keep their members under control.

PILGRIMAGES

Pilgrimages are commonly associated with medieval Christianity but they are actually much older. The ancient Greeks and Egyptians traveled to sacred shrines and sites, especially to those places that were connected with miraculous healing. The earliest Christian pilgrimages are believed to have taken place in the late 3rd century when Christians from the Roman Empire began traveling to the Holy Land to see and worship at sites associated with the life of Christ.

The three most prominent pilgrimage destinations were Rome, the Shrine of St. James in Compostela in northwest Spain, and the Holy Land. Traveling to and from these sites involved many months of travel for most Europeans. More commonly, people went on pilgrimages to minor shrines closer to their homes. There were many which involved only a day trip or only a couple of nights away from home. The journey of Chaucer's pilgrims from London to Canterbury was one that involved just a few overnight stops on the outward and return trips.

People from all levels of society made pilgrimages for a variety of reasons. Many pilgrims traveled to shrines or other holy places just as an act of devotion. Many others did it to ask for divine help, most commonly to cure some physical or mental problem. Some went to give thanks for some cure they had already received. Still others were people who had vowed to go on pilgrimage as part of their prayers for deliverance from some danger, such

as a shipwreck. And some sought to atone for their sins and ask for God's forgiveness.

This last reason for going on pilgrimage was not always freely chosen by the pilgrim. Rather, secular and ecclesiastic courts sometimes ordered offenders to go on pilgrimages as part of their punishment. Some of these pilgrimages were quite short but did serve the purpose of publicizing the person's guilt and humbling him or her. Other penitential pilgrimages were very long and involved traveling to the most distant sites such as the holy city of Rome, Compostela in Spain, or the Holy Land itself. In extreme cases, pilgrimages to all three were ordered. This effectively exiled the offender for several years, with the possibility that he would not survive all the arduous travel. For those who did come back, they had to prove that they had completed the prescribed pilgrimage with a certificate signed by the presiding priest at each shrine.

Not all those who freely vowed to go on pilgrimages fulfilled their promises. The Church approved the alternative of having the person donate an amount equal to the sum that he or she would have spent on the pilgrimage. Another option was to hire another person to go in their place.

The Church discouraged women from undertaking any pilgrimages, especially ones that would take them far from their homes. Church leaders feared for the physical and moral well-being of women going on long pilgrimages. To prevent pilgrimages from becoming an excuse for fleeing family obligations, the church sometimes required wives traveling without their husbands to have a paper signed by them that approved the pilgrimage. Despite all this, many women did go on pilgrimages in the Middle Ages. Some traveled as far as the Holy Land. However, women from one group which the Church did control did not go on any major pilgrimages. Nuns were told to not take any vows to go on pilgrimage and that they best served God by remaining in their abbeys. They were to be satisfied with taking mental pilgrimages by reading accounts written by men, such as priests and monks, who had made the actual trips.

Christians were not the only ones to take pilgrimages in the Middle Ages. While far less numerous than Christian pilgrims, there were Jews from Europe, primarily rabbis, who traveled to the Holy Land and visited various religious sites. These included the graves of Abraham and other patriarchs as well as the graves of famed rabbis. Sites of events such as the place where Abraham almost sacrificed Isaac and the stone on which Abraham was circumcised were also visited.

Beggars and Vagabonds

Beggars appear to have been a common feature of many towns and cities as well as the roads of medieval Europe. For those who could not work for valid medical reasons, such as a crippling physical condition, there was no shame in begging to make a living and it was the duty of every Christian to give charity to those who were truly in need. Poor people who were on pilgrimages were another group eligible for such charity. However, it was generally expected that beggars would not burden a single community by staying there indefinitely, unless their health did not permit them to move on. Instead, they were to make their way through life by traveling from one town or city to the next. As for pilgrims, they were expected to stay no longer than a single night before resuming their journey.

There was always a problem of false pilgrims and "sturdy" beggars. These were people who wandered across Europe and begged even though they were fit enough to earn a living. To combat this problem, some jurisdictions required beggars to register and prove that they were invalids. They were then issued a permit to beg. After the Black Death, when labor was in short supply, there were legislative efforts in England to force physically fit vagabonds to go to work. These efforts met with little success.

Lepers

Lepers formed a unique category of beggars. In the Middle Ages, the term "leprosy" was applied to true leprosy and to any other disease that caused severe damage to the skin. As the modern use of the word "leper" suggests, lepers were outcasts from society. Their disease was believed to be incurable and highly contagious and so people shunned them. There was no work that they were allowed to perform so they had to beg for a living. As part of their begging, they carried rattles, bells, or some noisemakers to alert people to their presence. This enabled healthy people to avoid coming in too close contact with them. Some lepers were fortunate enough to be admitted to Lazar houses. These institutions housed and fed lepers and also provided some medical care. While they were typically still required to beg to pay for their upkeep, lepers staying in Lazar house were freed from the endless wandering which society imposed on them.

II

TRAVELING BY LAND

In this section, the primary aspects of travel by land will be examined. These include the various modes of travel, the infrastructure built to support travel, and the risks travelers faced.

Walking

Quite obviously, walking was by far the most common means for getting from one place to another. While riding on a horse, mule, or other animal was preferable, not everyone could afford to own or even hire a riding animal. As a consequence, most people walked, covering distances that ranged from a few miles to the nearest town to thousands of miles traveling to reach and return from distant pilgrimage sites. In the case of pilgrimages, even those who could afford to ride sometimes chose to walk as an exercise in humility. Walking was also the typical form of travel for armies on land. Only special, fast-moving raids were conducted exclusively on horseback. Otherwise, armies marched along, traveling only as fast as the slowest part of their baggage train of carts and wagons.

Walking had the advantage of requiring a minimum of equipment. A pair of leather shoes or boots sufficed in most cases. However, shoes and boots in the Middle Ages typically had soft soles and none of them had arch supports. Walking on soft ground or on trails of packed earth was likely not that uncomfortable, but crossing rocky areas must have led to many sore feet. Still, medieval people, especially the large majority who worked the land, were accustomed to such hardships. Tough, calloused feet must have been quite common. They spent long days on their feet, sometimes even barefoot. Illustrations of agricultural activities depict unshod farmers reaping and threshing grain. Pilgrims sometimes went barefoot as well. Trodding unshod along the road to a shrine was a sign of piety and penance.

Besides providing little cushioning for the foot, most medieval footwear appears to have provided only limited protection from the elements. Shoes were typically very low-topped and even boots typically reached only a few inches at most up the wearer's ankle. In wet conditions, whether in the mud or snow, even shod feet likely became damp quite quickly. By the beginning of the 12th century, a piece of footwear called a *patten* was developed to cope with this problem. Pattens were detachable hard soles about one to two inches thick and made of wood or thick layers of leather. The patten was fitted with one or more straps, often including one that encircled the ankle, which fastened over the top of the wearer's shod foot. They looked something like a pair of heavy sandals. The pattens helped elevate the wearer's shoes above the level of any puddles, mud, or other hazards that might otherwise dampen the wearer's shoes and feet. However, pattens were best suited for short walks around town since walking in them was somewhat awkward. They were impractical for long hikes where they would likely become mired in the first deep mud puddle and would, in any case, be dangerous to use on uneven surfaces such as rocky terrain.

Another accessory for walking was a broad-brimmed hat. Most were made of straw or felt but some were made of leather. Both for long and short walks, these hats provided relief from the glare and heat of the sun. They also provided some protection from rain and snow. Pilgrims were sometimes depicted as wearing such hats. They often pinned badges, souvenirs of their pilgrimages, onto their hats. In addition to hats, cloaks were worn to provide protection from cold or damp weather.

For long walks, it was common to carry food for the journey. Food was packed in bags or purses worn on the belt or in bags shaped like haversacks or modern women's shoulder bags worn slung over one shoulder. The shoulder bags were often associated with pilgrims and referred to as *scrips*. As part of the ceremony to begin a pilgrimage, a priest formally presented the pilgrim with a scrip as well as a walking staff.

Travelers sometimes carried water as well as food. Medieval canteens were typically made of leather and were called *costrels*. They were made by soaking leather to soften it and then drying it over forms to create the required shapes. Some were pear-shaped. Others were made in the form of small kegs. Regardless of shape, the pieces of leather were stitched tightly together and the seams sealed with tar. While most appear to have been made of leather, at least some costrels were made of staves of wood just like kegs and barrels. Whether of wood or leather, their opening was at the top and was corked with a wooden plug. They were also commonly fitted with a shoulder strap or other handle. However, at least one illustration shows a keg-shaped costrel mounted on a man's belt somewhat like a modern military canteen.

As for routes, walkers could follow the same roads as those who rode but they could also walk along paths suitable only for pedestrians. Most of these trails were short pathways that connected villages to one another but others covered long distances across moors and through other wildernesses. Some of these tracks were already ancient when the Middle Ages began, dating back many hundreds of years to the earliest settlement of the land. Following well-established paths raises another point about travel in the Middle Ages: maps were extremely rare for much of the period and those maps that did exist were usually impractical for providing useful directions. The development of practical maps and other means of finding one's way will be discussed in detail later in this book.

MAN-POWERED TRANSPORTATION

As part of traveling in general, walking was a common way of moving materials from place to place and a variety of containers were constructed to hold these materials. For example, illustrations show people, often women, with large sacks of grain slung over their shoulders, laboriously trudging to nearby mills. In a few instances, women are even shown balancing the grain sacks on their heads. Besides grain, bags could, of course, hold a nearly infinite variety of goods, from charcoal to fresh produce. In addition to bags, bundles, such as ones made up of sticks for kindling, can be seen on the stooped shoulders of people in a number of medieval pictures. Still other pictures show meat pie vendors walking through the streets with planks loaded with their wares, balanced atop one shoulder.

Another simple means of carrying things while walking was to use a pole. (See illustration 1.) A sturdy pole was placed across the top of one shoulder with a load at each end of the pole to balance it. Poles often were notched or turned up slightly at their ends to help prevent loads from sliding off. Buckets of water were often carried this way. In many medieval

Illustration 1. In this scene of activities on the bridges of Paris in the early 14th century (detail from a full page in *Life of St. Denis*, 1317), a team of men are pulling a sledge loaded with a large barrel of wine. While sledges made moving loads easier, it is doubtful that these men would be hauling such a heavy load very far. They may be moving the barrel from a river boat docked nearby to a tavern. On the right side, a man is carrying a pole which has a bucket on each end. He is probably a water-seller. These men loaded up their buckets at public fountains and at the riverside and then sold the water to whoever needed it (courtesy of the Bibliothèque Nationale de France, FR 2092, fol. 4V).

cities, water carriers were a frequent sight as they delivered water or sold it to passers-by on the street.

Baskets were another common container for carrying and people were frequently shown carrying large baskets filled with produce or other items either in their arms or, more rarely, balanced atop their heads. Baskets could be strapped to the back as well. Such baskets appear to have often been about two to three feet in height and about a foot in diameter. They were wider at the top and tapered toward the bottom. Fitted with shoulder straps, they were worn like backpacks. These baskets were open at the top so they could be easily loaded with a wide variety of items. Babies are sometimes shown riding on their parents' backs in baskets made of wicker or in cloth slings. Baskets were employed in a wide variety of settings, from carrying grapes from the vineyard to the wine

press to moving loads of earth or stones on construction sites.

Baskets were not the only devices for carrying material on building sites. Construction workers also shouldered mortar boards, lugging cement from the mixing troughs up to the stone work where it was needed. Another device seen in many illustrations of building across Europe was the litter. Carried by a pair of men like a modern medical stretcher, this device was used to move loads of stone and other materials that were too heavy for a single man. The handles were occasionally fitted with long leather straps which fitted over the carriers' shoulders. These straps enabled the men to lift with their shoulders as well as their arms. Despite the introduction of the wheelbarrow from China during the 13th century, these litters remained in use through the end of the Middle Ages. Illustrations from the 15th century show the two methods being used side by side. Wheelbarrows were sometimes shown with shoulder straps just like those used on litters. (See illustration 2.)

Besides serving as pack animals, men were also used as draft animals. The Bayeux Tapestry, from the late 11th century, shows two men using harnesses made of leather straps to pull a small, open-sided wagon loaded with helmets and spears. An early 14th century French manuscript also depicts four men in similar harnesses hauling a large wine barrel mounted on a small wheeled frame. (See illustration 3.) Other illustrations from this manuscript show carts fitted with handles on each side so that one man could push while the other pulled. Another image is of six men hauling a sledge loaded with another huge barrel of wine (see illustration 1). On paved streets, water may have been thrown on the stones in front of the sledge to make it easier to slide.

The use of men as draft animals was used only to cover short distances. And such means of moving goods appears to have been most common within cities, in neighborhoods where streets were so narrow and turned at such sharp angles that horse carts could not be used. Additionally, horse carts were sometimes banned in some cities because their iron-rimmed wheels broke paving stones. (See illustration 4.) Large, heavy carts also helped

Illustration 2. On the left side of this scene (detail from a full page in *Life of St. Denis*, 1317), a man is using a wheelbarrow to move several large bundles. The wheelbarrow originated in China and was introduced to Europe in the 13th century. The man has a strap around his neck that is connected to the barrow's handles to help him lift more of the weight with his back. On the right side, a beggar carries an infant in a sling on his back. Slings and packs were often used to help carry all types of loads. On the river below, a barge loaded with barrels of wine is towed by two men in a rowboat. These river craft are built like smaller versions of the seagoing ships of the age. They are clinker-built and taper to a point at both ends. On the wine barge, the man is using a large steering oar like a rudder to guide his boat (courtesy of the Bibliothèque Nationale de France, FR 2091, fol. 111).

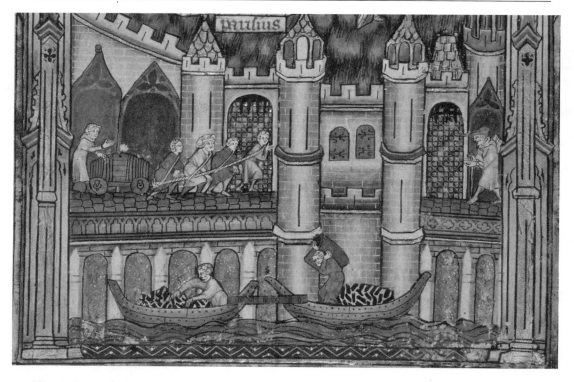

Illustration 3. **In this scene of life in Paris (detail from a full page in *Life of St. Denis*, 1317), a team of men are again hauling a large, heavy barrel of wine. This time, they have placed the barrel on a frame with small wheels, somewhat like a modern dolly. The job is still difficult. On the river, two boats carrying charcoal have docked and are starting to unload. The citizens and businesses of the city consumed huge amounts of both charcoal and firewood and so deliveries such as this were commonplace. (Courtesy of the Bibliothèque Nationale de France, FR 2092, fol. 1.)**

cut ruts into unpaved streets and churned up the surface of muddy streets.

In illustrations of city life, the men lugging the sacks and hauling the loads were likely to have been professional porters. Porters were employed to move anything that needed to be moved, from loading and unloading cargo on ships to delivering barrels of beer or wine. While the distances they covered were short in comparison to those traveled by horse carts and pack mules, these men were essential to the functioning of medieval ports and cities.

Men also carried loads much further than short trips in a town or city. Bearers carried loads up and through the Alps. Pack animals were often used but men on foot were an essential part of any group traveling through mountainous terrain. The bearers carried supplies for the travelers as well as small but valuable goods for merchants. Additionally, bearers were often local men who knew the routes through the mountains so, like Sherpas in the Himalayas, they could act both as guides and carriers.

Before moving on, there are two specialized methods of foot-based transportation that should not be overlooked: skis and snowshoes. In Scandinavia, skis have been in use for traveling cross-country since the Neolithic Period. They appear to have been used in Russia since that time as well and medieval skis have been found in both regions. During the Middle Ages, they continued to be used for winter travel, enabling people to move rapidly over the snow. They also allowed hunters to move quickly in pursuit of game and were even used in combat. Unlike modern skiers, medieval skiers commonly used only a single stick or pole to push themselves along and provide balance. At times, some skiers appear to have used no sticks at all.

The Scandinavians also used snowshoes, but they appear to have been less common than skis. While skis seem to have been limited to Scandinavia and parts of Russia during the Middle Ages, snowshoes were used in the Alps at least as early as the 14th century. In the high Alps, men from hospices wore snowshoes when searching for lost travelers.

Riding and Hauling

The next most common form of land transportation was riding. Riding was obviously much preferred over walking. Riding is fatiguing but far less so than walking. However, the cost of owning a riding animal put this form of transportation out of reach

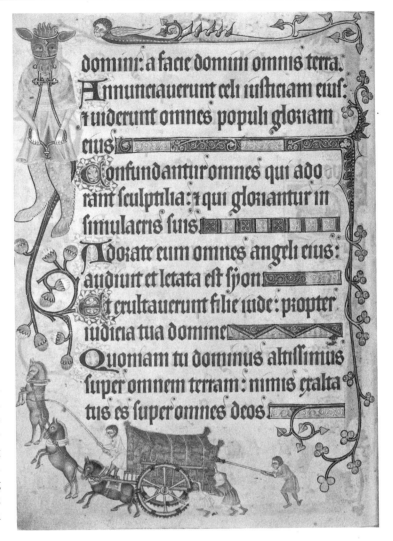

Illustration 4. The cart: This cart is loaded to capacity. Like many medieval carts, its sides resemble ladders placed horizontally. These open sides were lighter than solid ones. By keeping the cart light, heavier loads could be carried. Saving weight was important because, as the scene illustrates, moving the fully loaded cart was difficult enough without having any extra weight to pull. The wheels are typical of the vehicles of the entire Middle Ages. Rather than being made of solid boards, the wheels are carefully crafted with spokes and fellies. These wheels are as strong as any made of slabs of boards and are much lighter and easier to pull. These wheels also have metal rims that are fitted with spikes or studs to give them extra traction. While suitable for use in fields and on country roads, wheels with rims such as these were banned in many cities because they would break paving stones.

The horses: The horses are wearing padded collars which permit them to pull with their shoulders. This was a medieval innovation that improved the pulling capability of horses. Earlier harnesses pressed against the horse's throat, which made it difficult for the horse to breathe. These horses are harnessed in a single line. Harnessing in file like this was common and made good use of the horses' pulling power. These horses need all the advantages possible because they are not particularly large or strong. Even if the artist distorted their size, the fact that men are having to push the cart suggests that these horses are pulling at the limit of their strength. Larger, stronger draft horses would not be bred until a century or more after this scene was painted (© The British Library Board. All Rights Reserved 8/31/2010. License Number: PAUNEW01. Add. MS 42130, f.173v).

of most people in medieval Europe. Still, large segments of society, most notably the nobility, members of the higher levels of the clergy, and other comparatively wealthy people such as prosperous farmers and successful merchants and craftsmen could afford to maintain horses to ride. As an alternative, horses and mules were often available for hire and were rented by both poorer people and the well-off alike when the need arose. Even royalty rented extra riding, draft, and pack horses when moving their large households between estates. (Their exchequers, or financial officers, often found this to be more cost-effective than maintaining a huge number of animals which were only needed occasionally.)

Besides moving people, animals also provided the muscle for moving cargo. In fact, people sometimes served this purpose as well. Still, medieval society should certainly not be viewed as backwards since the development of steam and internal combustion engines only began to replace animal- and manpower in the 18th century and did not fully replace them as the primary movers of goods and people until the 20th century in industrialized countries. Even now, oxen, water buffalos, and other animals still serve to haul plows and wagons in some parts of the world.

The riding animals of medieval Europe were all equines; that is, horses, mules, and asses. Europeans only encountered exotic mounts such as camels and dromedaries when traveling in the Middle East and Asia.

RIDING HORSES

Riding horses were referred to by a bewildering variety of names: Arabians, Barbs, palfreys, rounceys, trotters, pacers, amblers, coursers, and jades. Some horses were used for both combat and riding, most notably the Arabian and Barb as well as the hobby and the jennet. There was also the destrier, a type of horse used exclusively for warfare. Before we look at the individual types of horses, it would be useful to first address the problems in identifying horses used in the Middle Ages.

Breeds of Horses

Manuscript illustrations provide innumerable images of medieval riding horses. However, connecting those images to the names and characteristics given for the various types of horses can seldom be done with any reasonable degree of certainty. This may sound ridiculous to any person today who is interested in horses. After all, there are established breeds of horses whose colors, height, and other characteristics are readily identifiable and must conform to set standards. And, indeed, existing breeds of horses did develop from their medieval forebears, but very few breeds in the modern sense of the word existed in the Middle Ages. For example, the Arabian of the Middle Ages is recognizable as the same breed of that name today. However, many other types of horses, such as the comfortable riding horse called the *palfrey*, cannot be identified with any modern breed.

The lack of identifiable breeds was a consequence of the lack of organized breeding programs in medieval Europe. Selective breeding to create lineages of horses, all with the same desirable traits, was practiced by the Romans and produced the fast, strong horses that ran in the chariot races as well as those that served in the Roman cavalry. However, with the collapse of the Roman Empire in western Europe in the 5th century A.D., such large-scale horse breeding fell into disuse. In the 8th and 9th centuries, the Christian kingdoms remaining on the Iberian Peninsula and the Carolingian empire revived horse breeding and began developing better warhorses. In the following centuries, nobility throughout Europe obtained the necessary breeding stock and implemented programs to improve the qualities of warhorses. As time went on, increasingly stronger horses were bred to meet the changing needs of the battlefield.

As this indicates, planned horse breeding was directed at meeting military needs, not the everyday needs of transportation and agriculture. The breeding of cart horses and plow horses received far less attention, if any. Some nobles did keep horses specially bred for pleasure rather than warfare, such as ones for comfortable riding or for speed in hunting or racing. But even on noble estates little seems to have been done to improve the quality of their working stock. This may seem short-sighted now, but the view then was that a superior stallion should not be wasted in trying to breed up ordinary riding and farm horses. It was considered far more important to focus on developing better warhorses. One might think that at least the farmers, carters, and others who owned horses and relied on them for their livelihood would have striven to breed better draft and riding horses. Some may have tried to mate their best mares with the best available stallions but few owned enough horses for such attempts to produce significant results. Further, unless such efforts were constantly kept up for generation after generation of horses (and their breeders), any improvements would be negligible and short-lived. It was not until the late 16th and early 17th centuries that concerted efforts were made to improve the quality of draft and riding horses. For example, to develop larger and stronger horses, Henry VIII issued decrees requiring landowners to maintain horses of large size and forbade the grazing of small horses on common land. These efforts laid the groundwork for the development of the Shire horse and other breeds of large, strong horses. Other identifiable breeds also evolved and proliferated in the post-medieval period. Hunters and thoroughbreds, descendants of the coursers of the Middle Ages, also developed into formal breeds as the nobility and well-to-do turned their efforts from breeding warhorses to developing horses for the pastimes of racing and hunting.

Returning to the Middle Ages, the many manuscript illustrations of horses do give us some general information about medieval riding horses, such as their stature and color. There are also surviving documents that provide a few clues as to the relative quality of different types of horses. For example, some household accounts of the nobility record the cost of horses purchased for their families or for the use of their servants. Other relevant documents include contracts for military service in the late Middle Ages. These contracts sometimes included provisions to indemnify knights and other men-at-arms for the loss of their horses and so the horses were appraised at the start of a campaign. From this information, one expert has estimated that, in the 14th century, a cheap riding horse, commonly called a *rouncey*, cost about 24 times an ordinary draft horse. Further, the price of a high-quality riding horse, a *palfrey*, was 400 times that of the draft horse. And that of a good warhorse, a *destrier*, was 800 times greater. While exact prices varied greatly from place to place and over time, these documents and estimates confirm that the cost of a horse went up in proportion to its quality. Additionally, the evidence reveals that, like any other commodity, prices of horses went up when demand increased, such as when a military campaign was imminent.

Applying the relative costs of horses confirms that in depictions of noble men and women riding their horses are most likely palfreys while those of their attending servants are rounceys. Additional clues can be gleaned from other documentary sources such as romances and other works of fiction, including *The Canterbury Tales*. The descriptions of the characters sometimes include mention of the sort of horses they ride. The type of horse usually reflects the rider's social status. For example, a middle-class merchant might ride a rouncey while a farmer rides an *affer* or *stott* (names for the ordinary cart or farm horse). Thus, while we cannot identify medieval horses with the same certainty as modern breeds, we can come to some useful understanding of what the various names mean and what horses the artists were attempting to portray.

One final point: archaeology has been able to provide little direct physical evidence about medieval horses. However, the few horse skeletons from the Middle Ages that have been recovered, along with surviving saddles and other horse equipment, confirm that the horses of medieval Europe were generally smaller than modern ones. Most modern breeds are at least 15 hands (60 inches) high and many easily reach 16 hands. While some horses in the Middle Ages appear to have reached 15 hands in height, the average height for horses is estimated at only around 13½ hands (54 inches), so some medieval "horses" would be considered ponies by modern standards.

Now, on with the cavalcade of the horses of the Middle Ages.

Arabians, Barbs, and Spanish Horses

Arabians and Spanish horses were the two most sought-after breeds of horses in the Middle Ages. Arabians were available either from Spain or directly from the Middle East. This breed originated in the Arabian Peninsula and was noted for its toughness and speed. While the first Arabs were likely first introduced to Spain by the Romans, the greatest numbers were brought to Spain by the Moslems during their conquest of the Iberian Peninsula in the 8th century. During their long occupation of what are now Spain and Portugal, the Moslems brought in many Arabians as well as Barbs. The *Barb* is a horse breed from North Africa and its name is a shortened form of Barbary, the name then commonly given by Europeans to the African coast from Libya to Morocco. The Barb is smaller than the Arabian but shares many of its characteristics such as stamina and strength. Returning to the Spanish horse, it appears to have developed from the interbreeding of native horses with the imported Arabians and Barbs. These Spanish horses are likely the ancestors of the modern Andalusian breed.

Arabians and Barbs were used for breeding high-quality horses, especially warhorses. The same characteristics which made them good riding horses (strength, endurance, and speed) made them very desirable as warhorses as well. Nobility across Europe bought horses of both these breeds as well as horses de-

veloped from these breeds and added them to their stud farms. From these efforts, this genetic stock was gradually spread across Europe and infused in many regional breeds. Not surprisingly, Arabians and Barbs were so expensive that only the nobility are recorded as purchasing them. They were also given as rare and valuable gifts, suitable for kings and emperors.

Palfreys

Unlike the Arabian and the Barb, the *palfrey* was a not a breed in the modern sense. Instead, palfrey was a name given to the best quality of riding horses. As mentioned previously, they were the most expensive riding horse as well. The name palfrey is derived from Latin *paraveredus*, a name designating the horses used by couriers in the late Roman Empire. The word gradually changed to *palefridus* and from there became "palfrey." Paraveredus is also the root of the German word for horse, *Pferd*. The Roman paraveredus was not noted as being a horse of any outstanding characteristics and, apart from the name, there is no evidence to connect it genetically or otherwise to the medieval riding horse.

The palfrey was a calm horse with a smooth gait and was the riding horse of choice for the nobility. Medieval illustrations show that it was popular with both noble men and women. (See illustration 5.) Allowing for the distortions of perspective common in medieval artwork, the palfrey appears to have had fine features and been a horse of medium height and build.

Rounceys

As with the palfrey, the *rouncey* (or *rouncy*) was a type of horse rather than a specific breed. In the 11th century, *runcinus* or *rincus* meant a plow horse in medieval Latin. Like paraveredus, its form and usage changed over time and, by the 13th century, it had evolved into *rouncey* in English and *roncin* in French and now designated a class of riding horses. In German, *runcinus* became *Ross*, another word for "horse."

While the term *rouncey* came to indicate a better grade of horse than a nag pulling a plow, the social status of those named as riding rounceys suggests that these horses were not as good as palfreys. For example, squires and the servants and men-at-arms who accompanied knights were often mentioned as riding rounceys. However, these riders could seldom afford to own a horse, even a rouncey. This is revealed in documents regarding military service from across Europe, which often specified that each knight, in addition to his destrier, would bring several horses, typically including several rounceys, for his retinue. Thus, the rouncey was of sufficient quality that it did not reflect poorly on a knight to provide such mounts for his party. And so, the rouncey was most likely a decent riding horse of middling quality and price.

Hackneys

In more recent times, *hackney* has meant a breed of horse and a type of horse-drawn coach. In the Middle Ages, the hackney, or *haquenai* in French, was yet another type of riding horse. The hackney is first mentioned in the 14th century. In the group of pilgrims in *The Canterbury Tales*, the canon, a clergy man of comfortable means, rode a hackney.

Hobby

The Irish *hobyn* or *hobby* was a small, sturdy horse bred from stock from Spain. In Spain, it appears to have originated from the native Spanish Asturian breed and may have contained strains of Barb as well. In Ireland, the hobby, which was also known as *haubini* in France, was crossed with local breeds. The result was a small horse which would likely be

Illustration 5. **This party of elegant noble ladies and men are riding palfreys. These graceful horses were bred as riding horses. They were quite expensive but these riders are clearly wealthy and could afford the luxury of superior horses. The gentility of the women is proven by their use of sidesaddles. While there were exceptions, this was considered the proper way for ladies to ride (© The British Library Board. All Rights Reserved 8/31/2010. Harley MS 4431, f.81).**

considered a pony by modern standards. In war, lightly armored soldiers rode the hobbies but did not fight as cavalry. Instead, they dismounted and fought on foot. In England, these soldiers came to be called *hobelars*. By the late 13th century, hobbies were exported to Scotland where they were well-suited to the fast-moving raiding tactics used by the Scots against the English. Small and tough, the hobby provided good mobility in difficult terrain. The English were impressed by the performance of the Scottish hobelars and hired several hundred Irish hobelars, complete with their hobbies, in 1296. In peacetime, the hobby could serve as a mount for ordinary riding. And after the Middle Ages, the name "hobby" came to mean a small riding horse with an easy gait.

Jennets

The *jennet*, in French *ginet*, was developed on the Iberian Peninsula. The name "jennet" was derived from the Spanish *jinete*, which meant a horseman who rode in the *la jineta* style, that is, with the stirrups shortened so that the rider's legs were tucked up close to his body. Over time, jinete came to designate the rider, his horse, and a combat tactic. Jinetes were lightly armored cavalrymen armed with lances or javelins who rode fast mounts and used their speed to strike at the enemy and then move out of range just as quickly. Light, fast, tough horses were best suited for this type of combat. Some of these horses appear to have been Barbs although many were likely a cross between Barbs and native Spanish horses, with the characteristics of the Barb dominating the mix. As with the Barb, the jennet was a comparatively small horse but, again like the Barb, was appreciated for its toughness and speed. By the 17th century, the jennet was being used in England to breed small, elegant riding horses.

Destrier

While the hobby and jennet had qualities that made them generally desirable and useful in peacetime as well as in war, the *destrier* was a specialized warhorse that had little use outside of the battlefield and tournament ground. Its name was derived from the Latin word *dextrarius*, meaning "on the right side." This may have been based on the custom of having the knight's squire use only his right hand to lead the horse when not in combat.

As discussed previously, considerable effort went into breeding warhorses so that they had the speed, stamina, and strength needed in combat. Additionally, as the weight of armor for both man and horse increased over the course of the Middle Ages, the destrier had to evolve to meet the challenge. In the early Middle Ages, well-built and strong but not particularly large or tall horses appear to have been used as warhorses. By the 14th century, depictions of warhorses show them as relatively tall, powerfully-built horses. By the 15th century, a knight's plate armor weighed approximately 60 to 70 pounds and a horse's armor weighed 50 pounds or more. Stronger horses were needed to bear this load and still provide vital mobility on the battlefield. Further, destriers were bred for increased height as well. The nature of medieval combat made height important for the knight. To use modern terminology, tall horses gave knights the "high ground." This added height allowed knights to inflict more damage to their opponents. Knights used impact weapons: lances, swords, maces, and others. When going up against other mounted knights, a height advantage could allow a knight to strike higher up on his opponent with his lance. This could possibly increase the chance of toppling an enemy from his saddle or at least hitting his head, throat, or upper chest, all vital areas. The height advantage was more clear-cut when a mounted knight attacked foot soldiers. From atop his horse and wielding his sword or other hand weapon, the knight could rain blows down on the heads and shoulders of the infantry men.

The destriers of the 15th century were likely the largest of their day but they were not giant, lumbering draft horses, despite the common misperception that only draft horses would be capable of carrying an armored man. Surviving armor for horses as well as contemporary illustrations from across Europe prove this point, revealing that they were about 15 hands (approximately 60 inches or five feet) high at the shoulders. The average height for horses in the Middle Ages is estimated at around 13½ hands (54 inches) so the warhorse did stand well above its contemporaries. However, most modern breeds are at least 15 hands high and many easily reach 16 hands. Further, the current breed standards for the Shire horse (the traditional English heavy draft horse which is often thought to resemble a destrier) require a minimum height for stallions of 17 hands (68 inches), with an average height of 17.2 hands (68.8 inches, about five feet, nine inches) for the breed. This average height is almost a full nine inches taller than the estimate for an average destrier. Given the increase in girth and weight that goes along with the extra height, there is no question that, while the destrier was a very powerful and robust horse and the largest of its day, it was far more compact than a modern draft horse.

Despite all the effort put into breeding warhorses, they ceased to exist soon after the end of the Middle Ages. Developments in weapons and tactics made the heavily armored knight obsolete so the destrier was replaced by tall but lighter horses suited to the new style of combat in which armor was considerably reduced and handguns were used along with sabers. Thus, like other domesticated animals, once the need for it had passed, the great horse was no longer bred and became extinct. The genetic strains of the destrier likely survive but have been scattered. We can only try to find resemblances in modern breeds using images and descriptions of warhorses.

Gaits

Besides the names given above, horses were often deiscribed by their gait. The most common were *amblers*, *pacers*, and *trotters*. As with the names, the gaits provided little or no clues as to the breed. For example, trotting is simply one of the natural gaits of horses. As for ambling and pacing, some horses can amble or pace naturally and many others can be trained to do so. When trotting, the horse moves its diagonally opposite legs at the same time. That is, the left front and right rear legs move together and the right front and left rear do the same. Trotting produces a somewhat jarring ride as the horse's back moves up and down with each complete stride. The rider can be bounced up and then dropped back down by this motion. Experienced riders learn to relax and move with the horse. Pacing and ambling provide greater comfort and are less fatiguing for the rider. This was particularly

desirable for long rides, for novice riders or those who seldom rode, and for those who simply wanted to be more comfortable. In pacing, the horse moves both legs on the same side (left front and left rear, right front and right rear) at the same time. As a result, the up and down motion is smoothed out but there is a side-to-side rocking movement instead. Still, it is more comfortable than trotting. Finally, for ambling, the horse moves its legs one at a time rather than in pairs. This provides the smoothest ride with no bouncing up and down and no rocking from side to side.

A horse's gait was an important factor in its value. This is sometimes reflected in records of prices for horses which reveal that trotters were significantly cheaper than amblers. The difference in cost may have been driven by the extra expense in training a horse to amble as well as by the greater desirability of a smoother ride. While there is no indisputable evidence, it seems likely that palfreys were amblers.

Other Descriptions of Horses

Lastly, there are riding horses which are given no specific name or gait. These horses are simply referred to by their gender (most often mares) or by their color, such as roan, bay, dun, or grey. Horses with more complex coloring were described with more sophisticated adjectives such as *lyard* (*liard* in French), meaning fine spots of white on a grey background, or *bausond* (*balzano* in Italian and *baucyn* in French) for a pattern of larger white spots on a background of any color. Other names for horses included *coursers, jades, affers,* or *stotts*. Coursers were fine horses noted for their speed and suited to racing and hunting. On the other hand, the names jade, affer, and stott are all comparable to the modern *nag* and so provide only the insight that the animal was a plain working horse or, worse, was old, worn out, or just plain ugly in the eyes of the person describing it (see illustration 4). Finally, the majority were just call "horses."

As all of the foregoing suggests, it is very difficult, if not impossible, to determine the breed and qualities of most medieval riding horses. Perhaps the most useful way to think of all these different names and descriptions is to compare the cars of today. There are scores of different makes and models of automobiles, from imported luxury cars down to small economy cars. And when one adds in the various options for enhancing performance or comfort, there are hundreds of possible combinations. Applying this analogy, a palfrey would be an expensive luxury car with a leather interior and powerful engine. A rouncey on the other hand would be a sensible, reasonably priced mid-sized car. Many others could be considered economy cars, some used and in bad condition. Still others, as we will see below, were the tractors and trucks of their day. These might not be the best comparisons but the surviving evidence for medieval horses has too many gaps for any closer analogies.

MULES AND DONKEYS

While horses were the preferred animal for riding, mules and, more rarely, donkeys (the domestic ass) were also used as mounts. Mules and donkeys were more affordable than horses but riding one typically showed that the person was of lower social status than one who could afford to ride a horse. However, the sure-footedness of both the mule and donkey did make them useful in rough and mountainous terrain as well as on poorly maintained roads. They could also survive by foraging better than horses.

A mule is the offspring of a male donkey and a female horse. While they have become a byword for stubbornness, mules generally have a calm temperament, which makes them quite suitable for riding. Compared to the donkey, the greater size and strength of the mule made it more desirable as a riding animal and so donkeys seem to have been ridden only by those who had no other choice. Still, there were exceptions. Mules and donkeys were sometimes seen as more suitable mounts than horses for members of the clergy since the use

of these more humble animals recalled Christ's humility in entering Jerusalem riding a donkey. However, this seems to have seldom deterred most clerics from riding horses whenever they were available. Pilgrims used donkeys as mounts in the Holy Land. This too may have been a sign of humility but, in the late Middle Ages, the Moslems who then controlled Jerusalem and the rest of Palestine banned pilgrims from riding horses and permitted them to hire and ride only donkeys.

Saddles

Whichever animal one rode, a saddle was essential. As they still are today, saddles in the Middle Ages were made from wood, leather, metal, and material for padding. A saddler began by constructing the wooden saddletree. This was a stout framework that formed the foundation of the seat for the rider. The saddletree was built to place the weight of the rider on either side of the horse's back. Having the saddle rest directly on the spine would seriously injure the horse. The saddletree was then covered in leather and the girth straps for securing the saddle to the horse were also added at this stage. The leather foundation was built up in the front and back to create the pommel (the upward projection at the front) and the cantle (the one at the back of the saddle). These gave the rider a firmer seat in the saddle. On ordinary riding saddles, the pommel and cantle rose a few inches, just enough to give the rider a comfortable and secure seat, but on saddles for warhorses the pommel and cantle were much larger. The higher pommel and cantle gave the knight a much firmer seat, with the cantle rising several inches and curving to enclose his lower back to prevent his being knocked off his horse. A layer of padding, perhaps made of tow (flax fibers) or other durable yet pliable materials, went over the base layer of leather. A final layer of leather or cloth covered the padding. The saddler finished by fitting the buckles to the straps although lorimers, the craftsmen responsible for making bits and other metal fittings for horses, sometimes challenged the saddler's right to do this.

Saddles were sometimes decorated. Besides being covered in colorful cloth, some saddles were painted or decorated with metal badges. (Again, the lorimers, as well as painters, protested when saddlers performed such work themselves.) In addition, surviving saddles for jousting reveal that decorations with carved panels of bone were sometimes inserted into the sides of these saddles.

Sidesaddles and Pillions

Unlike men, women generally did not ride astride horses in the Middle Ages. Modesty and propriety, as well as the impracticality of straddling a horses while wearing a long dress, dictated that women rode with both their legs on one side of the horse. (See illustration 5.) As a consequence, they used sidesaddles, known as a *sambue* in France. Unlike an ordinary saddle in which the seat faces forward, the seat of a sidesaddle is turned to one side of the horse. Women also rode on *pillions*. These were cushioned extensions added to the back of an ordinary saddle that permitted a woman to ride sidesaddle behind a man.

While the majority of female riders rode either on pillions or sidesaddles, there were a few that rode like men. For example, in the 1410s, Queen Isabeau of France had riding trousers specially made for her so that she could ride astride her horse. However, exceptions such as this were so rare and unusual that they merited special mention in the chronicles and other records of the time.

DRAFT ANIMALS

Although they were held in far lower esteem than riding horses, medieval society could not have functioned without the armies of draft animals that slaved away in the fields and on the roads. Without the oxen and horses that pulled the plows, Europe would have starved. Further, until the advent of the steam locomotive, these animals hauled the carts and wagons which carried everything society needed, from grain to building stone to passengers.

Oxen

For most of the Middle Ages, the work of pulling plows, carts, and anything else that needed hauling was performed primarily by oxen. Horses gradually became more common than oxen as draft animals but they never fully displaced oxen for heavy hauling. The ox possessed several attributes which made it an ideal draft animal. For one, the physiology of the ox's shoulders and neck made it easy to harness. Oxen were fitted with wooden oxbows that placed the stress of pulling on their shoulders and chest. Straps or ropes attached to these yokes harnessed the oxen to the plow or cart they pulled. The ox was also strong and had a generally placid temperament. Further, as a ruminant, it fed primarily on grasses and so could be easily maintained by being put out to pasture for most of the year and being fed hay in the winter. In this last respect, oxen were cheaper and easier to keep than horses, which could not live on grasses alone. They required oats or other grains to stay healthy. Finally, at the end of its life, the ox became a nutritious (if rather tough) foodstuff and provided a hide to be turned into leather. These factors explain why it had been used a draft animal for millennia before the Middle Ages and continued to be for some time afterwards.

The ox, like all other medieval livestock, was smaller than its modern descendants. But it was still the strongest draft animal of the time. Further, to increase pulling power, oxen were most often used in pairs or teams rather than singly. For example, for pulling the heavy plows of the late Middle Ages, teams of six to eight oxen were considered ideal. For heavy hauling, even more pairs of oxen were often harnessed together to form more powerful teams. Another example can be found in royal accounts from 14th century England which record the use of teams of ten oxen to pull wagons loaded with an estimated four tons of lead each. Even larger teams were recorded, including a single one which contained 26 pairs of oxen. This team was used for hauling stone for the construction of cathedrals. Oxen were an essential feature of cathedral construction. In a unique recognition of the ox's contribution, the builders of Laon cathedral included 16 statues of oxen high up in the towers they helped build. But such recognition was exceptional. Oxen went unrecorded in most cases. Instead, when a cart or wagon was hired, it was assumed that a suitable number of draft animals came with it. Thus, there are numerous entries in construction and shipping contracts for carts and wagons but rarely any mention of the animals that pulled them.

Draft Horses

As discussed previously, medieval horses, like oxen, were significantly smaller than their modern counterparts. Immense and strong draft horses, such as the Percheron, Clydesdale or Shire horse, were not bred until well after the end of the period. This is borne out by the pictorial evidence which does not show medieval draft horses as being especially large or powerfully built. (See illustration 4.) Yet horses were increasingly used as draft animals over the course of the Middle Ages. The horse certainly did not completely replace the ox, but it gradually took over a larger role even for heavy hauling. This growing use of the horse can be attributed to improvements in harnessing and a growing availability of horses.

The horse harnesses developed in the Middle Ages were a significant improvement over those used by the Romans. Based on pictorial evidence, the Roman harness appears to have had a wide strap or collar that ran across the horse's neck. When the horse was pulling a heavy load, the collar was drawn tight against the horse's throat, restricting its breathing and blood flow. This problem prevented horses from pulling heavy loads or being used in agriculture to pull plows. Even if the collar had been positioned so that it did not impair the horse, it only harnessed the pulling power of

the horse's chest. Recent archaeological finds have confirmed the existence of a second form of Roman harness which rested on the top of the neck in front of the horse's shoulders and withers. (The withers are located where the horse's neck and back meet, between its shoulders. It forms a slight lump against which the harness can rest.) This harness in no way interfered with the horse's breathing but it only harnessed the force of the shoulders and not that of the horse's chest. Further evidence of the low pulling power of Roman horses is found in Roman laws on the use of roads, which include limits on the weights that could be carried by horse-drawn wagons. These restrictions set weights which are low even by medieval standards. This suggests that Roman horses, hampered by their harnesses, could only pull relatively light loads and that the weight limits were to protect the horses from being injured by pulling heavy loads. In the Middle Ages, solutions were developed for this problem. The first was the breast strap which appeared in the 6th century. This was actually formed by a combination of straps. One strap encircled the horse's girth behind its shoulders. The other was connected to the first strap at the sides of the horse and went around the horse's breast. This placed the pressure of pulling on the chest rather than the throat. However, within a few centuries, a better system of harnessing was developed and replaced this system of straps. The new method was to use a padded collar which rested against the horse's *withers* and the breast (see illustration 4). This kept pressure away from the throat while maximizing the horse's pulling power by harnessing the force of both the chest and the shoulders. Straps or ropes called *traces* were attached on both sides of the collar and then back to the cart or plow being pulled. This type of collar has been in use up through the present.

The second factor which likely led to the increased use of horses for hauling was the growing availability of horses. In the Roman Empire, horses appear to have been bred primarily for the use of high-ranking citizens, for the military, for horse racing, and for the government's courier service. Some were used as draft animals but they were more commonly employed for pulling passenger vehicles, which were relatively lightweight, rather than heavy freight wagons. The restricted use of horses continued into the early Middle Ages since the majority of horses were owned by the nobility who bred them for their own use for riding or warfare. The nobility continued to breed horses throughout the Middle Ages, but ownership and breeding of horses by commoners proliferated and horses became readily available on the open market. While oxen remained more numerous, the horse population of medieval Europe expanded over the course of the period to the point that draft horses became a common sight on farms across Europe.

With the improved collar and the growing number of horses available, horses were increasingly used as draft animals. The horse was faster than the ox and could pull heavy weights when harnessed in teams. Horses also generally had greater stamina than oxen and so could work more hours per day. However, the ox was still generally stronger than the horse, so more horses were usually needed to haul the same weight that a smaller number of oxen could move. Still, records indicate that, by the late Middle Ages, eight horses were strong enough to pull a plow just like oxen and, with their superior speed, likely completed their jobs in less time than a comparable team of oxen. The use of horses on farms steadily increased during the Middle Ages but horses came to be the primary plow animal only after the period. As with plowing, horses had an expanding role in hauling vehicles. From the beginning of the Middle Ages, horses were the only animals depicted pulling passenger vehicles. The greater speed of the horse was put to good use, as teams of horses could quickly move these comparatively light vehicles. In addition, horses had prestige value. Passenger coaches were primarily owned by the wealthy and noble and having a coach drawn by fine horses was another opportunity

to display one's high status. As for heavy hauling, with the improved collar, horses could pull significantly heavier loads than their ancestors could. Gradually, horses came to be commonly used for hauling carts and wagons in most of Europe.

As with oxen, horses were typically used in teams when hauling, their greater numbers used to make up for the limited strength of each horse. Single horses are depicted performing the relatively light task of harrowing fields. When plowing, they were shown harnessed side-by-side in pairs like oxen. But, when pulling carts, horses were more often depicted as harnessed in a single file, forming a single line instead of two lines as when harnessed in pairs. Whether in single files or files of pairs, harnessing in file maximizes traction for the number of animals available. By having all the animals in a straight line in front of the vehicle, as much power as possible is directed to pulling the vehicle forward. None is wasted in any sideways motion such as would occur if the animals were harnessed side-by-side in a row extending beyond the width of the vehicle. While many depictions of horses in file show two horses, one ahead of the other, another advantage of harnessing in single file is that it allows more easily for the use of odd numbers of animals. In many manuscripts, horses were shown in odd numbers in single file (see illustration 4).

The use of large teams of draft horses and other animals, either in single or double file, did not end with the Middle Ages. Up into the 19th century, in Europe and the United States, express passenger coaches used teams of up to four pairs of horses. When rail service was not available, cargos too were moved by large numbers of animals. Perhaps the best example from the United States comes from the late 19th century. Teams of 20 mules were used to haul huge wagons loaded with tons of borax across deserts in southern California. Mules were used because they were hardier than horses and could more easily survive the rigors of the desert. Interestingly, while they were frequently used as pack animals, mules rarely appeared as draft animals in medieval Europe. This was a change from the days of the Roman Empire, when donkeys and mules were often depicted pulling wagons and carts.

Other Draft Animals

In addition to equines and oxen, a few other animals were pressed into service as draft animals. On the northern fringes of Europe, Lapps, natives of the northern regions of Scandinavia, used tamed reindeer to pull sleighs and sleds, a practice which has survived to the present. Also in the far north of Europe, teams of dogs were used to pull light sleds. Pulling sleds appears to have been the only use of dogs as draft animals in the Middle Ages. There are no written records of dogs being used to pull vehicles. There is a single medieval illustration of a huntsman riding in a cart pulled by a team of three hunting dogs. But this illustration is part of a series of marginalia that includes many absurd scenes, such as a dog in a cart pulled by two rabbits and a knight fighting a giant snail. Thus, the image cannot be taken as proof of dog-drawn carts. However, in some parts of Europe after the Middle Ages, dogs were used to pull small carts. In Belgium, for example, dogs were used to pull little milk delivery carts up until the early 20th century. There may also be some confusion about dog carts since, in the 19th century, the name "dog cart" was given to a type of light, horse-drawn passenger cart, originally used to transport hunting dogs out to the field.

PACK ANIMALS

Commonly referred to as *sumpters* (*sommier* in French), pack animals were used to transport any items that could be broken down into loads small enough to fit on their backs. Horses, mules, and donkeys were used as sumpters. Depending on the size and strength of the animal, loads ranged from about 200 pounds up to 300 pounds. Pack-saddles, panniers, and other specialized con-

tainers allowed them to carry a bewildering array of items. Some were fitted with huge leather bags for carrying water. Others carried bags or sacks that could contain anything from a merchant's wares to the bedding or even the treasury of a great lord on the move. Still others labored carrying building stones just small enough to fit into their panniers. And some were express carriers of perishables, carrying live fish packed in wet grass from the fishponds of some noble estate to a specially favored recipient. Those peasants who owned horses were sometimes subject to carrying duties as part of their obligations to their lord. They had to appear in person along with their horse and carry whatever their lord needed carried. Sumpters were also available for hire along with men who guided or drove them. In France, these men were often referred to as *muletiers*, which suggests that mules were widely used as sumpters in France. Mule drivers came to be called *muleteers* in English but sumpter drivers in medieval England were typically called sumpter men, and horses rather than mules appear to have been the most common pack animal in England.

Estimates for the carrying capacity of medieval packhorses range from 200 to 300 pounds. This is significantly less than the weight a single horse could have moved by pulling a cart, which is estimated at a minimum of about 800 pounds. A further handicap of pack animals was that they had to be completely unloaded when stopping for the night while draft animals only required unhitching, which was substantially less burdensome. Still, pack animals could negotiate trails and rough roads which were impassable for carts and wagons. They were essential for moving goods along the steep and narrow paths through the passes of the Alps. Pack animals could typically move faster than carts and wagons as well. Additionally, for small loads, such as the stock in trade of a traveling peddler or shipments of compact but very valuable items such as coinage, pack animals were far more appropriate in size and carrying capacity than carts and wagons.

The Expense and Burdens of Maintaining Riding, Draft, and Pack Animals

As indicated in several references above, owning animal for riding, hauling, and carrying was expensive. Some, such as the ox, were comparatively cheap to maintain while horses, on the other hand, could be very expensive.

First, there was the cost of obtaining the animal. Ideally, households bred their own animals, but this was not always an option and they often had to purchase them in the open market. So, how much did they cost? Providing meaningful prices for anything in the Middle Ages, including horses, oxen, and other livestock, is extremely difficult. The period spans a thousand years and there were periods of inflation and depression with prices and wages fluctuating just as they do today. Additionally, there are no precise "exchange rates" between modern and historic moneys. Only rough estimates can be made. So, as previously mentioned, the best that can be done is to compare the prices of items at a particular time and place in the Middle Ages and see the relative values. For example, in the early 14th century in England (before the Black Death):

Warhorse — 50 to 100+ pounds
Palfrey —10 to 50 pounds
Courser —10 to 50 pounds
Rouncey — 5 to 10 pounds
Hobby — 2 pounds
Cart Horse —⅝th of a pound
Pack Horse —⅝th of a pound
Farm Horse —¼th of a pound
Ox —½ to ¾th of a pound

(Note: These figures are drawn from a different source than the price estimates previously discussed and do not yield the exact same results. However, they do reflect comparable relative differences in the prices of these animals and include information on draft and pack animals which the first source lacked.)

At the same time a quarter of wheat cost from ³⁄₁₀ to ¾ of a pound. (A quarter was eight bushels of grain, approximately enough to provide bread and other cereal dishes for one person for a year.) While bearing in mind that some of these figures are averages and others are based on a very small number of documented sales, these numbers show that the purchase of a horse or ox required a substantial outlay of money. Half to ¾ of a pound for an ox might not sound like a lot of money but to a subsistence farmer such a price could be a significant portion of a year's profits. The fact that this was a relatively high cost was reflected in the common practice of pooling resources with neighboring farmers to have enough oxen to form a team for pulling a plow.

If one had the money, it appears to have been not that difficult to find someone willing to sell one a horse or ox. Horse fairs were a regular feature in medieval cities. The best description of one comes from the late 12th century. As part of his description of London, William Fitz Stephen, secretary to Thomas a'Becket (the future martyred saint), wrote about the horse fair which took place every Saturday in Smithfield, just outside the city walls. Every type of horse, from rounceys to destriers, was available. Impromptu races were held to show off the qualities of the finer horses. Lower-quality horses, such as plow and cart horses, and cattle were sold at a separate market at which farm animals were sold.

Buyers did well to examine their purchases closely since sellers did their best to conceal any defects in the animals. But even back then, it was possible to sue for egregious swindles. Additionally, a wise buyer also established that the seller was the legal owner or his authorized agent before purchasing since selling stolen horses and other livestock was not unknown. Out in the countryside, this problem was taken seriously, and in some areas a buyer had to comply with rules intended to thwart the sale of "hot" horses and cows. These requirements included informing village officials of the purchase, formally identifying the seller, and displaying the animal in the common pasture for a time. Failure to comply with these rules could be punished by forfeiture of the animal. These requirements were primarily for instances when an animal had been bought outside the village and its immediate environs since local sales were easily verified. However, even these transactions were often done before witnesses to avoid any later claims by either the buyer or seller.

Purchasing an animal was just the start of the expenses. While it should be obvious, it is all too easy to forget that animals could not simply be ridden or driven and then parked like cars or trucks when they weren't needed. To stay healthy, they required constant care: shelter, feeding, treatment for any illness or injury, and exercise to keep them in shape for their jobs.

Horses required additional expenditures for food since they could not survive entirely on grass and hay. They needed grains in their diets and were typically fed oats and wheat chaff. They were occasionally fed peas and other legumes as well. When kept in the city, they were sometimes fed "horse breads" made with beans. It is estimated that, because of their dietary needs, horses were 40 percent more expensive to feed than oxen. This estimate is for farm horses. Higher quality horses may have consumed feed that was two to three times more expensive than that fed to the common ox.

Shoeing of horses and oxen was common across medieval Europe. The lack of differences between late Roman and early medieval horseshoes make it difficult to pin down where and when the use of horseshoes occurred. In any event, the practice had been adopted throughout Europe by the 10th century at the latest. Shoeing was relatively cheap. Around the middle of the 14th century, it cost one and one-half to two pence per shoe. (One pence was 1/240 of a pound.) This included the cost of the shoe and the labor of nailing it onto the horse's hoof. Since horses' hooves grow, the shoes needed to be removed several times during a year so that the hoof could be trimmed. This meant pulling out the nails that attached the shoe and then nailing them back on after the hoof was trimmed. This cost one-half to one pence. Records for shoeing oxen are ex-

tremely scarce but it is likely that the costs and the need for periodic removal and refitting were comparable to those for horses.

Given the expense of upkeep, it is no surprise that riding and draft animals were routinely available for hire in much of Europe for much of the Middle Ages. As mentioned previously, commoners, clerics, nuns, and the nobility, including royalty, took advantage of these forerunners to modern car and truck rental services. The renter paid a suitable fee which was likely based on the number of days the animal was to be used. He then had to pay only for the food and care of the animal while he was using it. The cost of shoeing and maintaining the animal between rentals was the responsibility of the owner. This arrangement was far cheaper for the renter than owning an animal. However, the expense of rental could become a matter of dispute when an animal was injured, became sick, or died while in the custody of the renter. The rental agents often claimed that the renter owed reparations for the damage or loss of the animal. The renter, on the other hand, sometimes counterclaimed, asserting that the animal was defective before he took it and that he owed nothing. Further, the renter could demand that he be compensated for any veterinary care he paid for. Such disputes were likely as acrimonious as any today between rental car agencies and customers over scratches and dents.

Renting was not always an option. For long distances and one-way trips, it was often impossible to find anyone willing to rent a riding animal. Instead, travelers often bought a mount and then sold it when they reached their destination. Additionally, even renting could be costly, especially when hiring draft animals and carts. While some draft animals were hired alone to move wagons and carts owned by the person renting the animals, it was common to hire the animals along with the wagons and the carters who drove the wagons. In most cities, there were freight companies that provided such hauling service. This service was usually quite expensive since one had to pay the wages of the carters for both the outbound trip and their return trip back to their homes as well as for the rental of wagons and draft animals. For long haul jobs of raw materials such as timber and stone, the transportation costs often greatly exceeded the base value of the items being moved. Still, for lesser moving jobs and especially for the occasional need for riding horses, renting was cheaper than owning.

THE FINAL USE OF HORSES AND OXEN

Regardless of whether they were cheap draft horses or expensive riding horses, all horses were slaughtered when they came to the end of their useful lives. They were usually skinned and their hides made into leather but their meat was typically not used as food. For centuries before the Middle Ages, this was not so. Saxons in England as well as Germanic peoples in mainland Europe sacrificed horses and ate their flesh as part of their worship of the Norse god Woden. This practice continued into the early Middle Ages but as Europe became increasingly Christianized this and all other pagan rituals came to be condemned by the Church. Beginning in the 8th century, popes decreed that all consumption of horse meat must stop because of its connection to paganism. This ban spread across Christian Europe and the eating of horseflesh came to be limited to times of famine. Yet, the taste for horse meat has persisted and there are several countries in modern Europe where horse is consumed. The most notable, perhaps, is France. The French reversion to eating horse meat allegedly started during the French Revolution when horses, symbols of the hated aristocracy, were slaughtered to feed the poor. The killing of horses for human consumption was formally legalized in France in the 19th century and continues to the present day.

As for oxen, these animals too were slaughtered when they were no longer productive. Their hides were tanned and made into leather. Their horns were cut off and the outer layer separated from the inner core. The outer layer of horn could then be boiled and split to form a sheet of a plastic-like material that could be made into handles for knives and other useful items. There were no taboos against eating ox meat and it likely provided a welcome, if tough, addition to the table.

Vehicles

The subject of vehicles of the Middle Ages immediately conjures up images of crude ox carts with massive wheels made out of planks of wood. As with many other assumptions about the crudity of medieval people and the quality of their workmanship, this popular perception is largely baseless. While less than a handful of vehicles have survived from the Middle Ages, there are many illustrations of a wide range of vehicles. These reveal a variety of wagons and carts which were well-built and suited to the purposes to which they were put (see illustrations 4 and 6.)

TYPES OF VEHICLES

Vehicles in medieval Europe were referred to by a maddening variety of names. There were *plaustra*, *biga*, *wains*, *carra*, *carecta*, *quadriga*, *tumbrels*, *chars*, *chariots*, and many others. Many of these names were relics of the Roman Empire but they came to refer to vehicles quite unlike their Roman predecessors. Further, in some cases, these terms overlap with one name covering both two- and four-wheeled vehicles. In other cases, the terms appear to have designated different sizes of the same vehicles. Given this confusion, for the purposes of this book, vehicles with two wheels are called carts, four-wheeled cargo vehicles are wagons, and vehicles designed to carry people are passenger vehicles.

Carts

By far, the most common vehicle of the Middle Ages was the two-wheeled cart (see il-

Illustration 6. **In this scene of the bridges of Paris (detail from a full page in *Life of St. Denis*, 1317), a coach is crossing into the city. Although there are no records of commercial coach service at this time, this coach is likely a public one rather than a private coach. It is packed full of passengers whose faces are visible through the coach's windows. The driver is riding postillion on the horse harnessed nearest to the coach. Riding postillion was common since wagons and coaches were rarely built with seats for the driver. Below, three boats are delivering wine. In one the wine merchant is bargaining with a customer while a man in another boat, possibly one of the boatmen, samples some of the wine (courtesy of the Bibliothèque Nationale de France, FR 2091, fol. 125).**

lustration 4). These vehicles were extremely useful and were used to carry an infinite variety of things from building stones and crops to spoils of war. The widespread need for carts and their importance is reflected in documents of feudal obligations. Peasants, for example, were sometimes subject to cartage duties. They had to supply a cart with suitable draft animals and serve in person to drive the cart. They then had to carry whatever load their lord needed moved. Similarly, some records of military services reveal that vassals serving their lords on campaign were expected to bring carts along with their men-at-arms. The carts were essential for carrying food and other supplies the army needed. For example, when conducting a campaign in France in the mid–14th century, Edward III, king of England, was recorded as having 6,000 carts, each

pulled by four horses. While this figure must be an exaggeration, Edward certainly had a vast number of carts to carry food, tents, weapons, and armor for the thousands of men in his army. Further, he had carts loaded with hand-mills for grinding grain into flour, portable ovens for baking bread, and forges for shoeing horses and other metal work. On the return from a successful campaign, the carts would be loaded with plunder.

Carts were also needed for peaceful pursuits such as building cathedrals. Whether the quarry was nearby or miles away, carts were essential for carrying stones to construction sites. The importance of carts in building churches and cathedrals can be seen in the donation of the use of carts and draft animals. Such donations were considered as commendable as gifts of money. Whether in war or peace, medieval society could not have functioned without carts.

Carts were typically drawn by either oxen or horses. As previously discussed, oxen were more common than horses as draft animals in the first half of the Middle Ages. Over time, horses took over as the primary draft animals for all vehicles. Beginning in the 13th century, most illustrations show horses rather than oxen pulling carts. Using a cart greatly enhanced the load an animal could move. As previously discussed, a packhorse could carry from 200 to 300 pounds but with a cart a single horse could haul up to four times that weight. And heavier loads could be moved by adding more horses to the team. Additionally, a cart had the added convenience that when halting for rest the cart horse merely had to be unhitched, while a packhorse had to be completely unloaded.

Wheels

Interestingly, in illustrations of carts, even those from the earliest years of the Middle Ages, there are no depictions of wheels made of layers of solid planks such as are commonly shown in movies set in medieval Europe. Instead, a wheel in the Middle Ages was typically composed of a rim, spokes, and hub, just as it had been for centuries before the Middle Ages and would be for the centuries that followed (see illustrations 4 and 6).

In antiquity, the Romans, Celts, and many other peoples made wheel rims from single pieces of wood by carefully bending them to form the circular rim. The wood was likely steamed or soaked in water to make it pliable enough to bend. They also made wheels with rims composed of several pieces of wood. These pieces were called fellies and each was carefully shaped to form a segment of the curve of the wheel's rim. When joined together, the fellies formed the complete circle of the rim. Wheels with rims made of a single piece of wood appear to have been considered superior to those made of fellies since the former were more expensive. The construction of wheel rims from single pieces of wood dis-

appeared in the early Middle Ages and rims came to be made only of fellies.

Medieval wheelwrights were quite skilled. They carefully cut the curved surfaces of the fellies so that when they were finally joined they formed as perfect a circle as possible. They shaped the spokes, making them slender but strong. United, the hub, spokes, and fellies formed a durable, solid unit. In illustrations from throughout the Middle Ages, examples of these well-built wheels can be seen on vehicles from royal coaches to humble farm carts.

Making wheels with spokes instead of layers of planks had several benefits. A solid, plank wheel would have required far more wood than a wheel with spokes. Medieval artisans sought to avoid such a waste of material. Like many craftsmen before and since, medieval wheelwrights strove to make the most efficient use of their materials and the construction of wheels with hubs, spokes, and fellies produced the strongest wheel with the least amount of wood. People likely resorted to making plank wheels only if no local craftsman could make spoked wheels and no such wheels could be obtained through trade. These circumstances appear to have been rare.

Using layers of planks would also have produced very heavy wheels. A cart or wagon fitted with such wheels would have weighed much more than a comparable vehicle with spoked wheels. The heavier plank wheeled cart or wagon would have required more animals to pull it than the one with spoked wheels. If additional draft animals were not available, the load of the plank wheeled cart or wagon would have to be reduced to a level that could be pulled by the existing team of animals. In contrast, using spoked wheels reduced the weight of the cart or wagon. As a consequence, more of the pulling power of the team of draft animals could be applied to moving the load rather than the deadweight of the cart or wagon. This enabled draft animals to haul larger, heavier cargoes.

While it cannot be determined, wheels may have often been left with their wooden rims exposed instead of being fitted with metal rims to protect the wood. The availability and cost of the iron needed for the rim likely dictated whether or not a wheel was finished with a metal rim. Thus, a typical farm cart may not have had a metal rim but, as indicated in records of expenditures on maintenance, wheels on vehicles owned by the nobility appear to have been routinely fitted with iron rims. The intended use of the cart may have also determined whether or not it would be iron rimmed. The wheels of a cart built to carry only light loads were subject to less stress and wear than were the wheels of a cart which carried heavy cargo. As a consequence, there was less of a need to protect the wheels of a light-duty cart with metal rims than there was for the wheels of a heavy-duty cart. Iron rims were made in sections which were nailed to the wooden rim so that they overlapped and protected the joints between the fellies. The Romans had metal rims which were made of a single band of iron which was heated and then fitted around the wooden rim. As the metal cooled, it shrunk so that it fit tightly on the rim. Unfortunately, this technique was lost with the collapse of the Roman Empire and was not used again until the 18th century. It then went on to become the standard method for affixing metal rims on wagon wheels. Returning to the Middle Ages, the outside of the wheel's rim was sometimes studded to improve traction. These wheels were well suited to rough roads but in cities they could crack and break paving stones. As a consequence, horse-drawn carts with iron-shod wheels were banned in some cities. The surfaces of bridges were vulnerable to such damage as well and iron-shod carts were banned from bridges in Toulouse and London. However, it is unclear whether these bans applied to all carts with iron-rimmed wheels or only those with studded rims. The latter seems more likely.

The pairs of wheels were mounted on the two ends of the cart's axle. In most illustrations, it appears that cart axles were attached directly to the bottom of its bed. However, it is more likely that they were fixed to a frame under the bed. As with wheels and axles for many vehicles before and since the Middle Ages, the cart's axle was stationery and did not rotate. Instead, the wheels rotated freely on the two ends of the axle. This allowed the wheels to turn independently of each other, which permitted the cart to roll more easily, especially when turning. Turning requires having the wheel on one side turn faster than the opposite wheel. This is as true for automobiles today as it was for medieval carts. The wheels were held on the axle by metal or wooden wedges which were fitted into holes in each end of the axle. Based on post-medieval examples, these wedges would have needed protection from being worn away by the constant rubbing of the hub against them. While it is not clear from the illustrations or accounts of expenditures on wheel construction and repair, it is possible that some form of collar or washer was fitted on the axle between the hub and the wedge. This would protect both the wedge as well as the outside end of the hub from damage. This was the solution used after the Middle Ages. If this method was not used, the wedges would quickly wear out and require frequent replacement.

The inside of the hub was sometimes fitted with a metal collar and the axle was also protected with a metal band. Making these surfaces of metal made them more durable. The Romans had used this same technique. Experts disagree over when this improvement was reintroduced but it was clearly in use by the 14th century at the latest. As with rims, this use of metal may have been limited by the cost and availability of iron as well as by the use for which the cart was made. Whether of wood or metal, the hub and axle end required constant greasing. This lessened the friction between the hub and axle and so cut down on the wear on these parts. This grease was made of animal fat.

One other use of metal in making wheels was the reinforcement of hubs with metal bands. These bands encircled the outside of the hub and helped keep it from splitting.

Cart Construction

The bodies of most carts were made of a flat bed constructed atop a frame. The bed was fitted with stake sides (see illustration 4). The stake sides were formed of uprights topped by a horizontal bar. Together, the uprights and bar looked like a ladder laid on its side. Some carts had sides made of thick wickerwork around the uprights but open sides were more common. Sides made of planks may have existed. One wagon with planked sides has been excavated but, as discussed in the section on wagons, this vehicle might be an anomaly.

Cart bodies were rarely made with a seat for a driver. For ox-drawn carts, the driver walked alongside the cart. For horse-drawn carts, the driver normally rode postillion. (See illustration 6.) Riding postillion meant riding one of the horses pulling the cart, usually the one harnessed closest to the cart. Riding postillion was not limited to carts. Wagons, both cargo and passenger, were guided in this same way. For controlling the team, the driver was equipped with a long whip.

For harnessing horses to the cart, two shafts extended from the front of the cart. In some instances, the horse was secured between the shafts by straps attached to other straps which went across the horse's chest and another encircling the horse just behind its shoulders. As discussed in the section on draft horses, during the early Middle Ages, these straps were supplemented and then largely replaced by the padded horse collar. The padded collar more effectively harnessed the horse's pulling power. Ropes or long leather straps called traces attached the collar to the cart. These can be most clearly seen on carts to which several horses were hitched in single file.

While single files of draft animals were used to haul carts, pairs of animals harnessed side by side were sometimes used for moving heavy loads. Oxen were most commonly used in pairs. Carts built to be pulled by such teams had a single pole projecting from the center of the front of their frames instead of a pair of shafts. The pole went between the draft ani-

mals and they were then harnessed to either side of it. When more power was needed, additional pairs of animals were harnessed in file in front of the first pair. When using a single pair of oxen, the pole could be attached directly to the center of the ox yoke. Some poles were long enough for a second pair of oxen to be similarly harnessed. When the length of the team exceeded the length of the pole, ropes were tied to the center of the yokes and then back to the pole. Horses were harnessed in a slightly different manner in the early Middle Ages. Since the horses were not yoked like oxen, the central pole was attached to the chest and girth straps of the horses. This does not appear to have been a very satisfactory method of harnessing since the stress of pulling was unevenly distributed. The horse's side next to the central pole was under more strain than its other side. In contrast, for oxen, this uneven stress was lessened by the rigid, wooden yoke which spread the strain of pulling more evenly on both shoulders of the ox. The flexible straps of the horse's harness, on the other hand, could only bend under the pressure. The introduction of the padded collar helped balance some of the stress but did not solve the problem. This changed in the 12th century when the pole began to be supplemented with *whippletrees*. Whippletrees were bars of wood that were mounted on the pole. They were centered on the pole and attached so that they could pivot. Alternatively, they could be attached to the pole or the front of the cart by lengths of chain or rope. The traces from the collars of the horses were attached to the ends of whippletrees. By attaching to traces on both sides of the horse instead of straps on just one side, the whippletree spread the stress of pulling more evenly on both sides of the horse. This also made more effective use of the horse's pulling power.

The use of whippletrees had several other advantages over harnessing directly to the central pole. Additional teams, each fitted with their own whippletree, could be easily added on to the line of horses pulling the cart. The flexible connections of the whippletrees made turning easier as well since the team could now move more in the direction of the turn. Before, their movement was limited by the rigidity of the pole so they could not turn as sharply. The flexibility of the traces and the chains and ropes of the whippletree also allowed the horse to pull more smoothly, especially when starting out. This lessened the stress on both the cart and the horse. The whippletree did have one disadvantage over the central pole. When going downhill, horses or oxen harnessed directly to the pole could slow down and act as brakes for the cart. With the whippletree and its flexibility, the animals could do little to slow the cart. One solution to this problem was to immobilize the wheels. This could be done by tying a rope or attaching a chain to the cart's frame and then running it through the spokes of the wheel and then tying or attaching the end back to the frame. Another alternative was to chain or tie a wooden beam or log to the bottom of the cart's frame in front of the wheels. As the cart moved forward, the beam was dragged back against the wheels, slowing or stopping them from turning. Another method which was used in later centuries and which may have been used in the Middle Ages was to attach a specially made piece of wood that fit the bottom of the wheel. Sometimes called a drag shoe, it immobilized the wheel and turned it into a skid or runner. Since it went under the wheel, the shoe had the added advantage of protecting the wheel's rim while the wheel was being dragged. All these methods could be used for wagons as well, in which case it was the rear wheels that were immobilized. Finally, for very steep grades, one possible solution was to unharness the team and then place them behind the cart. Harnessed to the back of the cart, they could then move slowly forward, acting as brake as the cart eased down the slope.

Not all carts were horse- or ox-drawn. As previously mentioned in the section on walking, some carts were small and light enough that men could pull them. Some of these carts were made so that one man could pull while another pushed. This latter type is probably best described as a barrow. Both the ordinary man-powered cart and the barrow were well suited for moving goods within towns and cities. While their loads were typically lighter than horse- or oxen-drawn carts, these carts and barrows greatly increased the weight men could move. For example, with these vehicles, men moved heavy loads such as large barrels of wine that weighed several hundred pounds or more, transporting them from the dock where the wine arrived to customers around the city. In the narrow streets of medieval cities, barrows and carts hauled by men likely had an advantage over horse-drawn carts since it was easier to maneuver them in tight spaces.

Wagons

For the purposes of this book, wagons were four-wheeled vehicles which served the same purposes as carts but had larger carrying capacity. Again like carts, they were used to carry a great variety of items such as building stone and enormous loads of hay. Wagons were typically drawn by teams of draft animals rather than by single beasts, but some wagons were illustrated as being pulled by a lone horse.

The most complete wagon that survives from the Middle Ages comes from a Viking-age burial in Norway. This wagon is built with sides made of overlapping planks, much the same as the planking on the hull of a Viking ship. However, such construction may not have been common since the wagon was likely specially built as a hearse rather than as a functioning wagon. Instead, as with carts, most wagons appear to have been stake-sided and could easily be loaded with a variety of things, from armor and camp supplies for soldiers to sacks of grain for farmers.

The construction of wagons largely mirrored that of carts:

- Wagons were typically pulled by pairs of animals and so a pole rather than pairs of shafts were used to harness the draft animals. As discussed above, whippletrees were used to supplement the central pole.

- As with carts, wagons were usually built without seats for a driver who either walked alongside the team pulling the wagon or rode postillion.
- Like carts, wagon axles were fixed in place and wheels rotated on the ends of the axles.

One problem with wagon wheels and axles was turning. Unlike a cart, a wagon could not make sharp turns. On a wagon, both axles were fixed in place and the front wheels could not be turned from side to side as they can be in a car today. Since the wagon's wheels could not be turned to steer the wagon, the driver had to use the strength of the draft animals to pull the entire wagon over in the direction of the turn. At some point, this problem was solved by mounting the front axle so that it could pivot and point the front wheels in the direction of the turn. When this improvement was developed is a matter of debate. The Romans had some form of pivoting axles but these went of out of use with the collapse of Rome. Evidence of the rediscovery of this feature is difficult to pin down. Medieval illustrations of wagons were not typically drawn in sufficient detail to answer this question with certainty, but for most of the period the images strongly suggest that the axles were fixed. However, based on depictions of wagons from the 15th century, the pivoting front axle had been rediscovered before the end of the Middle Ages.

As for braking, the same methods that were used for carts were used for wagons. Usually only the rear wheels of the wagon were slowed or immobilized.

Passenger Vehicles

Passenger vehicles were often referred to as *chariots*. Chariot is an Old French word derived from the Latin *currus*. The word chariot is somewhat misleading. While there are early medieval illustrations of people riding in two-wheeled chariots, most of these depictions are of mythological or ancient historical events

and the riders are such figures as the Pharaoh of Egypt pursuing the Israelites.

In the Roman Empire, passenger vehicles were common. There were both two- and four-wheeled versions. All were horse-drawn. Horses were used in part because of their speed. Passenger vehicles and their loads were typically far lighter than cargo wagons and so horses could move them at some speed. Oxen were quite unsuitable for quick movement. Oxen were also unsuitable because of their low status; horses were used in part because of the status they connoted. Having a fine team of horses to draw one's carriage was a display of wealth. In the Middle Ages, horses continued to be used for pulling passengers for these same reasons.

Following the collapse of the Roman Empire in western Europe, passenger vehicles became extremely rare. Their use increased very slowly over the course of the Middle Ages. One reason for this limited progress was the negative attitude of the nobility towards passenger coaches. The Romans had considered riding in a coach as a suitable means of travel for anyone, including senators, generals, and emperors. Medieval noble men, on the other hand, viewed riding in a vehicle rather than on horseback as demeaning. This bias is reflected in one Arthurian tale in which Lancelot desperately needs transportation but can find no other means than a cart. Seeing him riding in a cart, people along the way assumed that he was a disgraced knight who was on his way to execution. A man walked or rode a horse, but he never rode in a wagon or cart unless he had been seriously wounded or was too old or sick to ride.

For noble women, on the other hand, riding in a wagon could be quite desirable, if the wagon was suitably luxurious. These deluxe coaches had low, solid sides rather than the staked sides common to most other wagons. The sides were frequently brightly painted. Above the sides, these coaches were covered with high, arched canopies made of cloth or leather. In this respect, they resembled the covered wagons used by American pioneers. The canopies were made of the best material the noble owner could afford. This gave her the opportunity to display her status. The sides of the canopies were fitted with flaps that could be opened to provide light and air for the passengers. In good weather, the canopy could be removed entirely. The external decorations were sometimes completed with carvings on the frames supporting the canopy. In one illustration of a coach, the ends of the frame have been carved into a variety of heads. Interestingly, this same coach is also fitted with chains that stretch across the openings at the front and back of the wagon. These chains are safety belts that help keep the ladies from falling out of the wagon. As for the coach's driver, he rode postillion like most other drivers of wagons and carts. Having a seat at the front of the coach for the driver was not developed until some time after the Middle Ages.

The interiors of these luxury coaches were also fitted out to the best of the owner's budget. One countess had the inside of her coach's arched cover lined with samite, a costly fabric. She also had velvet curtains and decorative hangings. There were also pillows and cushions covered in expensive fabrics which provided some comfort, but the ride must still have been quite bumpy since these wagons typically had no suspension system to absorb shocks and soften the ride. Passenger vehicles in the Roman Empire had had suspension systems in which the passenger compartment was suspended from metal bars attached to posts at the four corners of the vehicle's frame. The bars were mounted so that they could swing and transform some of the jolting on rough roads into a more gentle rocking of the passenger compartment. This form of suspension system disappeared with the collapse of the Empire. Eventually, medieval Europeans rediscovered the concept of suspension systems and built some coaches with riding compartments suspended by bars similar to those used by the Romans or by chains attached to posts at the four corners of their frames. Alternatively, the compartment was sometimes slung on large leather straps attached to the wagon's

frame. All these devices provided some relief from the rough ride. Instead of being jolted by each bump, the bars, chains, or straps smoothed out the ride by converting the bumpiness into a swaying of the passenger compartment. However, coaches with these suspension systems were very rare. They appear to have been first developed in what is now Hungary possibly as early as the late 10th century. Their construction and use spread slowly to other parts of Europe. By the late 14th century, they were in use in Germany and France. The Hungarian origin of coaches with suspension systems is reflected in the word "coach," which is derived from the name of the town of Kocs in Hungary. Given the discomfort of riding in a coach with no suspension system, it may come as no surprise that most noble women appear to have opted to ride on horseback instead and saved luxury coaches for ceremonial occasions.

Noble women were not the only ones who owned coaches. In France, as part of their efforts to show off their wealth, wives of rich bourgeois sometimes bought coaches and teams of horses. The horses were finest they could afford and the coaches were made as sumptuous as their budgets could bear. This and other displays of wealth by commoners were opposed by the nobility, who hated such pretentious behavior by their social inferiors. It was an irksome reminder that some bourgeois were wealthier than some members of the nobility. As a consequence, sumptuary laws were enacted in several regions of Europe. Under the guise of upholding public morals and promoting thrift, these laws sought to prohibit spending on expensive luxury goods. They were especially concerned with clothing and sometimes set out regulations dictating the materials and accessories that were appropriate for the clothing worn by each level of the social hierarchy. Some of these laws went beyond clothing and extended to coaches. A law in Paris issued in 1294 banned outright any commoner from owing a coach.

By the later Middle Ages, there may have been commercial passenger coach service in some areas. Such a coach appears to be depicted in an illustration made in the early 14th century (see illustration 6). It shares some similarities with a royal coach. It has low solid sides apparently topped with a canopy. It also has decorated knobs extending from the canopy frame. However, in place of flaps, its side openings are in the form of a grill. This suggests that sides could be of wood rather than fabric but it is likely that the grill is formed by the uprights and crosspieces of the frame-supporting canopy. Unlike the royal coach, this coach is smaller and much more crowded. Three men and two women, all very close together, appear in the coach's windows. Their appearance suggests that they are sitting on benches.

Given the noble bias against men riding in a vehicle, the presence of men strongly suggests that this coach is for non-noble passengers. Commoners, men and women alike, were likely more practical than the nobility and traveled in coaches when it suited them. The fact that commoners did not generally own coaches along with the crowding of this coach suggests that this may have been a public conveyance. Unfortunately, apart from this illustration, there is no other evidence of public transportation at this early date. And the existence of regularly scheduled coach service over long distances was not recorded until the 17th century. However, such services, especially more local services, likely did exist earlier. A large and well-populated area like Paris and its surrounding towns could

easily have provided a market for some form of public transportation. Further, the series of illustrations in which this image appears is of everyday scenes of the bridges of Paris, which suggests that such a vehicle was not an uncommon sight. Thus, this coach could well have been a public coach, making its usual run into the city from a nearby town.

Litters

Another form of passenger vehicle was the litter. (See illustration 7.) The litter had no wheels. Instead, it was carried suspended

Illustration 7. **This is a rare illustration of a litter. Litters were considered appropriate only for invalids and women. This noble lady looks quite comfortable resting on her pillows in the well-upholstered compartment. The horses must have had matched gaits to provide a smooth ride. If they were out of sync, the litter would have pitched up and down (© The British Library Board. All Rights Reserved 8/31/2010. License Number: PAUNEW01. Harley MS 4431, f.153).**

between two horses. The litter had a small passenger compartment with room for one person. Some were constructed with a chair inside for the passenger but most appear to have been built so that the passenger could ride while reclining instead of sitting upright. Reclining litters were furnished with mattresses and pillows. Such litters were well suited for moving the elderly and the sick or injured since these passengers could comfortably lie down while traveling. Like the passenger coach, the litter had a framework covered by a canopy to shelter its occupant. Long poles were attached to each side of the litter. The poles were then harnessed to the sides of two horses, one horse in front and the other in back. The litter likely had a smoother ride than a coach since the horses absorbed the bumps in the road, but if the horses did not have matching gaits the ride could still have been uncomfortable. Also, there are no descriptions of what happened when the lead horse relieved itself. One hopes that the litter was attached far enough back.

Sleighs

In regions of northern Europe, especially in Scandinavia and Russia, transportation was adapted to the cold weather and took advantage of the freezing of the marshes, lakes, and rivers as well as the deep snow that covered the ground. In many areas of the north, travel over land was actually much easier in the winter than in the summer. Muddy roads and marshes hindered travel in the warm months but the ice and snow of winter created seasonal roadways ideal for travel in sleighs. Sleighs were commonly drawn by horses but Laplanders and other inhabitants of the far north used reindeer, as they have up to the present. As with later sleighs, medieval sleighs had an open passenger compartment atop two runners.

Sleighs were subject to the same traditions as vehicles elsewhere in Europe. Like wagons and coaches, sleighs were usually guided by men riding postillion. Further, as with coaches, the nobility generally considered riding in a sleigh to be suitable for women,

children, the sick, and the elderly. Noblemen typically rode on horseback even in the winter. However, unlike coaches, sleighs were sometimes driven just for pleasure. At these times, it was proper for a man to be the driver and for him to sit in the sleigh.

Other Vehicles

In addition to ordinary carts, wagons, and passenger vehicles, there were also a number of other vehicles which could be found in medieval Europe.

Sleds

In addition to sleighs for transporting people, there were also sleds or sledges for carrying cargo over ice and snow. Some were constructed with light frames resting on two runners that looked like long skis. Others were built with two large, sturdy runners and a box or frame on top. Light- to mid-weight sleds were pulled by dogs. One 15th century map has an annotation written on Siberia stating that dogs were used to pull sleds in this region. For heavier sleds, horses and reindeer were used. Like carts, sleds could carry a variety of loads. In the far north of Russia and Scandinavia, the natives loaded them with heavy bundles of furs to take them south to trading outposts. Surprisingly, large sleds, sometimes called sledges, were used in warmer settings as well. As mentioned previously, they were used to move heavy items, such as large wine barrels, through city streets as revealed in this scene from early 14th century Paris (see illustration 1). Sledges were used out in the countryside as well. Horse- or ox-drawn sledges could move heavy loads of logs, rocks, or building stones across soft and damp ground in which a cart would have become mired. Additionally, since the sledge had runners instead of wheels, there was no risk of breaking an axle under the stress and strain.

Tumbrel

The *tumbrel* or *timbrel* was a specialized form of cart. While the name *tumbrel* has come to refer to any two-wheeled cart, it originally meant a cart that was built so that it could empty its load by tipping down at the back. Admittedly, any cart could dump out its contents by unharnessing its team and lifting up its shafts, tipping the back end of the cart down. The tumbrel, on the other hand, was built so its bed could be tipped independently of the rest of the cart. Since the tumbrel carried loose materials, it was likely made with solid sides of planks or wickerwork of woven laths to keep its load from slipping out. Tumbrels are primarily recorded as being farm carts and appear to have been commonly used for carrying manure. This could have been because they could quickly and easily dump their loads and so minimize the time and effort spent on the unpleasant task of unloading them. However, manure was not collected and dumped simply to get rid of it. Manure was prized as a fertilizer and the tumbrel could have been used to help spread it on gardens and fields. While being pulled along slowly with its bed slightly tipped, the tumbrel would gradually drop its load. Farm workers walking behind the cart could spread the dropped manure with shovels.

Tumbrels may have also served as an early form of garbage truck in some cities. Over the course of the Middle Ages, large cities such as London employed men to periodically clean the streets and carry the waste off and dump it outside the city. Tumbrels were well-suited for this task. The street-cleaners could load the tumbrels with mounds of loose garbage and then easily dump it all at a waste site well outside the city walls.

Military Vehicles

Armies in the Middle Ages moved their supplies and loot using the same carts and wagons used by civilians. However, there were two uniquely military vehicles.

Amphibious Wagon. In the 8th and 9th centuries, Charlemagne and other Carolingian rulers used amphibious wagons called *bastarnes* for crossing rivers in the course of military campaigns. Bastarnes were described as well-built wagons which could cross rivers while keeping their loads of supplies safe and dry. According to one Carolingian edict, bastarnes had to be capable of actually floating across rivers when necessary. To accomplish this, the bastarnes were waterproofed by sealing joints in their frames with wax, pitch (tar) and tow (coarse fibers from the flax plant). This technique was similar to that used for sealing joints in shipbuilding. Additionally, one of Charlemagne's orders specified that a layer of cow hides was to be secured over the coverings of the bastarnes. The coverings were likely cloth tarpaulins stretched over the bastarne's bed to cover its load. The additional layer of hides provided a waterproof covering that would shield the load of supplies from any water coming over the side of the wagon. It could have also protected the bastarne itself from being swamped by preventing water from pouring into the bed of the wagon. Unfortunately, we have only the written description of the bastarne. None have survived, nor are there any illustrations of one. As for their use, there is one reference in an account of a military expedition to Spain by one of Charlemagne's sons in the early 9th century. Interestingly, despite their apparent utility, there are no records of bastarnes or similar wagons being used after the era of the Carolingians.

Wagenburg. The wagenburg, which can be literally translated from the German as "wagon castle," was a term for a fortified camp made up of wagons. The wagenburg was made up of the baggage wagons and carts which were a common and essential part of any army. The wagons were formed up to create an enclosure, much like the American pioneers in the West "circled the wagons" when attacked. Drawing up the wagons and carts to form a temporary defensive camp was not unusual in the Middle Ages and such use of wagons can also be found in classical antiquity.

In the 15th century, the Hussites developed specialized wagons to improve their wagenburgs. Named after their leader Jan Hus, the Hussites were considered heretics by the Church and so a war ensued to suppress them.

The war took place in Bohemia, a kingdom whose territory was located primarily in what is now the Czech Republic. The Hussites improved on the circling the wagons technique by building specially modified baggage wagons that provided protection for their men-at-arms. The sides of the Hussite war wagons were made of strong planks of wood and were tall enough to shelter the defenders standing behind these walls. The sides had slits or other openings to allow the defenders to attack with firearms and other missile weapons. When traveling, these wagons were placed along both sides of the convoy to provide a protective screen for the ordinary wagons, their passengers, and others riding and walking along in the column. When used to create a defensive encampment, the draft animals were unhitched and the wagons drawn up end-to-end to form a circular enclosure. To make the wall of wagons more secure, the wagons were chained to each other. Further, an additional board was hung below the frame of each wagon to prevent anyone from crawling under. While the image of a heavily armored wagon perhaps bristling with firearms might sound like a forerunner of the modern tank, the Hussite wagons were used exclusively as defenses. Even when on the march, these wagons always stayed with the column. They were never driven into enemy formations for attacks.

Infrastructure and Logistics

Traveling around medieval Europe by land required the same basic needs as land travel has always needed: Some sort of road or trail to travel on, means for crossing obstacles such as rivers, and a place to eat and sleep while en route.

ROADS

The Romans left behind them a system of roads which covered much of Europe and extended into the Near East and across North Africa as well. The Roman transportation network at its height included tens of thousands of miles of road with a significant portion paved with stone or gravel. The remainder were dirt roads.

Roman roads were famed for the quality of their construction. Important primary roads were built with foundations of layers of gravel topped with fitted, dressed stones to provide a firm, hard surface for traffic. The total thickness of the road bed and pavement could reach 30 inches or more and raised the road above the surrounding ground. In addition, ditches were dug parallel to the road on both sides. These ditches, along with the drainage provided by the layers of gravel underlying the road and the height of the road itself, ensured that the roads were well drained. Good drainage lengthened the lifespan of the roadways and prevented them from being turned into muddy messes by heavy rains or spring thaws. As a result, main Roman roads were passable in all seasons. However, while primary roads were carefully constructed to ensure durability, other paved roads were less well built. Many miles of these "paved" roads were covered with gravel. While not as durable as a highway of carefully laid paving stones, gravel roads did have several advantages. They could be constructed more quickly and more cheaply. They were also easier to repair. Potholes could simply be filled with dirt and additional gravel and then compacted to restore the road surface. Properly constructed, graveled surfaces also drain well so that the roads were less muddy and less prone to rutting than dirt roads. They also provided better traction than both dirt roads and roads paved with smooth stones. Finally, as for the thousands of miles of lesser roads, these were bare dirt and ranged from cart tracks that ran from agricultural fields to the nearest villages to roads that connected the villages to one another and to the roads that fed into the main road system.

Many Roman roads did survive into the Middle Ages but they gradually deteriorated through lack of maintenance and through intentional destruction by people using the roads as a source of building material. Still others fell into disuse as the destinations they connected lost their importance or even disappeared in the years following the collapse of the Empire. However, some major routes, such as that in England between Dover and London, remained important and continued to be used through the Middle Ages and beyond, through a combination of the original Roman road and later repairs, replacements, and additions. In fact, across Europe, some modern roads follow the courses of Roman roads, the remains of which are buried beneath them.

It is estimated that most Roman roads had severely decayed by the 10th or 11th centuries so new roads had to be built. Along with new roads to replace some of the old ones, entirely new roads were also constructed to connect towns and cities that were newly founded or that had risen in importance since the age of the Roman Empire. For example, Paris was just another provincial town during the Empire but as it grew in importance in the Middle Ages, new roads were built to improve its connection with other cities.

Road Construction and Maintenance

While there is little documentary or physical evidence of the roads built in the Middle Ages, most were likely quite primitive, with many being poorly constructed and poorly maintained. This assumption is supported by the numerous edicts of rulers demanding that their subjects keep roads in good condition. Even in the final centuries of the Roman Empire in western Europe, emperors issued orders reminding citizens that those whose land adjoined a road were responsible for its maintenance. The Carolingians who ruled most of western Europe in the 8th and 9th century repeatedly issued similar commands to their subjects.

Why were rulers, whether Roman emperors or medieval kings, concerned about the construction and maintenance of roads within

their realms? Roads served military and economic ends. In both the Roman Empire and medieval Europe, roads had strategic military value since they provided a means to move troops rapidly around a region. Such use of roads did not end with the Middle Ages. In the 1930s, for example, the German autobahns were built in large part to facilitate movements of troops and matériel. Roads also had significant economic value. With the decline of the Empire, roads deteriorated and travel became dangerous as order broke down. While trade initially contracted in the early Middle Ages, merchants still needed to move goods from suppliers to consumers. Any area that could provide passable, safe roads attracted merchants who needed reliable routes for transporting their goods to markets. In exchange for making travel safer, rulers levied tolls on merchants and other travelers passing through their domains. Some of these jurisdictions, most notably the county of Champagne, were able to further capitalize on providing safe routes by establishing trade fairs which attracted large numbers of merchants. Taxes collected on sales at the markets provided yet another source of revenue.

The combination of tolls and strategic advantage also led nobility in the vicinity of the Alps to improve access to passes through the mountains. In the 13th and 14th centuries, new roads were built and existing ones improved to facilitate travel through the Gotthard, Brenner, and Septimer passes in the Alps. These roads made it easier for merchants to travel between Italy and the rest of Europe. Besides collecting tolls from this traffic, controlling these roads enabled local lords to have some control over the passes as well. They could protect themselves from enemies by blocking passage through the mountains.

Yet despite the money to be made by attracting a greater stream of merchants, most nobles were greedy and routinely diverted the money raised through tolls. Instead of spending the money on the upkeep and improvement of roads, most lords treated the tolls as just another source of revenue and spent them as they wished. Higher authorities sometimes sought to correct this problem. For example, Carolingian rulers ordered those nobles who collected tolls to spend them on maintaining the roads that generated these funds. These edicts were unsuccessful and, despite the tolls that were collected, the problem of roads being poorly maintained persisted throughout Europe in the Middle Ages,

Royal and noble involvement in road building and maintenance continued throughout the Middle Ages. For example, like the Roman and Carolingian rulers before him, the king of England in the 13th century ordered that all major roads be maintained by those whose land was next to a road or through which a road passed. And obstructing a road was made a criminal offense. Further, in 1285 as part of an English edict to suppress violent crime, the land for 200 feet on either side of a road was to be cleared of all brush and trees to deprive brigands of cover and so protect travelers from attack. The encroachment of forests on roadways was a serious problem in some areas but there is no evidence that such massive clearance was ever carried out. It was difficult enough to keep roads and their ditches free of undergrowth. Some rulers went beyond merely ordering their subjects to maintain roads and actually provided funding as well. In 14th century Germany, the Holy Roman Emperor granted some cities the right to levy a tax to pay for the upkeep of public works, including roads and bridges.

Royalty and the nobility were not the only ones involved in road building and maintenance. Some road construction involved both nobility and commoners. For example, in 1203, the countess of Champagne in France hired builders to pave a road between two major towns within the county. Instead of being paid upon completion of the job, the contractors received a share of the tolls collected from traffic on the completed roadway. Groups of merchants themselves sometimes paid for road building. For example, in the 14th century, citizens of Ghent (a city located in what is now Belgium) paid for the repair of a road leading to Paris, a major market for the woolen goods and other merchandise from Ghent. Individual merchants sometimes paid for road improvement as well, most commonly by bequests in their wills. These men knew road conditions first-hand and the need for their repair. Such donations were seen as acts of piety and Christian charity since they benefited all of society.

Roads were also built by the governments of the Italian city-states. In the 13th century, Florence and Pisa both undertook road-building campaigns to improve their connections with their surrounding territories and to other cities. Pisa built roads to cities further inland as part of an effort to encourage these cities to continue using the port of Pisa for their overseas shipping. Florence improved roads both to cities that were allies and to ones that were potential enemies. These roads served both trade and strategic military purposes, as the city's armies could more quickly move along the paved roads both to defend against and to attack hostile neighbors.

Forms and Types of Roads

We now know who ordered roads to be built and maintained and who financed these efforts. Now, what were these roads like? Many were simply dirt roads. Throughout Europe, the remains of some of these roads survive in the form of sunken roads. Sunken roads, called "hollow ways" in England, were formed by centuries of cart and wagon traffic. The wheels of the carts and wagons wore deep ruts in dirt roads. Coupled with natural erosion, these roads were cut deeper and deeper into the ground until they were significantly lower than the surrounding land. As might be expected, these low-lying roads turned into muddy trenches in wet weather. However, even dirt roads lying on higher, better drained ground still could become mires during rainy weather and spring thaws. Covered in a deep layer of mud, some roads became virtually impassable for wheeled traffic. In fact, carts and wagons often made matters worse as their wheels churned up the mud, making it an even deeper and stickier mess.

Better-made roads were covered in gravel. This provided a firmer surface than bare dirt and also facilitated the drainage of water. Gravel was also used to patch holes and ruts in surviving Roman roads. In some areas, the increasing construction of gravel roads has been attributed to the increased use of stone in building over the course of the Middle Ages. Stone chips were a natural by-product of the quarrying process and perfectly suited for use in surfacing roads, so the chips were spread on top of the roads around the town or city to which the quarried stone was carried. At least as late as the 16th century, quarry waste continued to be used in this way.

As discussed previously, gravel roads did have some advantages over roads made of paving stones. The hard and relatively smooth surfaces of roads paved in stone were far more slippery in wet and icy weather than gravel roads. In fact, the more yielding surface of the gravel road provided better traction in all weather. The relative softness of gravel roads also meant less wear and tear on horses' iron-shod hooves. Beginning in the Middle Ages, horses were routinely shod with iron horse-shoes that were nailed to their hooves. These shoes gave horses better traction on soft surfaces. However, on smooth, hard pavements, the repeated shock of the impact of the shoes on the road surface could injure a horse's hooves and legs. Even today, this is a problem for police horses which are ridden on city streets. The modern solution is to fit these horses with tough and resilient rubber or plastic shoes that cushion their hooves.

Besides providing a surface which appears to have been better suited to the traffic which used them, gravel roads were also easier to patch and repair than paved roads. As mentioned previously, one simply had to fill in any holes with more gravel. However, not all holes were properly filled in. Brushwood and bundles of sticks or just dirt were used as infill and the holes quickly reappeared.

In some parts of England, farmers created massive potholes by digging up roads to get marl. Marl is a type of clay laced with various minerals and it can be plowed into fields to enhance their fertility. Farmers dug up marl wherever they could find it, even if a deposit ran beneath a road. Some of these potholes grew so large and deep that travelers allegedly could drown in them.

The next step above gravel roads were those paved with cobble stones. These were far rarer because of the time and material needed to construct them. Few people could afford the expense of such building. In the Middle Ages, the earliest routine use of cobblestone pavement appears to have been in cities and towns. As with roads in the countryside, the dirt streets in medieval towns and cities turned to mud in wet weather. To solve this problem, urban governments paid for streets to be paved in stone. Public squares and main streets were paved first and gradually side streets were also covered with stone. Finally, some cities and towns paved the roads approaching them for some distance as well.

Some roads took the form of dikes or causeways. Some examples of this can be found in northern Italy. Because the low ground was often swampy, roads had traditionally been built along mountain ridges. This required travelers to follow indirect routes and to cope with rough terrain. Over the course of the Middle Ages, some swamps and marshes were drained. By the 13th century, dikes built as part of drainage projects sometimes formed the foundation for elevated roadways as well. In addition to dikes, earthen causeways were also built specifically to raise roads above the surrounding marshes. These roads were paved in gravel or stone to improve drainage and prevent the underlying dikes and causeways from deteriorating into muddy mounds. In one case, Florence went even further and planted trees every four feet alongside a dike. The tree roots helped stabilize the sloping sides of the dike and, in turn, provide a firmer foundation for the road.

In some instances, causeways were built out of wood instead of earth. In Scandinavia, for example, wooden causeways were built across the marshy bottoms of valleys. Causeways could be quite long and were sometimes supported by hundreds of posts driven into the damp ground. More rarely, causeways were made of stone. One such roadway survives in England.

As the wooden causeways of Scandinavia indicate, earth, stone, and gravel were not the only materials used in the construction of roadways. In Russia, Scandinavia, and elsewhere in Europe, log roads were built by simply laying the timbers directly on the ground with no supporting piles. This was done in marshes and other areas of soft soil. Laid side by side, the logs created roadways with a firm surface. Using logs spread the weight of passing traffic over a larger area and thus lessened the likelihood that the road would be forced down into the soft ground beneath it. The buoyancy of the logs may have also helped prevent the road from sinking. This use of logs actually pre-dates the Middle Ages and survived for centuries afterward. Even today log roads are built in isolated areas with rough terrain and soft ground. They are often called "corduroy roads" because the ridged surface resembles the texture of corduroy fabric.

Temporary roads existed in northern and northeastern Europe during the very cold months of winter. While winter meant rain and boggy roads for much of Europe, winter brought snow and freezing temperatures in Scandinavia as well as in what are now Russia, Poland, Latvia, Lithuania, and Estonia. Road surfaces hardened, making them easier to use, and snow-covered ground could be traversed by sleighs and sledges. These same vehicles were used on the temporary roadways created by the freezing of marshes, rivers, and lakes. These frozen waterways facilitated travel into regions which were largely isolated during the warmer and wetter months. Thus, while the weather was bitter cold, movement was easier than in warmer months.

Besides being classed by the type of materials used in their construction, roads were also ranked according to their width. For ex-ample, in part of France in the 13th century, a compilation of local traditional laws broke roads down into the following categories:

Path — Approximately four feet wide, suitable for pedestrians and pack and riding animals, no carts.
Cart Road — Approximately eight feet, wide for one cart and for cattle led on bridles.
Way — Approximately 16 feet wide, for two-way cart traffic. Cattle could be herded in lines, not in loose herds, and they were not permitted to graze along the roadside.
Road — Approximately 32 feet wide, for two-way traffic with ample room to pass. Herds of cattle being driven to market could graze on vegetation along the side of the road.
And last:
Royal Road — About 64 feet wide and suitable for all traffic. Further, these roads were to be laid out on as straight and level a course as possible.

Similar classifications appear in other countries. In Byzantium, the surviving eastern half of the Roman Empire, there were pedestrian paths, packhorse trails, cart roads, roads, droving routes, paved roads, military roads, and imperial roads. While their widths were not specified, they were likely comparable to French standards. Returning to western Europe, English laws indicated that a royal roadway was to be 30 to 34 feet wide while a code of German laws from the 13th century had a more modest standard for king's roads: a minimum of 13 feet, enough to allow two carts to pass easily. This last figure is probably the most realistic estimate for the width of most primary roads. However, it is possible that for road widths of 30 feet and above the authorities were including the shoulders of the road and not just the roadway itself. The reference to permitting cattle to graze while being herded along the way suggests that the measured width of the road included some open, grassy areas as well as the beaten or paved surface of the road itself. These grassy shoulders could have easily extended several yards on either side of the road and at least partially complied with edicts stating that brush and undergrowth be cleared away from the sides of the road to deprive highway robbers of cover. Shoulders also likely encompassed the ditches needed to keep the road drained.

Besides natural encroachment by forests and scrub, medieval roads and streets were under constant pressure from those people whose land adjoined the road. Out in the countryside, farmers sometimes plowed and planted the shoulders as well as the roadway itself. These farmers saw more value in extending their cultivated lands than in having a passable road. Similarly, in towns and cities where homes and other buildings were tightly packed together, citizens often encroached on public streets. Some did so on a recurring basis, such as butchers who slaughtered animals in the streets in front of their shops. Others took the more permanent measure of building their houses and shops up to and over the property line. This led to the gradual narrowing of the streets. Over the years, streets which could once have accommodated a horse-drawn cart were reduced to a width that was barely passable by a pack mule. Civic officials did have the authority to keep the streets open and in some situations were able to force the removal of obstacles in the roadways. However, in general, it was very difficult to push back all the encroachments.

With all the problems of primitive construction, poor upkeep, and encroachment, it is difficult to believe that medieval roads functioned at all. Yet despite these problems, these roads still served as arteries for travel and trade across Europe for centuries. Every year, untold thousands of pedestrians, riders, and carts used the paths, trails, and roads that crisscrossed medieval Europe to reach destinations ranging from the nearest village to cities and shrines many hundreds of miles away. The ending of the Middle Ages and the advent of the Renaissance did nothing to change these conditions. While there was always some gradual improvement, concerted efforts to improve roads across Europe did not begin until the late 17th century.

Road Workforces

Who actually performed the manual labor of constructing and maintaining roads? In much of Europe, peasants owed services to their lords in exchange for holding their land. In France, part of these labor services typically included maintenance of roads on the lord's land. This and other labor obligations were known as corvée. However, not all peasants in Europe were required to work on roads as part of the obligations of their land tenure. Additionally, over the course of the Middle Ages, most peasants' personal service obligations were increasingly commuted to cash payments instead. Further, even under corvée, the peasant's obligation was usually limited to the maintenance and repair of existing roads and did not extend to the construction of new roads. Thus, some road maintenance was performed by peasants as part of their corvée obligations while hired laborers were often used for both building and repairing roads.

General laborers, whether peasants performing their corvée duties or paid workers, were essential for both maintenance and construction of roads. Some of these workers dug or cleared drainage trenches. Some shoveled dirt to build up the height of the road bed while others shoveled gravel to make the surface of the roadway. For building new roads, specialists such as woodsmen were need to cut down trees if the new route ran through forests. Additionally, for paved roads, stonemasons were needed to cut and place stone blocks. These masons were likely less skilled than those who constructed stone buildings but they were still specialists who knew the basics of working and laying stones. Together, these men built and repaired the roads of medieval Europe.

Traffic Regulations

Besides trying to regulate road sizes and usage, there were even attempts at traffic control. As mentioned above, some roads were wide enough for only one cart. So what happened when two carts traveling in opposite directions met? The same code of German laws that categorized road sizes established an order of right of way to cover such situations. When two carts met, one of them had to pull off onto the side of the road to let the other pass. According to the German code, the cart with the lighter load yielded to the heavier cart. An empty cart yielded to any loaded cart. A rider on horseback yielded to any cart, loaded or empty. And last, pedestrians yielded to all other traffic. A French code simply stated that right of way should be yielded to the vehicle, pack animal, or man which was carrying the heaviest load. These orders of precedence were not some legalistic creation. Rather, it recognized the relative ease with which one vehicle or other road user could get off the road and then back on again. However, the French code also factored in another reasonable consideration and stated that most perishable cargo should be given the right of way.

FORDS, FERRIES, AND BRIDGES

Inevitably, roads ran into rivers and travelers had to find some way to cross them. Fords, ferries, and bridges were used to accomplish this. All three of these had been used for millennia.

Rivers and river crossings were an important factor in the development of many large towns and cities in the Middle Ages. Besides providing water for drinking and sanitation, rivers provided a relatively cheap and easy means of transportation. As a result, many cities grew up at points which were important to river traffic, such as at the confluence of two major rivers, at the highest navigable point on a river, or at the lowest point at which a river could be bridged. For most of these cities, bridges and ferries provided a means for crossing rivers. Some towns and cities did have natural crossings in the form of fords but these were increasing replaced by bridges over the course of the Middle Ages. Whether it was a

ford, a ferry, or a bridge, a river crossing usually brought an economic advantage to any nearby town or city. Some revenue came from the tolls that bridges and ferries generated but, more importantly, a river crossing often bought increased trade as land-based and river-based routes intersected.

Fords

Fords are naturally shallow spots in streams and rivers. They are shallow enough that men and horses can safely wade across them. Fords were found throughout medieval Europe, as place names remind us. Frankfurt am Main in Germany is located where the Franks forded the Main River. While in England, a shallow spot where cattle waded across one river came to be called Oxford.

Fords, like bridges, were of strategic importance. For example, in the events leading up to the battle of Agincourt in 1415 during the Hundred Years' War, Henry V of England and his army desperately sought a safe crossing of the Somme River. The French had destroyed all the bridges in the region to trap the English but Henry and his troops located a ford and escaped across the river.

Fords were important for more than just military operations. They provided routes for routine but vital activities as well. For example, in 1359, a famine in Flanders was worsened by heavy rains which raised the level of the Somme River so that fords were impassable. This prevented carts of grain from the west from reaching the cities and towns of Flanders.

Fords have the advantage of being simple and easy to use. Unlike bridges and ferries, there is little needed to maintain a ford, perhaps just a few guideposts to mark its location. However, the Romans did pave some fords, placing large stones to create a firm roadway on the river's bottom. Similarly, throughout the Middle Ages, people sometimes improved fords by adding stepping stones or creating submerged causeways to make fords even shallower and safer to cross. On the downside, because fordable shallows are naturally occurring features they were not always conveniently located. Travelers seeking to cross a river might have to go miles out of their way to reach a ford. Additionally, during rainy weather and spring thaws, rivers often became deep, raging torrents and so fords became impassable. Even during drier weather when rivers were generally calmer and shallower, fords could be treacherous to use. Straying from the path of the ford could be fatal. Travelers who failed to carefully follow the route of a ford could end up stepping into deep spots in the river bottom and drowning. Slipping on the wet stones that often made up the ford could also be fatal. Those who lost their footing could be quickly swept downriver. These dangers might seem unlikely but the fords ranged widely in depth from ankle-deep to waist-height. These fords were considered suitable for pedestrians but some fords were so deep that they could only be crossed on horseback. Using any ford safely was sometimes a challenge.

One last point about medieval fords: Today, many of the fords which were usable in the Middle Ages have disappeared. Some are buried underneath the bridges that replaced them. (See illustration 8.) Since fords were shallow spots and were already well-established points for crossing rivers, they were ideal locations for bridges. Other fords have disappeared in the last few centuries as a result of measures to control flooding and improve the navigability of rivers. As part of these programs, there has been a concerted effort to contain the flow of rivers in Europe and force them into canal-like channels. This has typi-

Illustration 8. This bridge at Barnard Castle in the north of England is believed to have replaced a ford. The bridge was built in the 14th century. Although it was repaired in the 16th century, it retains all of its original features. It is made entirely of stone and is anchored firmly to strong abutments on each end. Its central pier rests on the river's bed and is likely laid directly on bedrock. The pier has a cutwater on its upstream side to deflect the current and any floating debris. Its arches are high above the level of the river in this picture but, during spring floods, these arches are needed to allow the high water to pass safely under the bridge.

cally eliminated the shallows or marshes which formerly existed along a river's shoreline. In contrast, as part of modern channeling of the rivers for flood-control, improved navigation and other purposes, many rivers have been made much narrower and deeper. Their shallow edges, along with any surrounding marshes, have been eliminated and many rivers are now easily eight feet deep or more right at their edge. Because of these changes to rivers, it is extremely difficult to locate exactly where fords once existed.

Ferries

Another means of crossing a river or lake was to use a ferry. Ferries appear to have been quite common and are recorded at sites across Europe. Many of these records are found in inventories of an area's resources and merely state that the ferry existed and how much money it generated in tolls. Other evidence of the existence and location of ferries can be found in some cities and towns that have streets with "ferry" in their names which indicate that they once ran down to a ferry dock. Even in cities with bridges, ferries continued to operate, probably because it was often easier and faster to move goods and people on the water rather than through narrow and congested streets. Additionally, when a bridge was damaged and rendered impassable by floods, ferry services were needed until the bridge was repaired and such repairs took months or even years to complete.

Ferries were also recognized as having strategic value. In the 8th and 9th centuries, the Carolingian rulers stated that their nobles should maintain good boats as well as good bridges. Mentioning boats and bridges together suggests that the boats were to be used for river crossing as were the bridges. So the nobles were responsible for keeping boats for crossing rivers where there were no fords or bridges. This was part of the Carolingian policy of maintaining an infrastructure to facilitate moving troops and supplies across their domain.

There have been no finds of any medieval vessel which can be clearly identified as a ferry. Additionally, there appear to be no medieval illuminations of ferries. Thus, we can only develop an image of medieval ferries and their operations based on the limited documentary information, available supplemented by descriptions and examples of post-medieval ferries.

Medieval ferryboats ranged from canoe-sized up to large barges. Small ferries were rowed or poled across the water by the ferryman. These ferries could only accommodate a few people at a time. Small ferries were suitable for minor river crossings although they could be used on rivers of any width for carrying small groups. For bigger rivers such as the Danube and Rhone, larger ferries operated, and the largest appear to have been shallow-bottomed barges. They could accommodate 100 or more passengers along with horses and other animals, although horses were often tethered behind ferries and swam across rivers. Oddly, even large ferries are rarely recorded as carrying carts or other vehicles. It is unclear how large ferries were propelled. Some seem to have used a combination of sails and oars but the wind could not always be relied upon. Medieval ferries do not seem to have employed the "chain" method of propulsion used by later ferries. This method involved stringing a chain across the river. The ferryman or groups of men lifted the chain out of the water and hauled the ferry along by laboriously pulling on the chain hand-over-hand. Stout rope could be substituted for chain but ropes would present a hazard to any river navigation because, while chain sank and rested on the river bottom when not in use, rope would typically float in the water. Thus, ferries moved by pulling on ropes strung across the river would only have been suitable for rivers with little if any river traffic. But there is no evidence that the chain method was used either with chains or with ropes in the Middle Ages and so propulsion was limited to poles, oars, and sails.

Some evidence about ferries comes from

a few medieval stories, including accounts of some divine miracles. In one miracle story, a person was saved from drowning when a ferry sank. The ferries in these stories were typically described as grossly overloaded with hundreds of passengers. The villains in these stories were greedy ferrymen who tried to pack in as many passengers as possible on a single voyage. Ferrymen encountered on pilgrimage routes were especially criticized for being avaricious and charging pilgrims as much as they could. Given that ferries were often the only way to cross a river, especially in remote areas away from towns and cities, pilgrims and other travelers were at the mercy of ferrymen. Such excesses encouraged the building of bridges along pilgrimage routes.

Bridges

The ruins and the few surviving intact medieval bridges make it appear that they were all massive stone structures but, like the Roman bridges before them, many medieval bridges were made wholly or partly of wood. Given the perishable nature of wood and the frequent rebuilding of bridges on the sites of earlier bridges, there is little physical evidence of medieval wooden bridges. What little we have comes from the dredging of rivers, which occasionally turns up the remains of wooden pilings that once formed the foundations of bridge piers. There is also some limited documentary evidence, often in the form of accounts of the reconstruction of bridges lost in floods, and a few manuscripts include illustrations of wooden bridges.

Motives for Building Bridges

In the Middle Ages, bridges were built for three principal reasons. First, bridges had economic value. Their tolls provided a source of revenue. Further, providing a river crossing attracted travelers, including merchants who needed reliable routes for reaching markets to buy and sell merchandise. Goods bought, sold, or even that simply traversed a region could be subjected to taxes or duties, generating

money for the region's ruler. Second, bridges had a military value. Bridges allowed a ruler to move his troops more easily around his country and respond to any threats with greater speed. Bridges could also be used defensively to block river traffic, including waterborne invaders such as the Vikings. Bridges, combined with a good road system, also ensured that a ruler could more quickly receive information from around his realm and beyond. Finally, the building of bridges was one embodiment of Christian charity. A bridge provided a safer means of crossing a river than fords and ferries and so building a bridge could save the lives of innumerable travelers, including pilgrims on their way to shrines. This helping of complete strangers was believed to be good for the souls of those who donated to bridge-building campaigns.

Bridge Construction

In the age of the Roman Empire, the construction of bridges, like the construction of roads, was guided and ordered by the central government in Rome. With the end of the Empire in western Europe, the construction of bridges fell to the various rulers that governed the fragmented remnants of the Empire. In the early Middle Ages, these rulers could seldom muster the resources to build major new bridges. However, as time went on, new bridges were built on the sites of old bridges as well as at new locations to carry the roads built to connect newly founded or important towns and cities. For both new and older bridges, considerable effort was focused on their maintenance, as will be discussed later in this section.

Types of Bridges

As during the age of the Romans, there were three types of bridges in the Middle Ages: those made entirely of wood, those made primarily of stone, and those made of a combination of wood and stone (see illustrations 8 and 9). There were also pontoon bridges made of boats lashed together, but these floating bridges were used only in emergencies such as

Illustration 9. **This is the Pont St. Bénézet in Avignon, France. The first bridge on this site was built in the late 12th century as the result of a charity campaign started by Bénézet, a shepherd. The bridge originally had 22 arches. The first bridge was largely destroyed by flooding and neglect and was rebuilt in the 13th century. The piers of both bridges were anchored directly to the rock of the riverbed. By the late 17th century the bridge was in ruins again and never repaired. The building on one of the piers is the Chapel of St. Nicholas. Donations collected at the chapel were used to pay for the maintenance of the bridge.**

when a conventional bridge had been damaged or washed away by flooding.

Wooden Foundation Bridges. As with roads, the width and quality of the bridge was based on the traffic it was expected to carry. While no physical remains have been found, the rare pictures of pedestrian bridges show that they were simple affairs made of wood and were suitable only for crossing streams and other minor obstacles. The smallest pedestrian bridges were made of a single plank laid across a stream. Planks were also used for track ways across marshy ground and had been for millennia. Larger pedestrian bridges were supported by two parallel rows of posts that were driven into the streambed with large, two-handed mallets or hammers. Along the top of the posts, two timbers ran the length of the bridge. These were sometimes further sup-

ported from underneath by braces springing from the posts. The decking was of planks laid across the two timbers. Such bridges were only a few feet wide and may have typically lacked railings.

For heavier traffic such as carts and horses, there were bridges that were larger versions of the pedestrian bridges. One example from the 10th century can be found in Denmark. A half-mile-long bridge was constructed across a marshy valley. This bridge was like an elevated boardwalk with the roadway just a few feet above the surface of the marsh. At least 2,500 posts, or piles, were used to support the roadway which was some 16 to 20 feet in width. The piles were arranged in parallel rows, each a few feet apart.

While none survive, there were larger versions of the Danish bridge that spanned small rivers. These had much larger piles to withstand the force of the flowing water. Hewn into long shafts from single trees, these huge timbers were driven in parallel rows into the bed of the river or stream being crossed. Oak was sometimes used for pile but elm was the preferred wood since it was more resistant to rotting. The Romans often fitted the ends of their piles with iron points to make it easier to drive them firmly into the riverbed. Examples of Roman piles with iron heads have been dredged up from the Main River in Germany and elsewhere. Many piles in the Middle Ages were also fitted with iron points. When iron heads were not used, the end of each pile was typically sharpened to provide a point to ease driving it. Too large to be driven manually, these piles were driven in by pile-drivers. Like the Roman machines before it, a medieval pile-driver was made up of a winch, a tall vertical frame, and a heavy weight fitted into channels in the frame. The weight was winched up to the top of the frame and then released, driving the pile into the riverbed. When crossing larger rivers, pile-drivers could be mounted on barges. Alternatively, the pile-driver may have been started on the ground at the shoreline. As each pile was driven in, the pile-driver could have been gradually moved out from the shore, supported by the piles that had just been driven in. To complete the bridge, the piles were connected with a wooden framework. Braces supported the framework and sometimes cross-braces connected the piles to strengthen the bridge. As with pedestrian bridges, a deck of planks was laid over the timbers on top of the piles. The roadways created by the decking appear to have been eight feet or more in width. These larger wooden bridges were often fitted with railings.

While the bridges founded on rows of single piles were more suitable for spanning wider rivers than were the pedestrian bridges, they were not strong enough for crossing very wide or deep rivers. Larger, stronger bridges were needed. These bridges had foundations made of many piles driven close together,

forming pilings that were far more resistant to the stresses of the river's currents than single piles. Creating a firm foundation was even more important for larger bridges than for the smaller ones. For larger bridges, piles were ideally driven down until they reached a solid layer, preferably bedrock, underneath the riverbed. However, bedrock, hard clay, or layers of other similar materials were not always within reach. In these instances, the piles were driven in until they were firmly seated in the river bottom. Because they could create firm foundations in otherwise soft river beds, wood pilings were often used where it was difficult or impossible to construct stone foundations.

Depending on the diameter of the piles and the size of the bridge, hundreds or even thousands of piles were needed, each one laboriously driven in. Together, these groups of piles formed pilings. The pilings extended to some height above the level of the river. The pilings served as the base for the bridge piers. Piers were placed relatively close together. This was necessary because the gap between each pier had to be narrow enough to be spanned by the timber framework which would support the bridge deck. Narrower spans were also sturdier and could better withstand the stresses both from the traffic they carried and from natural forces such as floods. The wooden spans were supported from underneath by braces projecting up from the bridge piers. The framework was strengthened by cross-bracing between the long beams that made up the primary structure of the span. Plank decking was laid over the framework to create the roadway and railings completed the bridge. Again, no wooden bridges survive to reveal exactly how wide the finished road was. They presumably varied based on the type and volume of traffic expected. Some wooden bridges may have been only wide enough for a single cart to pass while other, more important bridges located in high traffic areas in major cities were likely 12 feet or more, wide enough for two lanes that permitted carts to move in both directions.

Stone Foundation Bridges. For bridges

with stone foundations, the Romans typically went through the laborious process of creating cofferdams. Cofferdams were enclosures created by driving piles into the river bottom. Cofferdams were typically made of two rings of piles. The space between the rings was filled with clay to create a watertight wall. Once the enclosures were complete, the water was bailed out so that the riverbed was exposed. When possible, the section of riverbed was excavated and a solid stone foundation built, firmly anchored in the river bottom. Alternatively, piles could be driven into the bed enclosed by the cofferdam and a stone foundation built on top of the piles. Driving the piles was easier with the riverbed exposed than it was to drive them under the water of a flowing river. Cofferdams were typically left in place after the construction was completed. There was simply no reason to go through the laborious task of dismantling them. Further, they formed protective barriers around the foundations that shielded them from erosion and other damage.

In the Middle Ages, cofferdams appear to have been kept in use for bridging relatively shallow rivers. It was easier to construct a cofferdam in shallow water than in deep water. In general, however, it appears that cofferdams were uncommon until the 15th century, when this method was generally revived.

Some stone bridges did not require piers set into the river bed for support. Some bridges were placed where the rivers were narrow enough to be spanned by a single arch. For such a bridge, stone abutments were built on both sides of the river to form solid foundations for the arch. Other examples of this type of bridge can also be found in mountainous regions. For example, the bridge over the Schöllenen Gorge in Switzerland was built with a single arch that was anchored directly in the exposed bedrock of a mountain on either side of the valley. Stone bridges such as this were quite impressive both for their setting and their construction. The bridge over the Schöllenen Gorge was known in the Middle Ages as the *Stiebendebrücke*, which meant "the bridge that hangs in the foam," a reference to

the mist and spray generated by the fast flowing River Reuss below. As for its construction, the bridge had to cross the gorge, which was approximately 40 feet wide, with a single arch since it was impossible to build piers up from the bed of the river at the bottom of the narrow canyon. Further, one side of the canyon was a nearly sheer cliff while the other was a steep slope. Yet medieval builders were capable of meeting this challenge and constructed a stone arch to bridge the gap. Stone arches for bridges were built using the same methods employed in building arches in cathedrals and other buildings. A temporary wooden framework was constructed to support the arch while it was being built. Masons then laid wedge-shaped stones called *voussoirs* over the wooden frame to form the arch. When completed, the arch was self-supporting and the wooden framework was removed. A stone roadway was then built across the top of the arch. (See illustration 10.) While this building technique was used for all stone arches, constructing a graceful arch high above a river between the two faces of a gorge was an impressive achievement. When completed, the Stiebendebrücke was relatively narrow, only wide enough for pedestrians and pack animals. However, the trails that ran to and from the bridge were also narrow and pack animals and people on foot were the only traffic on them as well. The Stiebendebrücke was built in the last decade of the 12th century or in the first decades of the 13th. Centuries later, it came to be known as the Teufelsbrücke, which meant the Devil's Bridge. It was given this name because legends grew up that building a bridge to cross such a major obstacle could only have been accomplished with supernatural aid.

Not all bridges with stone foundations were completed with stone superstructures. Both Roman and medieval stone bridge piers were also used to support wooden frameworks and decking like those previously described for all-wooden bridges.

Wood and stone were not the only materials used in bridge building. As the Middle

Illustration 10. This scene of bridge building is from a 15th century chronicle of the city of Bern, Switzerland. The man-powered crane was a common feature of medieval construction sites. Cranes similar to this one were also used for unloading ships and boats in harbors. Stone for the bridge is being brought in by a barge that is a larger version of the three-plank river boat, although the artist has drawn the barge too small to carry such a large load of stone. Moving stone by water was ideal for bridge construction but it was also used for other construction projects when possible since it was cheaper than carrying it by cart or wagon (courtesy Burgerbibliothek Bern, Mss.h.h.I.16, p. 81).

Ages progressed, bricks came to supplement stones in building both the foundations and the arches of bridges.

Like wooden bridges, stone bridges were built in various sizes. Not all stone bridges were massive structures. Small, all-stone bridges were built to span streams and small rivers. Examples of these bridges can be found in out of the way spots across Europe. Many were built of stone rather than wood because large supplies of building stone were readily available. In addition, some were built of stone because the streams and rivers they crossed, while small most of the year, were subject to torrential seasonal flooding. Properly con-

structed, a bridge built of stone rather than wood was less likely to need regular rebuilding.

Some small bridges are as narrow as four to six feet and were built for horses as well as pedestrians to cross. In England, for example, some of these surviving bridges are referred to as "packhorse" bridges. However, some bridges now called packhorse bridges were actually built to accommodate vehicles, primarily carts. Generally, those eight feet wide or wider were built for carts. Even today it is possible to drive over some of them in a car, although they are only wide enough for one-way traffic.

Bridges expected to handle higher volumes of wheeled traffic were made larger and wider. For example, one surviving stone bridge, the Pont Vieux at Carcassonne, France, built in the late 13th century, is a little over 15 feet wide for most of its length, just wide enough to handle two-way cart traffic. The Pont Vieux was part of one of the main routes into Carcassonne, which was then a fairly large and important town, and so likely handled a steady stream of wheeled, mounted, and pedestrian traffic into and out of the town.

Wood and Stone Foundations. During the Middle Ages, there were alternative methods to the cofferdam for creating foundations with stone and wood. One was to drive piles into the river bed without a cofferdam and build the stone foundation directly on the piles. As with all wooden foundations, this method was commonly used where the bottom of the river was soft and the pilings could not be driven into clay or other firm material. For this reason, wooden pilings supporting stone foundations were frequently built on tidal stretches of rivers where the river beds were covered with sand. Surprisingly, these foundations were very strong. The pilings were driven deep into the wet sand and held securely in place. Some of these foundations lasted for centuries, although regular maintenance was required. To complete the wooden foundation, a grid of timbers was sometimes laid atop the pilings to create a flat surface for the stone piers to be built upon.

Another method that mixed wood and stone involved dumping rubble into the river until it reached the water's surface. Piles were then driven in to surround the mound of rocks. This piling contained the loose rubble and held it in place to create a firm foundation. The rubble core was sometimes compacted as well. The core was leveled to form a flat base for the construction of the pier.

In another method, piles were driven into the river bottom to form enclosures, but, instead of cofferdams as the Romans had, the enclosures were simply filled with rocks and gravel. The filling was held in place by the piles, which extended for several feet above the level of the river. The filling was compacted and rammed down to make it a more solid foundation. The pile-driving equipment already on site may have been used for this job. Once the core inside the pilings was complete, a frame of timberwork and a layer of masonry were constructed on top of the core, creating a level, stable surface upon which the bridge piers were built.

With all these types of foundations, stone arches were built on top of the piers and a roadway laid on the surface formed by the arches. An additional feature common to these types of foundations was a protective layer of additional piles driven all around the pilings. These piles did not support the bridge piers. Instead, they shielded the pilings from erosion and damage from debris carried by the river. This surrounding ring of piles was known in England as a starling. Starlings could be quite large. The London Bridge completed in 1209 (not the current Tower Bridge which was built in the 19th century) provides a good example. Its starlings were effectively small, man-made islands. Their size provided good protection for the pilings and the bridge piers. But the starlings suffered constant wear and tear. The maintenance for London Bridge and other bridges with starlings included the near-constant driving of additional piles to keep the starlings intact and the bridge foundations secure. Another drawback was that, as new piles were added, the starlings grew. This narrowed the space between the adjoining starlings and constricted the flow of water under the bridge. This increased the erosion caused by the river. The partial damming of the river also caused water to back up behind the bridge, which could contribute to flooding upstream.

The starlings for London Bridge were pointed on both the upstream and downstream sides. This feature, called a cutwater, helped break up the flow of the river so that these sides of the starling were not hit by the full force of the river's current. The wedge shape of the cutwater split the current, lessening its force. Since the Thames is a tidal river, it needed cutwaters on both ends of the starlings, but in most instances bridges' cut-waters needed only to face upstream, toward the oncoming water (see illustration 8). The wedge shape of the cutwater also channeled any floating debris, including chunks of ice in winter, into the open spaces between the star-lings. These materials would otherwise have accumulated on the face of the starling and caused damage. Use of cutwaters was not unique to starlings. Roman stone bridges had used them, as did many medieval bridges with stone foundations.

Drawbridges. Drawbridges are most commonly associated with castles but they were also built as part of ordinary bridges. Most medieval bridges were built relatively low to the water. The low clearance between the surface level of the river and the bottom of the bridge often impeded the passage of boats. Barges and small boats could typically pass under the arches of most bridges but larger boats, especially those with high masts, could not. Building bridges high enough to accommodate all sizes of river traffic was not feasible. Bridge height was limited by how high the piers and arches supporting the bridge could be built. Lower arches and shorter piers were usually more structurally sound than those built to greater heights. Ad-mittedly, in some instances, medieval builders were able to build quite high and constructed bridges in which the underside of the bridge was 20 feet or more above the water level. But even some major bridges appear to have had clearances as low as 15 feet or less under their arches. To cope with the problem of low clear-ances, major bridges on navigable rivers were often equipped with wooden drawbridges to permit larger ships to pass. The pivoting end of the drawbridge was mounted in a gate- or bridge-house which contained the winches that raised the drawbridge by winding up the ropes or chains connected to the free end of the bridge. Drawbridges were typically located in the center of the bridge where the river was at its deepest. When the drawbridge was raised, tall ships could pass through the bridge and move up or down the river. Drawbridge

openings were regularly scheduled, although they might be limited to just a few times per week. In tidal areas, drawbridge openings for ships going upriver were sometimes timed to coincide with the rising high tide. At that time, the downstream current was lessened by the incoming movement of the tide, which made proceeding upriver easier. Drawbridges could also contribute to the defensibility of a bridge. They could be raised or even destroyed to block passage across the bridge.

Sizes and Qualities of Bridges

As outlined before, bridges, whether of wood, stone, or a combination of the two, var-ied in width and overall size depending upon the traffic they were expected to carry and the conditions (wide river, narrow stream, etc.) where they were sited. Particularly large bridges were needed in some urban settings. In important cities, such as London and Paris, wide bridges were required to keep the flow of pack animals and carts moving. From trade goods to foodstuffs, this traffic was vital to a city's existence and so bridges in most major cities were built large enough to accommodate two-way traffic. In the late Middle Ages, the roadway on London Bridge was 20 feet wide, although its usable width is estimated to have been reduced to 12 feet by the houses and shops built along it.

For centuries, even such important bridges as the ones in London and Paris were built of wood. Gradually, more bridges were built of stone, many in hopes that the stone construction would better withstand the vio-lent floods which repeatedly washed away wooden bridges. In some cases the expense of building in stone was repaid with the durabil-ity of the new bridge. However, building in stone was no guarantee of permanence. The collapse of major bridges was not uncommon. Even stone bridges could be damaged by severe floods destroying one or more of their piers and arches. In Paris, for example, floods com-pletely or partially destroyed the city's bridges four times in the course of the 13th century. In other cases, poor construction, often the result of a lack of understanding of the various stresses placed on the bridge, caused bridges to fail. This problem would persist for centuries after the Middle Ages until civil engineering became a more precise science. Still, stone bridges were generally more durable than wooden ones and some intact medieval stone bridges can still be found scattered across Europe. And some of these bridges are still in use today.

Floods were not the only nemesis of bridges. Wooden bridges were also susceptible to fire. For example, in 813, the bridge at Mainz in Germany burned. It was replaced with a bridge with stone piers and a wooden superstructure. Similarly, London's bridge burned in the late 12th century and was replaced with a stone bridge set on wooden and stone foundations. Bridges made entirely of stone were clearly more fire-proof although any houses or shops built on them were still vulnerable.

Bridge Maintenance

In the late Roman Empire, all citizens were responsible for maintaining the roads and bridges near where they lived. This obligation was continued into the early Middle Ages. In the 8th and 9th centuries the Carolingians, rulers of much of western Europe, issued decrees ordering their subjects to maintain roads and bridges. The Carolingian rulers stated that maintaining good bridges was part of a count's duty. Similarly, in the 9th century, Alfred the Great of England declared that bridge maintenance was an obligation for every man who held land. So, continuing the Roman practice, people living near roads and bridges were expected to appear in person and carry out the maintenance themselves. This was another use of corvée labor.

Examples of this forced labor can be found in many instances in the early Middle Ages. For example, in the 9th century, the Carolingian ruler Charles the Bald ordered his subjects to work on several bridges during his reign. However, it should be noted that work on some of these bridges was recognized as being so onerous that the workers were granted exemptions from any future calls for laborers for public projects. In another example, in 1097, the king of England resorted to compulsory labor to rebuild a bridge lost to flooding. He forced residents of London and the surrounding area to turn out and do the work themselves.

Needless to say, the persons compelled to do this work resented it and many likely lacked the skills (as well as the will) to do the work at hand. Over time, rulers came to tax residents near bridges to provide the funds needed for bridge maintenance instead of requiring them to personally perform the work. This transition can be seen in the English example from 1097. This appears to have been the last time that an English king called for such forced labor from his subjects. When bridge repair was needed in 1110 and again in 1125, the local residents paid additional taxes instead of serving in person. This progression of commuting labor services to cash payments occurred across Europe and there are no further examples of large-scale use of corvée labor for bridge work after the 12th century. Construction and maintenance of bridges increasingly became jobs for professional builders such as masons and master carpenters. However, very few appear to have specialized in bridges. Instead, bridge work was just another project for them, along with constructing cathedrals, castles, and other structures.

Bridge maintenance was a never-ending problem. The piles of bridges with wooden or wood and stone foundations needed constant, routine replacement as rot and damage from the flow of the river gradually ate away at the pilings and piers. For those bridges with starlings, maintenance of the piles was especially important. If a pile gave way, the filling could slip out and destabilize the starling and the pier it supported. To address this problem, additional piles were frequently driven around each pier to keep the rock and earth core firmly enclosed. This process gradually narrowed the space between piers and often created problems for river traffic.

Even above the waterline, stone bridges were not immune to the passage of time and the battering of floodwaters. The piers and arches that supported the bridge deck required routine inspections and maintenance to head off collapse. Unfortunately, these efforts were not always enough and full and partial bridge collapses sometimes happened, especially in the wake of flooding. In some instances, ferries were used until the bridge had been repaired. In others, wooden arches and roadways were built to span the section that had collapsed. These temporary measures sometimes remained in place for months or even years.

All this stress on maintenance may seem excessive, but bridges rapidly decayed and became impassable without routine, periodic repairs. For example, in one account from the 10th century, the roadway of a bridge in Meaux in France was so full of large holes that it could be crossed only at great risk. Travelers told of having to use loose planks as well as their wooden shields to cover the holes so they and their horses could cross. They would cover a hole, cross it, and then move the shields and boards on to the next hole. They reached the other end of the bridge only after repeating this process many times.

Tolls and Other Contributions to Bridge Building and Maintenance

While we do not know how many bridges charged tolls in the Middle Ages, all major bridges are known to have levied tolls. One answer could be that tolls were levied at all bridges with sufficient traffic to justify employing a toll-collector and so many small bridges were likely toll-free. Tolls were charged even on bridges which were built as acts of charity. These bridges were originally free of tolls but the need for money for maintenance led to their conversion to toll-bridges. Oddly, for many bridges, tolls were even collected from boats passing under them. Given that bridges impeded rather than helped river traffic, these tolls must have been particularly galling to the boatmen. As with tolls for roads, bridge tolls were routinely treated as ordinary income by the local lord and diverted to other purposes despite the repeated directives from kings and emperors that tolls were to be used only for the maintenance of the bridges.

Charitable Donations. Some funding for the construction and maintenance of bridges came as charitable donations. By contributing to building or maintaining a bridge, a donor was being a good Christian, helping his fellow man on his journey through life and perhaps saving him from drowning while attempting to cross a river. Aiding pilgrims by building bridges along routes to religious shrines was seen as especially laudable. This religious element in bridge building can be found across medieval Europe. For example, in London, contributions for the maintenance of the bridge were referred to as gifts "to God and the Bridge." In Scandinavia, even as early as the time of the region's conversion from paganism to Christianity, the financing of bridges was done for the benefit of the soul. Rune-stones near some bridges commemorated the name of the benefactor who had the bridge built and stated that it was done for the good of his or her soul and often the souls of family members as well.

To encourage donations for the maintenance or reconstruction of some bridges, the Church even offered indulgences to the donors. In exchange for contributions of cash or labor to a bridge project, an indulgence granted a donor remission of the punishments for his sins. The religious aspect of bridge building was also reflected in the practice of building chapels on bridges. Such chapels were found across Europe (see illustration 9). The donations taken in were divided between the maintenance of the chapel and that of the bridge.

Charitable gifts for bridges came both from living donors and from bequests in wills. Some of these donations were in the form of rents from properties. (Donations of this type were not rare in the Middle Ages. Income from properties was often among contributions made to churches and other religious foundations.) To manage these properties and other gifts and to oversee their expenditures, administrative groups were sometimes formed. One such organization was a corporation founded for the bridge at Rochester in England which has continued in existence to the present.

In addition to corporations, in southern France in the late 11th and early 12th century, there were also religious fraternities dedicated to the building of bridges. The bridge construction which these groups supported was often considered an act of charity, as was the building of some other bridges paid for by free-will donations. Initially, no tolls were charged for their use. However, the free use policies were short lived, as were the fraternities themselves.

Taxes. Donations alone never covered the expenses of bridge upkeep. And even in those instances when local lords did not divert the funds to other purposes, tolls were often inadequate to meet the high costs of maintenance. So, as discussed previously, this led kings across Europe to renew the decrees that the towns and parishes near bridges must pay to maintain them. However, kings sometimes recognized how burdensome this requirement was and included authorizations for these communities to levy special taxes and tolls to pay for the maintenance. In exchange for paying the additional taxes, local residents were often exempted from paying tolls for using the bridge.

Other Funding. In some instance, primarily in large cities, bridge construction and maintenance became a wholly local matter. Residents in the vicinities of bridges would decide whether it was worth the expense based on financial considerations: would the bridge generate enough revenue in tolls and trade to repay the investment?

Other Roles of Bridges

In urban areas such as London, Paris, Pisa, and Florence, major bridges often served as locations for shops and housing. One reason for this was that space was limited within the city walls. The rents from these shops and houses were another source of revenue for the upkeep of the bridge. Again, chapels were also a common feature of major bridges and were found across Europe.

Besides shops and housing, bridges were sometimes the site of mills as well. (See illustration 11.) Mills for milling grain were built under the arches of large bridges. While these locations were ideal for mills, they had the negative effect of limiting river traffic by decreasing the number of arches open for the passage of boats.

In addition to residential and commercial uses, bridges served military functions as well. Bridges provided a route for troops, and control of them meant that one could defend and block river crossings. For example, in 1450, citizens defending London against rebels held the bridge and prevented the enemy from entering the city. In some instances, to facilitate defense, some bridges were fortified and given towers that resembled those of castles. One such bridge survives at Monmouth in Wales. (See illustration 12.) Built in the late 13th century, the bridge at Monmouth has two towers connected with a gallery that straddles the bridge. The towers and gallery were fitted with a gate and formed the first line of defense for the town behind them. Another fortified bridge with three towers, built in the 14th century, can be found at Cahors in France. In some instances, bridges could not be adequately defended and were destroyed to block the advance of enemy forces. The ease with which these bridges were destroyed strongly suggests that many were either entirely wooden or had wooden superstructures which could be easily torn up to make a bridge impassable.

In addition to blocking river crossings, bridges were also used to block traffic on the rivers that flowed beneath them. When the Vikings raided France in the 8th and 9th centuries they sailed and rowed their ships far up rivers to reach rich targets well inland. To counter these attacks, the Carolingian rulers of France tried to maintain bridges which served as obstacles to the Viking ships. Despite

Top, illustration 11. This is a rare depiction of water mills mounted under the arches of a bridge (detail from a full page in *Life of St. Denis*, 1317). Here, three grain mills mounted on boats are moored under a bridge in Paris. On the left and right, men are carrying large sacks of grain to the mills (courtesy Bibliothèque Nationale de France, FR 2092, fol. 73V). *Bottom, illustration 12.* In the 14th century, this tower was added to the bridge at Monmouth, Wales, as part of the town's defenses. Fortifications such as these were built on bridges across Europe to defend important river crossings as well as to protect towns and cities. Unfortunately, only a handful of these fortified bridges remain and this is the only one left in the United Kingdom.

these efforts, the Vikings were often successful in breaking down bridges and opening rivers so their boats could travel further inland. Additionally, the destruction of the bridges disrupted communications and impeded the movement of land-based defenders who were attempting to respond to the Viking attacks.

One method of attacking bridges which was likely used by the Vikings can be seen in an example from the early 11th century. According to one Norse saga, Olaf, future king of Norway and saint, was assisting the English king Ethelred in his war against the Danes. Olaf and Ethelred's combined fleets sailed to London. While the English still held London, the Danes held London Bridge and the suburbs south of the Thames. The Danes had fortified the bridge and were using it as a platform for attacking ships attempting to reach London. Olaf had his ships fitted with roofs to shield his crews from projectiles dropped from the bridge. With these ships, Olaf's men reached the bridge's pilings, secured ropes to some of the piles, and then pulled away as quickly and forcefully as they could. They succeeded in damaging several pilings and destabilized the bridge, forcing the Danes to abandon it. This incident may have been the basis for the children's nursery rhyme of "London Bridge Is Falling Down." However, the rhyme in its current form has been dated to the late 13th century, when it was a criticism of Queen Eleanor. Eleanor was generally unpopular and was made more so when her husband, Henry III, gave her the tolls collected on London Bridge as a gift in 1281. This grant may have had an element of revenge in it: Previously, in 1265, Londoners had stood on the bridge, yelled insults at her, and pelted her with eggs, garbage, and filth as she attempted to pass under the bridge in her barge. This hail of trash halted the queen's progress and forced her barge to retreat. This experience may have contributed to her decision to spite the residents of London and spend the toll money on her own interests rather than on the bridge. As a consequence, the bridge suffered severely from a lack of maintenance. Thus, "London

Bridge Is Falling Down" was describing the current state of the bridge while "my fair lady" was a sarcastic reference by the Londoners to the queen.

Suspension Bridges

Before closing this section, there is one form of bridge which is conspicuous by its absence: the suspension bridge. A modern engineer might question why medieval Europeans did not build simple forms of suspension bridges which would have typically required fewer pilings and piers and created other savings of time, effort, and materials.

The earliest known suspension bridges were built in the Himalayan Mountains at some time before the 3rd century B.C. In the earliest suspension bridges, a pair of ropes, one above the other, was strung across the void to be spanned. Placing his feet on the lower rope and holding onto the upper rope with his hands, a person crossed the bridge by inching along sideways. In the 3rd century B.C., more advanced suspension bridges began being built in China. A pair of ropes was strung across the gorge to be spanned. A wooden walkway of parallel planks was then laid across and attached to the pair of ropes. One or more additional pairs of ropes were strung above the walkway. These pairs of ropes were then connected to the primary pair of ropes by stringers. Stringers are shorter lengths of ropes that connect the primary pair of ropes and the other pairs of ropes. The upper pair of ropes served both as a railing for the bridge and as an additional support.

Most Chinese suspension bridges used ropes made of bamboo. Near the end of the 3rd century B.C., the Chinese began using iron chains to build suspension bridges. By the 6th century A.D., chain bridges were numerous in China but were primarily built in the mountainous regions of the south-central provinces that bordered the Himalayas. However, even after the advent of iron chain suspension, bamboo ropes remained the more common cabling material.

Suspension bridges were also developed

in Central and South America, independently of those in Asia. The earliest suspension bridge built in the Americas was built by the Mayans in the 7th century A.D. These bridges were constructed with ropes made of fibrous material from plants.

Returning to Europe, suspension bridges were virtually unknown until after the Middle Ages. There appear to be only two mentions of possible suspension bridges in classical antiquity. As part of their invasion of Greece in 480 B.C., the Persians were recorded as building a bridge using ropes made from papyrus fiber. According to the one other record, Alexander the Great had a bridge constructed using iron chains in the 4th century B.C. However, it is possible that the ropes and chains were used to bind together boats for a pontoon bridge rather than to make a suspension bridge. As for the Romans, despite their engineering expertise, they did not develop suspension bridges.

While there were no suspension bridges in medieval Europe, there were structures which used some elements of the suspension bridge. These were wooden walkways on Alpine passes which were hung from chains attached to the sides of mountains. The first recorded one of these partially suspended walkways was built in the early 13th century A.D. It was called the Twärrenbrücke which meant "Transverse Bridge." The Twärrenbrücke was built across the face of a cliff to connect a pathway to a bridge over a gorge. Holes were carved into the cliff face and beams were inserted into the holes. Planks were laid on top of the beams to form the walkway. Iron rings were mounted on the cliff face at some height above the walkway. Chains connected the outer edge of the walkway to the iron rings on the cliff. Thus, the wooden walkway was supported from below by the beams projecting from the cliff and from above by the iron chains. Unfortunately, the Twärrenbrücke was destroyed by a flood in the 18th century, leaving only the beam sockets and iron rings behind. However, a similar wooden walkway is just barely visible in mountains in the back-

ground of a painting by Pieter Bruegel from 1567. This walkway is supported from beneath by props or beams sticking out from mountainside but there are no chains visible. Still, regardless of the means of support, like the Twärrenbrücke, this narrow walkway is shown as running along the face of the mountain where the natural trail is unsafe. Interestingly, the Romans in the 2nd century A.D. built a similar structure on part of a road along the Danube River. Like the one in the Bruegel painting, this walkway was supported solely by timbers which were set into holes carved into the face of a cliff. Thus, there may have been a tradition, starting with the Romans, of building wooden walkways in mountainous regions, but there is insufficient evidence to prove that medieval builders were actually familiar with the Roman examples.

In the centuries after the Middle Ages, true suspension bridges were developed in Europe. Europeans began to design and build suspension bridges in the late 16th century. A few of these early bridges were made with ropes. Most used chains. Regardless of the materials, all these bridges were built with plank walkways supported by pairs of ropes or chains strung across the void to be spanned. In the early 17th century, descriptions of the suspension bridges in China began filtering into Europe. These influenced later bridge designs and provided additional inspiration for building such bridges. Still, suspension bridges remained extremely rare in the Western world until the early 19th century. This was due in large part to the fact that virtually all European and American suspension bridges were designed to be built with chains, wires, and other structural elements made of metal. The methods and forges needed to produce iron on a scale large enough for building suspension bridges were only developed in the Industrial Revolution.

FOOD AND SHELTER

For any trip which could not be completed in a single day, travelers needed a place to spend the night and something to eat. There were a variety of institutions to meet these needs. Some catered to specific classes of travelers such as merchants and pilgrims. Others were open to anyone who could pay.

Some travelers sought to avoid the uncertain availability of suitable food by bringing or buying their own supplies and preparing meals themselves. But shelter for the night was generally sought at inns or other hospitable institutions. When no accommodations could be found or when there was not enough room to house the entire party, travelers sometimes used tents. The use of tents was most commonly recorded for armies on campaign and for nobles traveling with large numbers of followers. Sleeping rough outside was the last option and sleeping this way in cities and towns was grounds for arrest since being out after curfew was prohibited.

In the Roman Empire, the government built and operated a network of guest houses along the Empire's roads. These were placed at intervals about one day's journey apart. In addition to food and shelter for travelers, they also provided stabling and feeding for their horses. Fresh mounts were also available. However, these facilities were intended only for the use of official travelers rather than for the general public. Only messengers and others traveling on public business who had been issued the appropriate documents were authorized to stay at these rest stops. These official travelers did not pay for their accommodations and food. Instead, the local inhabitants near the rest stop were usually obligated to provide the necessities or pay for them. Government rest houses appear to have continued in use in the eastern half of the Roman Empire, but with the collapse of the western Empire in the 5th century these facilities disappeared in western Europe.

Private travelers in the Roman Empire stayed in inns. Towns which had official rest stops frequently had an inn as well. However, even at this early date, inns frequently had bad reputations. Travelers complained of innkeepers taking advantage of them by overcharging

them and by providing poor quality food, drink, and accommodations. If at all possible, Roman travelers preferred staying with family or friends along their route. And it was not unusual for this network of potential hosts to be expanded to include friends of family members, relatives of friends, and the friends of friends. In these instances where the traveler did not personally know the host, the traveler's relative or friend likely provided a letter of introduction that vouched for the traveler and asked that he be accepted as a guest. The practice of staying with friends, relatives, or others to whom the traveler had more tenuous connections continued through the Middle Ages to the present day.

Among the barbarian tribes which came to occupy western Europe, there was a tradition of private hospitality. People were expected to take in travelers and house them. They also either fed the stranger or provided him with the facilities for preparing his own meals. Tradition forbade the host from charging for these services but the traveler might have repaid his host with news from the lands through which he had passed. In an age before newspapers, television, and other forms of mass media, a person bearing fresh information from outside the vicinity was often a welcome guest. The traveler may have also performed some work for his host as well. There were limits on this hospitality. Guests were expected to stay a maximum of three days and then move on. In the 8th century, the Carolingians who ruled much of western Europe made the provision of hospitality a legal duty. The law codified the services to be provided by the host and the conduct expected of the guest. Again, a three-day limit was imposed.

Besides the barbarian tradition, private hospitality was also part of Christian practices. Taking in travelers was an act of charity in accordance with the New Testament. Specifically, in the Gospel according to Mark, Christ says "For I was hungry and you gave me meat: I was thirsty and you gave me drink: I was a stranger and you took me in.... Inasmuch as you have done it unto the least of my brothers, you have done it unto me."

Thus, every traveler was considered an embodiment of Christ. In practice, the hospitality provided likely conformed to the laws of the Carolingians.

While some people continued sheltering and feeding strangers as an act of Christian charity, the tradition of individuals providing hospitality to travelers gradually disappeared across Europe. The tradition persisted the longest on the northern and eastern fringes of Europe, where it lasted into at least the 12th century. Providing hospitality to strangers became more a matter for religious institutions as monasteries and hospices became providers of food and shelter for travelers.

Although providing accommodations for strangers continued to be a charitable act, the housing and feeding of travelers increasingly became more of a commercial matter. By the 11th century, the number of inns across Europe was greatly expanding. This growth was most pronounced along trade routes and in cities and towns which were centers of commercial activity such as those in northern Italy.

Monasteries

In accordance with the precept that every stranger was an embodiment of Christ, monastic orders had a spiritual obligation to provide hospitality to all travelers. In their striving to be ideal Christians, monks made the provision of food, drink, and shelter to those in need part of their mission. Of course, such charity was limited by the resources available to a monastery. The quality and quantity of the food and drink and the comfort of the accommodation varied according to the social standing of the guest. Poor travelers such as common pilgrims could usually expect only broth, bread, and beer or low-quality wine and a place to sleep. The most basic sleeping arrangement was a spot on the floor where the traveler could curl up under his own cloak. If a monastery could afford it, there might be beds in an area set aside for visitors. While descriptions of guest beds in monasteries are lacking, accounts of beds in inns indicate that these beds were likely large and had mattresses stuffed with straw, although better-quality ones were stuffed with feathers.

While monks slept alone in individual beds in their dormitories, guests were housed apart from them and likely shared beds with other travelers. Except for a nightcap of some sort, people in the Middle Ages typically slept naked. Having several people in a bed had the advantage of warming the bed. Given that most rooms did not have their own fireplace or other source of heat, this warmth was likely welcomed in cold weather. Interestingly, sharing a bed, even with strangers, was a common practice, although, if at all possible, a traveler slept with others from his party.

In descriptions of hospices for pilgrims, accommodations for travelers were recorded as being divided by sex so that men and women slept apart. This practice was almost certainly observed in monasteries as well. The only exceptions were likely for noblemen traveling with their wives. However, persons of such rank were housed in private accommodations apart from the common travelers.

While common travelers had to be content with basic accommodations and food, nobility, whether traveling on pilgrimage or other business, expected the best the monastery could afford. In addition to being served the best food and drink, the nobility were housed in the best accommodations available. This was usually in the house of the abbot, although many monastic communities built guesthouses especially for important guests. Monasteries located along major routes often had several guesthouses to cope with the high volume of traffic.

Ideally, the buildings for housing and feeding guests, both rich and poor, were located at the outer edges of the monastic compound. This was done so that the guests would not disturb the monks in the performance of their duties.

Pilgrims and other non-noble travelers were expected to spend only one night or at most three nights and then push on in their travels. Exceptions were made for the sick and injured, who could stay on while the monks tended to them. There were problems with the nobility abusing monastic hospitality. Those nobles who made donations to a monastery felt that they had a legitimate right to routinely impose on the monastery. Even nobles and royalty who were not donors felt free to use monasteries as though they were their own property, staying as long as they liked. In some instances, monasteries were nearly bankrupted by these freeloaders. A few rulers recognized that this was an unfair burden on the monasteries. King Edward I of England enacted a law in 1275 to try to limit such impositions but the problem persisted and went unchecked in much of Europe.

On rare occasions, nobles, kings, and queens did show some conscience and made donations to compensate their religious hosts. For example, when traveling on a military campaign in 1306, King Edward I of England stopped as Lanercost Priory in the far north of England. He had intended to remain for only a few days but became so ill that moving him was considered out of the question. His brief stay ended up lasting five months. During this time, the canons of the priory were forced to live in cramped quarters while the king, the queen, and their entourage occupied most of the complex. While the royal party did supply much of their own food, the strain on the priory's resources was great. Edward recognized this and, in the spirit of his own law from 1275, made donations to the priory and paid for the repair and improvement of some of its buildings. Still, gifts from travelers were seldom enough to cover all the expenses of hospitality and religious communities had to bear the excess costs out of their existing funds. These shortfalls were sometimes so great that the communities were left with insufficient funding to cover their ordinary operating expenses. This problem could leave monasteries almost bankrupt and led some to limit the number of travelers they hosted.

While sheltering travelers was a burden for most monasteries, a few monasteries were located especially so they could help travelers. As early as the 8th century, some monasteries were built in the Alps to provide food and shelter for those crossing the mountains. They were sited at critical locations such as the bottom of passes so that travelers could rest before making the long journey over the mountains. Monasteries along other pilgrimage routes also cared for travelers on their way to shrines.

Hospices and Hospitals

Today, the word *hospice* is most commonly associated with institutions that care for the elderly or terminally ill. However, the term originally referred to institutions that provided food and shelter to those in need, such as the poor and travelers. The first hospices were built by the Christian Church in the 4th century A.D. Early hospices were referred to by the Greek word *xenodochia*, which means "house for strangers" or "guest house." From the 4th century onwards, bishops ordered the construction of xenodochia in their dioceses to provide charity to those in need. Xenodochia served both as hospitals to care for the sick and as hospices to shelter the poor as well as travelers such as pilgrims. The mixing of hospice and hospital functions continued for many centuries. This was true even at one of the most famous hospitals of the Middle Ages, the hospital in Jerusalem operated by the brothers of the Order of the Hospital of St. John of Jerusalem." The Hospitallers cared for the sick and injured, especially pilgrims who became sick either on their long journey or during their stay in the Holy Lands. The hospital also provided food and shelter to pilgrims and others who were healthy but were poor and in need. The healthy were kept apart from the sick and women were housed in a facility separate from the men. This segregation by health condition and by gender appears to have been a standard practice for hospices and hospitals.

While staying in a hospital was not uncommon for travelers in the early Middle Ages, hospices became the primary religious institutions for housing pilgrims and other travelers in need. Like hospitals, hospices were typically founded and operated by religious orders and funded by donations from the pilgrims who used them. Hospices could be found across Europe along the major pilgrimage routes. Some were located in towns and cities, including one in Paris that provided accommodations to pilgrims passing through the city. This hospice lodged and fed 16,690 pilgrims in a single year. Other hospices were located in more remote and sparsely populated areas. In these regions, hospices were sometimes the only lodging available. Hospices were often positioned so that they were one day's journey or less apart. Thus, the pilgrims could count on finding shelter at the end of a long day of walking.

One major hospice was built at Compostela in Spain to care for the great number of pilgrims who came to worship at the shrine of St. James. As with the hospital in Jerusalem, it mixed health care with hospitality. Sick and injured pilgrims were cared for in accommodations in a separate ward within the hospice. While sick pilgrims could stay on until they recovered or died, healthy pilgrims were given free food and lodging for only three days. On the fourth day, they were expected to be on their way. The three-day limit on hospitality seems to have been observed at all hospices.

The primary pilgrimage routes from northern Europe to Italy passed directly through the Alps. Pilgrims passing this way were on their way to Rome and to port cities, especially Venice, where they could board ships bound for the Holy Land. Hospices were built in the Alps to assist pilgrims and other travelers in negotiating the treacherous terrain. These hospices supplemented the monasteries that already existed in the region. From as early as the 11th century, hospices were being built, some located at the tops of the Alpine passes. Like the monasteries, these hospices provided food and shelter for the travelers and enabled them to rest up during their arduous passage through the Alps. The poor ate and stayed for

free while those who could afford it paid for their room and board. Staffs of the Alpine hospices provided travelers with information about weather and road conditions. They also rang the bell of the hospice's chapel during bad weather and in the morning and evening in the winter. This was done so that travelers could find their way to the hospice by following the sound of the bell. The staffs also patrolled the surrounding areas for lost travelers. The hospices also had cemeteries for those travelers they were unable to save. Winter was, of course, an especially difficult time for crossing the Alps, and the bodies of some travelers were not recovered until the spring when the melting of the snow revealed them. While dogs may have been used to help search for travelers, this practice is not recorded in the Middle Ages. The first evidence of the famed St. Bernards which originated at the hospice on the Great St. Bernard Pass dates back only to the 17th century.

While the hospices of the Alps are perhaps the most famous, the hospices in the Pyrenees Mountains in southern France and northern Spain were also well known in the Middle Ages. These hospices were along the routes to Compostela in northern Spain. The shrine of St. James in Compostela was one of the most popular pilgrimage destinations in medieval Europe.

Like the Alps, the Pyrenees were a major obstacle for pilgrims. Snow storms, difficult terrain, and wolves claimed many lives every year. Hospices were built to shelter pilgrims in this hostile environment. One of the most famous of these hospices was at the pass at Roncesvalles. This hospice was notable because of the pass's connection to the legendary hero Roland. At Roncesvalles, Roland and his companions valiantly defended Charlemagne's army from a treacherous attack by the Basques, the natives of the Pyrenees. The Carolingian forces won the day but Roland and the rest of his warriors died in the effort. These events were immortalized in *The Song of Roland* and the story was spread throughout Europe. The hospice at Roncesvalles received many donations and was noted for the high quality of its accommodations.

All religious orders that operated hospices and hospitals depended on donations to pay their expenses. Many, if not most, donations came from those who had stayed in these institutions. Donations ranged from a few pennies from poor travelers up to grants of land and property rents from wealthy, noble travelers. For example, the order of Hospitallers was particularly favored and received endowments of lands scattered across Europe. Other sources of revenue for hospitals were the clothes and other personal goods of travelers who died while at the hospital.

There was one other charitable institution which served as both hospice and hospital: the *hôtels-Dieu* found in many French cities. Hôtels-Dieu were established for the care of the sick and the poor. They also provided food and shelter for pilgrims and other travelers. However, the charters and endowments of some hôtels-Dieu limited their care to only pilgrims and the sick so healthy travelers were turned away.

Inns

While monasteries and other religious houses fed and housed both poor travelers and noble ones, they did not routinely extend their hospitality to merchants and others who could afford to pay for their meals and accommodations. These travelers were expected to stay in inns. In fact, some monasteries built and operated inns nearby to capitalize on the need for food and shelter. Instead of being a burden, travelers were now a source of revenue for these monasteries. Some travelers preferred staying in inns anyway since accommodations were usually more comfortable than those provided to ordinary travelers in monasteries. At an inn, a traveler could expect to find a bed, food, drink, and usually stabling for his horse as well.

Locations of Inns

By the 11th century, inns could be found in many parts of Europe. Increasing trade drove the demand for accommodations. Merchants traveling abroad needed places to stay in the cities and towns in which they did business. In addition to the merchants, the pack animal drivers and carters who moved the merchants' goods also needed rooms for the night. As a result of this traffic, inns developed in major cities and along trade routes. They became especially common in areas with high levels of urbanization and commerce, such as in northern Italy. Southern France, especially in the 14th century, also had a large number of inns because of the presence of the papal court in Avignon. While engaged in Church business at the courts of bishops, archbishops, and the pope, clergymen routinely stayed in inns in these cities. Inns in major cities such as Avignon, as well as capitals such as London and Paris, were also patronized by government officials attending to business in the courts of law and ministries of their rulers. Foreign delegations also stayed at inns in the capital cities, if they were not important enough to merit grander accommodations in the palaces of their hosts.

Away from cities and larger towns and from the main trade and pilgrimage routes, inns appear to have been rather scarce. Spain was noted for having few inns except in major cities. Travelers complained of having to sleep on the floor in the poor accommodations they could find. But Spain was not alone in lacking inns. In the rural regions of England, Germany, and northern France, inns appear to have been few and far between. But this seems to have been true throughout much of Europe, with the exception of Italy, which, particularly in the north and central regions, seems to have been well provided with inns.

Within towns and cities, inns were often located on the main thoroughfare so that travelers could easily find them. These inns were also well placed for serving travelers who were just passing through on their way to another destination. Inns were also located near important places such as major markets or government buildings. In Paris, for example, merchants often stayed near Les Halles, the central market. By sleeping nearby, they could easily and quickly get to the market as soon as it opened in the morning. In Rome, the Vatican was the primary attraction for clergymen with business in the ecclesiastical courts so they stayed at inns close by. In walled towns and cities, inns sometimes clustered just inside the wall near the main gates so that travelers would find them immediately upon entering the city. Interestingly, inns could also be found just outside the gates as well. These inns were placed to take advantage of the nightly closure of city gates. Travelers who arrived too late to enter the city needed a place to stay until the gates reopened in the morning and so these suburban inns took care of them. London and Southwark provide an example of this arrangement. London Bridge closed at night so late travelers coming from the south stayed in inns in Southwark on the southern shore of the Thames.

Advertising of Inns

Innkeepers used sign boards to advertise their establishments. In fact, inns were usually required to display signs to indicate their business. The symbol of the inn's name was also painted on its sign board. In an age when the majority of the population was illiterate, having the inn's name also rendered as a picture made it much easier for customers to find a particular inn. Inns had a wide variety of names. Some were named after saints while others were named after animals, both real and imaginary, such as "The Black Horse" or "The Dragon." Others were named after objects such as "The Crown" or "The Star." Some had names and symbols such as the coat of arms of the local ruler. In some cases where the innkeepers had emigrated from another region, they used some symbol of their homeland for their inn's name. For example, "The Shield of Brittany" was operated by a Breton innkeeper in a city far from Brittany. By advertising a connection with Brittany, the innkeeper may have attracted traveling Bretons who wanted some "down home" hospitality.

Some innkeepers went too far with their advertising. Oversize signs hanging out into the streets were a hazard to passing horsemen. Other signs were so large and heavy that they threatened to pull down parts of the buildings to which they were attached. Some sent men out to accost travelers and persuade them to stay at their inns. One 15th century pilgrim who was approaching Venice by boat encountered one such agent who was approaching in another boat. When the pilgrim told the man that he had already made his own arrangements for the night, the man began disparaging the inn the pilgrim had chosen and became so agitated that he fell out of his boat.

Accommodations at Inns

The floor plans of inns varied greatly. Some were ordinary houses with just one or two rooms for guests. Others were quite large with numerous rooms for guests along with stables for their horses. Large inns were sometimes constructed with blocks of buildings forming a square that surrounded a central courtyard. The entrance to the courtyard was through a gatehouse on the side facing the street. This side of the complex often included the accommodations for the innkeeper and the common room for eating and drinking. Another side was formed by the block containing the guestrooms. A third side held the kitchen, store rooms, and, perhaps, a room for brewing as well. The stables, including storage for fodder, made up the fourth side. The central courtyard provided a secure space for guests' carts and wagons. Other inns were not so elaborate and were simply formed by connecting several contiguous townhouses. In these inns, the residential block and stables faced directly out onto the street. Whatever their configuration, the essential features of an inn were some number of bedrooms, a kitchen, and a common room for meals and drink, as well as for socializing, gambling, and transacting business.

The sizes of inns varied greatly. In very small inns, a traveler might sleep in the same room or even the same bed as the innkeeper and his family. Such tight quarters are humorously depicted in Boccaccio's *Decameron*. Such small inns may have been the only accommodations available in villages and in some towns, especially the smaller ones. In cities and large towns, on the other hand, civic regulations sometimes required an inn to have at least two rooms for guests and some inns were much larger than this. For example, in the city of Aix in the south of France, among the 27 inns recorded, most inns had 7 to 12 beds and could accommodate 15 to 30 guests while the two largest inns had 18 to 20 beds and could normally accommodate 30 to 40 guests. In one of these inns, 20 beds were divided among 12 rooms. In general, having two beds per room appears to have been common although three or four beds were sometimes crammed into a single room.

Beds in inns were routinely shared. Sleeping two, three, or four to a bed appears to have been common but up to ten or more guests might be forced to bed together when accommodations were in short supply. While beds holding so many people were sometimes quite large, with some measuring up to seven feet wide, sleeping in such close quarters was obviously uncomfortable. In cold months, having several people in a bed provided welcome warmth, but, in warm months, the presence of a number of hot, sweaty bedmates must have been very unpleasant. Ideally, a traveler shared his bed only with other members of his party, but sharing beds with strangers was often unavoidable. Although this practice was common, there were problems with sharing rooms and beds with strangers. Records of crimes reveal that guests sometimes stole money and other valuables from their bed- or roommates. Fighting was also a problem. In one instance, a brawl broke out when an innkeeper brought in another guest to share a bed after having assured the earlier guests that they would have the bed all to themselves. In other cases, some guests provoked fights by rolling in drunk and disturbing the other guests who were already settled in bed. However, only those instances in which a crime occurred made it into the records. The majority

of stays at inns were peaceful and uneventful, if uncomfortable, and so went unnoticed.

The furnishings of the guestrooms varied with the quality of the inn. At a bare minimum, rooms contained a bed with a mattress and sheets. In the best inns, bed linens were washed frequently and mattresses were regularly restuffed. In the seediest inns, linens might have been washed only when they became so dirty that guests refused to sleep in them and mattresses were allowed to become thin and lumpy. Better inns also provided pillows and blankets for their guests and some even included nightcaps as well. Besides mattresses and sheets, beds sometimes had curtains and canopies. While these features are considered a sign of luxury today, they were more common in the Middle Ages. Curtains kept out cold drafts and trapped warm air. These were important features in an age without central heating. In addition to beds, guestrooms sometimes had chairs or benches as well as chests and tables. Again, higher-quality inns were more likely than low-quality ones to provide such furnishings. Further, in addition to furniture and clean, comfortable bedding, the better-quality inns also provided guests with wash basins, towels, a rod for hanging up clothes, and candlesticks. Candles themselves were of sufficient value that innkeepers often charged additionally for them.

The few financial accounts and records of inn patrons indicate, not surprisingly, that good accommodations were more expensive. Some inns appear to have catered to high-end travelers such as the nobility and those clerics and merchants who could afford to pay for their comfort. Pack animal drivers, carters, and others with less to spend stayed in cheaper inns. However, even a traveler who could afford one could not always find a decent inn. Poor accommodations could command high prices when a town or city was packed with merchants attending major trade fairs or with pilgrims observing religious festivals. Inns located in relatively remote locations where there was little or no competition also appear to have charged dearly at times. In these situations, a well-off traveler might pay to stay in an attic or a loft in a stable. In some cases, travelers searching for accommodations encountered inns that also served as brothels. While brothels and inns were usually two separate institutions in medieval cities and towns, prostitution was an activity long associated with inns.

Humans were often not the only guests at inns. Horses were a common means of transportation and so most inns provided stabling for their customers' mounts. The cost of stabling a horse, including its feeding, could be as much as the cost of the room. Some inns even functioned as livery stables and guests could hire horses. Further, for a suitable fee, some inns stabled and fed horses during the day for non-guests while they went about their business in town.

Long-term Accommodations

While most guests at inns stayed only a night or two, inns sometimes provided long-term housing. In university towns and cities, students who could afford it sometimes took rooms for the term of their studies. In some cases, students could stay at inns run by people from their home country or who could at least speak their language. For example, in the university city of Bologna, Swiss émigrés ran an inn that catered to students from German-speaking countries. Masons and other workers building cathedrals were another group that might take up long-term residence in a city, staying on until the job was done.

The Bad Reputation of Inns

While many inns offered safe, clean accommodations, inns in general had a bad reputation. Lice, bedbugs, and particularly fleas were common problems. Fleas infested the bedding as well as the rushes covering the floors. In an age when fleas were a common pest, they must have been truly horrible in some inns to have rated comments about how it was impossible to sleep because of the constant biting and itching.

Food was another common source of complaints. Breads and cheeses were some-times wormy. Meat was tough and unidentifiable. As a consequence, those travelers that could afford it brought their own fresh ingredients with them or purchased them locally and then prepared their meals themselves, using the hearth or kitchen at the inn in which they were staying. Some travelers went even further. Nobility, high clerics, and others who could afford it had their own cooks travel with them to prepare their meals.

Some innkeepers took advantage of their guests, especially foreigners, and overcharged them. Court records also reveal that some innkeepers even stole from their guests' rooms. In one case, a guest repeatedly asked for the key to lock his room but the innkeeper kept putting him off. While the guest was absent from his room, a small chest of valuables he had placed under the bed was stolen. The guest brought charges against the innkeeper. He was convicted and ordered to return the chest and its contents.

There were other illegal activities at some inns as well. Inns and taverns had the reputation of being the haunts of prostitutes, thieves, and professional gamblers with loaded dice who cheated unwary travelers. Another problem was brawling, often fueled by drinking and arguments over gambling. These quarrels could easily prove fatal, as most men in the Middle Ages carried knives. Guests were sometimes attacked and robbed by local residents. In one particularly tragic case, a woman staying alone in an inn was attacked by a number of local men who dragged her out into the street and raped her.

Taverns and Other Sources of Food and Drink

While inns routinely offered food and drink, travelers often ate and drank at other establishments. Taverns provided drink and usually food as well but typically did not offer accommodations. Traditionally, taverns primarily served wine while alehouses served ale and beer. Taverns had even worse reputations than inns for being dangerous for travelers.

Again, gambling and prostitution were often connected to taverns.

In cities, food was also available at cook shops that provided a variety of ready-to-eat food and bakers in most towns could provide meat pies. In an account of London in the 12th century, one traveler marveled at all the ready-to-eat foods that were available. However, prepared foods, even those served at inns, were often viewed with some suspicion. As strangers to the city or town, travelers did not know the reputations of local food vendors. This tempted unscrupulous bakers and cooks to sell them substandard foods, such as meat pies made with spoiled meat and other unhealthy items. While they also tried to sell these disgusting items to local customers, these cooks and bakers likely viewed travelers as especially good targets for this foul practice since travelers were likely to quickly move on and not be repeat customers. Further, because they often stayed for only a short time and were strangers to the town, travelers were unlikely to complain to the authorities. Again, seasoned travelers cooked their own meals to avoid this problem.

Specialized Accommodations for Merchants

There were other accommodations in addition to monasteries, hospices, and inns. Merchants who came from other countries also had specialized residences in some cities. These were often complexes which housed both them and their merchandise. These enclosures also served to protect the merchants during times of anti-foreigner unrest. Foreign merchants frequently enjoyed exemptions from taxes and duties as part of government efforts to encourage trade. These privileges angered local residents who had to pay these taxes.

German merchants had compounds in a number of cities. Some of these complexes included living quarters, warehouses, administrative offices, an assembly hall, and stalls for selling goods. On the shore of the Thames in London, German traders lived in the *Stalhof.*

The English called it the Steelyard, which suggests that the complex was named after the steel imported by the Germans. However, the origin of the name "Steelyard" is unclear. It may have been taken from a type of scale for weighing merchandise called a *steelyard.* (But steelyard scales had been invented by the Romans and had been widely used for centuries, so it is difficult to understand why such a scale would have been considered so distinctive as to merit naming the compound after it.) The Germans also had a trading station called the Peterhof in Novgorod in Russia. This was surrounded with a palisade for protection. The Peterhof was a small compound and the church there was also used as a warehouse and treasury. In Venice, the German compound was called the *Fondaco dei Tedeschi,* the Fondaco of the Germans. The word fondaco was derived from the Arabic *funduk,* which was a building or compound used to house merchants and their goods. Many Italian merchants engaged in trade with the Moslem world and had firsthand experience using funduks and took this concept back home. In the Middle East and North Africa, some Italian city-states had trading compounds in Moslem cities as well as in those cities held by Christians during the era of the crusades. In the crusader-held lands, Italian city-states such as Genoa and Venice were given quarters in some port cities in exchange for the valuable support they provided to the crusaders. Within these quarters, Italian merchants had their own churches, bakeries, baths, and other facilities in addition to warehouses and accommodations. Cemeteries were also a part of some merchant compounds.

Having foreign merchants residing in a single location, whether in an inn or fondaco, had advantages for both merchants and their host governments. For merchants, these accommodations often provided a measure of security and convenience. Additionally, innkeepers who had experience in dealing with foreign businessmen and the resident staffs at trading compounds could provide a range of important services. These included advising on local conditions, both political and commercial, and setting up meetings with local merchants. Brokering business deals between local and foreign merchants was so commonly performed by innkeepers in Bruges that they belonged to the same guild as professional brokers. In fact, use of local brokers was sometimes required by law. This allowed the authorities to keep track of trade with foreigners. It also made money for the brokers since the foreigners had to pay for their services. Innkeepers also gave other assistance such as providing secure storage space for merchandise and arranging for its packing and shipping. Further, some innkeepers made loans, stood as sureties for loans and other business dealings, and collected debts. However, these financial services were not done casually. It is most likely that they were performed only when the innkeeper and his customer had developed a relationship of trust based perhaps on repeated contact or on recommendations by trusted third parties.

To provide all these services, innkeepers needed some way of communicating with their foreign guests. Those innkeepers who routinely dealt with guests from other lands appear to have learned some foreign languages from their repeated contact with such travelers. In other cases, the innkeepers spoke other languages because they themselves were immigrants. For example, German innkeepers could be found settled in Venice because of the trade connections between German countries and the city-state. Swiss innkeepers were drawn to Bologna by the money to be made in catering to university students from German-speaking countries.

For their part, travelers also sought to bridge the language barrier. Over the course of their journeys, many appear to have tried to learn enough of other languages so they could at least communicate their basic needs, such as ordering a meal or booking a room. Merchants who routinely traveled abroad likely went further and picked up enough of other languages to enable them to transact business.

Having merchants and other travelers stay at inns which specially catered to foreigners or in trading compounds also served local security and economic interests since it helped track the arrival and movement of foreigners. In Paris, inns were required to submit lists of all foreign guests every night. In one Italian city, a foreigner could not get a room at an inn until after he had registered with civic authorities. Such practices were motivated, in part, by a fear that foreigners could be spies. Alerting the local authorities to the arrival of foreign merchants also served the more mundane purpose of tracking them to ensure that they complied with local trade regulations. These regulations sometimes required foreign merchants to contract business only through approved local brokers. This ensured that the appropriate customs and taxes were paid on the transactions.

Tracking foreigners did not end with the Middle Ages. For centuries afterwards, travelers often had to present their passports when registering at inns (and later at hotels) in many parts of Europe. Passports sometimes even had to be surrendered to the hotelier so that information about the traveler and his movements could be copied and passed on to the local authorities.

Accommodations for the Nobility

The nobility had other options for accommodation, besides extracting hospitality from monasteries and paying for stays at inns. In much of medieval Europe, nobles held lands scattered across the country so when traveling they were sometimes able to arrange their itineraries to allow them to stay at their own properties. Traveling from one estate to the next was a routine matter for the nobility. These stays enabled them to see how their properties were being managed, to administer justice to their subjects, and to consume the foodstuffs that comprised some of the rents paid by their tenants.

In addition to having estates around the country, higher nobility, both lay and religious, often maintained townhouses in capital cities. London and Paris were perhaps the best examples. Archbishops and dukes owned homes in these cities so that they could reside in suitable splendor while attending the royal court. Interestingly, these properties were often rented out when the owner was out of town. Even the nobility weren't averse to making a profit from travelers needing a place to stay.

Besides staying at their own manors and townhouses, nobles also stayed at the properties held by their vassals. As with monasteries, the cost of furnishing such lodging was often a heavy financial burden on those subordinate nobles "graced" by the visit of their superiors. The visiting overlord sometimes compensated his host with gifts, but the privilege of entertaining a great lord did have some value in itself. Such a visit gave the host an opportunity to enhance his reputation by furnishing his lord with the best food, accommodation, and entertainment he could muster. In the status-conscious world of medieval nobility, successful handling of a superior's visit was important and could improve the host's political standing as well as his social stature.

In addition to availing themselves of the hospitality of their vassals, the nobility also stayed with relatives, friends, and acquaintances just as other members of medieval society did. Further, some nobles developed reputations of being especially gracious and generous hosts and welcomed any fellow nobility who happened to be traveling through their lands. However, such gallant behavior seems to have been more common in fiction than in real life.

When staying in towns and cities away from their homes, royalty had one other option for finding accommodations. They could simply requisition housing. Harbingers, who were officials that went in advance of royal parties to make arrangements for food and shelter, surveyed the available accommodations such as at inns and religious foundations. If these were insufficient to host the royal entourage, the harbinger had the authority to make residents vacate their homes to provide rooms for the party. The homeowners were paid for providing the accommodations but it is unclear where they went to stay while their houses were occupied. Additionally, when the king or emperor was staying for some time, properties were sometimes modified to satisfy his needs. This could include building additional rooms or connecting townhouses by cutting doorways through their walls. Owners were paid for the damages or, as in some cases, officials of the royal party arranged for carpenters to repair the houses.

Accommodations for Armies

With many hundreds or even thousands of men on the move, finding sufficient food and shelter was a tremendous problem. In the early Middle Ages, the men who served in armies raised by levies imposed by their rulers typically had to bring their own rations with them. The Carolingian rulers expected their men to carry enough food to last for the entire campaign. Over the course of the Middle Ages, soldiers came to expect that their leaders would provide food. This food could come from stockpiles brought by the nobles commanding the armies. More commonly, food was obtained by requisitioning or by raiding. When an army was campaigning within its own lands, supplies were usually obtained by requisitioning them from farmers. The farmers often had difficulty obtaining payment for their produce but had little choice but to turn it over. When the army was in enemy lands, foodstuffs were plundered from the local inhabitants. Armies could devastate wide areas in their search for food. This destruction was also carried out to deprive the enemy of food.

For shelter, armies improvised. When out in the field, the nobility typically lived in tents they had brought with them. However, if there were any towns or villages in the area, housing was commandeered for the nobility. Common soldiers seem to have sometimes had tents as well but were frequently expected to rough it. Like their leaders, they would seek out any buildings in the area to use as shelter.

When they were encamped for long periods such as during sieges, soldiers built huts or shacks for themselves. During the Hundred Years' War, Edward III of England went even further and had an entire town, complete with a marketplace, built to house his men during the siege of Calais.

Accommodations for Jewish Travelers

Jews from the Middle East, North Africa, and Muslim-held Spain, as well as from long-established communities within western Europe traveled for a number of reasons. Some traveled for business and others for religious purposes, either as scholars seeking out learned rabbis or as visitors to religious sites. In the early Middle Ages, Jews appear to have been able to travel around Europe as they had in the days of the Roman Empire. In these centuries, they seem to have been able to stay in inns just like any other travelers, but hospices and other Christian institutions appear to have been closed to them. However, one account describing the hospice at Roncesvalles claims that it was open to all travelers, including Jews. Still, the fact that this was specifically mentioned suggests that it was an exception to the usual practice. As for accommodation at inns, there is insufficient information to determine their policies towards Jews. Given the rising anti–Jewish sentiments over the course of the Middle Ages, it seems likely that they were increasingly unwilling to accept Jews as customers. Instead, most Jewish travelers stayed within the Jewish communities scattered in the towns and cities across Europe. In the larger and more wealthy communities, they could find lodging in guesthouses built and maintained by the local residents. Where guesthouses were not available, travelers were taken in to private homes. Travelers were expected to pay for their accommodations but allowances were made for the indigent, especially scholars.

Staying within Jewish communities was likely preferred by Jewish travelers over staying at ordinary inns. In a Jewish guesthouse or private home, they could observe their religious practices among their fellow Jews, including dietary laws. Obtaining kosher meals must have been virtually impossible when traveling away from Jewish communities.

Final Accommodations

Finally, there were places for the eternal rest of travelers. Travel was an arduous and frequently dangerous activity and some travelers never made it home. Embalming was primitive and so moving their bodies long distances was usually impossible. Instead, those far from home were usually buried near where they died. As mentioned previously, hospices along pilgrimage routes and hospitals had graveyards for those whose pilgrimages or other travels ended in death. These cemeteries ensured that a traveler could expect a proper Christian burial even while far from home. Traditionally, hospices and hospitals claimed the clothing and other personal belongings of the dead as compensation for the care they provided to the deceased. Cemeteries for travelers were also found in more secular locations. For example, the trading outpost at Novgorod had a cemetery for foreign merchants who died there. Those traveling from Russia to the Byzantine Empire along the Dnieper River noted several cemeteries for merchants who had died along this route.

While most people had to be content with a burial near where they had died, the nobility often made arrangements to be buried in churches, cathedrals, or abbeys at their homes. If they had died within a few days' travel from their home, their bodies would be quickly moved home for burial before they rotted. If the death occurred in winter, the cold would help delay putrefaction and increase the length of time that the body could be moved. In some instances, all the internal organs were removed and the body embalmed. This technique was used for high nobility so that their bodies could be moved in a stately funeral procession to their resting places. In these situations, while the body was buried in the religious institution designated by the deceased, the heart and other organs were often buried at the nearest church, monastery, or cathedral. When death occurred so far away that the body would severely putrefy, even with embalming, before reaching the deceased's home, the body was often boiled until the flesh came away from the bones. The bare bones were then carried home for burial. This process was used for King Louis IX of France in the 13th century. Louis died on crusade in North Africa. Tradition dictated that, as king of France, he had to be buried at the abbey of St. Denis near Paris. His heart and other organs were removed and then his body was boiled in wine to remove all the flesh. En route to Paris, Louis' heart and other organs were buried in a monastery in Sicily while his bones went on to St. Denis. In rare cases, in accordance with the deceased's wishes, his or her heart was removed, preserved, and sent to some especially favored religious institution for interment. Richard the Lionheart of England had his heart taken to Rouen Cathedral while the rest of his internal organs were buried in a church near where he died and his body went to Fontevrault Abbey for burial.

HAZARDS AND ASSISTANCE

Travelers on the trails and roads of medieval Europe faced many obstacles, both natural and man-made. Medieval travelers were confronted by potentially lethal dangers ranging from rain-swollen rivers to murderous robbers. And, more mundanely, they had to endure poorly maintained roads and the harassment of paying tolls imposed by all the petty lordships through which they passed.

Various aids to travel were developed to cope with these hazards. The most basic aid to safe travel was to be part of a group of travelers rather than travel alone. In general, the larger the group the better. Women especially needed to travel as part of a group for their own protection. Traveling with others offered some deterrence against bandits, particularly

if some or all of the party was armed. For their mutual protection, merchants always tried to travel in groups because they were choice targets for highwaymen. Having traveling companions also helped when confronting natural obstacles. It was safer to ford a river or trek through mountains if someone was there to help in case of an accident.

Natural Hazards

Rivers and mountains formed the two most difficult natural features for land travel in the Middle Ages. Further, weather, vicious animals, and darkness could make travel dangerous.

Rivers

As previously discussed, fords, ferries, and bridges were the most common means for crossing rivers. Where these were not available, travelers had to take the risk of crossing without any help. Such a crossing might not be very dangerous if the river was not particularly wide and its water level was low, such as during the hot, dry months of summer. However, trying to cross a river, or even a large stream, on one's own during the spring thaw and rainy months of the year was only for the desperate. The deep water and fast-moving currents were killers. Even using a ford or ferry at such times was dangerous. Fords became impassable. Ferries would be difficult to control and could even be capsized. Severe flooding could damage bridges as well and leave them unusable. Thus, rivers could be major obstacles for cross-country travel. In fact, the power of rivers to divide the land and make it difficult to cross from one side to the other had long made rivers effective boundaries for political and social entities. This practice predates the Middle Ages. For example, the Romans used the Rhine River as the border between the Empire and the Germanic barbarians. This use of rivers continued through the Middle Ages, with rivers forming the borders between states ranging from small counties up to empires. However, as will be discussed in the section on water-borne travel, some rivers, even those used as dividing lines, provided easy movement of cargo and passengers over long distances.

Mountains

Like rivers, mountain ranges, too, were sometimes used to mark the boundaries between one country and another. Rising high from the surrounding plains, mountain ranges such the Alps and the Pyrenees provided impressive and very visible lines of demarcation between the lands on one side of the mountains and those on the other. Further, as with rivers, mountains could only be crossed with some difficulty and so they provided a physical barrier and reinforced political divisions between the lands. Also like rivers, there were a limited number of points, the passes, at which the mountains could be safely traversed.

The Pyrenees and the Alps are the two principal mountain ranges in Europe. The Pyrenees form the border between modern-day France and Spain and separate the Iberian Peninsula from the rest of Europe. The Alps sweep across France, Switzerland, Austria, and Italy and form a barrier between Italy and the more northerly countries of Europe.

The Pyrenees were crossed by many travelers, ranging from merchants to armies. However, pilgrims were the most noted travelers. Thousands every year formed a steady steam of traffic from France down through the Pyrenees and on to the shrine of Saint James in Compostela in northeastern Spain. The two primary passes through the Pyrenees were near its western end. It was possible to skirt the Pyrenees around its eastern end near the Mediterranean, a route used by merchants bringing goods down to trade in the east and south of the Iberian Peninsula. However, this route was impractical for most pilgrims since it would have taken them hundreds of miles out of their way. So instead, pilgrims and other travelers commonly crossed the mountains through two passes near the western end. One pass was at an altitude of over 3,000 feet while the other's elevation was over 5,000 feet. Sur-

prising, in the early Middle Ages, many pilgrims climbed up to the higher pass. They did this to avoid Basque bandits that frequented the lower pass. Finally, in the 12th century, the local nobility suppressed attacks by the Basques and more pilgrims used the lower pass.

Mentioning crossing the Alps or any other major mountain range conjures up images of mountain-climbers using ropes and ice axes to scale nearly vertical cliffs. Fortunately for travelers in the Middle Ages, passes provided routes through the mountains which were far less dangerous and physically demanding than climbing up and over mountain peaks. Still, using passes to cross mountains involved climbing, albeit gradually, up several thousand feet and then back down again. Further, while many passes had been used for centuries or even millennia before the Middle Ages and had well-defined routes, they were still rocky and unpaved and bad weather made even the best trails dangerous.

Passes were largely natural features. Most were made up of valleys that cut through parts of the mountains. Some valleys cut directly through parts of mountains and enabled travelers to avoid having to scale mountain ridges. More commonly, passes, such as those in the Alps, were made up of a series of valleys. Following a trail up through a valley, travelers gradually ascended as they went from the lower end of the valley at its mouth up to the higher end at its top. From there, they would cross into the next higher valley and repeat the process until they crossed the mountain. To descend, the process was simply reversed and travelers made their way down a series of valleys. Thus, they avoided having to scale the heights of the mountains, but they still often had to climb along the ridges between the valleys.

Following the valleys was less dangerous and less strenuous than trying to climb directly up the side of the mountain, but it was not without risk and placed great physical demands on the travelers.

Valleys were not lined up in a neat,

straightforward route directly through the mountains. They were typically at angles to one another and so created switchback trails that zigzagged through the mountains. Travelers had to walk much farther than if they had been able to go in a straight line but this pattern of trails did keep the incline of the ascent to a manageable level.

When possible, trails proceeded up the floor of the valley from its mouth to its top. However, trails frequently ran precariously along the sides of the valleys, well above the bottom of the valley. This was often necessary because of rivers running through the valley floors. Some of these rivers were torrents running through narrow rocky channels they had cut in the floors of the valleys. Other rivers created marshy ground in the bottoms of valleys which also made travel difficult.

Finding points for crossing rivers among the valleys was sometimes difficult and some routes could be used safely only in the late summer and early fall when water levels were usually at their lowest. Along some routes, bridges were built to provide safe crossings, but bridges in the mountains remained scarce through the end of the Middle Ages.

The trails varied greatly in size and quality. Some were wide and relatively smooth but many were narrow and uneven and made walking treacherous. Coupled with the steep slopes that the trails often ran along, straying from the path could lead to a fatal fall.

Even the best trails were typically unsuitable for wheeled traffic. Riding on horseback was possible on some trails but not all. The vast majority of travelers crossed major mountain ranges only on foot. Horses were led rather than ridden. Sumpter animals were sometimes used but merchants often employed men to carry their goods, especially on narrow and poorly maintained trails. Some merchants believed that using such packmen kept their merchandise in better condition than having it carried on the backs of horses or mules. Still, trails were gradually improved to facilitate more traffic. On some passes, the trails were made safer and easier to use. For example, a

new track for carts was built through one pass in the late 14th century. A few were opened by the construction of bridges that spanned previously uncrossable chasms, such as the Stiebendebrücke, which was described earlier in the section on bridges.

Throughout the high range of the Alps, there was a risk of avalanches, both of rocks and of snow. In the winter, water froze, melted, and refroze in cracks in and between the rocks. This process widened the cracks and loosened the rocks so that they could easily fall apart and cause an avalanche. These rock falls could block trails.

Snow avalanches were also a problem as massive snowfalls accumulated on the steep peaks and ridges. In the late Middle Ages, Alpine natives fired guns before entering an avalanche area in hopes that the shots would safely bring down the avalanche. This may have been a forerunner of the modern technique of using small explosive charges or light artillery fire to trigger avalanches. But it is a myth that noise alone can be a trigger. Rather, it is the force and impact of the explosion or projectile that causes the avalanche.

The high altitudes of the Alps do not appear to have caused any problems for travelers. This may have been due to their slow progress up the mountains, which allowed them to gradually become accustomed to the thinner air.

Aids for Crossing the Alps. The Alps posed unique challenges for travelers and some specialized means were developed to cope with these problems. Some travelers, like modern hikers and Alpinists, used walking sticks to test the trail ahead of them. When traveling through snow-covered regions, some wore goggles or masks with slits to counter snow-blindness.

There were also more elaborate devices and methods to help people and animals negotiate steep slopes. The simplest was to have the travelers sit on a leather mat. The guides could then either pull the mat up the slope or hold on to it as it slid downhill. For going down the slope, the guides acted as brakes to slow the descent to a safe speed. Travelers with horses held the reins of their mounts, who followed behind the mat.

Oxen were sometimes substituted for humans in moving the mats. For going uphill, the oxen could simply pull the mats. However, while the written descriptions are difficult to interpret, it appears that in some instances a long rope was used to harness the oxen to the mat. The rope was run up the slope and around a stout tree or rock at the top of the slope. (A rock would have been the only object available if above the tree line.) With this arrangement, the oxen started at the top of the slope and plodded downhill, pulling the mat at the other end of the rope uphill. For going downhill, the oxen simply walked slowly up the slope, easing the mat down the slope. This enabled the oxen to act as brakes and control the speed of the mat's descent.

Besides being pulled along behind the mats, horses were sometimes placed on the mats to move them up- or downhill. Another method for lowering horses down a steep descent was to lay them on their sides with their legs bound together and then slide or drag them down. This technique was not always safe. Horses were recorded as being maimed or even killed in the process.

Another aid to crossing the Alps was the *marruccis* or *marones*. These were local residents who were hired to serve as guides to parties traveling through the mountains. Some appear to have been hired to be porters as well as guides, serving a role similar to the Sherpas of the Himalayas. The marones were described as wearing especially warm clothing, heavy mittens, and high boots with soles fitted with metal spikes. They also carried long poles to probe for the trails buried beneath the snow. Unfortunately, one of the few mentions of these guides involves a disastrous attempt to set out in severe weather in the middle of winter. In exchange for a large payment, a group of marones agreed to guide a large party of pilgrims despite the dangerous conditions. The marones had only gone a short distance when an avalanche fell on them. Some were killed

and others were injured. The pilgrims fled in terror back to the village below. Marones were also employed by the hospice of St. Bernard to guide and rescue pilgrims.

Weather

Weather conditions posed many problems for the medieval traveler. Rain turned roads into mires and washed out bridges. As discussed previously, swollen with heavy rain or the runoff from spring thaws, rivers and even large streams turned into torrents that could not be crossed. Flash floods could catch travelers unawares, especially in the mountains. Low-lying areas flooded as well and were difficult to cross unless causeways had been built to carry traffic.

Rainy weather also had an impact on the baggage carried by travelers. Rain collected on the top of chests with flat lids and could soak in and dampen the chests' contents. To avoid this problem, chests were made with curved lids so that the rain would run off.

Mist and fog also hindered travelers. Trails could easily be lost in a dense fog. In the mountains, losing sight of the trail could have fatal consequences.

Freezing weather both helped and hindered traveling. Many lakes, marshes, and even rivers were easier to cross when frozen. However, the severe cold needed for such deep freezing was generally limited to the north and northeastern parts of Europe, such as in Scandinavia, the Baltic states, Russia, and Poland. For much of the rest of Europe, winter was no friend to travelers at all. It just brought bitter cold and damp. Many roads became a mixture of mud and ice.

Around the Mediterranean, the climate was milder except at higher elevations in the Alps and the Pyrenees. As previously discussed, heavy snow and biting cold made crossing these mountains dangerous. Cold in the mountains was sometimes so severe that the eyelids of horses froze shut, men's beards became stiff with ice, and one monk found that his ink bottle had frozen solid.

In general, those who could avoided traveling in winter. Still, many travelers could be found riding and plodding along roads in winter. Kings and their retinues went about their business across their lands, although Christmas provided an excuse for a lengthy stop, preferably at some comfortable palace. Armies, too, braved the weather when needed. And pilgrims, clerics on church business, and secular diplomats and messengers carried out their missions, even if it meant crossing the Alps in the depths of winter.

Hot weather appears to have caused fewer problems for travelers than winter. Late spring through early fall was the preferred season for traveling in medieval Europe. The conditions of roads were generally best in these months. Rivers and streams were usually at their lowest levels so they could be crossed with relative ease. However, the high heat of late summer was exhausting, especially for those traveling long distances on foot such as pilgrims and soldiers. Many pilgrims who traveled to the shrine of St. James in Compostela could attest that the summer sun was merciless in southern France and Spain. The hot weather also raised clouds of flies and other biting insects. These same regions were noted for their dryness as well and finding drinking water was a problem at times. In periods of drought, water may have been scarce in other parts of Europe as well. However, except for during such extreme conditions, water levels in most of Europe were rarely so low that drinking water could not be easily found, even at the height of summer.

Animal Attacks

Apart from flies, wasps, mosquitoes, and other bugs that plagued travelers in hot weather, the only other animals recorded as attacking travelers were wolves. Bears and boars attacked people but only when cornered, such as during a hunt, or when their young were threatened. Unlike bears and boars, wolves were willing to closely approach people when searching for food. (Bears in North America have only recently developed this habit as garbage created by humans has become a regular food source for scavenging bears in some areas. People in the Middle Ages obviously generated garbage as well but it contained far less edible material. Further, unlike bears in parks today, bears in medieval Europe seldom came into contact with humans, except when being hunted, and so did not come to associate humans with sources of food.) Wolves occasionally followed armies and fed on dead horses as well as human corpses after battles. They also encountered people while preying on sheep, cattle, and horses. Herdsmen tending these animals as well as farmers out alone were most at risk of wolf attacks. Travelers were also at risk since they too were often isolated and had no shelter from attack. It is not surprising that wolf attacks on travelers appear to have been most common in remote, sparsely populated areas. Because of their danger to people and livestock, bounties were offered across Europe for killing wolves.

Wolf attacks appear to have been most common in the winter when prey was scarce. Driven by hunger, wolves would even enter villages or larger settlements in winter in search of food. During some severe winters, it was possible to find a wolf literally at one's door. While the wolves were primarily seeking domesticated animals, people who came out to defend their animals or who were simply outside at the wrong time could be attacked by ravenous wolves. Pilgrimage routes through the Pyrenees were noted for wolf attacks in the winter. Remains of those killed by wolves were collected in the spring along with the bodies of pilgrims who had frozen to death. However, it is likely that many of those believed to have been killed by wolves had actually died of other causes and their corpses were later fed upon by wolves. Still, travelers, as well as their horses, who were exhausted from traveling and weakened by the cold must have been attractive prey for hungry wolves.

Wolves usually hunted in packs and so were able to overwhelm individual and even small parties. Traveling in large groups was the best defense as wolves were less likely to attack when clearly outnumbered. Displays of force and brandishing weapons may have also helped to frighten the wolves away. However, wolves often hunted between dusk and dawn and could surprise unprepared travelers in the dark. In one instance, wolves attacked a group at night and panicked their horses, scattering them. The wolves then hunted down some of the fleeing horses. The travelers luckily emerged unscathed, as the horses, rather than the travelers themselves, were probably the wolves' targets from the first.

Night

Perhaps the most mundane natural hazard was nightfall. Staying out in the open at night was avoided if possible. Those who were out at night risked attack by animals and by bandits. There were those who planned ahead for camping overnight and were prepared to protect themselves, but most travelers tried to reach some town, city, or hospice where they could be sheltered for the night.

As for actively traveling at night, this was usually done only by accident either as a result of losing one's way or miscalculating the time to reach one's destination. While rare, there were some activities which forced travel at night. These included the carrying of especially important messages by couriers and the maneuvering of armies under cover of darkness.

Moving by night was difficult. Carrying torches for long periods was impractical so one had to rely on what natural light was available. If one was moving in open country on a night lit by a full moon, travel might not be too difficult. But on a moonless night or when traveling through the cover of a forest, the darkness was so deep that it was easy to get completely lost. Today, in an age when it is difficult to escape artificial outdoor lighting, it is difficult to image just how dark night could be. It should also be remembered that the seasonal lengthening and shortening of the day also impacted travel. Far less ground could be covered before nightfall in December than in June.

Even within towns and cities, walking at night was also a problem. There were virtually no streetlights. A few important places such as city gates might be illuminated at night but the majority of streets would only be lit by the faint glow from windows of homes and taverns and inns. Even this limited light disappeared as people went to bed and taverns and inns closed for the night. To walk safely, one had to carry a torch or candle. The wealthy had servants to carry the lighting for them. Torch carriers may have been available for hire but documented instances of this practice date only to the 17th century. Oil lamps do not appear to have been used for walking outdoors. They may have yielded too little light or were too easily extinguished by breezes to have been practical. Candles would have been easily blown out too, so it is likely that they had some form of guard to shield them and direct their light. Fully developed lanterns with candles or oil lamps do not appear until some time after the Middle Ages.

In some cities, carrying a light after dark was required by law. This allowed the night watch to see them and see that they were not engaged in any wrongdoing. Those who were without a light or were out after curfew were presumed to be criminals. Even where having a torch or candle was not formally required, the same presumptions applied. Having a light may have also provided some deterrence against being robbed, which appears to have particularly been a danger within cities. Besides the darkness, drinking likely contributed to robberies at night since many people out at night were probably heading home from the tavern and so their senses were dulled with drink, making them easy marks.

Man-made Hazards

Not all impediments confronting travelers were naturally occurring. Some man-made obstacles, such as tolls, were simply nuisances but they could be expensive. Others, such as robbery, were dangerous and potentially lethal.

Tolls

The most common and annoying problem inflicted on travelers was tolls. As discussed in previous sections, medieval travelers had to pay a variety of tolls: for roads, for bridges, for ferries, and sometimes for mountain passes. The burden that tolls imposed on merchants and other travelers was recognized from almost the outset of the Middle Ages. In the 8th and 9th centuries, the Carolingians who ruled most of western Europe attempted to prevent their subordinates from disrupting travel by imposing tolls and then diverting the funds into their own pockets instead of using the revenue for maintenance and improvement of the roads and bridges. In some later instances, tolls were also designated as paying for policing roads or providing armed escorts to protect travelers from robbers, but the lords who levied the tolls continued to take the money and leave the travelers on their own. Throughout the Middle Ages, rulers across Europe repeated these efforts to force tolls to be spent only on legitimate purposes. But at all times, these measures were only good to the extent that they were actively enforced and the fact that such orders had to be repeated indicates that it was a hard habit to break. Once a ruler's focus had moved on to another issue, his vassals usually reverted to their former ways and charged whatever tolls they could get away with, using the money for their own purposes rather than for the public good.

Temporal rulers were not the only ones concerned with excessive tolls. The tolls levied by some greedy lords were such a problem that the Church took action to rein them in. In 1179, the Third Lateran Council (a high-level convocation of the most important clergy) threatened those persons who imposed new tolls or increased existing ones with excommunication, the highest punishment the Church could inflict. However, even the wrath of God did little or nothing to deter unfair toll collecting.

While nobles were the most noted exploiters of tolls, they were not the only ones who inflicted tolls on the traveling public. Some towns and cities had the authority to collect tolls on bridges in or near their borders and some even levied tolls on travelers simply for entering their limits. These and other tolls fell most heavily on merchants since the tolls were actually taxes or duties and were usually based on the value of the merchandise they were carrying. Some of these towns and cities were as zealous as any noble in pursuing their rights to tolls. Some patrolled the surrounding regions to ensure that merchants were not taking unapproved roads to detour around toll stations. In one case, a group of merchants was caught making a diversion some miles outside a town instead of using the road passing through the town. The group was forced to agree to never avoid the tolls again.

The clergy also benefited from tolls. Some were given donations of land which included any tolls owed within the region. In some instances, the proceeds of tolls were directly donated to religious institutions.

Another group of toll collectors had no authority other than force. According to one travel guide for pilgrims, the Basques on the routes through the Pyrenees extorted money from pilgrims and called it "toll collecting." The Basques forced the pilgrims, who were ordinarily exempt from tolls, to pay for the privilege of passing through their lands. Those who did not pay were reportedly beaten or even killed. Similar "toll collecting" could likely be found in many areas distant from authorities where bands of armed men operated freely.

Why were tolls so common and such an effective means of raising revenue? First, the traveler had little choice but to pay the toll. His only other option was to somehow bypass the road, bridge, or other toll point and this was rarely practical. Second, travelers generally lacked any means for challenging the authority for imposing the toll. The only way they could succeed was to appeal to some authority above that levying the toll. Raising such an appeal required money and usually political connections as well and appears to have worked in few cases. Third, tolls usually fell most heavily on foreigners, not local people. As a consequence, the people residing near the collection point were less likely to oppose the toll. (In some ways, this aspect of tolls is still used today in the rationalization of taxes on rental cars, hotels, and other services patronized primarily by visitors to a city rather than by residents.) Local residents likely became concerned only if the tolls were adversely affecting trade.

Various groups of people were exempted from paying tolls. The poor were often exempt simply on the grounds that they truly could not afford to pay. Most prominently, clerics and pilgrims were not subject to tolls because they were traveling on God's business. Additionally, the Church opposed any hindrances, especially monetary ones, to its activities. University students were also usually included under the exemption of clerics since, for most of the Middle Ages, virtually all university students were clerics as well.

Not all jurisdictions extended the privilege of free passage willingly. Some limited the exception for clerics to the clerics alone and not to their servants. For example, monks might be allowed to pass for free but monastic servants moving supplies to the monastery would be taxed. In some cases, monasteries and convents were granted a limited number of free passes per year for their shipments.

The fact that there were repeated orders to cease imposing tolls on clerics suggests that tolls were still collected any time a noble thought he could get away with it. At times, exemptions were abused. Some jurisdictions established fines for merchants who tried to disguise themselves as pilgrims. It was worth trying to dodge tolls in this way since tolls were often actually taxes or duties and the amount assessed was based on the value of the items being carried.

Bandits

Robbery on the open road was not unknown in the days of the Roman Empire. At times, imperial soldiers were stationed at points along the major roads to police the area and deter criminals. Unfortunately, it appears that the soldiers did not make an effective police force. Their limited numbers coupled with the hit-and-run tactics of highway robbers made capturing criminals difficult.

With the collapse of the Roman Empire in western Europe, law enforcement on the roads completely disappeared. Travel became even more hazardous. One consequence was the shrinking of trade. Part of this was caused by the decrease in markets, but it was also caused by the lack of security on the roads. Merchants had little guarantee that they could move their goods safely to customers. Gradually, order was restored as local lords provided some security on roads as part of establishing and maintaining control over their lands. Still, there were no regular patrols and robbery remained an all-too-common threat on the open road. And merchants remained the preferred prey of highwaymen since they typically carried money or at least valuable goods.

Who Became Bandits? A variety of men turned to banditry over the course of the Middle Ages. Some were just individual men who chose to make a living waylaying travelers. Some were already outlawed criminals when they took up banditry, while others were men accused of crimes who fled to forests to escape justice and became robbers to survive. These men may sound like potential Robin Hoods but none are recorded as ever sharing their loot with the poor.

While some robbers were highwaymen who acted alone or with a small group of accomplices, others were part of organized gangs. Some gangs of bandits were quite large and well organized. This was particularly true of the bands of brigands formed from groups of military veterans. These men served in the armies of their lords in wartime but their services were not needed in peacetime. Those who were select retainers of the nobility stayed on with their lords but, unlike modern standing armies, most men-at-arms were not kept in readiness for the next conflict. Instead, they were given their final pay and laid off. They were expected to return to the peaceful occupations from which they had been drawn. However, fighting was the only job most of these men ever knew. This was especially true of the mercenaries who were employed in increasing numbers over the course of the Middle Ages. In particular, the Hundred Years' War between France and England created martial employment for thousands of men for decades. During lulls in the war, there were spaces of relative peace which left the warriors unemployed. Used to combat and marauding, these men applied their skills to make a living. They went beyond being mere gangs and were actually small armies. They held towns for ransom and sacked those that refused to pay. Even the papal city of Avignon paid tribute to avoid being attacked. Needless to say, merchants and other travelers captured by these men were treated no better than townspeople. All were robbed, some were killed, and those who were wealthy enough were held for ransom.

Not all bandits were commoners. Some gang leaders were knights and some were even nobles, although most were only minor nobility. Still, even higher nobility sometimes dabbled in robbery in the form of detaining travelers and extorting money for their release. The most famous case of this was the seizure of King Richard the Lionheart by Duke Leopold of Austria, who extorted 100,000 marks of silver in exchange for Richard's release. Duke Leopold's actions were especially heinous since Richard was returning home from the Third Crusade and crusaders, like pilgrims, were to be allowed free and safe passage on their travels.

Even the clergy, while not engaged directly in robbery themselves, was not above abetting brigands. For example, one archbishop of Cologne allowed a gang of bandits to use one of his castles as a base. This was stopped only after a duke from a neighboring region defeated the archbishop's men and then destroyed the castle.

Banditry in medieval Europe was not limited to Christians. In the early Middle Ages, Moslems were notorious bandits. In the late 7th and the early 8th centuries A.D., the Moslems swept through the Middle East and North Africa. They went on to invade Europe in the 8th century. Their attempted conquest was checked by Charles Martel at the battle of Poitiers in A.D. 732. They then retreated south but still held Sicily, parts of southern Italy, and most of the Iberian Peninsula. They used these holdings to continue raiding other parts of Europe.

In the late 9th century, Moslem pirates from Spain successfully invaded the southeastern coast of France in the area currently known as the French Riviera and established a stronghold there. Some of the Moslems pushed further east from their base and seized control of several important passes in the western and central Alps. Here, they robbed merchants, pilgrims, clergymen, and other travelers. In addition to robbery, Moslems were known to kill travelers as well. In one instance, the Moslems killed a group of English pilgrims by dropping stones on them from a vantage point above the trail. Moslems also sold some of their victims into slavery in Spain, North Africa, and the Middle East. Captives of high rank were held for ransom instead. In A.D. 972, they kidnapped Abbot Maiolus. He was the respected head of the important abbey of Cluny and a friend of many high-ranking nobles. Maiolus was released after his ransom of 1,000 pounds of silver was paid by his abbey but his kidnapping brought international attention to the problem in the Alps. In response, Count William I of nearby Provence led campaigns against the Moslems from A.D. 972 to 975 and succeeded in driving them out of both the Alps and the Riviera. With safety restored, increasing numbers of merchants and travelers used the western and central passes of the Alps.

There were also Moslem bandits in the Holy Land. Pilgrims were frequently robbed and sometimes killed or enslaved by Moslem raiders along the principal routes between pilgrimage sites. Such attacks continued even after the European conquest of the Holy Land. Pilgrims tried to deter the bandits by gathering their parties together and traveling in larger groups. Around A.D. 1120, more aggressive steps were taken to defend pilgrims with the foundation of the Poor Fellow Soldiers of Christ and of the Temple of Solomon, better known as the Knights Templar. One of the primary functions of this military religious order was to protect pilgrims. It mounted patrols along the major pilgrimage routes and fought the bandits. Soon after the creation of the Templars, another military order was founded, the Order of the Hospital of St. John of Jerusalem. In addition to caring for sick and poor pilgrims, the Hospitallers also took action to shield pilgrims from attacks. Still, despite these efforts, pilgrims remained targets of highway robbery through the end of the Middle Ages.

In addition to the land-based attacks, there were also raids by Moslem pirates. They plied the coasts of Italy and the southern coast of France. Here they raided shipping traffic as well as towns and roads along the shore. Again, travelers and local residents seized along the shoreline were killed, kidnapped and sold into slavery, or held for ransom. Pirates from Moslem states along the north coast of Africa were the most notorious of these raiders. This threat persisted through the Middle Ages. In later centuries, the problem grew worse. From the 16th century through the early 19th century, thousands of Europeans were taken and enslaved by the pirates every year. Many were captured on ships at sea but most came from raids on coastal areas across Europe, from Iceland and England to Spain and Italy. It was not until the 19th century that forces of the United States and several major European countries finally suppressed these pirates and ended this threat to those who lived, worked, and traveled along the shores of Europe.

Not all attacks of travelers took place on the open road. Taverns and inns could also be dangerous for travelers. Particularly when drunk, a lone traveler could be an easy mark for local robbers. Some authors in the days of the Roman Empire as well as in the Middle Ages complained of this problem and the role some tavern and innkeepers played by turning a blind eye to these crimes in exchange for a cut of the take.

Combating Banditry. For merchants and other ordinary travelers, the most practical means of combating the threat of highway robbery was to travel as part of a large, armed group. Robbers preferred easy targets and likely avoided attacking when they did not have a clear advantage over their potential victims.

Traveling as part of a group was essential for women. Women were rarely armed in the Middle Ages. None were recorded as ever traveling armed and so they were especially vulnerable and appear to have been particularly at risk of being raped along with being robbed. For their own security, they simply had to be accompanied by trusted men. This can be seen with pilgrimages where women were always part of a larger company of travelers, at least in part for their own protection. Records of the travels of noble women also provide evidence that ladies always traveled with at least a few armed male retainers. Similarly, nuns took along one or two of their nunneries' male employees when traveling any significant distance. But there is one form of protection which was never used by women travelers: chastity belts. Some inventive tour guides in Europe point to chastity belts in their collections and claim that ladies wore these to protect themselves while on the road. But chastity belts are a fantasy created centuries after the Middle Ages. There is absolutely no evidence of their use or even their existence in the period.

Ordinary people were not the only ones who feared assault and highway robbery. Even government travelers relied on the strength of numbers and arms to deter bandits. For example, a royal money shipment in England in the early 14th century was accompanied by 12 men-at-arms. Obviously, ordinary travelers could not field such an impressive force of guards but they could at least have enough comrades to make it appear that they were not easy prey.

In theory, at least, travelers could also rely on help from local governments for protection. Part of the nobility's obligations to their people was to protect them from crime. This including protecting travelers within their lands since making the roads safe was, in theory if not in practice, one of the motives for collecting tolls and assessing taxes of merchandise carried by people passing through their domains. The vigor with which rulers executed this obligation varied greatly. Beginning in the 14th century, some German nobility began providing armed escorts for merchants traveling across their lands. However, the merchants had to pay the lords for the protection, including the full wages of the escorts along with the cost of their food, drink, and lodging. The guards also expected tips. Merchants came to regard the escort services as another costly burden on trade. The most notable case of noble rulers taking their role as defenders of travelers seriously was in the county of Champagne in the late 12th through the 13th century. Here, the counts and countesses encouraged the development of trade fairs and part of their strategy was to protect merchants coming into their lands. This program was a success and was improved through negotiations with neighboring regions to provide similar safeguards for merchants. This expanding zone of cooperation benefited the merchants as well as the rulers who exacted tolls on their merchandise. Another part of the policy of the counts of Champagne was to obtain reparations for merchants whose goods were stolen en route to the fair. This is explained in the section on reparations below.

While reparations made merchants whole economically, they were of little consolation in more violent attacks. Although active policing of roads was rare, there were other groups in addition to rulers which attempted to protect travelers. For example, in 1241, Lübeck and Hamburg concluded a treaty of friendship that included sharing the expense of keeping the road between the two cities free of brigands. Lübeck and Hamburg belonged to the Hanse, a trade association of cities and towns along the Baltic and North Sea coasts, and the road between them was a major trade route that was very appealing to robbers. Unfortu-

nately, the details of these cities' attempts at securing their roads were not recorded.

In Europe, robbers were seldom caught in the act. Instead, when the problem of banditry reached intolerable levels, the most common response from the local lords and from citizens who took the law into their own hands was to hunt down the criminals to their bases and attempted to destroy them there. At times, however, nobility and city governments joined together to fight banditry within a large area. Such leagues were formed in Germany in the 14th and 15th centuries and were successful in rooting out robbers and making roads safer for all travelers. In those instances in which bandits were caught, they were executed publicly, in part to satisfy the community's desire for revenge and to deter other brigands.

For the large groups of men-at-arms turned marauders, different tactics were required. The companies of brigands in France, including the one that blackmailed Avignon, were encouraged to go on crusade, but that offer failed. Instead, many found employment in the incessant wars between the Italian city-states. Most of those smaller groups which stayed behind were gradually hunted down or broke up.

War

While robbery was a constant threat, the worst man-made obstacle to traveling was war. Wars in the Middle Ages ranged from very localized hostilities between rival families of the petty nobility up to international struggles between the great powers of the day. These latter wars could reduce safety on the roads to the level of the early Middle Ages as civil order was disrupted by the destruction caused by the opposing armies.

The Church made efforts such as the Peace of God in the 10th century to protect noncombatants such as clergy, nuns, and pilgrims as well as ordinary citizens, including peasants, and merchants in wartime. People from these groups were to be safe from the fury of armies both at home and when traveling. Unfortunately, these worthy attempts had little success and most people caught in a war zone were always at risk of robbery, assault, and murder by soldiers. However, there were rare exceptions such as during the invasion of France by King Henry V of England. In this instance, Henry restrained his men from marauding for the unique reason of wanting to demonstrate that he regarded the French as his rightful subjects and did not want to alienate them from his cause.

Besides the direct risks of injury and death to the traveler, wars also hindered him by closing travel ways. This appears to have been less of a problem for pilgrims. Their claim to peaceful passage seems to have generally been respected along the traditional roads to shrines, although noble pilgrims often took the extra measure of obtaining a safe conduct from the belligerents to protect themselves. For other travelers, crossing war zones was more difficult. Safe conducts were sometimes adequate for them as well but they likely tried to simply avoid war-torn areas entirely if possible. This could force them to go considerable distances out of their way.

Reparations

In some instances, rulers were held liable for robberies committed in their lands. A merchant would complain to the lord of the land that his goods had been unlawfully seized and seek reparations under the theory that the lord was responsible for maintaining order within his lands and had failed to do so. If the lord failed to make reparations, the merchant could then complain to the lord of his homeland. That lord could then order the seizure of goods of merchants from the land in which the robbery had occurred. The merchant would then be compensated out of the proceeds of this merchandise. However, there were larger political concerns that likely affected whether this remedy was granted. For example, if the merchant's home country was attempting to maintain good relations with the other country, the ruler would likely not order a potentially provocative action such as the seizure of goods.

Alternatively, if a merchant's country was already hostile to the other land, then taking the goods could be used as part of a larger policy of harassing the other country. If the nations were actively at war, a ruler would not hesitate to grant the authority to seize goods from merchants of his opponent in the name of reparations. This sort of reprisal was a particularly common remedy for seizures committed by ships at sea and is discussed further in the section on the hazards of sea travel.

The most noted rulers who carried out a policy of seeking reparations for thefts from merchants were the counts of Champagne. As part of their program to foster trade fairs within their realm, the counts used economic pressure to force other rulers to protect merchants within their own lands. For example, in one instance, merchants traveling to the fairs in Champagne passed through the lands of Piacenza in Italy and were robbed there. In response, the counts banned any merchants from Piacenza from attending any of the fairs in Champagne until the stolen merchandise was returned or other suitable compensation was made. The value of the trade carried out at the Champagne fairs was so great that the Piacenzans made reparations to get the ban lifted.

Travel Aids

While the dangers and risks of traveling were daunting, there were a few aids to help people through their journeys. As discussed previously, the most important forms of assistance were the food and accommodations provided by monasteries and other religious institutions to pilgrims and other travelers. Some of the other basic help travelers needed were directions to get to their destination and a means of communicating with the people of the foreign lands through which they passed.

Directions
How did a person in medieval Europe find his way to his destination? The most common way for medieval travelers to find out

where they needed to go was to ask someone for directions. Whether out in the country or in a strange city, this was the best and easiest way to find one's way. This was so common that an English-to-French phrase book from the 14th century included asking for directions among the essentials for travelers. Directions appear to have been given in terms of landmarks such as churches, crossroads, and prominent natural features. In cities, confused visitors could be guided by references to public fountains, distinctive buildings, and other similar points.

As this suggests, most Europeans knew the areas immediately surrounding them but generally only vaguely knew directions for destinations further away. There were significant exceptions to this:

• Many of the nobility traveled widely. They traveled to the capital and other important cities to attend their lords' courts. They moved between their own estates, which could be quite scattered and far-flung. Some were also part of military campaigns into other countries.

• Some of the clergy, particularly among the higher ranks, were also well traveled. Monks were sometimes transferred between abbeys. New bishops had to travel to Rome to be formally confirmed in their new positions. Other clergy had to go to Rome on a wide variety of Church matters. Bishops, archbishops, cardinals, and abbots were summoned to attend Church councils which were held in a variety of locations over the course of the Middle Ages. Some clergy were even sent beyond the limits of Europe on embassies to the Far East and brought back information on distant peoples and their lands. And some monks and other clergy learned the geography of Europe without ever traveling by reading the maps and manuscripts in monastic and cathedral libraries. Admittedly, much of this information was flawed but it still gave some idea of the relative location of important places and a sense

of the distances between them. More practically, clergymen could stop at abbeys, churches, and other religious institutions along the way to get directions from the local clergy.

• Many merchants traveled extensively across Europe and beyond in pursuit of profit. Italians routinely traveled to the Low Countries and England as part of the trade in wool and wool cloth. Italians from many city-states could also be found in the Near and Middle East buying spices and silks to sell to the wealthy across Europe. Germans traveled east to Russia to obtain furs while Norwegians brought timber to sell in England. All these merchants had firsthand knowledge of the geography of wide parts of Europe and other lands.

• Finally, people who went on pilgrimages, from ordinary peasants up to the nobility, gained knowledge about areas away from their homes. Such travel ranged from a short trip to a local shrine only 10 to 12 miles away up to a journey of thousands of miles to reach the Holy Lands. All these pilgrims increased their knowledge of the lands around them in proportion to the length of their trip.

Still, while many people did have an understanding of geography beyond the lands around them many others did not. For example, the horde of peasants who formed the ill-conceived and ill-fated People's Crusade of 1096 had little understanding of how far it was from Europe to Jerusalem. As they set out, many seem to have assumed that the next city in the distance would be Jerusalem. Thus, there was a wide mix of people with varying degrees of understanding of the geography of Europe.

Road Signs

There appears to have been no use of road signs in medieval Europe. In contrast, the Romans placed milestones along their primary roads. The stones gave the distance from that point to the nearest towns in either direction. Some also gave the distances to the principal towns or cities that the road connected. In at least some towns, there were carved stone plaques which provided similar information. While thousands of the Roman milestones survived, they were of little use to later travelers. As discussed previously, many sections of the Roman road system fell into disuse as new towns and cities developed and older ones declined or even disappeared. With such changes, the information on many milestones became irrelevant. However, no replacements seem to have been developed in the Middle Ages. There is no evidence of roads signs of any type. Neither mileposts nor signs indicating directions to the nearest town or city have been found and none were mentioned in contemporary documents.

In part, the lack of signs may be attributable to the low literacy rate among medieval Europeans. It could also be that they saw little or no need for such signs. Local inhabitants knew where the nearest villages or towns were and approximately how long it would take to travel there. If the traveler's destination was more distant, he could just ask people along the way for directions.

Itineraries

Maps were very scarce in the Middle Ages and were generally of little use to travelers. Itineraries were one alternative to maps. These had existed since the days of the late Roman Empire. They consisted of lists of the names of towns and cities along the route between two points. They also typically included rivers and other significant natural features. All the points were listed in the order they would be encountered as a traveler proceeded to his destination. The itinerary gave the distances between the towns and cities but did not provide directions. For example, a rare illustrated itinerary from 13th century England was drawn with the road running from the top of the page to the bottom with little paintings of towns and cities at intervals. But the road is not drawn to scale and no directions were

given between points. They are laid out as though the route formed a straight line from start to finish.

Most of the surviving itineraries were of routes from Europe to the Holy Land. In fact, the earliest pilgrim itineraries predate the Middle Ages and were created in the 4th century A.D. These itineraries were most likely composed by pilgrims who actually made the journeys. Travelers continued to create itineraries, and later travel guidebooks. Some itineraries were copied in monasteries by monks who had never left their cloisters, let alone visited the Holy Land or other pilgrimage destinations. Sometimes they copied authentic itineraries written by eyewitnesses but some included out-of-date information or inaccuracies written by travelers who exaggerated their experiences. Still, over the course of the period, accurate itineraries for a variety of pilgrim destinations did circulate and were copied.

Unfortunately, it is difficult to determine how much itineraries were used by pilgrims and other travelers. It is speculated that some people may have consulted itineraries held in local cathedral or monastic libraries before setting out. It is also possible that some may have taken itineraries with them on their journeys. The itinerary could have supplemented the directions given at hospices and other sources along the way and allowed the traveler to roughly calculate how much time it would take to reach the next stage in his trip. However, obtaining a copy of an itinerary would have involved the expense of hiring a scribe. Further, the traveler would have had to be literate to use the itinerary. Thus, the only likely users of itineraries were the relatively wealthy and educated, but there are no records of them taking such documents along on their travels. The only surviving itineraries are found in monastic and other institutional libraries. Perhaps the primary readership of itineraries were "stay at homes" such as monks, nuns, and other clergy who wanted to undertake a pilgrimage in spirit. They could consult the itineraries kept in their libraries. Still, it is possible that there were more itineraries that were actually used on travels but which wore out, unlike those carefully protected in libraries.

Travel Guidebooks

As with itineraries, travel guides date back to when the ancient Romans wrote guides for trips to Greece. These guides described sites, primarily those tied into mythology, to be seen. Like maps and itineraries, some guides may have been taken along when traveling but most were likely not. Instead, they may have been used to plan a journey or to amuse an armchair traveler.

The tradition of travel guides continued into the Middle Ages. Travel guidebooks usually provided more detail than itineraries although some contained only bland statements that listed travel times and an inventory of the sights seen. However, many included additional information including descriptions of the town and cities passed through on the way to the ultimate destination. Some even included details about the traveler's personal experiences and feelings as well as about the means of travel. Those written by the actual travelers typically contained the most accurate information although even these accounts sometimes contained embellishments taken from other travelers and from legends about marvels beyond those seen by the traveler. Further, some surviving guidebooks were composed by monks who often drew from several different original texts. Some of these books contained accurate information but others did not. The copyists had no direct knowledge of the subject and freely drew from all texts, whether truthful or not. Thus, additional inaccuracies and insertions of fanciful information crept into these guidebooks.

As with itineraries, guidebooks were primarily for pilgrimages to shrines. One such guidebook describes the four main routes through France that led to the Spanish route to the shrine of St. James in Compostela. It also provides information about the shrines to be seen en route as well as the local residents and dangers encountered along the way. The information is colored by the author's biases, particularly against some of the various inhabitants along the pilgrimage route. Some are described as immoral, others as dirty and lazy, while still others as dangerous robbers.

Another surviving guidebook describes the city of Jerusalem and all the holy sites to see there. As with the itineraries, these travel guidebooks may have been used to plan pilgrimages but their main audience was most likely people who never undertook pilgrimages but wanted to read about them. Again like itineraries, there is no evidence that these guides were actually taken along on a pilgrimage. Still, based on inventories of libraries in the Middle Ages and the numbers which have survived to the present, guidebooks clearly became more numerous. Thus, it is possible that at least some books were actually used by travelers.

Maps

As in classical antiquity, maps were scarce in medieval Europe. Like Roman and Greek maps before them, most medieval maps were maps of the world, called *mappae mundi* (singular: *mappa mundi*) in Latin. These maps represented the world in a very stylized manner, usually with the holy city of Jerusalem at their center. The maps were often oriented so that east was at the top of the map with Asia occupying the upper half of the disk. Europe was in the bottom left-hand quarter and Africa in the right. The principal seas and rivers divided the continents and formed a "T" shape. There were several variations of *mappae mundi* but they generally maintained the same positioning of the continents. Major cities such as Rome, Constantinople, and Jerusalem were marked on these maps as well. These maps provided little if any practical guidance for travelers and appear to have never been used for that purpose. Instead, all of these world maps were kept in libraries in monasteries and other major religious institutions, where they were studied by scholars.

One significant exception to the disk-shaped *mappa* is the Peutinger Table. This map is believed to be a 12th or 13th century copy of a 4th century A.D. original. While its projection is extremely distorted by its scroll-like construction, the Peutinger Table provides a roughly accurate depiction of the inhabited world from the Atlantic to eastern Asia and from North Africa to the northern edge of Europe. Another exception is the Gough Map. This map, made in England in the 1360s, depicts England, Scotland, and Wales in some detail. The map includes over 600 cities, towns and villages as well as roads, rivers, and other important features. The map is approximately four feet by two feet and appears to have been made for use by the royal government of England. It seems to have been kept in London, where it was probably used for administrative purposes, although its exact purpose and use is unknown.

Some historians believe that there may have been practical maps of travel routes or of relatively small areas suitable for travelers but that these have been lost because they were worn out through repeated use or simply decayed over time. In part, this argument is based on the fact that many ancient maps drawn on perishable materials such as papyrus were destroyed by decay. Unfortunately, there is no documentary or physical evidence that such maps existed in the Middle Ages. The only extant small maps are of very small scale and are of towns, land holdings, and building complexes, primarily monasteries. While useless for guiding travelers, these maps did serve practical purposes. Some were created to be used as evidence in cases of boundary disputes and others were used for administrative purposes. Similar maps were created in ancient Greece and Rome. Both the medieval and ancient maps of this sort were the creation of land surveyors. These men were skillful and well equipped to accurately draw such maps but they could not map larger areas with the instruments and techniques available to them. Cartographers capable of creating larger maps did not appear until the 13th century and did not begin to flourish until the 14th century, but the maps they produced were sea charts, not land maps.

More accurate land maps were not developed until late in the Middle Ages but even then they weren't for travelers. Some were expensive pieces that were gifts for nobility and even for royalty. These and other late medieval maps were improved *mappae mundi* that incorporated more accurate information about coastlines drawn from sea charts called *portolans*. These maps and the remapping of the world will be addressed fully in the section on navigation at sea.

In the 15th century, some cartographers began drafting new styles of maps. Some maps were in the form of aerial views of cities. Typically, important buildings and other points of interest were drawn as pictures rather than as simple blocks viewed from directly above as in a modern map. These maps were rarely to a constant scale but still provided a good overview of the city. Maps such as these were first created in Italy. This style spread and, before the end of the 15th century, city and town maps in the form of simple sketches of streets with the street names appeared in England and the Low Countries.

Over the course of the 15th century and on into the Renaissance, the city-states of northern and central Italy commissioned maps of their territories. These depicted roads, cities and towns with their fortifications, mills, and other strategic features. The respective governments used these maps for administering their lands and for preparing their defenses for war. Some states began mapping the lands of their rivals as well. By the early 16th century, mapping enemy lands in advance of military operations was recommended by strategists.

One final point about mapping: most medieval Europeans did not believe the earth was flat. They knew it was a sphere. This issue will be fully discussed as part of maritime navigation in the section on sea travel.

Other Aids for Finding Directions

When traveling on land, the use of navigation techniques based on instruments and other methods was very limited. Certainly, travelers knew that the sun rose in the east and so could orient themselves for their day's travel. Scientific instruments such as astrolabes were limited primarily to academic use for most of the Middle Ages. By the end of the period, the astrolabe and other devices were beginning to be used at sea but not for land navigation. Similarly, navigating by the stars was done primarily at sea. While many land travelers likely knew how to determine north by looking for the Pole Star, traveling was rarely done at night and so this technique was of little practical use.

Guides

The ideal guide was a traveling companion who had already made the trip before. This was likely most common among merchants. They would have learned the primary trade routes from having served as an apprentice on previous travels. However, had any directions been needed, the porters, muleteers, and carters hired by the merchants to move their goods were likely well acquainted with the most common routes from having made repeated trips back and forth along them. In addition to directions, these men would likely have known the conditions along the routes and been aware of any problems. Ordinary travelers who had large amounts of baggage to move would also have engaged such men and would have benefited from their knowledge of the roads.

When an experienced traveler was not part of the group, guides were sometimes hired to lead parties. This was likely most common where trails were difficult to follow. Some local residents may have been willing to serve as guides out of a sense of Christian charity, although payment appears to have been customary or, in most cases, a requirement. Getting an opportunity to talk with strangers and get news and gossip from neighboring or even distant areas may have also been a motivation. However, guides were not always available. In some instances, local residents may have simply not wanted the inconvenience of escorting travelers some distance and then having to walk all the way back as well. Still,

if the traveler could pay a generous fee, persuading someone to be a guide must have been much easier.

Ordinary travelers were not the only ones who needed guides. While they tried to secure as much information about the geography of the land they were invading, armies sometimes needed guides. In these cases, local residents were persuaded to help either by bribes or by force. Armies also tried to gather as much information as possible in advance of invasion. This information was gathered from merchants and other travelers who had recently been in enemy territory. Merchants were considered such a regular conduit for information between countries that they were sometimes detained on suspicion of being spies. Another source of information was their own diplomats who may have been on peace missions to the enemy before the outbreak of war. For this reason, diplomats were typically viewed as spies. There were also men specifically employed as spies who infiltrated the enemy's lands to gather tactical and strategic information.

There was one type of guide that was quite different from those who led travelers along roads and trails. These unique guides were licensed by the government of Venice. From the 13th century until the end of the Middle Ages, Venetian galleys were the primary providers of passage to the Holy Land. Thousands of pilgrims passed through Venice every year on their way to Jerusalem and catering to these travelers was a lucrative business. By the 15th century, Venice had officially authorized guides called *tholomarii* who helped pilgrims find lodging. They also assisted pilgrims in converting their money to the local currency, buying the supplies needed for their trip, and booking passage on one of the galleys bound for the Holy Land.

Travel Documents

Passports and visas did not exist in the Middle Ages. However, there were other legal documents which travelers used to help in their journeys. One such document issued by rulers was the safe conduct. In a safe conduct, the traveler was given the protection of the ruler while traveling through his lands. The traveler, along with his possessions, was free to cross the issuing noble's lands without interference. Sometimes this included exemption from tolls as well. They were especially valuable for merchants since they protected the traveler's property as well as the traveler himself. Further, they were very useful during wartime since travelers, particularly foreigners, were regarded with heightened suspicion. Additionally, during hostilities, the goods of foreign merchants were sometimes subject to seizure.

As with most privileges conferred by rulers, obtaining a safe conduct appears to have required political connections with the noble's court or the money to buy the necessary influence. For example, a jewel merchant in the late 14th century had several expensive maps made and presented them as gifts to the kings of the lands through which he passed. His hope was that they would give him a safe conduct across their lands and possibly exempt him from tolls and other duties as well. As this example shows, experienced and well-heeled travelers would seek safe conducts for each of the countries through which they were passing.

In some instances, safe conducts were provided without documentation. Counts of Champagne as part of their efforts to encourage trade in their land assured safe conduct to all merchants entering their realm. Further, the business-savvy counts extended the sanctuary for merchants by obtaining similar safe conducts from nobles who ruled adjoining territories.

Safe conducts might even be extended to enemies. For a tournament held by Edward III of England, the king invited knights from across Europe and issued a general safe conduct so that they could attend. Safe conducts were also issued for citizens of enemy countries who were going on pilgrimage and needed to cross their opponents land. All pilgrims were supposed to be allowed free passage at all times

but it was wise to secure a safe conduct during hostilities.

Letters of introduction were another form of travel document. These were issued by the nobility and likely by merchants as well. Nobles wrote these for their subordinates or others such as favored religious clerks or troubadours. These letters identified the bearer's identity and rank and asked that he be extended the appropriate courtesies and hospitality. In some cases, these letters also appear to have served as letters of recommendation for employment since they described the merits of the bearer.

Language Barrier

In the Middle Ages, just as today, different languages were spoken in different regions of Europe and beyond and travelers had to cope with communicating with people who did not know their language. There were several different means for overcoming this problem.

Translators

The easiest way to overcome the language barrier was to employ a translator. However, professional translators were a rarity. In Byzantium, the imperial court had translators and provided them to visiting nobility and diplomats. (The translators also spied on their guests.) Courts in western Europe appear to have been less sophisticated than the imperial Byzantine court and relied on ad hoc translators rather than employing full-time translators. Nobles and diplomats appear to have sometimes traveled with their own translators if they lacked the necessary language skills themselves. Professional translators were also found in the Holy Land after its recapture by Moslems. Christian pilgrims employed Moslem men to act as translators and to help make travel arrangements. These men also helped the pilgrims navigate the numerous restrictions and tolls imposed on pilgrims by the Moslem bureaucracy.

The use of less formal translators was far more common. For example, in mid–15th century Venice, there was an inn operated by a German couple which catered to travelers from German-speaking parts of Europe. As previously discussed, having someone who could speak one's native tongue and was familiar with the local area was a great help. Such hosts could help their guests in making business or travel arrangements.

Learning Languages

Many travelers tried to learn enough of the local languages to communicate at least their basic needs. Some travelers were lucky enough to have someone in their group who knew some of the language. Merchants who had made many journeys before were likely a good source since they had to have basic understanding of the language in order to conduct business. A traveler could try to pick up some essential phrases from them. Similarly, some travelers tried to learn from their guides. In accounts of their travels, some pilgrims to the Holy Land after it had been reconquered by the Moslems recorded that they tried to learn some Arabic from their guides. As with language learners today, medieval Europeans appear to have had varying degrees of success in mastering new languages.

The value of knowing another language was well recognized. For example, in the 15th century, some cities in the Hanse trade association attempted to bar non–Hanse merchants from learning Slavic. These cities were attempting to maintain their monopoly on trade in Eastern Europe and wanted to prevent other merchants from being able to deal directly with the native people. How they hoped to block their competitors from learning Slavic was not recorded. Ultimately, this and all other attempts at saving their monopoly failed.

Phrase Books

While there appear to have been no multilingual dictionaries for travelers, there were phrase books. These were akin to modern phrase books for travelers in that they provided the words necessary for ordering food, booking a room, and other essential matters.

However, the details reveal some differences between modern and medieval societies.

The most complete phrase book is from the late 14th century. It was written for Englishmen to use in France and provides translations for use in a wide variety of common situations. One chapter covers all the details for arranging a stay at an inn. The traveler is presumed to be wealthy, likely a nobleman, and to be traveling with a servant. He orders his servant to travel ahead and make arrangements for the night. The servant arrives at the inn and reviews the accommodations. He confirms that the room has no fleas or lice. The hostess says it does not and adds that the rat and mice problem has recently been taken care of. The servant then goes on to buy the food for the evening meal and begins preparing it. The traveler arrives and orders the hostess to have all her maids brought out. He interviews the three maids and selects one to be his companion for his stay, promises her rich rewards, and then begins to flatter her. He has her dine with him and insists that she sit in the chair with him, likely on his lap. He continues to flatter her and makes professions of his love for her and then "frolics" with her. After frolicking, the traveler is in a good mood and gives small amounts of money and silk clothing accessories to the inn's staff. The evening then proceeds to drinking, dancing, and singing. When it is very late, the traveler retires to his room, taking the maid with him. The next morning, the traveler is hungover. He has breakfast. He gives the maid a fair sum of money and then leaves. It is interesting that this was such a common series of events that it was deemed necessary to provide the phrases for it.

A later chapter in this phrase book addresses a much more humble and austere travel situation. In this chapter, two companions banter while getting ready to go to bed. As was the custom, they are sharing a bed and sleeping nude. In bed, one complains to the other that he is crowding him and has cold feet. He also complains about the fleas infesting the bed and biting him all over. This is quite different from the deluxe accommodations in the earlier chapter.

The Language of the Church

One group within medieval Europe did not need to resort to phrase books or translators when speaking with any other members of their class regardless of where they came from. These were the clergy and they were trained to speak and write in Latin. Admittedly, there were some whose knowledge of Latin was weak, such as many common village priests who had learned to say prayers and perform masses and other religious offices in Latin but could not converse or compose letters in the language. However, great numbers, from monks and priests up to abbots, archbishops, and the pope, had sufficient command of Latin that all Church business was conducted in it. This use of Latin allowed the Church to hold convocations with representatives from across Europe. The pope and other officials could issue edicts and know that the recipients would understand them regardless of their nationality. More mundanely, the common use of Latin allowed monks to travel from a monastery to another in a different country and still be able to communicate with their brother monks. This was also true for scholars and university students, who were virtually all clergymen themselves for most of the Middle Ages. While drawn from nations throughout Europe, these students could debate each other, attend the same lectures, and study together because they all knew Latin. In fact, the use of Latin at universities was a requirement and those students who slipped into their native tongues were subject to fines.

The use of Latin by the clergy was imitated by secular rulers, particularly in the early Middle Ages. Government records and laws were written in Latin. Most of this documentation was written and read by clergymen employed in varying capacities by secular authorities.

Over time, Latin lost its place as a universal language. Governments gradually shifted to keeping records and issuing laws written in their local language. Even within the Church, while Latin continued to be the official language, it was difficult to maintain training in Latin. More priests as well as monks and nuns knew the Latin for their prayers, hymns, and other passages by rote rather than really understanding the language. Still, the better-educated clergy maintained the use of Latin through the Middle Ages and beyond.

The Language of the Jews

Comparable to the Church's use of Latin was the Jewish use of Hebrew. As part of their religious education, Jewish men learned Hebrew since it was the duty of every adult male to be able to read the Torah. In reality, not all Jewish men achieved proficiency in Hebrew, but many did and were able to read, write, and speak Hebrew. Thus, Hebrew was a universal language for Jews and enabled them to communicate with each other regardless of which country they came from. A Jew from Germany could speak with a Jew from France or from the Holy Land.

Religious Obligations

Just because people were traveling did not mean that they were freed from their religious duties. Ideally, one heard mass at the chapels, churches, and cathedrals along the way. Chapels could be found at all hospices. Hospices were built with chapels so that they could meet the spiritual as well as material needs of travelers.

The wealthy could attend mass at religious institutions as well but some found it expedient to hear mass without breaking their travels. This was accomplished by bringing a priest with them. Priests were a common part of a wealthy noble household so finding a priest to accompanying them was not a problem. They also brought along portable altars for the priests to say mass.

Noble households were not the only ones to travel with priests and portable altars. Armies often included them among their support personnel and baggage. Priests said masses before battles and heard the confessions of warriors who desired to have clean souls in case they died. After the battle, the victors sometimes had their priests sing a mass in thanks for their triumph. Henry V of England had this done after his victory at Agincourt.

Speed of Land Travel

The speeds of land travel in the Middle Ages were the same as they had been in antiquity and remained the same until the invention of the steam locomotive. A person walking could typically cover about 20 miles a day at most. However, a number of factors affected this figure. Carrying a heavy pack, hiking uphill and crossing difficult terrain slowed walking. When crossing mountains, speed might drop to two and a half to three miles in a day. While going downhill or having a good, level road, an individual's rate of travel would of course speed up. Additionally, since travel was rarely done at night, the length of the day affected travel time. In the longer, usually pleasant days of summer, more distance could be covered than in the short, cold days of winter.

People traveling by horseback could move faster but their speed was often impeded when they were part of a group which included people traveling on foot. Having part of a group riding while some walked was a common practice for both noble entourages and armies. Since they were limited to the speed of the slowest member of the group, a mixed party of riders and walkers typically averaged only 15 to 20 miles a day. Armies with both cavalry and infantry might only move 8 to 14 miles in a day, in part because of their baggage trains, which could include dozens if not hundreds of slow-moving carts and wagons.

When free of traveling with people on foot, a rider could achieve significantly higher speeds: 30 to 40 miles a day. Horses could move at faster speeds but only for short periods of time. Still, fast speeds were possible when travel was urgent and changes of mounts were used. For example, during an emergency, King Richard II of England covered 70 miles in a night with one change for fresh horses. Similarly, messengers using relays of horses appear to have routinely gone 40 to 60 miles a day and distances of 95 to 125 miles a day were possible, although these latter distances likely involved some riding at night. One example of such fast service was the courier service from Bruges to Venice which covered approximately 700 miles in seven days to bring information to and from Italian merchants and their trading outposts in northern Europe. In comparison, in the 19th century, riders for the Pony Express in the American West covered 200 miles in a day and a night, with the horses changed at stations every ten miles and riders replaced every hundred miles. This speed was comparable to the 235 miles per day and night achieved by the trans-Asian courier service run by the Mongol dynasty as reported by Marco Polo in the 13th century. Like the Pony Express, the Mongols had numerous relay stations along the route where the horses and riders were changed at regular intervals and travel was by day and night. In medieval Europe, messengers were able to get fresh horses but the system was not as developed as in 13th century Asia and 19th century America, which had numerous relay stations that allowed horses to be ridden at top speed.

At the opposite end of the spectrum, vehicles traveled slowly. Heavily loaded wagons and carts drawn by oxen often traveled only 8 to 12 miles in a day. Horse-drawn vehicles moved faster, around 15 to 20 miles in a day. As the speeds of horse-drawn coaches in the 18th and later centuries suggest, horses in the Middle Ages may have been capable of hauling wagons and carts at faster speeds. However, even if they could have moved faster, the generally poor road conditions of medieval Europe made higher-speed travel for vehicles dangerous, if not outright impossible. Additionally, while some were driven by men riding postillion, many carts and wagons were guided by men walking alongside them. This meant that the horses were limited to the speed of a walking man.

III

TRAVELING BY WATER

Travel and transportation on water, whether on rivers or on the seas, were essential to medieval society. Goods and people routinely moved long distances by water. The revival and expansion of trade throughout Europe drove the growth of shipping. And the increasing availability of shipping, in turn, promoted trade. In the next two sections, we will examine transportation on inland waterways and then turn to travel on the seas around Europe.

Inland Water Transportation

Water travel in medieval Europe was not limited to the surrounding seas. As they had been for centuries before the Middle Ages, rivers were major transportation routes and provided access far into the interior. Across all of Europe, from France to Russia and England to Italy, rivers were essential for moving a great variety of raw materials and finished products. These could be moved relatively cheaply to towns and cities along the length of the waterways. Some goods, ranging from wine and pottery to timber and grain, even found their way into international trade as barges reached deep-water ports at the mouths of rivers where their cargoes were reloaded onto seagoing vessels. Inland water travel was an essential part of trade in medieval society.

THE GEOGRAPHICAL EXTENT OF INLAND SHIPPING

Europe today has hundreds of miles of navigable rivers and canals. Barges carrying 500 tons or more of cargo can sail far inland, shuttling goods between seaports like Rotterdam in the Netherlands and river ports such as Basel, 500 miles upstream in Switzerland. The same major rivers used today, the Rhine, the Seine, the Dnieper, and many others, were used in the Middle Ages. Further, the much smaller size of medieval river craft enabled them to use hundreds more miles of small rivers and large streams and reach even further inland than their huge modern counterparts. Additionally, the scale of trade coupled with the relatively higher expense of land travel meant that it could be profitable to take small cargoes such as three or four large barrels of wine 20 or 30 miles inland from a seaport or a larger river port up to a town in the interior. Medieval river craft could negotiate the progressively narrower and shallower watercourses leading inland down to the point where they were only a few feet deep. As a consequence, water-borne transportation was available in large parts of Europe, including many places that modern navigation cannot reach.

Still, accessibility by vessels capable of carrying ten tons or more was important and towns and markets sometimes grew up at the furthest points inland that could be reached by these larger boats. For example, in England, Henley on the Thames was situated at the highest point on the river that could accommodate large barges. A market for wood and grain developed at Henley as these products were brought in from the surrounding areas to be loaded aboard bulk carriers and shipped downstream to be sold in London.

Rivers were not the only bodies of water used for transportation. Boats transporting goods and people also plied the lakes in Germany, Switzerland, and Italy. Further, voyages on inland waterways were often not limited to a single river or lake. For example, to reach the Russian trading center at Novgorod, Scandinavian and German merchants sailed across the Baltic Sea to the mouth of the Neva River. Here, they transferred their cargoes to smaller boats with Russian pilots to guide them. The boats appear to have been propelled by oars but some were also described as having a single mast with one square sail. These would have aided in both upstream and downstream travel. They then traveled up the Neva to Lake Ladoga, across the lake, and up the Volkhov River. At the rapids in the Volkhov, their vessels were pulled over the rapids by local men who were part of an organized group of boat-towers. To make it easier and safer to tow the boats, they appear to have been first unloaded and then reloaded once they had reached the other side of the rapids. Safely past the rapids, the merchants continued upriver and finally reached Novgorod.

In the early Middle Ages, some Scandinavian traders went even further and followed the Volkhov past Novgorod and up to Lake Ilmen. From there, they proceeded up rivers that led near the tributaries of the Volga and Dnieper Rivers. They then portaged their boats, carrying them across the land separating the rivers until they reached the rivers that fed the Volga and the Dnieper. Returning to the water, they took their boats hundreds of miles south to the Caspian and Black Seas to trade with merchants from Central Asia and the Near East. For the trip from Lake Ilmen, some of the traders appear to have used large log boats fitted with boards to raise their sides and increase their carrying capacity. These boats were rowed and had masts and sails like the other river boats.

How the traders accomplished their return trips is less clear. There is an account that outlines the return trip from the Black Sea to Novgorod by river so some must have made the arduous voyage north. The upriver trip must have taken significantly longer than traveling downstream and required hard work at rowing, although the sails likely helped on some stretches. The voyage upstream may have been somewhat eased by the relatively light weight of the cargos carried on the return trip. Going downstream, the boats carried heavy items such as blocks of wax, large bundles of furs, and slaves, while the upstream loads were usually lighter goods, including fine silks and other luxury items. Small coffers or bags filled with silver coins gained from trading were also carried, but these were not large enough to weigh down the boats. Still, some traders, primarily those using dugout canoes, appear to have disposed of their boats at the end of their southern voyage. References to making new dugouts each spring suggest that this was the case, but there are no descriptions of how they made the long return trip north by land.

CARGOS

An amazing variety of goods was transported on canals and rivers. Wine was perhaps the most ubiquitous along with grain. These items had to be moved in large quantities from production centers to markets in towns and cities. Wood, in the form of lumber, firewood and charcoal, was also needed by urban consumers and was brought to them by water. In lesser amounts but still vital to meeting the appetites of cities, all sorts of fresh produce was shipped in as well. All these goods were transported overland as well but carrying them by water was much cheaper and was the best way to move them in bulk.

The use of inland waterways was particularly well suited for moving heavy cargoes such as building stones (see illustration 10). The expense of transportation by land for these is estimated to have sometimes been so high that freight costs for a mere 12 miles cost as much as the stone itself did. For this reason, quarries near waterways were preferred, especially for supplying stone for large construction projects such as cathedrals or monasteries. In fact, in some instances, canals were built to connect quarries to navigable waterways. On the other end, canals were also dug to connect building sites to rivers. Some of these, particularly those for monasteries, continued in use after building had been completed and were used to bring in supplies and ship out products such as wool. Still, water transportation was not always available and much building stone was moved overland despite the expense. Additionally, except when traveling downstream, shipping by river or canal was usually slower than movement by land. As a consequence, goods which could be economically carried overland, such as cloth, which was comparatively light and had a value high enough to merit the costs, were routinely transported by wagon or packhorse.

Seagoing and Inland Traffic

Trade and traffic on inland waterways was not rigidly segregated from shipping on the sea. In Italy, for example, boats some 30 feet long but only a little over eight feet wide engaged in trade both along the coast and up rivers and canals. In England, coastal ships carried butter from York down the River Ouse, out to sea, down over 100 miles of coast, and then up the Thames to London. Unfortunately, not all such traffic was peaceful. The same rivers which permitted merchants to reach suppliers and markets also provided the Vikings with the means of penetrating far inland to carry out raids. London, Paris, and many other cities as well as monasteries found their positions on major rivers to be a liability in the centuries of Viking attacks.

Types of Inland Vessels

A wide variety of vessels were used on inland waterways. Wrecks of a few of these ves-

sels have been found and there are also some contemporary illustrations, but, as with land vehicles, there is a plethora of names for these craft. There were shouts, keels, crayers, barges, *navicula* (Latin for "small boat"), prahms, barches, *batella* (from the Medieval Latin *batulus*, meaning "boat") and others. Again, like land vehicles, it is difficult, if not impossible, to definitively match names to the physical and pictorial evidence. Still, crafts for use on rivers and canals can be broken down into general categories. Some were quite small, able to carry just a few people or a very limited amount of cargo. Others were large and capable of carrying loads weighing many tons. And there were some in between (see illustrations 2, 3, 6, 10, and 11). The types of vessels used depended on the waterway. Large barges could only function on the bigger rivers such as the Rhine and Main in Germany, the Seine and Rhone in France, and the Thames in England. There were smaller barges which could reach up the tributaries of the great rivers and even smaller boats that traveled along small rivers and large streams, as discussed previously.

Log Boats, Plank Boats, and Coracles

The simplest small boats were log boats. These were made of large, single logs scooped out to make a dugout canoe. Remains of log boats have been found in sites in western England and on the Continent. They were used on large streams, rivers, marshes, and lakes and were propelled and steered with a pole or paddle. When poling, the boatman stood in the rear of the craft. For paddling, there was a seat carved in the back of the canoe.

Dugouts varied widely in size. Examples found in England range from 6 to 12 feet in length. Larger canoes were built in eastern Europe. As mentioned previously, some Scandinavian traders used log boats large enough to carry several men plus trade goods in their voyages down the rivers of eastern Russia. The sides of these canoes were built up with planks to increase their capacity. The top row of planks was fitted with oarlocks or holes for oars so that they could be rowed rather than just paddled. Rowing was more efficient than paddling. Some appear to have been fitted with a mast for sailing. This would have provided welcome relief from rowing.

Other small boats were made of three planks. One plank in the shape of a pointed oblong was used as the bottom while two long planks formed the sides. Some plank boats added carved stern and bow pieces. This allowed the boat to be larger and have a greater carrying capacity with only a slight increase in the amount of wood used. Like the log boat, plank boats could be paddled or poled, although poling appears to have been most common. In this respect as well as in their general shape, flat bottom, and shallow draft, they were like the punts of later centuries. Plank boats could be used on all inland waterways and on the Continent they were used on estuaries as well.

Remains of various forms of the plank boat, including larger ones made out of multiple planks but retaining the same basic shape, have been found in England, Germany, and other sites in northern Europe (see illustration 10). Large versions of this boat continued in use on the Continent into the early 20th century and were sometimes fitted with a mast and sail. These boats were also sometimes fitted with paddle-shaped side-rudders. It is likely that larger medieval plank boats may have been steered this same way. The more recent plank boats were used for fishing and transport as they had been for centuries.

A third type of small vessel was made of hides stretched over a wooden framework. It was usually round or ovoid and some were shaped like halves of giant walnut shells. These were called coracles in England and Wales and curraghs in Ireland. Unlike the larger sea-going curraghs, they were small and light enough that a single man could carry one on his shoulders. Coracles and curraghs were propelled with a single paddle by a boatman who sat or crouched inside. The use of the coracle and the curragh was limited primarily to the rivers

of Ireland, Wales, and western England although, as discussed previously, there were larger, sea-going versions of the curragh as well. Additionally, the Magyars, a people from western Asia who invaded eastern Europe in the 9th century, used coracles for crossing rivers. The traditional curragh and coracle continued in use in Ireland and the United Kingdom into the last century and are still made today, although typically using modern materials.

A specialized form of boat related to the coracle was used in the Hundred Years' War. Along with other matériel for supporting his army, Edward III of England brought collapsible leather boats. These boats could carry three men. In part, these boats were used for fishing since fish were such an integral part of the medieval diet. Fish were essential for complying with Church dictates that forbade the consumption of other meats on Fridays, during Lent, and on the many other days of fasting and abstinence. These boats were also likely applied to the practical tasks of crossing rivers in the course. The number of boats was far too small to ferry large numbers of troops but was likely very useful for scouting parties and advance groups securing river crossings.

These small boats may sound very primitive and, in fact, some are difficult to differentiate from far earlier boats. Still, they were used throughout the Middle Ages and much later, although the log boat fell out of use by the end of the period. These boats stayed in use because they were well suited for ferrying people and goods across rivers and lakes and could travel up large streams and small rivers which were too shallow and narrow for larger craft. Admittedly, the small size of these three types of craft generally limited their usefulness. They could carry typically only a few people or a cargo of a few hundred pounds at most and they were suitable only for short trips. Still, particularly in areas with poor road networks, they provided vital connections to markets for consumers and producers far upstream in the interior.

Larger Boats

Larger river boats were referred to by names including barge, boat, barche, batella, navicula, and others. They varied widely in size. Smaller ones could carry only a ton or two of cargo while the largest carried around 40 tons. Most appear to have been able to handle cargoes around 10 to 12 tons.

To give some idea of the quantities such weights represented, a large barrel of wine called a *tun* usually held 252 gallons and weighed 2,240 pounds. For dry cargoes, a standard bushel of wheat today weighs 60 pounds but a medieval bushel is estimated to have weighed a little less than 50 pounds. For a boat of average size carrying 10 tons, this meant a load of 10 large wine barrels or approximately 400 bushels of grain, which had a volume of around 500 cubic feet. One expert has estimated that a boat carrying such a cargo of grain would have been around 60 feet long, 10 feet in breadth, and have a draft of 6 feet. At the upper limits, a vessel capable of carrying 40 tons of wheat had to be able to hold around 1,600 bushels. This would have been quite a large boat. Some of these larger vessels were of sufficient size that, outfitted with masts and sails, they were used for both inland and coastwise travel and sailed between nearby ports as well. However, their large size was both an advantage and a disadvantage since it limited how far upriver they could reach.

As for the shapes of these larger boats, these varied depending in part on the cargoes they carried, the waters they traveled in (small rivers, large rivers, lakes, coastal areas) and regional traditions in boat building. Like modern river barges, most had flat bottoms or had only a shallow keel (see illustration 10). Surviving wrecks of river craft confirm that they were commonly shallow draft and drew only a few feet of water. On many boats, the stern and bow were made in the same shape. Both the bow and stern were blunt and round on some while others had squared-off, straight sterns and bows. Still other boats looked like smaller versions of seagoing ships with pointed bows and sterns that curved upward (see illustrations 2, 3, 6, and 11).

All cargo-carrying river craft had a single, open deck. Those carrying bulk goods that could be spoiled by wet weather, such as grain, were fitted with canopies. By the end of the Middle Ages, some barges on the Rhine were constructed with enclosed cargo holds.

Log Rafts

As with other heavy, bulky goods, moving timber overland was expensive. Even for a relatively short trip, the freight costs quickly exceeded the purchase price of the wood. As a consequence, timber was moved by water whenever possible. Small amounts of timber, particularly that which had been finished into lumber, could be carried aboard barges but huge numbers of logs were moved in a different way. Vast numbers of logs were bound together to form rafts for moving the timber downstream to markets. Some of these rafts were so large that small cabins and galleys were built aboard them to house and feed the crew. Some carried cargo as well.

The rafts were controlled with bargepoles as well as steering oars. Since log rafts were used only for trips downstream, the sole job of the boatmen was to steer the raft and keep it in the main channel of the river. The number of men needed for controlling and moving rafts varied with size of the raft. While medieval figures are not available, some huge log rafts in the American northwest during the 19th century required 100 men or more.

The use of log rafts appears to have been most common on large rivers in northern Europe such as the Vistula in Poland. The biggest rafts were to be found on these rivers as well. Spring, when rivers were swollen by the melting of snow and spring rains, appears to have been the best season for moving these massive rafts. Smaller rafts could be operated during other times of the year and on smaller rivers such as the Vienne in France.

Passenger Boats

Passenger boats operated on waterways across Europe. As previously discussed, some of these were ferries used for river crossings. In harbors and in cities that spanned rivers, such as London and Paris, small boats served as "water-taxis," taking passengers to various points along the river or around the harbor. This was usually faster and easier than traveling by land. In addition, larger boats provided service between destinations further away. For example, in the late Middle Ages, passenger boats regularly traveled the Thames between London and Gravesend near the mouth of the river, a distance of over 20 miles.

In addition to the common passenger boats, more luxurious vessels also plied the rivers. These were the barges of royalty and nobility. Across Europe, the elite had their own luxury craft for traveling in style. Unlike the open decks of ordinary boats, canopies were a standard feature of passenger barges. Some boats, primarily those for long trips, even had well-furnished cabins to provide their privileged passengers with the comforts of home. In the late Middle Ages, some barge cabins had the luxury of glass windows. Traveling by barge was appealing because it was typically more comfortable than traveling overland. It was less fatiguing than riding a horse and was smoother and less jarring than riding in a carriage.

Passenger boats were used for both long and short journeys. In the late 8th century and early 9th century, Charlemagne traveled across parts of his domain by barge. Later, the kings and queens of England traveled up and down the Thames from the Tower of London to the palace at Westminster and between London and their estates further upstream. Most passenger barges were relatively light compared to cargo vessels and were propelled by crews of oarsmen so that they could move upstream as well as down with relative ease. Heavier passenger boats, however, were subject to the same limits as cargo barges and moved upstream only with considerable effort.

The best-recorded uses of passenger boats for long distances come from late 14th century France where, along some routes, barges provided speedy service. For example, in 1371, Duke Philip the Bold of Burgundy and his retinue traveled in six barges down the Sâone River to the Rhone River and then all the way to Avignon in the south of France to meet with the pope. The trip was entirely downstream and, even with putting into shore each night, it took only five days to cover about 200 miles. The return voyage was much slower. It is estimated that it took three to four weeks since these large barges had to be towed upstream by oxen, horses or men. In this case, the speed of upstream travel was around seven to eight miles a day in contrast to the 40-mile-per-day downstream speed. The slow movement of barges upstream meant that travelers typically chose a mix of means of transportation and traveled by land when water travel was simply too slow. Duke Philip did just this and left Avignon on horseback.

When using roads was impractical or impossible, river boats were sometimes used on journeys as short as 30 miles. Queen Isabel of England made such trip in 1311. It took two days but this was likely a much easier trip than had it been overland since four barges were required to move the queen, her retinue, and all of their luggage. Going by boat saved hiring carts and pack animals that would have otherwise been needed.

Seagoing Ships

Craft specifically constructed for travel on inland waters were not the only vessels found on rivers and canals. Seagoing ships were sometimes sailed or hauled miles upstream to ports. This was possible due to the relatively shallow draft of many ships. They could not go as far upstream as the flat-bottomed river and canal boats, but ports 30 or more miles inland were sometimes accessible, particularly when rising tides could be used to help move them inland and ebbing tides to carry them back to the sea. Perhaps the most extreme example of seagoing ships going up rivers is the Viking raiders who were masters of sailing and rowing their shallow-draft ships well upstream. They could reach inland targets such as Seville, Spain, 50 miles up the Quadalquivir River from the Atlantic Ocean, and Cologne, Germany, over 130 miles up the Rhine from the sea.

By having merchant vessels travel as far inland as possible, the need to unload cargo and reload it onto smaller craft was minimized. It saved money and time if a cargo could be delivered directly to a major market center rather than to an outlying port from which goods would either have to be transferred to land freight or reloaded onto smaller river-going or coastwise boats. However, transferring cargo could not be avoided when a ship was too large for a port's wharves or the port was too shallow for the ship's draft. The ships had to anchor offshore and their cargo was ferried to the wharves by smaller boats.

PROPULSION AND STEERING

River craft relied on several different means of propulsion. For traveling downstream, the current was the primary moving force. Man-made force was most frequently provided by the use of poles. As previously discussed, poles were used for propelling log boats and simple plank boats. For larger vessels, bargepoles were used. Boatmen moved their vessels with these long, sturdy poles by shoving one end of the pole into the riverbed at the bow of the boat and then walking back the length of the boat, pushing the boat along. This was done to move barges through slow running water as well as to push them upstream. Small barges could be handled by a single man when traveling downstream but larger crews were needed for moving upstream and for bigger boats when traveling down- or upstream.

The poles were also used to steer the boat. As shown in some illustrations, poles were even used for steering on barges outfitted with sails. Boatmen pushed their barges away from the shore to keep them in the main channel of the river. They would also use the poles to guide their vessels through swift water and away from rocks and other hazards in the river. Considerable strength and skill were needed to manipulate the poles for these tasks.

In addition to bargepoles, large oars, like those aboard seagoing vessels, were sometimes used to steer river craft. Steering oars on barges functioned like those on sea-going ships. The steersman stood at the stern of the barge and held the oar in the water (see illustration 2). By angling the blade of the oar, he directed the boat's course. As with using the bargepole, holding and moving the steering oar required strength. The steersman also needed to be experienced in the use of the oar as well as knowledgeable about river conditions and the course to be followed.

Besides poles, some river craft used wind power. Some boats were rigged with sails, usually a single square sail. These were most common for barges that operated in the relatively wide-open reaches where rivers met the sea. Examples of this could be found around the mouths of the Humber River in England and the Rhine in the Low Countries. Large sailing barges had been used on the lower Rhine since the days of the Romans. In England, sailing barges called *keels* continued in use on the Humber into the early 20th century. Sails were sometimes used on stretches of rivers further inland such as where the rivers wound through open plains. In some instances, sails could be used to move both up- and downstream when winds were favorable. One such example can be found in Italy, where boats moving grain from Ostia on the coast up to Rome used sails whenever possible. Seagoing vessels, too, used their sails to push inland although towing was common.

For traveling upstream, while bargepoles and sails were sometimes used, it was common to have boats towed. This was most often done by men or draft animals walking on towpaths along the riverside. Hauling boats has a long history. A carving dating from the age of the Roman Empire depicts a gang of men laboriously hauling a boat along a towpath. Towpaths, called *treidelpfad* in German, were established along some stretches of the Rhine River and were in continuous use from Roman times through the Middle Ages and into the centuries afterward. While draft animals were used for hauling, much of it was performed by men. Haulers appear to have been available anywhere boats regularly needed to be towed. For example, as mentioned previously, an organization of boat-towers pulled boats over the rapids on the Volkhov River in Russia so that merchants could reach the important trading city of Novgorod.

When being towed from the shore, the boatmen had to constantly use their bargepoles to push their vessels away from the shore since the natural movement of the hauling would have pulled the boats onto the shore. Based on accounts from England in the centuries immediately after the Middle Ages, some boatmen attempted to alleviate this problem by having the towing horses get down into the muddy edge of the river or canal. However, this method sometimes led to the death of horses and the boys who led them as they could founder in the muck and drown.

Men continued to haul barges well into the 17th century but the use of horses became more common over the course of the Middle Ages. Post-medieval figures from England indicate that six to eight men were needed to pull a small barge and that a single horse could do the same work. For large barges, six horses could replace 60 haulers. Obviously, using horses was far more economical and efficient than using men. Use of horses became so common that, in the 16th century, King Henry IV of France regulated the cost of hiring tow horses from relay stations. This indicates that teams of fresh horses were hired on a regular basis, likely every day. Accounts from 17th century England indicate that this was the practice for human haulers as well. They appear to have been day-laborers hired at towns along the canal or river. Fresh teams of men or horses would then be hired at the start of each day. However, in the Middle Ages, some

monasteries did employ haulers on a longer-term basis and one abbey even built a rest house for its crews along the canal connecting it to a quarry. Additionally, towing service was another obligation which tenants sometimes owed to their lords. For this, tenants who lived alongside rivers had to turn out to help pull their lord's barges. Presumably, they were expected to bring any draft animals they possessed or else do the hauling themselves. It is unclear whether they were required to make the entire journey or just provide service for a certain number of days. However, like many other servile obligations, this was commuted to a money payment by the late Middle Ages so that lords could simply hire professional haulers and boatmen to perform the work. In fact, most boats were privately owned and operated and were contracted out to carry cargoes like the land-based freight services. As with hiring horses and wagons, this was far more economical for most people, even the nobility, than maintaining their own boats. In some areas of Germany and France, boatmen organized into guilds and had monopolies on the river traffic in their regions. For example, the boatmen of Paris were recognized by the French kings as having the sole right to transport cargo along the Seine in the vicinity of the capital.

SPEED OF TRAVEL

As the previous sections makes clear, the speed of river travel varied greatly depending on whether a vessel was moving upstream or down. Barges could travel downstream relatively quickly, often as fast as or faster than travel by land. As mentioned above, the Duke of Burgundy traveled 40 miles a day, which was likely quite typical, but even faster speeds were possible. In some instances, 60 to 80 miles a day were covered. While sails and bargepoles could be used to move boats, the speed of the river's current was certainly the most important factor affecting a boat's downstream speed.

As for moving upstream, this was always

much slower than downstream travel and required significant effort. It could usually be done only with hard labor either with by boatmen with bargepoles or by men, oxen, or horses plodding along paths on the shore. A voyage that took only days on the downstream leg could take many weeks for the return trip. Some historians believe that upstream movement was aided by the types of cargoes carried. Downstream cargoes were often heavy goods such as grain, stone, and wood while lighter items such as pottery and other finished goods were more common for upstream loads. In fact, some vessels may have been virtually empty on their return trips from carrying cargoes downstream. This arrangement, when possible, would have been quite practical. Still, some heavy goods, particularly barrels of wine, initially traveled downstream from their sources but had to be brought upstream to markets. Thus, upstream movement was likely aided by the lighter weight of the cargo in many instances but, ultimately, some heavy loads did have to be moved upriver.

PORTAGING

Along some rivers, shallows or rapids blocked points between navigable stretches. To cope with this, boats were unloaded and their cargo carried by land around these barriers. The cargo could then be loaded onto boats at the other side of the rapids or shallows and the journey continued. When possible, the merchants' boats were also portaged so that it was not necessary to find and hire new boats on the other side of the obstacles. For some trips, it was necessary to move boats and their cargo between two bodies of water separated by land. As discussed previously in this section, examples of this can be found in Russia where Scandinavian traders crossed from one river to the next by portaging their boats. Using this technique, they were able to travel all the way from the Baltic down to the Black and Caspian Seas and back. Towns sometimes grew up at portage points such as Schaffhausen in Switzerland, where cargo was carried

around the Rhine Falls. These towns provided the workforces needed to move the cargo and boats. They also catered to other needs of boatmen, selling them food and drink. Not all portaging locations were so hospitable. In the early Middle Ages, merchants traveling the Dnieper River were vulnerable to attack by local nomadic tribes when portaging around rapids.

The need for portaging could also be driven by the weather. In times of drought, parts of some rivers became too shallow for normal navigation. Boats would unload cargo so that they would float higher in the water and pass over the shallows. The cargo was portaged and reloaded onto boats. Sometimes lightening the load was not enough and the empty boats either had to be hauled across the shallows or their cargo transferred to boats on the other side of the shallows.

IMPROVING RIVERS

To contain rivers and minimize flooding, dikes were built along the sides of some rivers. In Italy, these dikes sometimes served as roadways as well since they were elevated above the surrounding marshy ground. There were also some attempts to stabilize the riverbanks to stop erosion and channel the flow of the rivers. Keeping rivers within their existing channels was important both for navigation and flood control. Like the Mississippi in the United States up until the early 20th century, some European rivers, such as the upper section of the Rhine, would periodically cut new courses as part of severe flooding. These new channels flowed across previously usable land and left the old channels impossible to navigate. This latter problem was so common on the upper Rhine that local residents were obligated to place large poles along the riverbanks to mark which channel was navigable. After the Middle Ages, the construction of dikes or levees and other measures countered these problems by forcing rivers to remain in their existing channels.

Silting in was a chronic problem for all

inland waterways. To keep some rivers open to navigation, dredging was necessary. The primary examples of this come from the Low Countries, where estuaries were especially subject to silting in. One example of this involved the city of Bruges. As mentioned previously, Bruges made repeated attempts to cut a channel in the Zwijn River so that it could remain connected to its ports on the sea but these efforts ultimately failed. The primitive dredging equipment then available was simply inadequate for such large-scale operations. In the end, with the loss of direct access to the sea, Bruges declined economically. Most foreign trade relocated to Antwerp, which was still linked to the sea and continues to be a major port today.

Small rivers and even streams were sometimes maintained to keep them navigable. In England, one small waterway was kept clear by men with iron rakes and shovels hired by local ship owners.

THE DEVELOPMENT OF CANALS

Improving rivers was one means of facilitating inland navigation. Another was the construction of canals. Canals had been built in Europe for centuries before the Middle Ages to drain marshes and to supplement rivers as conduits for water-borne trade and some served a dual purpose of drainage and navigation.

Canal Building and Operation

The Romans had built canals such as the one connecting the port of Ostia to the city of Rome. Some Roman canals continued in use through the Middle Ages but, as with roads, new ones were built as well to improve inland water travel between locations which had not been significant in the days of the Empire.

The earliest medieval canal was built in an island off the Danish coast around A.D. 726. It was about a third of a mile long and 40 feet wide. It was used for moving ships across the island to provide a shortcut and

avoid treacherous straits nearby. Later in the 8th century, Charlemagne ordered the construction of a canal in southern Germany to connect the Rhine to the Danube. The canal would have enabled the rapid movement of the men and materiel around Charlemagne's empire but construction was soon abandoned. Even if it had been completed, the differences in the heights of the two rivers and the lack of skills needed to create locks of sufficient scale to overcome this difference would have made operation of the canal impossible. The remains of the aborted excavations can still be seen today. It was not until the 20th century that Charlemagne's dream was realized by modern engineering.

Canals of more practical size were built across Europe. Some were built as part of the massive drainage and flood control projects in the Low Countries. These were used for navigation as well and provided connections between coastal towns and those further inland.

Some canals were built specifically for shipping. There were several types of navigation canals. Some were diversions of existing rivers. An example of this can be found at Rhuddlan in Wales, where, as part of his castle-building campaign, Edward I of England had part of a river redirected into a two-mile-long canal. The canal was built so that building materials could be brought in for the construction of his castle at Rhuddlan. Once the castle was completed, the canal continued in use, allowing the castle to be resupplied directly from the sea. The canal also formed part of the castle's moat.

Other canals paralleled rivers. These channels were built to bypass obstacles in rivers such as rapids or shallows. One such canal was dug alongside the Thames River in the 11th century to restore the connection with Oxford by bypassing a section of river that was filling with silt. Parallel canals were also built to go around man-made obstacles such as the low dams or *weirs* built to hold water to power mills.

Canals were also built as spurs off rivers or other canals. Some canals of this type were dug so that stone and other building materials could be brought by barge to building sites for cathedrals and monasteries. This was done for the construction of cathedrals in both Milan and Pisa. Having a canal built as close as possible to the work site minimized or even eliminated the need to offload the cargo, load it on a cart, and then move it over land to the site. The cost and effort of digging the canal was lower than that required for bringing in the materials overland. For monasteries, after the building was completed, the canal was still used to ship in supplies. In cities, the canals continued to be used for trade and, occasionally, for defense when the canal formed part of a city's moat.

There were canals that connected bodies of water. The 8th century Danish canal mentioned at the beginning of this section was a canal of this type. A much more ambitious canal was built near the end of the Middle Ages to provide a link between the Baltic and North Seas. The seven-mile-long Stecknitz Canal, built between 1391 and 1398, connected two rivers and created a direct route by water between the important trading cities of Lübeck, on the Baltic Sea, and Hamburg, on the North Sea. This saved ships the time and risks of sailing all the way around the Danish peninsula, although only relatively small ships could use the canal.

There were also canals that were cut to connect cities to the sea. In the Low Countries, this was necessary because the North Sea shoreline has steadily progressed northwards so that some cities that had had direct access to the sea gradually found themselves landlocked. For example, in 12th century Flanders, the cities of Bruges, Ypres, and St. Omer (now in France) dredged canals to connect them to new seaports built on the new coastline. The seaport for St. Omer was Gravelines (now in France), Nieuwpoort for Ypres, and Damme for Bruges. Seagoing vessels could unload at one of these ports and have their cargos ferried up the canal to the inland city or, if the canal was large enough, the ships could sail directly to the city.

Keeping a canal in functioning condition required frequent maintenance. The sides of the canal naturally sloughed into the canal as the water eroded them so they had to be re-dug periodically. The flow of water through a canal was relatively slow. This meant that soil suspended in the water could easily settle out and fill the canal with silt. Aquatic weeds were also a constant nuisance and could gradually choke a canal if they were not removed. When too much silt and plant matter had accumulated, dredging was required. Unfortunately, there are no surviving records that describe how this task was performed. For smaller canals, perhaps the upstream end of the canal was temporarily blocked and men shoveled the muck and mud out. For larger canals such as the one between St. Omer and Gravelines, this would not have been possible. This canal was large enough to accommodate seagoing ships that could carry up to 600 tons of cargo. It must have been an expensive and laborious process that was similar to the initial dredging. If the canal was not regularly maintained, it would gradually fill in and the watercourse would seek out its natural route. This was often back into the main channel of its parent river. It is believed that many medieval canals have disappeared in this way.

Locks

Locks were structures built to compensate for different levels of water within the course of a river or canal. For much of many rivers' lengths, the water levels changed gradually and river craft could safely move up- or downstream. But in some locations, water levels changed abruptly as the river flowed down inclines. Here, the differences in water level caused the river's flow to speed up. The drops in the elevation of the river were sometimes accompanied by rapids, shallows, and exposed rocks. These conditions could throw a boat out of control and run it aground or smash it on the rocks. As mentioned before, portaging boats or at least their cargo was a common means of coping with rapids. To eliminate the need for portaging and to permit larger craft to operate, locks were developed to allow boats to move safely over stretches of rivers which had significant changes in elevation. Canals also needed locks. The dangers of rocks and shallows were eliminated by the smooth bottoms of the man-made canals but, like rivers, they flowed down from higher elevations. Without locks, there would have been impassable stretches with dangerously steep drops and fast-flowing water.

The simplest lock was the "flash lock." This was part of a weir, a low dam built across a river or canal. This barrier could span the entire width of a river but it was much more common for it to reach only partway out into the river. Many weirs were built to hold back water for driving water mills. This was necessary since most rivers did not flow fast enough to adequately turn the mill's wheel. By damming part of the river and then releasing the trapped water through a narrow channel, or *leat*, the water had sufficient force to turn a wheel at a speed sufficient to drive the mill's stone or other machinery. The flash lock was another opening in the weir and was much larger than the leat. The lock was made up of removable panels. It was used to regulate the level of the water held back by the weir and to permit boats to pass through the weir. When a boat needed to proceed downstream, the panels were quickly removed and the boat shot down the river on the sudden "flash" of freed water. The burst of water also helped temporarily raise the water level so that the boat could clear any rocks or shoals in the river downstream. For upstream movement, panels in the barrier were lifted, allowing free flow of water, and the vessel was poled or towed up the river. Along the Thames, some mill weirs were fitted with winches and ropes to pull boats upstream. Where there were no winches, draft horses, oxen, or groups of men performed the pulling. Flash locks were only suitable for relatively small differences in water levels so the hauling or poling, while strenuous, was quite feasible. Despite their drawbacks, flash locks continued in use in England

into the late 19th century. Flash locks were used on canals as well. For canals, the flash lock covered the entire width of the channel.

A swinging lock gate was first developed in the Low Countries in the 11th century. Initially, it was made of a single swinging gate which spanned a river or canal. It was swung open and, like the flash lock, released the vessel on a surge of water. Again, this was most suitable where there was only a fairly minor descent. On these locks, winches were used for pulling the gates open against the force of the water. Additionally, sluices in the gates, like panels in flash locks, were raised to lessen the water pressure to make it easier to open the gate. As for the barges, moving the vessel upstream again required hauling or poling but winches were also used to pull them.

Around the end of the 13th century and the beginning of the 14th, this system was improved by using pairs of gates to create the pound lock. To operate it, one gate was closed and the vessel entered the "pound." The second gate, the one behind the boat, was then closed and sluices were opened to either fill or drain the pound to equalize the water level with that of the river or canal the vessel was entering. When the water level was equalized, the first gate was opened and the vessel could proceed on its way. With pound locks, boats could be raised and lowered with more control than with flash locks and single gate locks. Additionally, these locks could compensate for greater differences in water levels than earlier, simpler locks. Pound locks appear to have been developed independently in Italy and the Low Countries. By 1304, the city of Pisa had built a canal with locks that allowed barges heavily laden with marble to travel from a quarry to near the building site of the city's cathedral. Around the same time, the city of Bruges built a form of double lock as part of the efforts to remain open for seagoing traffic. During the 14th century, pound locks were built on a number of canals in the Low Countries as well as in Italy. As with single gate locks, winches were usually needed to pull the gates open.

A technique not using locks was developed in the 12th century to cope with changes in water levels in some areas. A wooden ramp was built on the bed of the river or canal where the level of the river dropped. Since it lay on the bottom, water flowed continuously over the ramp. For boats going downstream, the ramp made the descent gentler and safer. As with locks, boats traveling upstream were pulled up the ramp by a rope attached to a winch or by draft animals or teams of men.

HAZARDS AND OBSTACLES

Travel on rivers was not without risk. As mentioned in a previous section, in 13th century London, the unpopular Queen Eleanor had insults and garbage thrown at her barge by irate citizens on the bridge. There were also more serious dangers with fatal results. In 1428 on the Thames River, a barge carrying the Duke of Norfolk and many others struck one of the supports of London Bridge. The barge quickly sank. The duke and two or three others made it onto a bridge support and were rescued but all the other passengers drowned.

Bridges were not the only hazards for river traffic. Dangerous rock outcroppings such as the famed Lorelei on the Rhine claimed many victims. Boatmen drowned when their vessels went out of control, smashed on the rocks, and sank. There were also treacherous currents as well as sudden drops in elevation that created rapids whose churning water could cause a boatman to lose control of his craft and wreck.

Darkness worsened these risks and could make even routine travel dangerous. As a consequence, barges appear to have routinely put in to shore for the night. Boatmen stopped in towns or cities where they could buy food and drink or at least fresh provisions for preparing their own meals.

Other obstacles to river traffic were not hazardous but did present problems for navigation. As previously discussed, some rivers were partly blocked by weirs. Some weirs extended too far out into rivers, leaving insuffi-

cient space for barges to bypass them. Others lacked adequate locks to permit passage of boats or the owners failed to open the locks when needed. On some stretches of rivers, there were many mills, each with its own weir, creating one obstacle after another. Besides blocking river traffic, weirs sometimes caused flooding on lands upstream since they slowed the flow of the river and held back water that would have otherwise drained downstream.

In addition to mill weirs, another hindrance were the fish traps found along many rivers. Some of these were incorporated into mill weirs, but some had weirs of their own, funneling the flow of the river into numerous wicker traps to catch the fish. Other fish traps were simply nets strung on stakes set in the riverbed. As with mill weirs, both fish weirs and lines of nets could narrow the usable width of a river to the point that it was no longer navigable. They could also contribute to flooding upstream. In England, there were occasional government inspections of the Thames for the purpose of removing and destroying fish traps and nets that caused blockages. This frequently led to confrontations between the government officials and the fishermen whose traps had been seized. The officials were sometimes faced with angry, armed mobs of fishermen who forced the officials to return the nets and traps. As a consequence, inspections did not significantly solve the problems caused by the fishermen.

The obstruction of waterways and the flooding caused by weirs and fish traps and nets sometimes led to lawsuits to remove or reduce them. In one instance, a large group of men, without the benefit of a court ruling, destroyed a weir that blocked nearly the entire width of a river. In England, royal edicts ordering the removal of all such obstacles were repeatedly issued but appear to have had little effect. Similar problems existed on the Continent.

Banditry and tolls were other man-made obstacles to river travel. Like travel on land, river traffic was subject to attack and plundering. In the early Middle Ages, even local nobility sometimes raided river boats passing through or near their lands. If not practicing outright robbery, many nobles attempted to extract as much money as possible from travelers, especially merchants, and so levied tolls on any river traffic they could reach. This problem seems to have been greatest in Germany on the Rhine, where nobles whose castles dotted the shores of the river demanded payment from the passing barges. Along with noblemen, high-ranking Church officials who held castles along the river levied tolls as well. Both nobles and churchmen became notorious for their tolls on the Rhine and Main rivers. They sometimes blocked the rivers with chains or ropes, particularly at bridges, or prevented the use of towpaths to enforce collections of tolls. This interference with trade reached crisis levels several times in the Middle Ages. In the late 12th century, for example, the Emperor Frederick Barbarossa had received so many complaints about tolls on the Main and Rhine that he banned all tolls on the rivers and stated that no merchants traveling on the river or anyone on a towpath hauling a boat was to be interfered with. Towpaths were to be considered the emperor's or king's highways and so were subject only to imperial or royal jurisdiction. Levying tolls or otherwise obstructing the use of these paths was subject to punishment. In England, the rivers themselves for as far inland as they were tidal were considered public highways and their use was subject to the king.

As with land travel, wars sometimes interfered with travel on rivers and canals. The destruction of bridges, a common occurrence in wars, could also block rivers and canals. Barges were also subject to attack anywhere a waterway passed through war-torn lands. For example, during the war between Poland and the Teutonic Order in the mid–15th century, barges of the German Hanse were sometimes attacked on rivers in the region of the conflict. This led the Hanse to arm their barges and operate them in convoys, sometimes of 100 or more vessels, for their safety. Also in the 15th century, the city-state of Venice built small

warships for use on rivers in their wars against rival cities.

There were also pirates on some waterways in eastern Europe and western Russia. Finns and Karelians attacked German and Scandinavian merchants on their way to Novgorod. The boats used by the Finns were called *uisko*, which meant "swimming serpent." This style of boat was adopted by Russian pirates. In the 14th century, these pirates ranged across the lakes and rivers of western Russia and attacked and pillaged cities and towns along the shores.

Seagoing Vessels

Some of the greatest technological advances in the period were made in the design and construction of seagoing vessels. These developments in naval architecture far outstripped the achievements of any earlier culture as well as those of any contemporary societies around the world. The fusion of the technologies of northern and southern Europe led to the creation of the fully-rigged ship near the end of the Middle Ages. With these vessels, Europeans broke out of their familiar waters and sailed the world.

Along with improvements in ships, Europeans developed navigational instruments and techniques which would make their voyages of exploration and discovery possible. Most navigational tools, such as the quadrant and the astrolabe, were known in antiquity and had been further developed by Moslem scientists for use in astronomy. By the end of the period, European navigators had taken these instruments and were using them at sea to guide their ships. This practical application of astronomical devices, combined with the evolution of maritime charts and improvements to the compass, made navigation more reliable, especially over long distances.

While improvements in ships and navigation gradually made travel by sea safer, great hazards, both natural and man-made, remained. Many ships and lives were lost to storms and shipwrecks. Piracy and attacks during wartime claimed them as well. Additionally, conditions aboard ships improved only incrementally. Crews and passengers were afforded more protection against the elements as decks and cabins were added and ships grew larger. But these accommodations were cramped and were often limited only to the ship's officers and privileged passengers. There was also little, if any, improvement in the quality and quantity of food and drink aboard ships. As would be the case for centuries afterward, keeping adequate supplies of edible food and drinkable water was a challenge and salted meat and ship's biscuit were staples of diet at sea.

A wide variety of ships were required to meet the needs of medieval society. They were used for fishing, for waging war, and for carrying goods and people. However, the distinction between ships used for war and those used for peaceful purposes was often blurred. There were few ships constructed solely for military service. Merchant cargo ships were often pressed into military service, primarily as troop transports, but they also served in naval combat when needed. The long ships of the Vikings were built for warfare and were occasionally used in battles on the seas, but they too were more commonly used as transports, landing parties of raiders and then retrieving them along with their plunder. In this section, all seagoing vessels that carried cargo and people will be reviewed.

There were many names for ships in the Middle Ages: *navis, nef, knaar, cog, não, carrack, galley, keel, buss, hulk, round ship, cocha,* and *long ship*. Some of these clearly denoted different types of vessels. Others were just generic terms for ships. Using illustrations from manuscripts, city seals, and paintings, and some recovered wrecks, it is possible to connect images with some of these names. There are written descriptions that help as well. Still, it is not always possible to authoritatively identify a vessel mentioned in a medieval document. One problem is that ships of the same general type often varied considerably, especially as they evolved into different forms of ships. The cog is one example of this. While sharing some basic features, a cog built in the 11th century differed significantly from one built in the 14th century. There were also regional variations. All this makes it difficult to clearly trace the evolution of ships over the period.

SHIPWRIGHTS AND CONSTRUCTION TECHNIQUES

Shipbuilding techniques differed greatly between northern and southern Europe. Broadly, there were two techniques for building ships: clinker building in northern Europe and carvel building in southern Europe. With either method, however, shipwrights had to have considerable skills to design and oversee the construction of ships. They had to determine what shape was needed to give the ship the best performing capabilities within the constraints of size and purpose set by the ship's buyer. They had to be able to visualize the completed ship and the components necessary to achieve that desired shape.

As with many other crafts in the Middle Ages, shipwrights learned through apprenticeships which involved watching ships being built and later working on their construction. Along with this hands-on training, the master shipwright would teach his apprentices based on his own experience. Shipwrights gained additional knowledge by observing any different ships that came into port. For most of the Middle Ages, ship building was learned exclusively in this way. Treatises on ship design began to appear in the first half of the 15th century. These were written in Italy and contain mathematical formulas, ratios, diagrams, and other information to assist in designing shapes of hulls. Given the advanced level of this information, it is obvious that some shipwrights had been using such scientific methods for designing ships for quite some time before these books were published. It is likely that papers such as these had been circulated and shared among shipwrights for several decades or more prior to the 15th century.

Clinker Construction

In northern Europe, up into the 14th century, the primary method of ship building was to construct the hull first and then insert the internal framing to strengthen the hull and hold it in shape. The hull was made of overlapping planks. The first row of planks, or *strake*, was nailed to the keel. Each succeeding strake was laid so that its lower edge overlapped the top edge of the strake below it.

From the outside of the hull, long iron rivets or nails, sometimes called *clinch nails*, were driven through the overlapped area. (See illustrations 13, 14, and 15.) On the inside of the hull, a square washer, or *rove*, was placed over the end of the rivet or nail. For rivets, the end of the rivet was hammered to spread it out. For nails, the nail's point was bent to one side and hammered down. Sometimes the rove was omitted and the nail's point was simply bent over and then hammered in. All these method accomplished the same goal of holding the strakes tightly together. When the hull was completed, wooden braces, curved to match the desired shape of the hull, were attached to

Illustration 13. This early 13th century illumination (detail from a full page in *Vie de St. Thomas de Canterbury*, c. 1230–1240) depicts the return of Archbishop Thomas á Becket to England from France. As was common in medieval illustrations, the people were drawn much larger than objects, in this case the ships, since the people and their actions were the focus of the picture. The ship is square-rigged and, judging from the nail heads, clinker-built, but using the reverse clinker technique in which the top edge of each row of planks, or *strakes*, overlapped the bottom of the row above it. In normal clinker-building, the lower edge of each strake overlapped the top edge of the strake beneath it, like clapboard siding on a house. The ship appears to be a hulk, judging by its banana-like shape and the rigging tied around the stern and stem of the upswept hull. It is steered with a large side rudder that is attached to the ship by two metal links. This arrangement allowed the helmsman to move the rudder freely and swing the rudder up when in shallow water or when beaching the vessel. The rudder also has a short handle mounted at its top, which gives the helmsman a more comfortable grip. The rowboat that is going out to greet the archbishop is built like the hulk. Such small boats were common but they are rarely depicted in medieval art and they have not been found in archaeological excavations (L30/1(37), detail, courtesy Conway Library, The Courtauld Institute of Art, London).

Left, illustration 14. This is the seal of the City of Winchelsea, England, from 1274. The ship depicted is likely a form of hulk. As with all other northern ships, it has a single square sail. It is clinker-built. Like the hulk in Illustration 13, this ship has a side rudder mounted on its right, rear quarter and it has a handle at the top to make it easier for the helmsman to control it. The ship has castles at the bow and stern. These are supported by posts that leave the space under the fortified tops open. The ship may be outfitted for war but it was common by this time for all ships to be outfitted with castles even in peacetime. In addition to the helmsman, the crew includes two trumpeters in the sterncastle that are signaling the ship's departure as well as sailors who are climbing and adjusting the rigging while two sailors near the bow are hoisting the anchor. (It should be noted that, as with Illustration 13, the ship is not in the same scale as the men aboard it.) *Right, illustration 15.* This seal of the City of Stralsund, Germany, dates from 1329 and has a detailed image of a cog. Stralsund was a member of the Hanseatic trading federation and cogs were the primary ships used by Hanse members throughout the 14th century. Like other northern ships, the cog has a single large mast amidships and is square-rigged. The part of the hull that is visible is clinker-built, but the bottom of the hull was usually constructed with planks laid edge to edge rather than overlapping. The bow of the cog comes to a very sharp point that has a straight edge rather than a curved bow as was common on earlier ships. The stern of the cog is nearly vertical, which is also quite different from other ships. The flatness of the stern made it easier to mount a centerline rudder. This innovation appears to have been introduced in the early 14th centuries. The helmsman holds the rudder's tiller. The tiller provides the helmsman with leverage that makes steering easier than when using a side rudder. This cog has a forecastle and a sterncastle. The helmsman would actually have stood under the sterncastle rather than out on the deck. (Again, it should be noted that the ship is not in the same scale as the man.)

the inside of the hull. Wooden pegs were driven through holes in the hull and into matching holes in the internal framing. This hull-first method of building was called "clinker" construction after the clinch nails.

While unrelated to the use of clinch nails, another common feature of clinker-built ships was that the strakes ran the length of the ship and gradually curved up towards the bow and stern. At the bow and stern, the strakes were nailed to the fore-and stern-stems, respectively. The stems were large, curved timbers that were attached to each end of the ship's keel. The stems formed the distinctive swept-up prow and stern commonly associated with

Viking "dragon ships." Both the bow and stern each came to a point and were virtually identical. Thus, these ships were sometimes referred to as "double-ended." All these features appear in Viking long ships as well as in contemporary and later merchant vessels of northern Europe.

Carvel Construction

In antiquity, the Greeks and Romans had constructed the hulls of their ships first, but using a different technique than clinker building. The planks, or strakes, of their hulls did not overlap. Instead, the planks were placed edge to edge and were held together by tenons. The tenons were small, rectangular wooden slats that were fitted into slots cut into the edges of the planks. When the planks were laid together, the tenons were locked in place with pegs. Once the hull was completed, an internal frame was built. Using tenons created a tightly constructed hull but required the labor of skilled carpenters. This style of construction gradually disappeared and, by the early Middle Ages, tenons were no longer used but the planks were still laid edge to edge. (See illustration 16.) To provide structural strength, the ship's frame was now built first and the planks of the hull were then attached to it. This building method came to be known as carvel construction. It was used throughout southern Europe.

In some ways, carvel construction was the reverse of clinker building in that the internal framing was built first and then the planks that formed the hull were attached to it. In carvel construction, the framing was carefully cut with the contours that formed the hull's shape.

Illustration 16. This is a Mediterranean round ship. The image dates to the late 13th or early 14th century but it displays features that were common to the round ship throughout the Middle Ages. While the image is stylized, it captures the tubby shape of such ships. The hull is carvel-built with the strakes laid edge to edge. It has two side rudders with one on each side of its stern. It is lateen-rigged with triangular sails held aloft by very long yards. These yards are so long that each is made out of two beams lashed or *fished* together. While this ship has two masts, single-masted vessels were also common. The front mast is raked forward rather being vertical. The raking permits the use of a large yard and sail (courtesy of the Bibliothèque Nationale de France).

Once the ship's skeleton of framing was complete, the planks were nailed onto the frames to form the hull. Another feature of carvel construction was that the strakes did not overlap. Instead, as mentioned above, the edges of the strakes butted up against each other. Carvel construction was used for building wooden ships up through the early 20th century. It is still used today for crafting wooden vessels.

Carvel and clinker construction each had their merits. Clinker building created a flexible hull. Sea trials of reconstructions of Viking long ships have revealed that this flexibility improved ships' ability to ride the large, rolling waves of northern waters without damage. However, there were limits on the effective size of long ships. With the relatively minimal framing of the long ship, it was possible for the ship to flex and twist too much if the ship was excessively long. Still, clinker-built ships were being constructed up through the end of the Middle Ages. The best recorded were navy ships of massive proportions, such as the English *Grace Dieu*, which is estimated to have had a displacement of 1,400 tons. But to build such ships, shipwrights had to stretch the clinker method to its limits. To provide a stronger and less flexible hull, some of these ships had three layers of planking instead of the usual one layer. Wrecks and other remains of clinker-built ships suggest that 100 feet was likely the longest practical length and most ships built using the clinker method appear to have been shorter than this, with many 75 feet or less. On the sea trials, reconstructions have shown that the flexing of the ship's hull, particularly in heavy seas, causes the seams between the planks to leak, despite the caulking of the seams. Constant bailing was required in such circumstances.

Besides the possible problems with structural integrity, construction of clinker-built vessels required the constant attention of a skilled shipwright. From the outset, it was necessary for the shipwright to ensure that the planks for the hull had been carefully split from the tree trunks in the correct shape and

to make optimal use of the strength of the wood's grain. The quality of the planks was very important since the hull itself gave the ship its shape. The large timbers of the keel and the fore- and after-stems had to be cut from trees carefully selected for having natural shapes that matched the desired components of the ship. Again, it was important that the wood's grain match the finished part of the ship so that the piece would be as strong as possible. For both the keel and the planks of the hull, it was also desirable to have the pieces as long as possible to minimize the number of joints. After all the timbers had been gathered and cut, the shipwright then began the painstaking task of assembling the ship. Throughout this process, especially when attaching the planks to the keel and stems as well as to the adjoining rows of planks, the shipwright had to continually gauge the curve of hull as it took shape to guarantee that the finished ship would have the desired form.

By the 14th century, planks for the hull were sawed rather than split from timbers. While the split planks were stronger, more planks could be obtained from a piece of timber by sawing than by splitting. Additionally, sawn planks were usually wider than split planks. This meant that fewer rows of strakes were needed. This sped up ship construction and minimized the number of seams that had to be kept sealed. Still, hull-first clinker construction was labor intensive and required careful craftsmanship.

Carvel construction created a more rigid hull that resisted being twisted by the actions of waves. Still, the placement of the planks in the hull edge-to-edge created long seams that were vulnerable to separating and leaking. It was essential to carefully seal all the joints with caulk. For safety, seams had to be inspected frequently and recaulked.

Carvel-building permitted construction of much longer ships than clinker-building. Since the primary strength of a ship was in the frame and not in the hull, ships could be built any reasonable length for which a frame could be built. For example, Venetian great galleys were built up to 150 feet long using carvel construction but strong, closely placed framing was required. A galley 110 feet long had framing with 95 ribs, nearly one rib every foot, to support the hull.

Another advantage of carvel-building was in the skills, materials, and money required for construction. An experienced shipwright was needed to design the ship's frame and then oversee its shaping and building. Once the frame was complete, the job was turned over to carpenters and caulkers. While the shipwright continued to supervise the work, he did not need to be constantly present since the task was to nail the boards to form the hull and deck and seal the seams between them. This required skilled carpenters and caulkers but they did not need the high levels of expertise required to form a hull using the clinker method.

As for materials, large, carefully selected long timbers were still needed to form keels and naturally curved pieces were needed to form the stem and key pieces of framing. Shipwrights appear to have often gone out and inspected the available trees to choose the ones that were needed. However, planking was far less critical than in clinker-building. Long, wide, straight-grained planks were desirable, but shorter pieces could be used as well since it was the frame behind the planks that gave the hull its strength. Additionally, unlike northern shipwrights, carvel builders had always used sawn rather than split planks. Again, this maximized the number of planks that could be obtained from a single tree and produced wider planks than if they were split. Carvel-building also required less wood since the planks of the hull did not overlap as in clinker construction. All this meant that more ships could be built using fewer trees. As forests near many Mediterranean ports dwindled, saving wood also saved the expense and effort of bringing timber in from sources some distance away. Having wider planks also reduced the number of rows of planks needed and so cut down on the number of seams, somewhat lessening the risks of leaking.

Besides saving transport costs, using fewer trees simply saved money. Having more of the work done by carpenters and caulkers who were paid far less than a shipwright saved more money. Building a ship was a commercial operation. Since their expenses of having the vessel built were smaller, the owners would recoup their investment cost more quickly and move on to making profits on each voyage the ship made.

Carvel construction eventually became the primary form of ship building throughout Europe but it took until late in the 15th century for northern shipwrights to fully adopt the technique. In some instances, it appears that individual ships' carpenters from the north learned the method while traveling in the south and then returned and taught it to others. This seems to have happened in Brittany and the Netherlands in the 1450s. Capture or abandonment of carvel-built vessels were other means of dissemination. The English captured eight large, Genoese-built carracks in the early 15th century and gained firsthand knowledge of carvel construction. Unfortunately, the English did not master the method quickly. Carpenters and caulkers from Venice, Portugal, and Spain had to be hired to maintain the vessels. It was not until a few decades later that the English built their own carvel ships. In the Baltic in 1462, shipwrights took advantage of the abandonment of a massive French carrack in the port of Danzig (now Gdansk) to examine the secrets of carvel-building. From these various events and likely many more that went unrecorded, carvel-building finally spread to northern Europe. By the end of the Middle Ages, carvel construction was the standard method for building most ships across Europe. Clinker construction remained in use in some parts of northern Europe through the 19th century but only for some relatively small vessels.

Waterproofing

Whether clinker- or carvel-built, the planks of ships' hulls were attached as tightly together as possible. Still, it was necessary to seal the spaces where the ends of planks were joined and the seams between the planks. This was all part of making the entire hull as watertight as possible. Sometimes the caulking material was laid in the seams as the ship was being constructed. More commonly, the caulking was driven into the seams after the hull was built. On clinker-built ships, caulking was usually driven into place with a hammer. On carvel ships, a mallet and caulking iron, which was shaped like a wood chisel, were used to force the caulking into the joints and seams. More caulking may have been required for carvel-built vessels since the seams between the strakes did not overlap. This increased use of caulk is suggested by the fact that references and payments to caulkers were far more common around the Mediterranean than in northern Europe.

Several different fibrous materials were used for caulking. Moss, wool, and animal hair from horses, cows, and goats were among the most common. Other materials included hemp, which was usually in the form of oakum. Oakum were fibers picked from scraps of old rope. Tow, which are coarse flax fibers, and strips of canvas, made from hemp or flax, were also used. Pine tar, pitch, or bitumen (asphalt or coal tar) was often mixed in to glue the fibers in place, fill in any tiny gaps, and make a more watertight seal. Pine resin and rosin were sometimes mixed in as well to make the compound stickier, denser, and even more waterproof.

After caulking was completed, the hull was covered entirely in hot pitch or tar to seal. After this coating had cooled and solidified, the hull was often painted or varnished. A final coating of tallow or grease was typically applied to finish the waterproofing and, in the belief of some, to help the ship slide more easily through the water.

In addition to the hull, seams between the planks of ships' decks were typically waterproofed as well to keep water, such as the spray from waves, from seeping into the ship.

PROPULSION

There were two ways to propel a ship: rowing and sailing. These remained the only means of propulsion until the introduction of the steam engine to ships at the turn of the 18th century.

Rowing

Vessels had been rowed for millennia before the long ships and galleys of the Middle Ages appeared. Rowing had several advantages. It was more reliable than sailing since it was not dependent on the wind. Further, in many situations, rowing could drive a ship faster than sailing over short distances. Vessels that were rowed were also more maneuverable than sailing ships. However, rowing was limited by the strength and stamina of the oarsmen. Peak speed could be maintained only for as long as the rowers could pull the oars. Additionally, depending on the size of the vessel, large numbers of rowers were sometimes required. Carrying sufficient food and water for all the men was a problem on long voyages. And the space needed for these supplies, combined with the room required for the oarsmen themselves, severely limited the cargo capacity of rowed vessels.

On the long ships and other rowed ships of northern Europe, each position was occupied by a single man with a single oar. The number of rowers depended upon the length of the vessel. A 90-foot long ship is estimated to have commonly had 25 to 30 oarsmen on each side of the vessel. Scandinavian oarsmen traditionally used their sea chests as their benches when rowing. As with any rowing, they sat facing the stern. Sitting this way allows the rower to pull the oar and push the vessel forward. This makes optimal use of the oarsman's muscles since he is able to deliver much more power by pulling than by pushing the oar.

In the Mediterranean, merchant and pilgrim galleys were originally *biremes*, that is, they had two men, each with their own oar,

Illustration 17. This picture of a pilgrim galley at the harbor of Rhodes in the 1480s has a wealth of details.

The galley: This is a large Venetian pilgrim galley. It is a lateen-rigged trireme with over 80 oars on each side. The rowers were positioned on benches on deck. As with the round ship, its extremely long yards are made from two timbers lashed together. It has a canopy on the stern which shelters the helmsman and the ship's master. The pilgrims slept below deck. Livestock can be seen in a raised pen near the stern. These animals were slaughtered to provide fresh meat throughout the voyage.

The harbor: The harbor is protected by a mole or breakwater. Thirteen windmills for grinding grain line the mole. This location exposed the mills to the strong winds coming off the sea. On either side of the mouth of the harbor, the ends of the chain used to close the harbor can be seen emerging from the water. The ends of the chain are secured in fortified towers. In the towers, massive winches pulled the chain tight to block the harbor. To open the harbor, as shown in this picture, the chain was slackened so that it sank to the bottom and ships could pass safely over it.

In the background: A fully-rigged ship is lying at anchor. This ship has three masts. The foremast and mainmast are square-rigged while the mizzenmast carries a lateen sail. The mainmast is fitted with a fortified crow's nest. This was a common feature on many ships in the late 15th century in both war and peacetime (91.283 Plate 6.1, detail, *Peregrinatio in Terram Sanctam*, Bernard von Breydenbach, 1486, ink on paper, photograph © The Walters Art Museum, Baltimore).

on each bench. In the early 14th century, a third oarsman was added to each bench. Galleys with three rowers per bench were called *triremes* (see illustration 17). (The additional oarsmen significantly increased the rowing power. A typical merchant trireme had 29 benches on each side. Twenty-five of the benches were manned by three rowers while four had only two rowers. Thus, triremes needed a minimum of 166 rowers but records reveal that they typically carried 175 so there were some extra men to relieve injured, sick, or just tired oarsmen. The higher number of rowers on the galley compared to that of a long ship was due to the heavier weight and greater size of the galley.

On the Mediterranean galleys, oars were 25–32 feet long and weighed around 120 pounds. To make them more wieldy, pieces of lead weighing 25–30 pounds were inserted into their upper ends to help counterbalance them. This added weight actually made it easier to move the oar. Galleys were also fitted with outriggers for the oars. These were long railings mounted along each side of the galley. The oars were attached to the outriggers with leather thongs. The outriggers provided a fulcrum for the oars that made rowing easier and more efficient. For a Viking long ship, oars are estimated to have ranged from 16 to 19 feet in length. The length of the oars depended in part on the size of the ship. Smaller rowing vessels had shorter oars.

Sails and Rigging

In the early Middle Ages, sails in northern Europe were made of long strips of woolen cloth stitched together to make square sails. While woolen sails have been found in use until the end of the period, they were almost completely replaced with canvas sails made from flax or hemp. In southern Europe, canvas sails were used throughout the period. The ropes used for rigging were also made from a variety of materials. In Scandinavia, early medieval ships' ropes were often made from strips of walrus hide and such ropes were

used as late as the 14th century. More commonly, ropes were made of hemp or flax, with hemp being the most widely used.

In medieval Europe, there were two types of sails: lateen and square. The triangular lateen sail was used in southern Europe while the square sail was used in northern Europe (see illustrations 13, 14, 15, 16, 17, 18, and 19). Both types of sails were suspended from a single yard, a long, round beam mounted on a mast. The middle of the yard was attached to the mast with ropes that permitted the yard to be swung around. Yards for lateen sails were much wider than for square rig. They were often as long as or longer than the ship they were mounted on (see illustrations 16 and 17). Some lateen yards were 140 feet long.

Each type of rig had advantages and disadvantages. In storms or very strong winds, the yard of a square rig could be lowered and the sail shortened to reduce its area in order to lessen the force of the winds on the ship and so maintain better control of the vessel. Sails were shortened by reefing. To reef a sail, the sail's lower edge was rolled up and tied off. By the 14th century, the area of the sail could be increased to make better use of the wind in fair weather. This was done by adding "bonnets." Bonnets were strips of canvas that were tied onto the lower edge of the sail to expand the amount of wind that the sail could catch. Lateen rigs lacked both these advantages. Lateen sails could not be reefed. To reduce the size of the sail, it was necessary to lower the yard, remove the sail, and replace it with it a smaller one. This took much more effort than reefing and required carrying additional sails. Some lateen-rigged ships carried up to four sails of various sizes for this purpose. With fair winds, the largest sail would be used to catch as much wind as possible but there was no means of increasing the area of the sail any further. The size of the sail was limited by the size of the yard. Additional canvas could not be added.

The lateen rig had some advantages over the square rig in that it had less drag and could sail using lighter winds than the square rig re-

Top, illustration 18. This 14th century illumination from the *Luttrell Psalter* depicts a hulk outfitted for war. Its castles are manned by an archer and a crossbowman. Its trumpeters are blowing their horns, possibly to announce its departure. A unique feature of this image is the centerline rudder. It is mounted awkwardly on the ship's curved stern. Ultimately, the fully-rigged ships that replaced the hulks were built with flatter sterns. These were better suited to the centerline rudder (© The British Library Board. All Rights Reserved 8/31/2010. License Number: PAUNEW01. Add. MS 42130, f.161v). *Bottom, illustration 19.* This picture from *Decretals of Gregory IX* shows ship-to-ship combat between two cogs. The ships are square-rigged, although the yard has been omitted from the cog on the left. They both have the angled sterns and bows that were the common feature of the cog. Centerline rudders are mounted on their sterns. They have forecastles and sterncastles. On the ship on the left, archers are using the added height provided by the castle to fire into the lower ship on the right. The men-at-arms are using a variety of weapons including a sword, a long club, and what may be a plank (© The British Library Board. All Rights Reserved 8/31/2010. License Number: PAUNEW01. Royal 10 E.IV, f.19).

quired. Lateen-rigged ships also tended to be more maneuverable than square-rigged ones. However, when sailing in adverse winds, the square rig usually performed better. To make headway when winds were blowing at an angle to the desired course of the ship, the sail had to be placed at angle to the wind so that it only caught part of the wind. On the square rig, this was done by turning the yard to one side. The ship then moved forward, although at an angle to its desired direction. By catching only part of the wind, the ship was kept closer to its course than if it were simply allowed to be driven by the full force of the adverse wind. To keep on course, the angle of sail was periodically switched from one side of the vessel to the other. This technique, called tacking, moved the ship in a zigzag along its course. This took much longer than if the ship had been able to sail before the wind, but it was the only way to make headway in unfavorable winds. Tacking was relatively easy with the square rig since the yard could be swung easily. However, it was possible to lose control of the ship if the wind caught the sail from the wrong direction as the yard was turned. This could further slow down the ship as it drifted or was blown off course until control was restored. Tacking was far more difficult with a lateen rig and required more manpower than on a square-rigged ship of comparable size. For the lateen, shifting the sail from one side of the mast to the other required loosening the lower edge of the sail and the ropes bracing the yard. With these loose, the entire yard was turned over, pivoting on the point at which it was attached to the mast. This operation moved the yard and the sail to the other side of the ship. The yard and sail were then resecured. As with the square rig, it was possible to temporarily lose control of the ship during this process. On larger vessels, with yards 100 or more feet in length, tacking was extremely difficult and shifting the yard required dozens of men.

A better sailing rig was a combination of the lateen and square sails. This type of rigging first appeared in southern Europe on ships called *coche* (singular *cocha*). The cocha, the southern version of the cog, was usually constructed with two masts. These ships carried lateen sails on both masts but, in the late 14th century, some were fitted with a square sail on the main mast and a smaller lateen sail on the mizzenmast, the mast near the ship's stern. This combination of sails gave the easy handling of the square-sail rig while the lateen at the stern provided better control turning turns and tacking. The lateen on the stern later evolved into the spanker, which was much easier than the lateen to move from side to side of the mast. The improved coche came to be called *carracks* and were the largest ships built in the Middle Ages. In the 15th century, a third mast was added to the front of the ship, providing additional space for more square sails. By the late 15th century, this combination of sails resulted in the creation of the fully rigged ship which dominated the seas for the next four centuries.

STEERING

A variety of devices were used to steer ships. The earliest means for steering a ship was an oversized oar or paddle. These remained in use for small vessels, particularly on inland waters, throughout the Middle Ages. On seagoing vessels, the steering oars and paddles grew larger as ships grew in size. They evolved into long, blade-shaped boards that were mounted on the sides of vessels (see illustrations 13 and 14). These were the first rudders.

In late antiquity, Roman vessels, both galleys and sailing ships, were fitted with pairs of steering oars. (Modern historians also refer to these as "side rudders.") These were mounted on each side of a vessel's stern and were moved in tandem to steer the ship. A helmsman was required for each oar and most ships carried four helmsmen so they could work in shifts as well as double up to control the oars in heavy seas. The Byzantines, the Italians, and others around the Mediterranean continued using paired side rudders well into the Middle Ages (see illustration 16). As late as the 14th century, pairs of side rudders were used on coche and galleys. For a time in the 14th century, some vessels were fitted with three rudders, with one on each side and another in the center of the stern. This was part of a transition from side rudders to centerline stern rudders.

Side rudders took the form of large wooden blades. Their length varied according to the size of the vessel. They had to be long enough to reach deep enough into the water so that the rudder could effectively steer the vessel. This meant having a rudder that reached at least to the depth of the ship's keel and even longer rudders appear to have been common. To cope with the extreme stresses placed on them, side rudders were usually formed from a single piece of wood to avoid having any joints that could weaken them. They were held in place with ropes or short lengths of chain (see illustration 13). The earliest rudders were turned simply by grasping their upper end and twisting. To make moving the rudder easier, a stout handle was added to the upper end. This was mounted perpendicularly to the rudder and provided the helmsman with a firmer grip on the rudder and better leverage for controlling it (see illustrations 13 and 14).

Single side rudders were also used. As with paired rudders, they varied in size. The longest surviving side rudders from northern Europe are approximately 20 feet long, but most appear to have been much shorter. Based on illustrations and archaeological evidence, single rudders were most common on Scandinavian and other northern European vessels. Single side rudders, sometimes called steerboards in northern Europe, were usually mounted on the right side of the stern (see illustrations 13 and 14). This positioning of the rudder gave rise to the term used by English mariners for the right side of a ship: starboard. German and other Northern European languages have similar words.

Over time, side rudders were replaced by a single centerline rudder. This is the type of rudder familiar to us today. It was a large blade mounted in the middle of the ship's stern on metal hinges formed of gudgeons and pintles (see illustrations, 15, 18 and 19). The rudder pivoted on the hinges. The rudder was turned from side to side using a tiller, a large wooden handle that projected horizontally from the center of the top of the rudder. The helmsman stood at the center of the stern and held the tiller to steer the ship (see illustration 15). This positioning of the tiller and hinges gave the helmsman some leverage when moving the tiller. Near the end of the Middle Ages, a further refinement was added to tillers on large ships. This was the *whipstaff*. With the whipstaff, the tiller was mounted so that it was below the deck. The whipstaff, a long wooden pole approximately five to six feet tall, was attached to the end of the tiller and projected up through a slot in the deck. The whipstaff was fixed to a pivot mounted on the deck. The helmsman steered by moving the whipstaff from side to side, which, in turn, moved the tiller. The whipstaff as well as the simple tiller remained in use for centuries and the tiller is still used today aboard small craft. The next major improvement in steering, the ship's wheel, did not evolve until the late 17th century.

Side rudders were more efficient and created less drag than a centerline rudder. However, there were limits on how large side rudders could be made. Further, very large side rudders were difficult to steer even with the addition of rope and pulleys to move them and hold them steady. These were important factors as ships grew larger and needed bigger rudders. Centerline rudders could be built to any size. They were constructed from several timbers instead of being crafted from a single piece of wood like a side rudder. Their size and thickness made them sturdier than side rudders. Further, the centerline rudder, in its position behind the ship, was more shielded and subjected to less stress than the side rudder. Thus, even though it was made of timbers joined together, this was less of a liability for the centerline rudder than for the side rudder. As for steering, the position of the centerline rudder and the arrangement of the tiller and hinges made it easier to move than a side rudder. Finally, in strong winds and heavy seas, ships were sometimes rolled from side to side. This could lift a side rudder mostly or completely out of the water, leaving the helmsman with little control over the ship. A rudder mounted on the stern did not have this problem and remained mostly submerged except under the most extreme conditions.

By the late Middle Ages, rudders were also typically attached to the ship's stern with chains. These had nothing to do with the operation of the rudder but were safety measures. Rudders sometimes came loose in storms and the chains kept the rudder attached to the ship. The loss of the rudder would be quite serious since it could leave the ship adrift. Some ships even carried spare rudders and this was made a requirement by some jurisdictions.

SUPERSTRUCTURES

In the early Middle Ages, ships usually had a single, open deck. This was either just the exposed inside of the hull or a layer of planks laid over the floor of the hull. Canopies or awnings were sometimes put up to provide some shelter from the wind, water, and sun, but there were no permanent structures. The only exception to this were the galleys of the Mediterranean. Continuing Roman tradition, these usually had a small structure on the stern for accommodating important passengers and the vessel's master (see illustration 17). However, even this shelter was often in the form of a framework to support a canopy rather than a solid, wooden cabin.

Over the course of the Middle Ages, structures became increasingly common on the decks of vessels. By the 12th century, the first superstructures were being built on the decks of sailing ships. These were platforms built on ships during wartime. Civilian vessels were converted for military use by the addition of wooden structures made of an open framework topped with a deck enclosed by wall (see illustrations 14, 15, 18 and 19). These were built on the sterns and bows of ships. They were called "castles." The castle on the stern came to be called the sterncastle and the one on the bow was the forecastle (which evolved into "fo'c'sle" among the terms used by English sailors). Castles were first used on warships to provide an elevated fighting platform. Since sea battles were fought with same weapons as land battles, height gave an advantage to those using arrows, crossbow bolts, javelins, and shot from slings could be used more effectively if one could fire down onto an enemy. (See illustration 18, 19). The sterncastle also sheltered the helmsman during the battle so that he could safely steer the vessel.

Castles became standard features aboard ships in peacetime as well as in wartime. By the 14th century, they were often constructed as part of the ship rather than as a later addition. They were also built with enclosed sides rather than open frameworks. In peacetime, the forecastles provided shelter for the crew. Under the sterncastle, the helmsman could man his position at the rudder and be protected from the weather as well as from attack during battles. However, his view of the sea ahead of the ship was now obscured and he had to rely even more on the navigator to call out directions. Apart from the helmsman and navigator, the shelter of the sterncastle was reserved for the master and the ship's officers. Eventually, the sterncastle, with the addition of internal walls, developed into more comfortable accommodations, which later included cabins for important passengers as well as ranking members of the crew. Beginning in the 14th century, additional decks were added to both the forecastles and sterncastles on some ships, creating more living and storage space as well as raising these structures to make them more effective fighting platforms.

SHIP TYPES

Many types of vessels were used over the course of the Middle Ages. These can be broken down into different types based on contemporary names, images, descriptions, and recovered wrecks. Unfortunately, there was no system of standardized nomenclature for ships during the Middle Ages, unlike later centuries when schooners, brigs, brigantines, etcetera, all had their specific features and could be classified accordingly. Further, ship types evolved over the course of the period. Taken together, this means that there is a considerable amount of guesswork involved in determining what features a particular vessel had at a particular point in time.

Another means of dividing the ship types is geographically. As discussed previously, for much of the Middle Ages, the countries of northern Europe had ship-building techniques and ship designs that were significantly different from those of countries surrounding the Mediterranean. We will divide the ships into the two primary regions and then examine the primary types of ship within each area.

The Mediterranean

In the Mediterranean, the two primary forms of vessels were derived from the Roman galley and round ship.

Galleys

Galleys had been used by the Egyptians, Phoenicians, Greeks, and Romans long before the Middle Ages. They were used as warships, fast courier ships, and passenger ships for important persons. This use of galleys continued into the Middle Ages in the Byzantine Empire. Some of the Italian states also continued the tradition, with galleys serving as warships. It was not until the 13th century that Genoa, Venice, and some other city-states began developing galleys for commercial service. While they still built war galleys, the Italians developed larger galleys, often referred to as "great galleys," to carry compact, high-value cargos such as spices. Later, some of the great galleys were placed in passenger service and ferried pilgrims from ports in Italy to the Holy Land (see illustration 17).

Medieval galleys have been described as sailing ships with oars. Galleys of classical an-tiquity often had masts and sails but these were small and used only for auxiliary power. They relied primarily on their rowers for propulsion. Medieval galleys relied far more on their sails. They were fitted with one or two large masts. Each mast carried a lateen sail. On the great galleys, these sail were quite large (see illustration 17). One contemporary account indicates that galleys typically sailed for at least half the time that they were at sea. The other half of the time included periods when both oars and sails were used as well as times when oars alone were used. Sometimes, oars were relied upon to such a small degree that the full complement of oars was not even taken on board to avoid accidentally damaging them. (This was a concern on leased galleys since those ships' masters or merchants who rented the galley had to pay for any wear and tear of the galley's equipment.) Rowing was done primarily when moving in and out of harbors, when becalmed, or when facing adverse winds. Besides simply being able to move against the wind, rowing could save a galley from being driven onto the shore by strong winds. This reliability regardless of the winds was the main advantage of the galley. Unlike sailing ships, galleys were less prone to being blown off course or forced to stay in port by adverse winds. This gave galleys a relative speed advantage since they could generally keep to their planned course. This also meant that galleys could keep to a schedule better than sailing ships, even if the galley's itinerary included frequent stopovers. Despite all the planned stops, the total time at sea was often shorter than on a sailing ship.

Galleys had large crews. As previously mentioned, Venetian merchant or pilgrim galleys commonly carried 175 oarsmen. There were also usually 25 other crewmen and ship's officers on such a galley. These included the master, the navigator, the helmsmen, and sailors for operating the rigging and sails and performing other necessary work. On Venetian galleys, the 175 oarsmen originally included 30 men armed with crossbows, but by the end of the 14th century these men were forbidden to row and served solely as men-at-arms. Along with archers and other men-at-arms, the large crews of galleys also served as defenders of the ship in case of attack. This deterred pirates. This high level of security was one reason that galleys were used to move valuable cargos. Merchants typically did not take out insurance on loads being carried in galleys because of the security and reliability of these vessels. This savings on insurance helped offset the higher shipping costs of using galleys. Because of their large crews and limited cargo space, shipping via galley appears to have cost twice as much as shipping on a sailing vessel. Fees for passage aboard galleys was similarly higher than passage aboard sailing ships but pilgrims and other passengers considered their greater safety and reliability to be worth the cost.

At the end of the 13th century, Venetians were building great merchant galleys that were 150 feet long. Carvel construction made building such large vessels possible. By increasing the width of the galleys, carrying capacity gradually increased from 150 to 250 tons. While greater cargo space was welcomed by merchants and shippers, the Venetian and Genoese governments limited further increases in size because it made the galleys slower and more difficult to maneuver. This compromised key advantages of the galley over sailing ships and made them unfit for use as military auxiliaries. Given that these governments relied upon impressed civilian ships to build up wartime navies, this was an important concern.

At their peak, the great Venetian galleys sailed to Egypt, the Black Sea, the Middle East, Flanders, and Southampton on the English coast, as well as ports on the Mediterranean coasts of France and Spain and along the north coast of Africa. Venetian commercial galleys continued into the early 16th century but gradually ceased operations between 1452 and 1535. The closing of the Black Sea and parts of the Middle East to European merchants by the Ottoman Turks and competition from large sailing ships, such as the carrack, contributed to the demise of the merchant galleys. The pilgrim galleys experienced a similar decline. In 1384, Venice sent six galleys and one sailing ship with a total of 600 pilgrims to the Holy Land. By the early 16th century, only one galley was sent annually and this was soon discontinued as the obsolescence of the galleys and changes in religious practices greatly diminished the numbers of pilgrims traveling to the Holy Land.

While galleys continued to be built for military use, merchant and pilgrim galleys were gradually replaced by sailing ships as improvements in sailing vessels deprived the galleys of most of their advantages. Developments in design and rigging created sailing ships that were more maneuverable and could operate under more diverse wind conditions. At the same time, it was increasing difficult to recruit the rowers needed to power the galleys and oarsmen came to be drawn from the ranks of criminals, vagrants, slaves, and prisoners of war. These rowers were often kept chained at their positions and could obviously not be trusted to defend the ship if it were attacked. Thus, the large crews of the galleys were no longer an asset in deterring pirates. Further, sailing ships became better suited to attack and defense than galleys. As decks were added, these ships stood taller in the water. This made it more difficult for many types of vessels, including galleys, to attack them. Since combat at sea still relied on missile weapons, such as arrows and spears, and on grappling and boarding, a vessel, such as the galley, that rode lower in the water than its target was at a great disadvantage. For example, there are accounts from the 15th century of vessels attacking carracks, which, being very large ships, towered above them. The attackers circled around the carracks and hurled missiles, but these did little damage since it was difficult to reach the much higher decks of the carracks. Ultimately, the attackers broke off and the carracks sailed on. The proliferation of gunpowder weapons further weakened the galley's position. There was little space for cannons aboard galleys. They were outgunned by the larger sailing ships that could easily carry large numbers of cannons. The galleys were also vulnerable to being fired down upon from the taller ships.

Round Ships

As their name suggests, round ships had relatively blunt bows and sterns. Many were rather wide in comparison to their length so they appeared stubby (see illustration 16). The hull was very rounded as well. The round ship's design dates back to the age of the Roman Empire, when it was the primary form of cargo ship. In the Mediterranean, it continued on into the Middle Ages in this role.

Round ships had one or two masts that carried lateen sails. For steering, they had large, long steering oars mounted on each side of their sterns. They varied widely in size, from 45 to over 100 feet in length. The smaller ones had a single, open deck. The largest ones had two or three decks.

The best documented round ships are those constructed for King Louis IX for France's crusades in the 13th century. They appear to have been a type of round ship referred to as a *buss*. The king's ships were especially big by contemporary standards. They were up to 115 feet in length. The double-decked ones displaced over 300 tons while the triple-deckers displaced 800 tons. These ships were designed for carrying both the crusaders and their horses. It is estimated that the triple-decked ships could carry 100 horses and 300 or more passengers. The horses were loaded on the lowest deck through large hatches on the sides of the ships. When shut, these hatches were sealed and caulked to prevent leakage. When not carrying horses, these ships are estimated to have had a capacity of 600 passengers or more.

Despite its centuries of use, the round ship does not appear to have been a particularly good design. Modern estimates of the speed of round ships range from one knot (one nautical mile per hour) when sailing against the wind and an average of two and a half knots, with a maximum of three knots, when sailing with the wind. In contrast, the square-rigged ships of the north appear to have averaged four knots when sailing with the wind and were capable of speeds of five knots or more with a good wind. Round ships were also susceptible to being blown sideways. On the other hand, it was possible to build very large round ships, as the example above illustrates. This was important because ships capable of carrying heavy bulk cargos were needed to move hundreds of tons of grain or alum (a mineral used in producing cloth) around the Mediterranean. Still, the round ship was eventually replaced by the cocha as the primary cargo ship in the region. As will be discussed in more detail below, the cocha was a version of the cog.

Northern Europe

There was a greater variety of vessels built in northern Europe, although all originated with the double-ended clinker-built vessels used throughout the region but most commonly associated with the Vikings today.

Long Ships

For the first half of the Middle Ages, most ships in the sea around northern Europe were square-rigged, clinker-built vessels which are typically referred to today as "long ships." These ships were designed to be rowed as well as sailed, although sailing was the preferred means of propulsion. They had an open hull which was either left exposed or covered fully or partially with a deck. They were steered with a side rudder that was usually mounted on the right side of the vessel's stern. However, while sharing many common features, these ships varied greatly in size and purpose.

A number of these ships have been recovered from wrecks and burials. The smallest is about 20 feet in length while the largest is nearly 100 feet. Half of the vessels are true "long ships"; that is, they were built as military ships. They are generally very narrow and long and were capable of high speeds both under sail and when rowed. Some merchant vessels have survived. These are wider than the long ships in proportion to their lengths. One wreck has been identified as a coastal trader. Another was an ocean-going trading vessel called a *knaar*. These ships are 40 to 50 feet long. While capable of being moved by oars, these ships were clearly designed more for sailing than for rowing. They have relatively few ports for oars and they appear to have carried small crews. Oars were most likely used for maneuvering in and out of ports. The ocean-going vessel was large enough that it could carry livestock on its open deck and some medieval illustrations show similar ships being loaded with cattle and sheep.

Hulk

The origin of the name hulk and how it later came to denote an old, decrepit vessel is unknown. The hulk was developed in the late 11th century and was built in much the same fashion as the earlier clinker-built ships with a few exceptions. Hulks were built with reverse clinker construction. Instead of each row of planks overlapping the top of the row below it, the lower row overlapped the bottom of the row above it (see illustrations 13, 14 and 18). Like earlier ships, the strakes curved up towards the bow and stern. However, they were not connected to a bow stem or sternpost. Rather, they continued up and were bound together with a metal collar or a ring of stout ropes. Because of its curved shape, the hulk has been called banana-shaped.

Like other northern ships, hulks had a single mast and carried a single square sail. Up through the middle of the 14th century, hulks were fitted with side rudders. The curve of the stern made it difficult to attach a centerline rudder (see illustration 18). Some later hulks were built with straighter sterns. With a straight sternpost, it was more practical to mount a centerline rudder in place of a side rudder. As with other ships, hulks were sometimes fitted with stern- and forecastles which eventually became integrated parts of the vessel.

Hulks were depicted as carrying passengers (see illustration 13) but they were primar-ily used as bulk cargo carriers. No wrecks of hulks have been found and pictorial evidence is unclear. Further, the hulk appears to have evolved greatly over the course of the period. Besides the straightening of the stern already mentioned, the hull became flatter and lost its banana shape. With its broad, flat hull, the hulk is described as having greater capacity than the cog and it appears to have become the primary cargo ship used in northern Europe in the 15th century. However, some of the improvements to the hulk were drawn from other ship types, particularly the cog, and so the hulk of the 15th century was a hybrid and not a purely lineal descendant of the hulk of the 11th century. But this problem of separating ship types is not unique to the hulk. Most ship types evolved over the centuries, often integrating superior features taken from other vessels, and it is difficult to clearly discern when a ship had changed so much that it became new type of vessel. In the end, the hulk disappeared as the much larger carrack became the most widely used cargo ship in the late 15th century.

Cog

The cog was a cargo ship first developed in northern Europe which originated in the 12th century (see illustrations 15 and 19). It was the successor of the long ship–style of vessel. Unlike those of the long ships, the sides of the cog were quite high. This enabled the cog to carry much more cargo. As for their overall shape, cogs were wide in relation to their length. This gave them a somewhat tubby appearance akin to the Mediterranean round ship. While they were not as fast as later narrower ships such as the caravel, they were capable of speeds of four to five knots. Additionally, they had large holds for bulk cargo and bigger cogs could carry 200 tons or more of goods. Cogs were used around northern Europe and formed the backbone of the Hanse trading fleets in the 14th century.

Like the long ship, early cogs were clinker-built, but this changed over time. By the 14th century, northern cogs were built using a combination of clinker construction and laying planks side-by-side rather than overlapping them. The floor of the hull was built with planks laid edge-to-edge but, as the hull began to curve up, the planks were overlapped and fastened together with clinch nails or rivets. While edge-to-edge construction was one of the hallmarks of carvel construction, there appears to have been no link to the Mediterranean style of building. The cog was still built hull-first, although, beginning in the late 12th or early 13th century, some framing was added as the hull was being built. This took the form of beams that spanned the width of the ship and were locked in place by the rows of planks that made up the sides of the hull. These through-beams were needed to provide rigidity and stability to the high-sided hull. They made the ship more resistant to being twisted by waves. The internal framing on the smaller, low-sided, clinker-built ships was inadequate for supporting and reinforcing the larger, taller hulls of the cogs. The use of through-beams became more common in later centuries. The Bremen cog, a ship built around 1380, was approximately 75 feet long and had five through-beams.

Rather than having a curved bow and stern like earlier northern ships, the cog had a straight bow stem and sternpost that were set into the ends of the keel. The bow stem projected out at a very pronounced angle while the sternpost was closer to vertical. The strakes curved up towards the bow and stern but not as much as on earlier clinker-built ships (see illustrations 15 and 19).

Cogs appear to have first been built with only a single open deck. During the 13th century, a second deck was added, creating a covered hold. The addition of the top deck was part of the development of higher sides of the cog's hull. The height of the cog was an advantage in combat since it provided a platform for raining arrows, javelins, and other missiles down on lower vessels. When used in wartime, castles were added to the bow and stern, which further improved the cog's height advantage. The castles came to be retained in peacetime,

although the castle at the bow grew smaller and was omitted entirely on some late medieval cogs. The cog had a single mast and was propelled by one square sail. Up into the 13th century, cogs were fitted with side rudders. In the 14th century, this changed and cogs were fitted with centerline rudders.

Northern cogs sailed south into the Mediterranean as early as the 12th century but did not significantly influence southern ship design until the end of the 13th century and the beginning of the 14th. Traditionally, the first notice of the fully developed northern cog is said to have occurred in 1304 when a party of Basque pirates sailed into the Mediterranean. However, the evidence indicates that the Genoese had begun developing cogs of their own at the end of the 13th century. The Venetians and Catalans soon followed. The result was the cocha. The square sail of the cogs seems to have been the primary advantage of the cog over round ships of the region. As previously discussed, the square sail could be handled more easily and with a smaller crew than the lateen sails that were common in the Mediterranean. The shape of the hull was also better than that of the round ships and the higher sides of the cog were desirable as well since they created larger cargo space than that on the traditional Mediterranean round ship. Further, using carvel construction, the Italians and other southerners were able to build larger versions of cogs than were possible with the hull-first clinker-building of the north. The cocha initially retained the pairs of side rudders used on the round ship but the centerline, sternpost rudder was quickly adopted.

Most coche had a single mast. Some still used a lateen sail but the square sail became more common. By the end of the 14th century, southern cogs were increasingly outfitted with two masts. One was large and mounted in the center of the ship and carried a large, square sail. The second mast was mounted towards the stern and carried a smaller, lateen sail. The square sail provided most of the force for propelling the vessel while the lateen sail greatly assisted in steering. This was an important step towards the eventual development of the fully rigged ship which would become the standard vessel of later centuries.

North Meets South

With the development of the cocha, northern and southern shipbuilding techniques began to merge. While northern shipbuilders did not implement southern methods until the mid– to late–15th century, shipwrights of southern Europe took the hull and rigging of the cog and began making changes and improvements in the 14th century. One result of this was the creation of the carrack.

Carrack

Over the course of the 14th century, Italian shipbuilders developed the carrack from the cocha. The carrack was a very large ship. It was designed primarily for hauling bulk goods such as alum and grain. Most carracks had capacities of several hundred tons and some even reached a thousand tons by the early 15th century. By the end of the century, some carried well over a thousand tons.

Unlike the galley, the carrack was well-suited to making the long voyages from the Mediterranean to the English Channel and North Sea. Carrack crews were much smaller than galley crews and the carracks' huge size allowed them to carry water and food for the crew sufficient for weeks at sea. This greatly reduced the need to make stops for resupplying. In fact, a carrack carrying hundreds of tons of alum from Phocea in Asia Minor sailed all the way to Southampton in England with only one stop in Malaga, Spain. Their smaller crew sizes also greatly reduced the expense of shipping. While a galley had a crew of 170 to 185 men and carried 200 to 250 tons of cargo, a typical carrack could have a crew of 70 and transport 600 to 700 tons. The reduced number of crewmen per ton of cargo cut manpower costs dramatically.

Illustrations typically show it as having a single, immense mast but later carracks had two or even three masts. As previously discussed, with the addition of the other masts, the carrack became the first fully-rigged ship, with two masts carrying square sails and one in the rear carrying a latten sail that made the ship more maneuverable. With the additional sails, carracks were also able to make better use of the wind and move faster.

Caravel

Caravels were lateen-rigged ships used primarily by Portugal and Spain. The caravel was a much smaller ship than the carrack. The earliest caravels appear to have been used as fishing boats and, by the mid–15th century, larger fishing caravels were sailing all the way from Portugal to the Grand Banks off Newfoundland to catch cod. Also beginning in the mid–15th century, the caravel was used in the voyages of discovery by the Portuguese and Spanish. Columbus' ships were all caravels, some of which were surprisingly small.

The caravel's advantages were that they were fast and maneuverable ships with shallow drafts. With their shallow drafts, they were well-suited for coming in close to shore to land parties of explorers. It also made them ideal cargo ships for delivering goods to ports around the Mediterranean. Their speed and handling improved the caravels' ability to dodge the Barbary pirates that increasingly plagued shipping in the Mediterranean.

Small Boats

In the 15th century, large vessels began carrying small boats. Commonly thought of as lifeboats today, these boats were used to ferry people to and from the ship (see illustrations 13 and 17). A pilgrim galley of the late 15th century carried two such boats, one small and one larger. The smaller boat appears to have required six rowers while the larger needed ten. The boats were carried on the sides of the ship's stern. Galleys' sterns were sometimes fitted with stairs leading down to the water so that people could easily board the boats. Some illustrations show large rowboats being towed behind large sailing ships. These boats were used for shuttling passengers and crews between the vessels and the shore. They are not recorded as being used as lifeboats.

Rowboats were also used to help maneuver sailing ships out of ports in a process called warping. Warping was necessary when it was difficult or dangerous for a ship to move out of a harbor under the power of its sails. This would occur when winds were unfavorable or when a harbor was difficult to navigate. To warp a ship, rowboat crews performed the backbreaking task of towing the ship far enough out of the harbor that it could raise its sails and safely move under its own power. Large sailing ships frequently moored some distance offshore to avoid the risks of navigating the shallows of harbors and this also had the advantage of reducing the need for warping.

At some point after the Middle Ages, special anchors were developed to help with warping. These anchors were light enough that they could be carried by the rowboats. A ship would send out the anchor on a rowboat, which would carry it out ahead of the ship and then drop it. The ship's crew then hauled in the anchor cable, pulling the ship out toward the anchor. This laborious process was repeated until the ship could safely raise its sails. This method of warping was also used to try to move a ship into the wind when it was becalmed.

Curraghs

There is one type of seagoing craft that does not fit in any of the categories discussed so far. This is the *curragh* of Ireland. As mentioned previously, small curraghs were used on streams and rivers but there were also much larger versions made of thick ox hides stitched together and stretched over a wooden framework. While they varied in size, some of these curraghs reportedly reached a length of 30 feet and were fitted with one or two masts that each carried a single square sail like other northern European vessels. Curraghs of all sizes were also propelled by rowing. Curraghs

appear to have been surprisingly seaworthy and some larger ones were recorded as making long voyages lasting several weeks. In the 6th century A.D., Saint Brendan of Ireland was said to have sailed around many parts of the North Atlantic in such a curraugh, ultimately reaching Newfoundland. In the late 1970s, a modern reconstruction of a large, two-masted curraugh successfully made this voyage and proved the feasibility of Saint Brendan's voyage.

The Crew

In the Middle Ages, as today, ships needed a number of men to sail them. Small ships had crews of only a half-dozen sailors while the largest required scores of men. In addition to the sailors, there were the ships' masters and other men with specialized skills that were vital to the ship's operation.

THE MASTER

The commander of the ship was the master. He was not referred to as "captain" during the Middle Ages. "Captain" referred to a military leader or officer, usually of armies, but the Italians did use the word *capitano* as a title for a commander in charge of an armed fleet. The application of "captain" to ships' masters was a later development that originated with such military practices. Among the Flemish and Germans, the master was called *schipp herr*, meaning "ship master." Over time, this title was adopted in English as *skipper*.

Masters did not undergo a formal apprenticeship, but they had years of experience at sea. In the early Middle Ages, it was possible for an ordinary sailor to work his way up to master but this became nearly impossible to do as the period progressed. Throughout the Middle Ages, most masters appear to have been from families of established masters or other relatively well-off families with connections to shipping, such as merchants who routinely traveled along with their goods. Sons from these families would sail with their fathers or be placed with others to learn the trade of sailing a ship. Completing this informal apprenticeship was no guarantee of employment as a master. They did not become one until someone had enough confidence in them to trust them with a ship.

Many ships' masters owned their own ships or at least a share in them. Ships were expensive and so it was common for several merchants and the ship's master to pool their money to buy and operate a ship. They could then either transport their own merchandise aboard the vessel or take on the cargos of other merchants for delivery. The master was paid based on his share of ownership. For example, if he owned a quarter share of the vessel, he received a fourth of the profits from a successful voyage. In addition, masters were typically allowed to bring along some merchandise of their own to trade for their personal profit.

Some masters were employees of ship owners rather than partners. This appears to have been most common in the Mediterranean, where galley masters were hired by the groups of merchants who owned the vessels. The masters, like the rest of the crew, were hired just for the duration of a single voyage. In addition to their pay, masters were typically granted the privilege of carrying along some merchandise of their own to trade. They were responsible for hiring and paying the crew. They could also fire them.

Sometimes, masters and even ship owners did not have complete control of selecting the crew. In 13th century Genoa, merchants who were traveling along with their trade goods were sometimes able to include a provision in their shipping contracts that entitled them to choose an experienced sailor to serve as a member of the crew. He was responsible for determining that the ship was seaworthy and carried adequate equipment and spare parts and reporting his findings back to the merchants. There were similar practices in

Venice. On Venetian ships, merchants had some authority over the hiring and firing of the crewmen. They were also responsible for confirming that the vessel was carrying the required arms and armor for the crew. They checked the ship's stores and rations as well to ensure that there were adequate supplies. The merchants were given these powers and responsibilities since, like the masters, their lives depended on the performance of the crew and ship.

While many masters were partners of the other owners of the ships and some were employees of the owners, all masters were the sole commanders of their vessels once the voyage began. There are some accounts that suggest that masters consulted with their crews about decisions such as whether the wind was favorable for setting out, but, for effective operation of the ship, the master must have had firm control and the final say on how the ship was run. He disciplined his crewmen as needed. He made the decisions about whether to run before a storm or put into port. He was the one ultimately held responsible for the safety of his vessel and the success of its voyage.

Aboard larger ships, masters had subordinates like modern ship's officers and mates to help supervise the crew and see that orders were carried out. Most were experienced mariners while some were likely young men in training to become masters. The navigator was also a ship's officer, as was the captain of the marines on those vessels that carried these men-at-arms. Even aboard ships that did not have marines, there was sometimes a master-at-arms who was responsible for keeping the ship stocked with weapons and armor for the crew to use in case of attack. In addition, some large pilgrim galleys carried ship's surgeons and cooks. Ships sometimes carried trumpeters as well (see illustrations 14 and 18). The Venetian government required all galleys to include trumpeters as part of their crews. The trumpets were used to announce the ship's departure, to warn other ships of the galley's presence to avoid collisions, and to make other signals.

Scribes were also employed aboard pilgrim galleys and some cargo vessels to assist the master by keeping records of important business transactions. With the master, he enrolled the crewmen when they were hired and kept track of their wages. On pilgrim galleys, he kept the passenger list and the passengers' contracts with the galley's master. The contracts were sometimes needed to settle the disputes that arose when passengers argued that they were not receiving the food and lodging that they had paid for. On cargo vessels, the scribe recorded the shipping contracts that the master made with merchants. He kept all the ship's financial accounts, including the weights and values of all merchandise loaded and unloaded from the ship and all the money received and paid out during the voyage. This financial information was used for settling accounts with the merchants. Besides keeping the accounts and recording the contracts made by the master, the scribe also wrote down contracts for others aboard the ship, including merchants, passengers, and crew members, when they engaged in any business dealings.

THE NAVIGATOR

Navigators were responsible for setting the ship's course and adjusting it as needed. They were often referred to as pilots. Like masters, navigators appear to have served informal apprenticeships. They learned how to navigate by the sun and stars as well as recognize the prevailing winds and currents of their routes. By the 12th century, at the latest, they were also using compasses. The skills, methods, and tools used by the navigator are discussed more fully in the later section on navigation.

Masters sometimes served as navigators as well. This was particularly suitable along well-established routes which the master had made many times during his years of learning his trade.

As with many masters, navigators were typically engaged for the voyage. Some may have developed working relationships with certain masters or ship owners and were able to serve on the same ships repeatedly. Many navigators appear to have specialized in certain routes or regions. They should have had the skills to navigate even in unfamiliar waters, and many did, but the nature of commercial shipping meant that vessels often sailed between the same ports or groups of ports so they developed particular skill in negotiating the hazards of these routes. An account of a pilgrimage to the Holy Land in the 1480s states that a navigator who entered unfamiliar waters was supposed to take his ship into the nearest port and relinquish his post to a local navigator who knew the sea ahead.

There were also specialized navigators who were "pilots" in the modern sense of the word. These were navigators sent out by ports to guide ships into harbor. Some ports had narrow entrance channels or other hazards such as shoals or peculiar currents. The port pilot took over from the ship's regular navigator to bring the ship safely in. He would also guide the ship out when it left. Port cities collected fees for this service.

THE ASTROLOGER

In the same pilgrimage account mentioned above, the author, a Dominican friar, states that the navigator of the large galley on which he was traveling was aided by astrologers. They watched the stars and winds and pointed out the way for the ship's course. They made weather predictions based on the stars and natural phenomena such as the schooling of flying fish and the smell of the bilge water. But they also used astronomical instruments to track the movement of the stars and could determine the time of night by the position of the stars. All this suggests that these men practiced both astrology and astronomy, along with a little prognosticating based on practical experience and some magic. This mixing of science and pseudo-science was not unusual. Even universities sometimes taught astrology along with astronomy. What is unusual is that a navigator would need assistance in determining direction by the stars and prevailing winds. Perhaps these specialists were needed for their ability to use astronomical instruments. Since the shipboard use of the quadrant, astrolabe, and other devices was still relatively new at the time, not all navigators may have been entirely competent in their use. It is difficult to determine how widespread the employment of such astrologers was since it is mentioned only in this author's account of sea travel. The astrological portion of their duties seems to hark back to ancient times when mariners relied on seers to read the omens and advise them of the gods' intentions.

THE HELMSMAN

The steersman or helmsman was responsible for the actual task of steering the ship (see illustrations 13, 14 and 15). Aboard smaller vessels, the master or navigator may have served in this role. However, this duty was most often performed by other members of the crew. Holding a steering oar, side rudder, or the tiller of a stern rudder on course was difficult and very tiring work. It took strong men to man the helm, especially in heavy weather or other dangerous conditions. Helmsmen were often recognized specialists. For example, on 13th century Italian galleys that were fitted with two steering rudders, one on each side of the ship's stern, four helmsmen were employed. This allowed the helmsmen to work in shifts and to have assistance when needed. Aboard smaller vessels, there may not have formally been a position of helmsman, but the duties were carried out by sailors who developed particular skill in this important task.

THE SHIP'S CARPENTER AND THE CAULKER

Some ships carried their own carpenters. These specialists could repair the ship either at sea or in foreign ports. Ships' carpenters appear to have often been journeymen ship-building carpenters. They served aboard ship to hone their skills. When their time at sea was finished, they would work in shipyards or, if fortunate, even establish their own yard when they were a master shipwright.

Some ships, most notably galleys in the Mediterranean, carried caulkers as part of the crew. The caulker was responsible for keeping the ship watertight by ensuring that the spaces between the planks of the hull were filled and tightly sealed with tar, pitch, and other materials. In constructing ships, Italian caulkers also performed extensive carpentry work since they were tasked to attach all the planks exposed to sea water, including the entire hull. Thus, they had the experience and knowledge needed to maintain and repair vessels.

THE SAILORS

The sailors performed the bulk of the work aboard the vessel and formed the majority of the crew, except aboard galleys, which had far greater number of rowers than sailors. They hauled up the anchor either by hand or, later, with the help of a winch or capstan. They raised and lowered the massive yards that held up the sails. They trimmed the sails and performed all the other myriad tasks that kept the ship running (see illustration 14).

Most sailors appear to have begun their training as ships' boys. These boys learned how to sail by performing small tasks around the ship. One such task was the important duty of turning the ship's sand- or running-glass every half hour. This was an essential part of the ship's navigation equipment. Throughout, they watched how the men worked and began helping them whenever they could. As their experience and knowledge grew, they became sailors themselves. With more years of service, they could be given additional duties and supervise other sailors, like modern mates and boatswains. A few may have even learned navigation. And, as previously mentioned, a select few advanced to being masters. However, such advancement was rare and most remained sailors all their lives.

THE OARSMEN

On galleys, large numbers of men were needed to pull the oars. One hundred and fifty to one hundred and eighty oarsmen were required for the typical galley used for trade or passenger service from Italy to the Holy Land in the late Middle Ages. These merchant galleys were built in the Italian city-states and operated from their ports. For most of the Middle Ages, rowers were free citizens. They were not criminals or slaves. Like the rest of the crew, they were paid professionals. They earned about the same wages as other laborers who performed strenuous work. Skilled oarsmen were needed to set the pace of the rowers' strokes. These specialists were paid more than ordinary rowers.

Having free men as oarsmen was important in the defense of the galleys. If attacked at sea, the rowers were issued weapons and fought alongside the rest of the crew. This meant that a galley had over 200 armed men to defend it. This made galleys very difficult to attack successfully and was one reason that galleys were used for high-value cargos such as spices. This protection was also a reason that galleys were popular as passenger ships for those who could afford them.

Finding sufficient numbers of oarsmen became a major problem. Many men considered the pay too low for the back-breaking work and harsh conditions. In 1330, the city-state of Venice had such difficulty finding oarsmen for its fleet of galleys that it began releasing men from debtors' prisons to serve as rowers. Some of these men were, in fact, oarsmen and other sailors who had fallen into debt. Along with men who could find no other employment, oarsmen were increasingly drawn from the ranks of these paupers and debtors. Still, they were all free men and not slaves or criminals and could be counted upon to defend their galleys. But the pool of free oarsmen continued to dwindle. As late as 1412, the Venetian government issued regulations requiring that oarsmen were to be well-paid free men and not slaves or convicted criminals.

This was still not enough to keep the galleys fully crewed. In 1443, the king of France authorized forcing criminals and vagrants to row the galleys of his navy. This practice spread throughout the Mediterranean for both merchant and naval vessels. By the end of the 15th century, many galleys were rowed by convicts and slaves, including captured Moslems. A few free men who were desperate for money also served as oarsmen. By the mid–16th century, galleys from Tuscany were crewed entirely by convicts and slaves. In Venice, navy galleys operated with free men as well as convicts and slaves up until the end of the 16th century. Some of the free men were provided through quotas levied on the city's guilds by the government. The rowers were divided based on their status. On some galleys, all the oarsmen were convicts or slaves while others had only free men as rowers. On military galleys, prisoners of war were sometimes used as oarsmen as well.

Galley slaves are typically imagined as being chained to their benches day and night and beaten to make them work. An account of a pilgrimage aboard a Venetian galley in the 1480s confirms that much of this was true. The rowers suffered harsh discipline with regular beatings. They were fed poor-quality food. They had no quarters. Instead, they had to sleep at their benches on the open deck. However, they were usually left unchained and were free to engage in other activities when they were not rowing, such as when the galley was moving under sail. They gambled for money, sang, played musical instruments, and even practiced some trades to earn money. For example, some made clothing or shoes and sold these to passengers or in port. Some sold fresh fruit and other foods they had picked up in port to passengers who were short on supplies. Others washed passengers' clothing for pay. Thus, they had some little freedom but were generally treated little better than beasts of burden.

The legendary Viking ships and other ships of Scandinavia were quite different from the late medieval galleys. Their rowers were all free men. Further, in addition to rowing, they performed all the other functions of sailors. Aboard Viking ships, they were warriors as well. On land, these men were the raiding party and at sea they were the ship's marines.

THE MARINES

Most vessels, even merchantmen, carried some weapons for their defense. Some even used them to commit acts of piracy. Merchant ships were sometimes specifically ordered to carry arms and armor for their crews. The best documented of such regulations come from the city-state of Venice, which required that weapons and some basic armor had to be supplied for the crew. Initially, sailors had brought their own weapons and helmets but, by the 14th century, ships' masters were responsible for furnishing this gear. This included helmets, shields, spears, axes, and other weapons. As mentioned previously, the regulations also required that a number of bowmen were to be included in the crews of galleys.

At times, professional men-at-arms were added to the crew for additional protection. These were marines who specialized in shipboard combat. Venetian shipping regulations sometimes required merchant galleys and sailing ships to carry a number of marines. Marines used a variety of weapons including swords and spears as well as missile weapons such as bows, crossbows, and javelins. These warriors served aboard ships to deter attacks by pirates or hostile warships. When deterrence failed, they would first shoot their bows and throw javelins when the attacking ship came within range. When the attacker came alongside, its crew would typically grapple the other ship and hand-to-hand combat, just like on land, would ensue (see illustration 19).

Conditions Aboard Ships

Besides the life-threatening dangers of storms and pirates, passengers on medieval ships also faced the simple discomforts of dismal accommodations, poor-quality food, seasickness, and boredom.

ACCOMMODATIONS

In the early Middle Ages, accommodations were primitive. In the seas around northern Europe, early ships were epitomized by the Viking long ship. As previously discussed, these ships had open hulls with no shelters for the crew or any passengers. Planking was sometimes laid directly over the floor of the hull to create a deck. This became standard over time but the ships remained open-topped. The crew lived and worked on the bare deck. As late as the 12th century, even royalty and high-ranking clerics were still depicted as traveling in open ships (see illustration 13). There were likely temporary canopies or tents erected to provide cover from the elements. A canopy would have provided shade from the sun as well as some limited protection from rain. The canopy would most likely have been placed on the vessel's stern, away from the spray breaking on the bow. Based on later practice, the ship's master, navigator, and any other ship's officers and important passengers would be the only ones permitted in this shelter.

In the Mediterranean, the Roman shipbuilding traditions persisted. Some oar-driven ships had open hulls like northern ships but most galleys, including all larger ones, were constructed with two decks. As with northern ships, one deck was laid on the floor of the hull. Since they had a deeper hull, there was room to build a second deck above the first. This formed a roof for the deck on the floor of the ship's hull. The space between the decks was the ship's hold. This cramped space was used for cargo and, on pilgrimage galleys, for passengers. On the top deck, there was often an area on the ship's stern that was covered by a canopy or awning (see illustration 17). This area was for the use of the ship's master and other VIPs. There were sometimes additional structures built on deck, most commonly at the bow, that provided some shelter for the crew. In the early Middle Ages, the stubby sailing ships of the Mediterranean were often depicted like northern ships in that many were open-hulled with a single deck. However, some clearly had two decks but none appear to have had any permanent shelters on deck. They, too, may have had temporary shelters in the form of canopies.

As discussed in the section on shipbuilding, as the Middle Ages progressed, a number of features developed that created enclosed spaces aboard sailing ships throughout Europe. The second deck became more common on ships across Europe and some large ships even had a third. As on the galleys, the hold between the decks was used for cargo but could also be used for passengers on pilgrim ships. There are few, if any, mentions of the crew occupying the hold. There were some very practical reasons for this. In general, holds were cramped. In warmer weather, their air was stale and hot. This was even worse on pilgrim ships, where the hold was packed with its living cargo. Accommodations below deck aboard pilgrim ships were noted for their foul air. Except in bad weather, it must have been far more pleasant to camp out on deck than below it. Further, aboard pilgrim galleys crewed with slave and convict oarsmen, these men were explicitly forbidden from going into the hold because of the risk that they would steal from the passengers.

Another improvement was the addition of a wooden structure on the stern (see illustrations 14, 15, 18 and 19). As mentioned previously, this was the aftercastle or sterncastle. It was first developed aboard ships used in military service. It was originally a raised wooden platform that provided men-at-arms with a higher position from which to fight. Like a wooden version of the canopy, it provided a sheltered space which was used as accommodations for the ship's master and others who merited such a privilege. Aftercastles became common aboard all ships, civilian as well as military. Walls and additional decks were eventually added to create compartments or

cabins. For example, on a late–15th century pilgrim galley, the aftercastle had three decks. The helmsman and the compass were stationed on the top deck. This deck was roofed with a canopy. The middle deck had accommodations for the ship's master and officers and for wealthy and important men. Ladies occupied rooms in the lowest deck because it was the most secure. This was the area where the master stored the most valuable items on the vessel and access was tightly controlled.

As with the ship's stern, a castle was added to the bow. This was the forecastle (later called the *fo'c'sle* in nautical terms). It, too, created a permanent covered space. This area was used for storage of ropes and other gear but was also claimed by the sailors as their accommodations. Merchants and any other passengers were not welcome in the forecastle.

So, if they were not permitted in the fo'c'sle and excluded from the accommodations in the stern, either because there was no room or because they could not pay for it, where did passengers stay on a cargo ship? They may have been left to huddle in their clothing or under blankets on the deck as the crew likely did. This would have been the only option in open-topped boats, particularly in the early Middle Ages. Later, some passengers appear to have been permitted to build temporary shelters on the deck. The earliest shelters were likely simple canopies or tents. Later in the period, merchants who were traveling with their goods are known to have built small wooden structures that have been described as small shacks. These were likely made up of prefabricated walls and roofs. As with tents and canopies, the shacks were set up every night and taken down and stowed every morning since the deck had to be kept clear so the sailors could perform their work unimpeded. In the later Middle Ages, under the terms of their shipping contracts, merchants traveling on galleys frequently had the right to some space in the aftercastle for sleeping and storing their personal belongings. A 14th century Venetian regulation on galleys specified that a merchant shipping a significant amount of merchandise was entitled to a space two feet wide for sleeping and was allowed to bring a chest, mattress, blanket, traveling bag, and arms for himself and his servant. The servant presumably had to find his own spot on the deck for sleeping. As aftercastles became a standard feature on most cargo vessels and grew in size, accommodations in cabins in the aftercastles became more common.

Passenger Ships

Many vessels would carry passengers on an ad hoc basis. Merchants or their agents would travel on cargo vessels along with their merchandise. Other people likely booked passage aboard any ship that happened to be headed to the right destination. This practice continued into modern times with people traveling on "tramp steamers." Not all sea travel involved finding space aboard a cargo ship. There were some ships which were built or, more commonly, temporarily modified to carry passengers.

In the Middle Ages, few ships were built solely for passenger service. Even at a busy crossing point such as that between Dover and French ports across the English Channel, there appears to have been no vessels that carried only passengers. Travelers had to find space aboard cargo ships. When large groups, such as retinues of kings, needed to cross, cargo ships were temporarily refitted for passenger service. There were occasional exceptions to this, as when a king or noble owned his own ship. These ships were permanently equipped for carrying their elite passengers in suitable style and comfort. However, even ordinary ships could be fitted with royal suites with surprising speed. The most common conversion of cargo ships into passenger vessels was during wartime (see illustrations 18 and 19). Cargo ships quickly became troop transports when needed. This was done during the Crusades to move men to fight in the Holy Land. In the Hundred Years' War, the English pressed vast numbers of ships into military service several times to take soldiers to France. Modifications

include adding the castles discussed above. They may have also involved constructing partitions to create living quarters or at least space suitable for men and their supplies. Similar alterations were needed to make stalls for horses. Since both the single deck of the open-topped ships and the holds of ships with two decks were typically open spaces with no walls to begin with, these modifications could be made relatively easily and quickly. They could be removed with similar ease to return the vessels to commercial service.

In a few instances, there were ships specially built to carry people. One example was the fleet constructed by William the Conqueror for the invasion of England in 1066. Another is from the 13th century when King Louis IX had ships built to take his crusaders to invade North Africa.

The most noted ships for transporting passengers were the pilgrim ships. Pilgrims sailing between Italy and the Holy Land accounted for the largest number of ships' passengers in the Middle Ages (see illustration 17).

The Pilgrimage Trade

Over the course of the Middle Ages, untold thousands of people made the pilgrimage from Europe to the Holy Land. In the early Middle Ages, the trip was commonly made by land through Asia Minor but this route became unsafe as Moslem Turks conquered that region. Pilgrims then began sailing from Europe to the Holy Land, primarily from ports in Italy. While exact figures are lacking, it appears that a few thousand traveled by galley and sailing ship every year until late in the Middle Ages when the popularity of pilgrimages declined.

The pilgrimage trade was a unique form of shipping. Transporting large numbers of people on a regular basis required reliable service and an infrastructure to support it. Both Genoa and Venice competed for the pilgrimage trade but Venice succeeded in becoming the primary port engaged in carrying pilgrims to the Holy Land for most of the Middle Ages. The success of the Venetian pilgrimage trade rested on the city's galleys. Although Genoa and other city-states also had galleys, Venice based a large part of its economy on them. In Venice, the state-run Arsenal built war galleys and some of the merchant galleys. Both government-built and private galleys were subject to regulation of their use.

As discussed in the section on ship construction, galleys were fitted with masts and sails but were also powered by oars. The oars were used for moving the vessel in and out of ports and when becalmed or facing unfavorable winds. These abilities made it possible for galleys to generally keep to a schedule and provide reliable and relatively fast service. Having large numbers of oarsmen also deterred attacks by pirates since these men could be armed to defend the ship. However, this advantage gradually disappeared as slaves and convicts increasingly replaced free men as rowers in the 15th century. The biggest drawbacks of the galleys were their limited cargo space and the expense of their large crews. This led to their being used primarily for moving compact, high-value items, such as spices from Egypt or fine, quality cloth from Flanders. They were also suited for carrying pilgrims who were willing to pay premium prices for reliable and relatively fast passage to the Holy Land. Passage on a galley was more expensive than on a sailing ship but those pilgrims who could afford it chose to travel by galley. Christian pilgrims were not alone in appreciating the advantages of the galley. Jews traveling between Europe and the Holy Land sometimes sailed aboard Venetian pilgrim galleys. One explained that this was because of the safety and reliability of the galleys.

Safety Regulations

To protect this valuable trade, the Venetians, beginning in the 13th century, enacted regulations and other measures to assist pilgrims in arranging travel and to safeguard them during their voyage. Some of these statutes addressed administrative matters but most directly addressed safety at sea. These measures protected the lives of passengers and crews but they were also good business for the city of Venice. Most regulations addressed overloading of ships. Overloading was a common problem since masters and ship owners made more profit with each additional pilgrim they could pack into their ships. But the city was willing to curb individuals' greed to maintain the city's commercial fleet and to protect Venice's dominance in the pilgrim trade. Losing ships because of overloading meant losing the revenue that the ships would have generated and it would hurt the city's reputation as the premier port for pilgrimages. In fact, the safety regulations may not have just protected Venice's position but may well have brought in more business for the city as pilgrims chose Venetian galleys over those of other cities because of their reputation for safety.

The Venetian government licensed the private galleys that were permitted to carry pilgrims. Pilgrims were advised to inspect several galleys before signing a contract for passage so that they could get the best accommodations they could afford. The *tholomarii*, official guides licensed by the Venetian government, could arrange meetings with ships' owners or masters so that pilgrims could tour their vessels. Unofficial guides also operated. These were servants of masters and ship owners of competing galleys. These men approached pilgrims and proclaimed the merits of their particular master's ship. Another form of advertising was the display of a large white banner marked with a red cross. This was set up on the dock next to a ship to indicate that it was available for pilgrimage bookings.

To avoid disputes, well-advised travelers carefully read their contracts for passage before signing. Besides designating the pilgrim's berth, the contract typically specified the food and drink to be provided by the master. The contract sometimes required that the ship be adequately crewed with both sailors and armed marines as well as oarsmen. This provision just confirmed the master's compliance with the Venetian laws on this point.

After the contracts were completed, the space assigned to each pilgrim was usually marked out in chalk on the deck in the ship's hold. The spaces were usually only two feet wide. In part, marking the spaces ensured that there was adequate space for each pilgrim and his supplies and other belongings. It was also done to prevent arguments over accommodations. Before sailing, inspectors toured the ship to be sure that there was a space for each passenger. Pilgrims were also advised to view their spaces before paying for their passage.

Prior to sailing, a safety inspector examined the galley to determine whether it was seaworthy. The inspector also confirmed that the galley was not overloaded by checking iron rods mounted on the side of the ship. These rods were marked with the level of the ship's waterline when the vessel was empty and the level when the ship was loaded to its maximum approved load. The rods were also marked in inches and fines were imposed based on the number of inches that the galley was below its safe level. An extra inch was sometimes allowed for the weight of the weapons, shields, and helmets the galley carried to arm its crew. For sailing ships, white crosses painted on the hull served the same purpose as the iron rods. Ensuring that the galley was not riding dangerously low in the water protected the pilgrims from greedy masters and ship owners who would have otherwise overloaded their ships.

Another safety measure was intended to protect the vessel after it was underway. As mentioned previously, for pilgrim ships and other vessels, the Venetians required that trumpeters be part of the crew (see illustrations 14 and 18). These men signaled the location of their ships with their instruments to warn other vessels and prevent collisions, like an early form of siren or air horn. Based on practices elsewhere in medieval Europe, warning trumpets were a common feature in busy harbors. One such horn has been found in London. Unlike shouting, the loud blare of the trumpets could be heard above the din and for some distance across the water. It caught people's attention. For Venice, this warning system was likely used on the open sea as well.

For both pilgrim and merchant galleys and ships, the Venetians often traveled in convoys. Vessels could drift dangerously close to one another. Trumpeting was the best means available to try to warn other ships while there was hopefully still enough time and distance to change course.

Accommodations Aboard Pilgrim Ships

As with the great ocean liners of the last century, accommodations on medieval pilgrim ships varied greatly. The greater nobility could afford to charter a ship for themselves and have it stocked with all the luxuries of home, with enclosed cabins with soft beds and windows as well as gourmet food prepared for them by their own chefs. Even aboard ordinary ships, wealthier pilgrims could book cabins adjoining those of the ship's master and officers and enjoy the best rooms available. But for most pilgrims, accommodations were limited to a space in the ship's hold that was just large enough to lie down in.

Regardless of any regulations and inspections, accommodations for common pilgrims on galleys were notoriously cramped and unpleasant. Space on the galleys was very limited and only 100 pilgrims could typically be packed into their holds. The pilgrims were placed with their heads against the inside of the hull and their feet pointed towards the ship's centerline. Their supplies were piled at their feet. This positioning made optimal use of space, enabling the maximum number of pilgrims to be crammed in. To make matters worse, as with all other medieval ships, the clearance between decks was low by modern standards and there were no portholes. The only light and air came from the few hatches in the deck above. Given that the pilgrimage sailing season was primarily during the warmest months of the year, the hot Mediterranean climate must have made it suffocating and sweltering in the poorly ventilated hold. Further, the deck on which the pilgrims were billeted lay directly over the ship's bilge. This was filled with sand to ballast the galley but there was also a well that collected the water that seeped into the ship. The foul, stagnant water in the well added a bad odor to the already hot, unpleasant air.

Most sailing ships used for transporting pilgrims carried as many or more passengers than the galleys. Most appear to have carried several hundred pilgrims but, by the mid–13th century, there were much larger ships sailing to the Holy Land. In 1250, one enormous sailing ship is recorded as carrying 1,100 pilgrims, plus a crew of 75. The number seems to be an exaggeration but, in the later Middle Ages, large sailing ships were sometimes built with three full decks and had a far greater capacity than an average galley with its small hold. Further, some ships of this type served both as pilgrim ships and as bulk cargo carriers. With their large, open decks, they could easily switch between carrying passengers and carrying bulk goods such as grain. At this time, such cargo vessels were reaching capacities of 500 tons and more. Thus, some very large pilgrim ships did exist and modern experts estimate that 1,000 pilgrims could have been carried on a single large sailing ship.

The surviving records of conditions aboard pilgrim ships are mostly about traveling by galley. However, conditions aboard sailing ships were likely the same. The ships may have been larger than galleys but that just allowed room for more passengers to be packed in, rather like on jumbo jets today.

Pilgrims were allowed on deck during the day but had to return to their allocated space to sleep. These tight quarters were nearly intolerable when all the pilgrims turned in for the night. Some people tried to take up more than their allotted space while others snored loudly or talked in their sleep. Some stayed up chatting late into the night. Others came to bed after the lights were out with their candles shining on the faces of those trying to sleep. To make matters worse, mice and rats would run across the sleepers. All these annoyances were too much for some passengers and fights sometimes broke out.

Pilgrims brought their own mattresses, sheets, blankets, and pillows. One guidebook advised that these items were essential and, according to the author, could be resold to another pilgrim when the journey was completed. The crew used mattresses as well. Hammocks did not come into use until after the Middle Ages. Hammocks may have been used aboard ships of the Athenian fleet in the 5th century B.C. but they soon disappeared, if, in fact, they had ever existed. There is one illustration of what appears to be a hammock in the margin of a 14th century English manuscript but it is not in a nautical context. Two men are suspending it from two letters in the manuscript. There is no other evidence of hammocks until the end of the 15th century, when Columbus is generally credited with the introduction of hammocks to Europe from the Americas. Their use spread slowly. For example, the British Royal Navy did not adopt them until the 17th century.

Near the end of the Middle Ages, when fewer people went on pilgrimages, there appears to have been some improvement in accommodations aboard the ships. Some travelers noted that they were able to hang sheets or even use collapsible wooden screens to provide some privacy.

TOILETS

Most early medieval sailing ships had no toilet facilities for the passengers or crew. They were expected to relieve themselves over the side of the ship. Aboard a galley, even in the early Middle Ages, there were more options. For the master and important passengers, a toilet complete with a seat was housed in a small projection off the ship's stern. For the crew and common passengers, such as most pilgrims, there were two toilets mounted on the ship's bow; one on each side of the galley's prow. Based on post-medieval examples, these toilets were wooden box- or barrel-shaped structures with a seat on the top and open at the bottom. The prow seems an odd place for the toilet but the stern was off limits to most people and going over the galley's side may have been impractical since the rowers and their benches and gear lined each side of the vessel. Other than off the stern, the prow offered the only direct drop into the sea. It was also constantly washed clean by the waves breaking on the bow. The limited number of toilets was often a problem. One pilgrim recorded that there were sometimes long lines for the toilets on his galley.

In bad weather, the spray and rain left passengers soaked when using any of the places designated as toilets. The same pilgrim said that some stripped naked before going from the hold out to the bow so that they at least had dry clothes to come back to. The lack of privacy aboard pilgrim ships, including when using the toilet, was used as an argument against letting women go on pilgrimage. Proper modesty could not be maintained in such difficult circumstances. The only exception might have been for ladies who could afford cabin space and had access to the more private toilets that emptied off the stern.

As more sailing ships were fitted with castles and cabins, sheltered toilets became far more common. For example, a merchant cog built in Bremen in 1380 had a toilet with a seat mounted at the stern of the vessel sheltered by the castle deck. As with galleys, it projected out from the ship. This toilet was still reserved for the use of the ship's officers and any privileged passengers on board. Ordinary passengers and crew were expected to relieve themselves elsewhere. While they could go over the sides of the ship, the bow became a preferred spot for this activity, as it was on galleys. Permanent structures like those on galleys came to be built into the bows of sailing ships. Over time, as castles were built on ships' bows, the toilets were more sheltered. These toilets came to be called "heads" because they were mounted at the "head" of the ship. This placement of toilets continued aboard sailing ships into the 19th century.

There is surprisingly little mention of the use of chamber pots. The main exception is a reference to small, bottled-shaped containers issued to pilgrims aboard galleys. These were for use at night. The pilgrims had to use the facilities on deck during the day but, given their cramped conditions, they were permitted to use the bottles at night rather than climb over all their fellow passengers to get to the toilets on the prow. But the bottles were not a good solution because they were easily knocked over. Further, when the seas were rough and it was not safe to go out on deck, some passengers simply relieved themselves in some corner of the hold. This, along with the vomit of the sick, seeped into the bilge which lay directly under the deck the pilgrims slept on. The stench of the polluted bilge water mixed with the odor of 100 unwashed pilgrims was described as being one of the worst smells imaginable.

Now, despite all this, it should be remembered that people in the Middle Ages did not enjoy being filthy. While there was a higher tolerance of body odor back then, they did bathe when they had the opportunity and, in fact, many appear to have enjoyed bathing, but ships lacked bathing facilities. As in later centuries, any light rainshowers were likely appreciated by passengers and crew for providing an opportunity for cooling off and rinsing off.

FOOD, WATER, AND COOKING

Providing food and drink for passengers and crew was a very difficult task, particularly for ships with large crews or large numbers of passengers and for ships traveling long distances. Simply keeping adequate supplies of food and water on hand was a challenge. Food often went stale or rotten in the damp sea air, especially in warm weather. Water, even when enough could be carried, would become foul and stagnant after a week or more at sea. Whenever possible, food and water were replenished, but it was not always possible to make landfall before supplies ran low. Finally, cooking required fires. These had to be carefully contained to prevent setting the ship ablaze.

Food

Aboard some pilgrim ships, passengers paid to have meals provided along with their passage. These were prepared by the ship's cooks. The quality and quantity of this food could vary so experienced travelers attempted to guarantee minimum portions and quality in their contracts for passage. Wealthy passengers often brought along their own food and cooks or else paid the ship's cooks to prepare it especially for them. Pilgrims of more modest means could still afford two meals a day with bread, meat, wine, and clean water furnished by the ship's master in accordance with the terms of contract for passage. More commonly, pilgrims cooked their own meals. They were permitted to cook their meals on the ship's hearths. Even those who paid for some of their meals prepared additional food from the supplies they had brought with them.

Guides for pilgrims advised them to bring with them a daunting list of food as well as dishes and cooking utensils. Small casks of wine and water, sausages and other preserved meats, hard cheeses, bread, fresh and dried fruits, sweetmeats (candies), and spices and herbs, which were used medicinally and for flavoring foods, were all considered essential. In one guide for pilgrims to the Holy Land, the author recommended bringing along fruit syrups as well since he had found them to be the best beverage in hot weather. However, packing enough supplies for the entire voyage from Venice to the Holy Land was not necessary since fresh supplies could be purchased as stops along the way.

Fresh foods were, of course, preferred over preserved foods. For example, while dried and cured meats were common items both in ships' food stores and among supplies brought by pilgrims, meat was carried in the form of livestock if possible. Pigs, goats, sheep, and even cows and oxen were kept in pens on the deck while chickens were kept in cages (see illustration 17). Pilgrims were advised to bring along a couple of live chickens of their own to provide eggs and meat during their journeys

to the Holy Land. Additional animals were purchased at ports along the way to replace those they consumed. Unfortunately, meat that was not cooked and eaten quickly became maggoty, especially in hot weather. Because of this problem, preserved meats were a staple of diet at sea. Ships often carried many barrels of salted beef, although salt pork was sometimes favored instead. To be made edible, the salted meats had to be soaked to remove some of the salt and to soften them. The process of soaking appears to have often been combined with making the meat into a stew or soup. This method of cooking helped ensure that all of the calories and nutrients of meat were retained. Dried beans, another durable foodstuff, were sometimes added to the soups or stews as well. However, despite drying and heavy salting, even preserved meats were not impervious to moist sea air. They gradually deteriorated and became infested with maggots.

Ships also carried barrels of salted fish. As was the custom in medieval Europe, fish was served on Friday and other fast days, that is, those days on which the Church forbade the eating of meat. Stocks of fish were essential for complying with this religious stricture. Fresh fish were served when available but do not appear to have been common. As with salted beef and pork, salted fish had to be soaked before eating.

The other staple of shipboard diet was bread, both in the form of loaves and in the form of ship's biscuit. Loaves of bread had to be consumed soon after they were brought aboard. They quickly went stale or became infested with weevils and worms. Ship's biscuit, a durable alternative to bread, was hard and cracker-like. It was baked twice so that no moisture was left in it and had to be soaked to make it edible. It was resistant to mold and insects but it, too, would eventually became infested with weevils. By some estimates, ship's biscuit provided over half the calories in a typical crewman's daily ration. Ship's biscuit, also called hardtack, remained a standard food on ships into the 19th century and was used as a survival ration for soldiers and others into the 20th century. Some versions of it are still made commercially today. As with meat, fresh supplies of bread were bought any time a ship put into port, providing welcome relief from ship's biscuit.

Fruits and vegetables were always in demand but in short supply. Lettuce salads with oil dressing were recorded as part of meals served on one voyage, but these were not always available. Oarsmen and other crewmen aboard pilgrim ships sometimes profited from these shortages by selling fruits to the passengers. From their experience with prior voyages, they knew that there was always money to be made by packing extra fruit, wine, and water to sell to pilgrims when supplies ran low. Again, pilgrims were strongly advised to buy more fruit, along with meat, eggs, bread, candies, and all other foods, any time they were in port since the supplies aboard ship could not be counted on to be adequate.

Water and Wine

Water, wine, and beer were the three most common beverages in medieval Europe. Beer was most popular in northern Europe and was sometimes carried for passengers and crews to drink, but water and wine were the primary beverages consumed aboard ships across Europe. Wine was popular both on sea and on land, in part because it kept well. It could be taken long distances and still be drinkable. Admittedly, wine could turn to vinegar over time or spoil in other ways but most wine remained potable for reasonable amounts of time. Wine was also more hygienic than water. Its alcohol inhibited the growth of bacteria. This was particularly important aboard ships since water in open or poorly sealed barrels became stagnant and contaminated. Such water was a breeding ground for disease. Records for some voyages indicate that much more wine than water was brought along.

Despite the popularity of wine, water was usually the most common beverage and thirsty crews and passengers drank as much of it as they could. Fresh water was always in demand. One pilgrim described the delight of the passengers when the ship's sailors returned with barrels of fresh water from a spring on shore. In the Mediterranean, navigators were expected to know of the sources of fresh water available on the lands along their routes as well as those in neighboring waters, in case they were forced off course.

Maintaining a supply of fresh water and wine was an important and difficult task. Simply carrying enough for a voyage was a challenge. Water and wine are heavy and bulky and large amounts were required. It is extremely difficult to estimate how much water or wine vessels carried. There is little evidence of how these liquids were carried and in what quantities. Further, ships varied tremendously in carrying capacity, crew size, and purpose. For example, a small cargo ship that sailed along the coast from between ports that were only a day or two's sailing apart required only enough water for a few days for a handful of men. Even larger sailing ships appear to have been able to carry adequate water along with their cargo. This was possible because crews on sailing vessels were relatively small. A crew of 25 could handle a ship with a capacity of 200 to 300 tons. But merchant galleys with their crews of over 150 oarsmen needed vastly more and galleys carrying pilgrims needed even more, possibly hundreds of gallons every day.

Sailing ships could carry large amounts of fluids as the wine trade proves. Massive tuns of wine were routinely loaded aboard cargo ships. And, with their relatively small crews, cargo sailing ships appear to have usually been able to carry sufficient water and wine for long voyages, although no ship passed up the opportunity for fresh supplies. Large pilgrim sailing ships could have also easily carried several tuns to supply the needs of their passengers and crew. But with several hundred passengers, even tuns of water were consumed at a rapid pace.

The problem was even worse for galleys.

Compared to many sailing ships, their holds were small. Further, on a pilgrim galley, most of the hold was filled with passengers. Fitting in tuns of water and wine was out of the question. Smaller barrels must have been used and there are references to water being brought aboard in barrels. But the supplies were still not sufficient for a long voyage. While it can only be estimated, a pilgrim galley likely carried only enough water for five to seven days. However, on a routine voyage, the galleys put into shore every three to four days, and sometimes more frequently, so adequate supplies of water were usually available aboard ship. Still, even if there was an adequate quantity of water, there were problems with it becoming undrinkable. Depending on how it was stored and other conditions, fresh water could rapidly turn foul. Passengers often complained of having to drink stagnant water that tasted and smelled bad.

Running Out of Supplies

As the previous sections reveal, many vessels, particularly galleys, had to stop frequently for fresh supplies of food and drink. But there was always the risk of storms, heavy seas, adverse winds, dead calms, and other problems which could leave a ship out in the empty wastes of the sea. A voyage that was expected to take a few days could take a week or more. Food and water could quickly run out while the crew struggled to get the ship to the nearest safe harbor. Accounts of travel on galleys reveal the desperation in such circumstances. To save water, none was given to the livestock on deck and the animals suffered terribly. The passengers and crew were forced to drink water that had gone foul in the heat. It was described as being murky or white and tasting awful. It was at these times that smart but unscrupulous crewmen could make a large profit by selling any food, wine, or water they had hidden away. This was also when the ship's master's and navigator's knowledge of the surrounding regions became critical. They had to know where the nearest island or other land was that could provide water and food.

Cooking

Cooking at sea was often challenging. Preparing meals on cargo ships was the easiest. Even with a relatively large crew, a single fire could suffice. On some vessels, mainly in the early Middle Ages, crewmen appear to have prepared their own individual meals but it is likely that having one sailor act as cook was common. On some pilgrim ships, passengers were also recorded as preparing their own meals. Multiple cooking fires must have been needed for such large groups. However, it also appears that meals were frequently prepared communally. This was certainly the case for the ship's master and other officers and for any wealthy passengers. And, as mentioned previously, some meals were included in fares paid by pilgrims, although many continued to bring along food to supplement that provided by the ship's master. It was obviously more efficient to have the crew's and passengers' meals prepared by one or two sailors than have everyone cook his own. Serving as cook was likely a collateral duty at first but, by the 15th century, full-time cooks appear among the crews of pilgrim galleys. And throughout the period, royalty, nobility, and other wealthy passengers frequently traveled with their own cooks.

Cooking Fires

Except near the end of the period, there were no permanent kitchens aboard medieval ships. Instead, temporary cooking facilities were set up on deck. As with cooking on land, the implements included pots suspended on tripods, gridirons and frying pans supported on legs, and other cooking vessels that were placed directly over open fires.

Aboard wooden ships, any fires, including those needed for cooking, were a great hazard. To lessen the risk of fire spreading to the rest of the ship, cooking fires were built in nonflammable enclosures. Sand boxes appear to have been most common. Evidence of one such box has been found in the wreck of an

11th century ship in the eastern Mediterranean where a charcoal fire contained in a box of sand appears to have been used for cooking. While descriptions are lacking, these sand hearths were likely made of a layer of tiles covered with sand and edged with tile or brick to hold the sand in. They appear to have been temporary. They could be easily assembled on the open deck and then taken apart and the sand swept up when the cooking was done. The sand could be reused. Metal sheets, with or without sand, may have been used as well. Again, these could be easily set up and removed to keep the deck clear.

Fires appear to have been allowed only on the ship's top deck. There were good reasons for this. The smoke generated by an open fire between decks would likely not have been adequately vented by the few hatches in the top deck. More importantly, even if the fire was contained in a sand box, the risk of fire spreading was much higher in this enclosed space.

More permanent fixtures were eventually built aboard ships. The first mention of cooking facilities aboard an English ship dates to the 1330s. At that time, a royal ship had an oven for baking bread. In 1340, another English royal ship was described as having a hearth and one or two ovens. These would have been constructed of bricks, tiles, and mortar. These fixtures were most likely part of an open air–kitchen on the top deck. A 15th century account of a pilgrimage includes a brief description of such a kitchen aboard a passenger galley. It was located on the top deck, near the stern. It was narrow and had only a small fire. However, the 14th century kitchens were likely bigger. Even on the largest galleys, space for amenities such as kitchens was limited, while large sailing ships typically had more space available on deck since they did not need to accommodate rowers. Further, the royal ships mentioned were used for combat and for transporting troops. They carried hundreds of sailors and soldiers and required large kitchens to feed them. Hearths and ovens appear to have become common aboard such

larger sailing ships by the end of the Middle Ages. For example, records of the construction of one large ship built in England in 1466 include payments for 800 bricks and over 250 tiles for the ship's oven. A royal warship built in England in 1490 had two massive ovens to feed its crew and complement of soldiers. These ovens were built with 6,500 bricks, 600 paving stones, mortar, and a large quantity of salt. One historian believes that the salt was used as an insulating layer under the ovens. The combined weight of these ovens must have been over three tons. However, the ship was huge by the standards of the day and had a displacement of 1,000 tons so the weight of the ovens was easily accommodated. Still, it was not practical for such a heavy fixture to be placed on the top deck. Based on later examples, such as the *Mary Rose*, a great ship of Henry VIII of England's navy in the 16th century, such large hearths and ovens were placed in the middle of the ship's lowest deck, straddling the ship's centerline. This helped to better balance the ship. This placement also sheltered the kitchen from the weather. Venting the smoke of the hearths and ovens appears to have been accomplished with chimneys that went up from the hold, through the intervening decks, and out onto the ship's top deck. While the chimneys seem to have been built of wood, they were lined with nonflammable materials. Some building accounts reveal that daub, a clay-based mixture, was sometimes used to coat the inside of the chimneys, just as they were on land. Thin sheets of lead were also used. One ship had a lead-lined wooden vent hood to trap and channel the smoke. Despite their location down in the hold, the hearths and ovens were well enclosed and ventilated and so the danger of fire spreading was limited. However, during battles and in heavy seas, the cooking fires were likely extinguished to reduce the risk of accidental fires.

Not all ships had cooking facilities, even of the most rudimentary kind. On smaller boats, there would have been no space to safely have a fire. Even aboard Viking long ships, which could be 70 feet or more in length, there was no cooking. Cauldrons and tripods for cooking over fires were brought along but these were used only on shore. When sailing long distances away from land, they had to make do with cold food. This was not that uncommon. Many mariners likely had cold meals because it was impractical to have a fire on their vessel. Many others may have simply found it easier to have cold food, especially on shorter voyages.

At times, even aboard a ship with a place for a fire, it could be difficult or impossible to light a fire and keep it lit. Since fire boxes and small hearths were out on the open deck until the end of the Middle Ages, wet weather would have put a stop to cooking. Heavy seas did as well since a fire could not be properly contained on the rolling, pitching deck. In these conditions, passengers and crew had to make do with a cold meal.

GOING ASHORE

Ships throughout the Middle Ages frequently came into shore during the course of their voyages. For example, while they slept aboard their vessels on long voyages such as those to Iceland and Greenland, the Vikings carried tents and slept in comfort on land when their travels permitted. These stops also provided an opportunity to cook a hot meal. And long before the Middle Ages, vessels in the Mediterranean often stopped at ports and shores of the sea's many islands and peninsulas to replenish their supplies of food and water. In the 12th century, crusaders sailing from Genoa sometimes stopped in Sicily for this reason on their way to the Holy Land. Coming into a harbor or into the shelter of land was also done to seek protection from storms. Sometimes this had unforeseen consequences, as in 1147 when a group of English crusaders bound for the Holy Land put in at the mouth of a river in northern Portugal to ride out a storm. Here they were contacted by the Portuguese and recruited to help them besiege Lisbon and push out the Moslems.

Firsthand accounts of putting into ports

or shores are most plentiful for pilgrim voyages from Italy to the Holy Land. As previously discussed, these ships could not carry adequate food and water for long voyages and needed to frequently put into shore to replenish their supplies. Again, this was comparatively easy in many parts of the Mediterranean, especially at its eastern end.

These stops often involved staying overnight. In some instances, this may have been to avoid sailing at night. This would have been particularly likely if the ship was passing through an area with hazards such as reefs or strong currents. These dangers were best confronted in the light of day. The stop also provided an opportunity for the passengers to disembark, get out of their cramped quarters, relax, and even sleep on the comfort of land. Some stopovers were so long that passengers hired residences to stay in. These stops also gave them the opportunity to pick up additional food and drink for their own personal supplies. Sometimes these stops lasted far longer than planned. Storms or adverse winds could keep a ship from sailing for days or even weeks. For example, one voyage from Italy to the Holy Land took nearly seven weeks, but three of those weeks were spent in various ports. Bad weather could also result in delays at sea by forcing a ship to take circuitous routes and call at ports far off the ship's planned course.

Whether at planned stops or in ports that were not on the original course, pilgrims often took the opportunity to sightsee and visit any religious sites in the region. In fact, frequent layovers are believed to have been considered an advantage of the galley over the sailing ship because they facilitated such tourism and broke up the voyage, providing welcome relief from their travels for both the crew and passengers.

SEASICKNESS

As with travel aboard ships today, many people in the Middle Ages suffered from seasickness when sailing. Even that consummate warrior-king, Richard the Lionheart of England, was laid low by seasickness on his voyage to the Holy Land. Other travelers to the Holy Land were equally unfortunate. Accounts of pilgrimages often include mentions of vomiting passengers. To make it worse, many became so sick that they could not get up from their places below deck. They threw up where they lay. The lists of items recommended for pilgrims included spices and medicines to ward off seasickness or at least treat its effects. For example, it was already known that ginger could help with nausea and a syrup made with ginger was recommended for soothing the stomach.

Some travelers had suggestions for other ways to avoid or, at least, lessen the effects of seasickness. These included recommending travel by galley rather than sailing ship, but this does not appear to have helped most passengers. One experienced traveler wisely advised pilgrims to minimize the consequences of nausea by not eating when the ship was in rough waters.

OTHER ILLNESSES

While seasickness was the primary illness to afflict ships' passengers, malnutrition and dehydration could also occur if a ship ran low on supplies or if the food deteriorated and the water became foul. Besides suffering the pains of thirst and hunger, passengers and crew were left weakened. With unhygienic conditions, including contaminated water, diseases such as dysentery could breed and quickly spread through the already weakened passengers and crew. Large numbers could die.

Infectious diseases that had been brought onto the ship could also decimate all aboard. In fact, the spread of diseases was sometimes associated with sea travel. This problem is best illustrated by the spread of the Black Death in the mid–14th century. The disease originated in Asia. In trading ports on the Caspian Sea, ships' crews and passengers came in contact with the disease. They then sailed to ports in eastern Europe and Italy, bringing the Black

Death with them. From these cities, the plague then spread further, both overland and by sea. It was in response to this epidemic that Venice imposed the first formal quarantine on vessels coming from ports which were known to be suffering from the disease. The practice of quarantine was intended to halt the spread of the Black Death by banning ships from entering port until sufficient time elapsed for the plague to manifest itself if the passengers or crew were infected. If it did, the ship was barred from landing until the disease had run its course and those who were sick died or, very rarely, recovered. For a vessel identified as a "plague ship," finding a place to land became difficult. For example, in the late 15th century, one pilgrim ship departed Venice while plague was striking the city. Ports along its route to the Holy Land refused it entry. While not recorded, these cities may not have been willing to accept the ship even if it underwent quarantine or the ship could not afford the delays the quarantine would have caused. When the ship reached the Holy Land, it was again denied clearance for landing and so the passengers had to bribe their way ashore.

Scurvy is one of the diseases most commonly associated with sea travel but it was not a problem aboard ships in medieval Europe. To some degree, it was prevented in the Mediterranean by the foods carried on ships. As mentioned earlier in this section, fruit, both fresh and dried, were recommended as part of the supplies for pilgrim voyages in the Mediterranean. These supplies, as well as stocks of vegetables, were often replenished during stops en route. However, some ships, such as those that were driven off course by adverse winds or becalmed, had inadequate supplies for their voyages. Further, in northern Europe, fruits and vegetables appear to have been far less common in ships' rations. But scurvy still does not seem to have been a problem. The most likely answer is that sailors were usually not at sea long enough for the disease to set in. Only with the voyages of exploration in the late 15th century did scurvy become a common problem for mariners. This was because they were often away from shore for months without any fruits or vegetables. Since it typically takes a month or more for the symptoms of scurvy to appear, it was simply not a significant threat for most sailors in the Middle Ages. Still, scurvy was not completely unknown in the period. The most severe outbreak of scurvy was noted during the First Crusade when, during their long march to the Holy Land and the siege of Jerusalem, the crusaders suffered extreme malnutrition, including a lack of fruit and vegetables.

Not all illnesses aboard ships were physical. Mental breakdowns also occurred. The stresses of sea travel and, perhaps, extreme fear of the sea appear to have exacerbated underlying mental problems of some passengers and caused them to go "mad." Madness was sometimes so severe that the afflicted attacked members of the crew or their fellow passengers and had to be restrained. Some committed suicide while others were recorded as simply dying while they were ill.

BOREDOM AND ITS REMEDIES

Boredom was another curse of sea travel. Until the advent of luxury liners, sailing was tedious for passengers, especially on long cruises. When the weather was fair and the wind was favorable, even the crew had time to be bored as they had fewer tasks to attend to.

Gambling was a common way to fill empty hours aboard ship. Betting on dice was the most popular. Playing cards first appeared in Europe in the late 14th century and card games first appeared on ships in the 15th century. The upper classes also played backgammon and chess to while away the time. Bets were placed on these games as well. Some people did not think that gambling was a suitable pastime, especially when on a pilgrimage or crusade. For example, on the return voyage from his disastrous crusade in Egypt, King Louis IX of France was so irate at one of his brothers for gambling aboard ship that he scooped up the dice and playing board and

threw them overboard. But even the clergy were not always so pious. Bishops and their retinues were recorded as gambling while on pilgrimage.

A more morally suitable activity for crusaders and pilgrims was prayer. Given most people's fear of water travel, constantly praying for a safe arrival was likely a good way for many passengers to occupy their time, although this may have caused some to dwelling on potential dangers surrounding them. Others sung hymns to make the time pass faster. Secular songs were also sung by passengers and crews and some played musical instruments, such as lutes, bagpipes, and flutes.

Sailors were recorded as engaging in physical exercise during idle time. This included lifting heavy objects, climbing the rigging, and other activities. This kept them fit and absorbed pent-up energy that might have otherwise been expended in less wholesome pursuits such as brawling.

There was another activity that was practiced aboard all ships which served to both combat boredom and improve personal hygiene. This was picking lice and fleas off oneself and one another. Vermin were a common problem and getting rid of at least some of them provided temporary relief from itching and scratching. This problem was not unique to sea travel. Infestations of lice and fleas were common everywhere and remained so for centuries. But even in the Middle Ages, some people found the practice somewhat distasteful. For example, one Italian city found it unseemly that picking lice was being performed in public and so banned it from some civic spaces.

Navigation

Without reliable navigation, sailing would be impossible. At the beginning of the Middle Ages, mariners used the same navigational methods used in antiquity, such as observing the rising of the sun and its movement west across the sky to determine which direction was east. Since land was in sight for all or part of a voyage, knowledge of landmarks was essential for masters and navigators. Knowledge of winds, currents, and locations of reefs and other hazards was also needed both in sight of land and out on the open sea. Additional techniques and tools for navigation were developed over the course of the period. These included the compass and sea charts. While some of even these improved methods may seem crude by modern standards, medieval navigators used them increasingly to guide their ships safely on innumerable voyages. These improvements facilitated the expansion of trade through shipping and enabled Europeans to embark on the voyages of world exploration at the end of the Middle Ages.

NAVIGATORS

In medieval documents, the navigator was often referred to as a pilot. The ship's master was often the navigator as well but on many ships, especially larger ones, there was a navigator who was responsible for safely guiding the ship to its destination. The importance of the navigator and his skills can be found in references scattered throughout the Middle Ages. Some French laws of the sea, dating to the 13th century, dictated that any pilot whose negligence caused the loss of a vessel could be executed.

Navigators learned their trade through experience rather than formal education. Further, they do not appear to have served formal apprenticeships. They may have been instructed in navigation while they also served as sailors. Some of these trainees may have been ordinary seamen who displayed an aptitude for navigation. Others were likely the sons of ship owners, masters, and navigators. Regardless of their origin, they had to have a grounding in how to sail before they could learn to guide a ship.

Learning navigation included firsthand observation of all the elements of nature which impacted a vessel and an understanding of how they affected a ship's course. The trainees also learned how to identify natural aids to navigation and use them to determine the ship's position as well as its heading. Besides learning through direct observation, their education also included listening to the navigator recount valuable information from his personal experience and from knowledge passed down through generations of mariners. Some of this lore could be applied to navigating anywhere but much of the information appears to have been specific to the routes the navigator had sailed and which the trainees expected to sail themselves. This included descriptions and locations of reefs and other hazards as well as safe anchorages and important landmarks, prevailing winds and currents, and other vital information. As this reveals, most navigators were trained primarily to sail within certain regions. For example, a navigator trained in the eastern Mediterranean was expected to recognize all the islands, coastlines, and ports in those waters and be able to find places where he could take on fresh water and other provisions even if he was blown off course. Given that he would likely spend most if not all of his career sailing in these same waters, all this specialized knowledge would serve him well. If he did venture outside his home waters, he could still apply his skills, such as being able to determine the heading of his ship and estimate the distances he had traveled, but he would have difficulty in recognizing and avoiding hazards and even in finding his destination if he had not been given directions. The best means of obtaining information about routes in other regions was through discussions with other navigators who had sailed there. This sharing of information was particularly important in the centuries before charts and sailing instructions were written down. Still, as mentioned previously, in theory, a navigator who entered unfamiliar waters was obligated to take his ship into the nearest port and turn his post over to a local navigator who knew the surrounding seas. But the decision to do this did not rest with the navigator. Part of the responsibilities of ship's master was to decide when it was necessary to employ a local pilot.

There were other navigators besides those employed full-time aboard ships. For some ports, there were harbor pilots who came aboard ships solely to steer them into port. These specialists knew the waters and any hazards on the approach to their harbors. They also knew conditions within their harbors, which was important since some harbors had peculiar patterns of currents. In exchange for this service, the ship's master had to pay a pilotage fee.

NAVIGATIONAL AIDS

Navigators used a variety of both natural and man-made aids for finding the information they needed to steer their ships. Some of these, such as the position of the sun and the direction of prevailing winds, had been used since man first sailed. While reading natural phenomena remained essential, man-made aids increasingly supplemented natural ones over the course of the Middle Ages.

Natural Guides

It was essential for the navigator to have a knowledge of all the elements acting upon his ship: tides, currents, winds, and weather. He also had to be aware of submerged rocks, sandbanks, and any other hazards along his route. To help him in guiding his ship, he learned to determine his position and heading from the sighting of the sun and stars and from recognizing landmarks along the coastline. The depth of the sea and the composition of the sea floor sometimes provided him with vital information as well.

The Sun

The most universal guide for navigators was the sun. Its rising and passage from east to west provided basic information for setting a ship's course. The elevation of the sun above the horizon at midday could also be used to find the ship's heading on a north-south axis. This information was especially useful for voyagers on the open expanses of the Atlantic and in the North Sea. By knowing his approximate heading, a navigator could determine if he needed to adjust his course. For most of the Middle Ages, such estimates were done based only on the navigator's knowledge of the highest position of the sun in the sky at various times of year. However, measuring the sun's height from the deck of a rolling, pitching ship and taking the reading at consistent times of the day must have made it difficult for this method to produce accurate results. Still, even these rough measurements yielded enough information to estimate the ship's latitude. By the end of the Middle Ages, this method had developed into true determinations of latitude, which improved the navigator's ability to determine both his position and his heading. Making the determinations was further enhanced by the introduction of the cross-staff, quadrant, and astrolabe, all instruments for measuring the altitude of the sun and other celestial bodies. These made the measurements more accurate, although taking readings was still hampered by the motion of the ship. These navigational tools and others are discussed later in this section.

The Stars

Nighttime navigation was dangerous in the Middle Ages. Landmarks as well as hazards were lost from sight and lighthouses were extremely rare. Still, sailing at night was often unavoidable. For directional guidance at night, navigators relied primarily on the Pole Star and other stars which were seen as closely orbiting the North Pole. These provided navigators with a reliable means for finding north. In fact, in northern waters, some navigators intentionally sailed at night so that they could use the Pole Star as a reference. This practice was recorded in the 11th century as being used by German navigators.

The rising and setting of other stars were also observed for some clues to direction, but were likely used more for determining time.

Again, the altitude of the brightest, most recognizable stars could have provided information for determining latitude but this and other more complex celestial navigation was likely not done until the use of the cross-staff, quadrant, and astrolabe became more common at the end of the Middle Ages.

Natural Landmarks

Except for long voyages across the North Atlantic such as those by the Scandinavians to Iceland and beyond, most sea voyages in the Middle Ages took place with land in sight for part if not all of the time. As a consequence, capes, islands, headlands, cliffs, estuaries, and other geographical features, even active volcanoes, were used as landmarks to guide ships through the seas surrounding Europe. Navigators could determine their location and direction from sightings of landmarks. They may have been able to estimate their speed as well as from the time it took to travel between two landmarks.

While landmarks were essential for most navigation, ships did not "hug" the coast to stay in constant sight of the shore. Sailing so close to shore would have been extremely dangerous since a shift in the wind could drive a ship in and wreck it on the shore or on rocks or shoals near the shore. Instead, ships sailed roughly parallel to the shore at a safe distance out to sea. Following such courses, ships frequently passed out of sight of land for varying periods of time. In part, this was caused by shifts in the wind, but in some cases it was intentional. For example, it was shorter and more efficient to cross the open water at the mouth of a bay than to precisely follow the contours of the bay. In other instances, sailing within sight of land was simply not possible. Even in the Mediterranean where there were many conveniently located islands and peninsulas along sea routes, there were still points which required crossing stretches of open water and sailing out of sight of land for some distance. The problem was even more pronounced in the North Sea and North Atlantic, where mariners sometimes spent days out of the sight of land, as when crossing from Norway to England, or even weeks, as in the case of voyages to Iceland and Greenland. When passing out of sight of land, navigators would note the last landmark they had seen and continue along their course. They would then look for the next landmark when their estimate of distance and direction indicated that it should be in sight. Presumably, if the landmark did not appear when expected, the ship would be sailed in closer to shore until a recognized landmark was found.

Winds, Currents, and Tides

Experienced navigators were aware of the prevailing winds along the different parts of their routes. The direction and characteristics of the wind coupled with the time of year provided clues to the ship's position and heading. Certain winds were known to be more prevalent at certain times of the year, such as the sirocco in the Mediterranean. This is a strong, hot wind which blows from the southeast and is strongest in mid-spring and mid-fall. A good navigator knew such information for all the principal winds in the region in which he sailed. To the greatest extent possible, he planned his sailing according to the prevailing winds. For example, in the North Sea the prevailing winds come from the east-northeast in spring and from the west in the fall. Thus, mariners from Scandinavia and elsewhere on the coast of the Baltic sailed west to England and the rest of western Europe in the spring. In the mid– and late–Middle Ages, this use of the winds aided Scandinavian and Baltic merchant ships in reaching the ports of western Europe, but in the early Middle Ages these same winds brought the Vikings to England. With their ships pushed along by the west winds, both Vikings and merchants returned home in the fall. Winds followed a regular cycle in the Mediterranean as well, with winds from the north generally prevailing in the spring and winds from the south in late summer and early fall. This pattern of winds set the schedule for the pilgrimage trade, with ships sailing from Italy to the Holy Land in the spring and returning around September and October.

Winds also provided clues to approaching weather based on their direction, speed, and other qualities, such as their relative temperature and humidity. Any clouds accompanying the winds provided the navigator with additional information as well.

Like winds, currents followed regular patterns of movement. Also like winds, the strength and direction of some currents changed with the seasons. With a knowledge of the location of particular currents and the direction they flowed, a navigator could determine his approximate heading and possibly his location as well. Currents could sometimes be found by their temperature since they often circulate across different climatic areas. Some brought colder water while others brought warmer. Further, as with winds, depending on their direction and the desired course of the ship, currents could be either a hindrance or a help in reaching a destination. Navigators knew the currents and likely tried to avoid unfavorable ones if possible, aiming for those which could speed the ship along its desired course.

Tides also affected the direction and progress of ships. While the tides in the Baltic and Mediterranean Seas are so small that they have little or no impact on navigation, the heights and strengths of tides in the North Sea and the Atlantic are much greater and significantly affect coastal shipping. Knowledge of the tides was important for avoiding hazards such as having a ship driven onto the shore by a strong, rising tide. On the other hand, tides could be used constructively to move a ship. For example, ships typically sought to enter harbors with the rising tide since it gave them an extra push towards the land. The increasing depth of the water as the tide rose also lessened the risks of running aground on any shoals or sandbars. For departing a harbor, the preferred time was at the beginning of the ebb tide. Water levels were still high and the pull of the tide was now reversed, making it easier for ships to put out to sea.

The impact of the tide was not uniform. The levels and force of the tides varied greatly depending on the location. The shape of the shore further affected tides. In narrow bays and especially in bays with wide mouths that quickly narrowed, the height and force of the tide could be remarkable. On broad, gently sloping shorelines, the movements of the tides were usually slower and less forceful.

Other Natural Guides

Voyagers in the North Atlantic also watched for the presence of drifting icebergs and noted their number, size, and the direction they were headed. Since they were carried along by the currents, the icebergs provided a very visible marker of the direction and speed of the currents. Additionally, because icebergs melt as they drift south, their size and contours gave clues as to how far they had traveled from their point of origin. In the most obvious cases, encountering large numbers of big icebergs or hearing the sound of icebergs breaking off ice sheets were sure signs that one was far off course to the north.

There were living guides as well. When sailing out of sight of land, the presence of birds could indicate that land was nearby. This clue was part of the Scandinavian navigation of the North Atlantic. However, the type of bird was sometimes a factor as well, since some birds roosted on land while others slept floating on the sea. Birds that frequented the shore were a surer indicator of the proximity of land although even these birds ventured far out to sea in their hunt for food. So the presence of birds was a good sign of approaching land but it could still be some distance away. In addition to free-flying wild birds, the Scandinavians traveling to Iceland occasionally brought along captive birds that headed for the nearest land when released.

Fish and whales were another guide to location used in the North Atlantic. Vast schools of certain types of fish were known to appear at particular spots in the ocean at various times of the year. Viking sagas mention this use of fish as reference points for sailing. Whales, too, acted as living signposts for some parts of the year since they were known to routinely gather in certain locations such as off the coast of Iceland. Like the fish, they were seasonal as well. Whales generally winter in warmer southern waters where the females give birth and feed on the plentiful food. They return to the north in the relative warmth of summer.

Finally, the presence and type of seaweed and other flotsam in the water could indicate location. Color of the water was sometimes a guide as well. Silt carried by waters from rivers could color seawater brown. This discoloration could travel for many miles out to sea and be an indicator that land was nearby.

Lighthouses

While natural landmarks were numerous, they could rarely be seen at night. To provide guidance at night, men burned lights on the shore. The earliest of these were likely simple bonfires on the shore to help fishermen find their way home after long days out. This simple but effective technique continued to be used as late as the 14th century in northern Europe. Over the centuries, more permanent structures were built for supporting lights. These included stone cairns and pillars. By elevating the light, it was visible further out to sea. The first lighthouse was built by the mid–7th century B.C. in what is now Turkey. This was at Sigeum, a promontory located at a strategic location at the southern end of the Hellespont (now commonly called the Dardanelles), the channel which connects the Aegean Sea to the Sea of Marmara. While the lighthouse at Sigeum served as a general reference point, most lighthouses were built to mark the entrances to important harbors. One of the most famous of these was the lighthouse or *pharos* at Alexandria in Egypt built in the 3rd century B.C. This massive lighthouse survived to the 13th century A.D., when it finally collapsed in an earthquake. The Romans built lighthouses

for their ports as well, such as the one at Ostia, the seaport for the city of Rome.

Another ancient navigational light was actually a natural feature. From as early as the 4th century B.C., Stromboli off the northeastern tip of Sicily was known as the "Lighthouse of the Mediterranean" because of the glow of its lava-filled crater, which could be seen from 50 or more miles away at night.

With the collapse of the Roman Empire in western Europe, all lights outside of the eastern Mediterranean as well as those around the French and English coasts appear to have gone out. There was no longer any central authority to maintain and operate them. Further, some historians have proposed that the lights fell out of use since they attracted pirates to the harbor towns which the lights had marked. There was likely a return to more primitive use of lights such as bonfires to guide fishermen home, but it took several centuries before lighthouses were again used outside the areas controlled by the Byzantine Empire to any significant extent.

Most early medieval lighthouses were built in the Mediterranean. This reflects that many were built on the sites of earlier Roman facilities and that the highly active maritime traffic of the Mediterranean called for them. However, some Roman lighthouses found outside the Mediterranean were eventually rebuilt and put back into service as well. For example, a lighthouse at Boulogne in France marked the harbor and provided a landmark for the shortest crossing of the English Channel. In the early 9th century, Charlemagne directed the light's restoration. While it is not known if this particular order was carried out, the Boulogne light was eventually put back into service. Other Roman lighthouses never went back into service. On the other side of the Channel at Dover, the Romans had built two lighthouses on the headland high above the harbor. In the early Middle Ages, one had collapsed beyond repair while the other was converted into a bell tower for a new church built adjacent to it.

Over time, lighthouses were built in new

locations. As in the past, these beacons were constructed to mark the entrances to ports. These were for harbors which had not existed in the time of the Romans, were previously too unimportant to merit lights, or were simply outside the bounds of the Empire. Most early medieval lighthouses appear to have been built in Italy. There was a lighthouse at Bari in Italy as early as 1070. The first lighthouse at Genoa is also among the earliest and is documented from 1160.

Illustration 20. This is the Tower of Constance at Aigues-Mortes in the south of France. This 90-foot-high tower is topped with a smaller tower that is fitted with an iron framework. This structure was a lantern that sheltered the tower's signal fire. This beacon marked the town's harbor so that ships could find it in the dark.

A few lights were built to mark reefs and other hazards, a practice which does not appear to have been done by the Romans. One such light was built on the Cordouan Rock, a small island that is part of a dangerous reef near the mouth of the Gironde River in France. Fires had been used to mark this point since the late 9th century. This reef was of special concern since the area was heavily traveled by ships going to and from the important wine center of Bordeaux. Still, it was extremely rare for lights in the Middle Ages to be built solely to mark hazards. The great age of building lighthouses atop or near treacherous rocks and reefs did not begin until the 17th century.

Medieval lighthouses took several forms. Some were purpose-built towers. Some were not truly lighthouses but were simply large, open metal braziers sometimes placed atop stone platforms. Other lights were built as part of another structure. One of the best examples of this can be found on the south coast of France. In the walled town of Aigues-Mortes, built in the 13th century, the largest seaward tower was topped with a small tower that was capped with a huge iron lantern. (See illustration 20.) Similarly, a priory on the coast of northern England had a brazier in the top of one of its towers and served as lighthouse.

While open braziers placed in exposed positions were a common feature of many medieval lights, this was far from ideal. Wind and especially rain could dim or completely douse the light and such weather conditions were precisely when lights were needed most. To protect the fire from the elements, some lighthouses were topped with a small, roofed stone chamber. These fireproof rooms had wide openings on the sides so that the fire could be easily seen but was still relatively sheltered. Another means of protecting the light was to enclose it in a huge metal-framed lantern. One of these was used at Aigues-Mortes. While the current lantern is a later replacement, the original lantern was over six feet in diameter and six feet or more in height. To protect the fire from wind and rain, the lantern frame was fitted with panes of thin, flattened, translucent cow horn. This material was commonly used for windowpanes in the Middle Ages since glass was expensive. Metal lanterns glazed with horn or glass were increasingly used and came to be the standard fitting for lighthouses.

Regardless of the form of the light, keeping the fires burning must have been a challenge. Most used wood, but by modern estimates a wood-fired light large enough to be seen at a reasonable distance would have required approximately a ton of wood to stay lit just one night. Some lighthouses in the later Middle Ages burned coal, but the amount needed would still be near a ton. Some lighthouses around the Mediterranean burned oil. For example, the lighthouse at Bari was burning oil in 1070 while a document from 1326 mentions that both lights at Genoa were being fueled with oil. Although the type of oil is not specified, it was most likely olive oil since this was used for domestic lighting in the region. In oil-fired lights, the oil was placed in a large, flat pan. Wicks were floated in the pan. Large amounts of light could be generated by burning numerous wicks at the same time. Oil was likely more efficient than coal or wood but large quantities were still needed to fuel the light night after night. Regardless of the fuel, obtaining sufficient supplies must have been difficult and expensive and carrying them up to the top of a lighthouse must have been a constant struggle.

While most lighthouses were public works, religious institutions or even hermits operated lights in some instances. In late 12th century Ireland a group of canons established a light on the coast marking a point of land near the entrance to the port of Waterford. (Canons were priests who lived communally under rules somewhat comparable to those of monastic orders.) In the 14th century, Prince

Edward of England had a 48-foot-high tower built on the Cordouan Rock to replace earlier smaller towers and installed a religious hermit there to operate the light. At that time, the Cordouan Rock was of interest to the English crown because, as mentioned previously, it lies at the entrance of the Gironde River, which leads to the port of Bordeaux. Bordeaux was an important port for the lucrative wine trade and was then part of the lands belonging to the kings of England. In the 15th century, on his own initiative, a hermit in the north of England built a tower topped with a light to mark a dangerous stretch of coast. The involvement of the Church in the operation of navigational lights may seem odd but the work was an act of Christian charity since it helped prevent shipwrecks and saved the lives of mariners and passengers.

One religious organization, Trinity House, persisted in building and operating lighthouses in England even after the Middle Ages. Trinity House was originally a charitable religious fraternity established in the 13th century for the assistance of seamen and their families. In 1514, it was granted a charter by King Henry VIII and later, by an act of Parliament, it was confirmed that it was authorized to build and maintain lights and other navigational aids. While it gradually became a secular organization, Trinity House continues to administer many lighthouses and navigational buoys as well as light ships around the British Isles.

Whether lights were operated by religious men or by laity, their funding was usually derived from tolls levied on passing ships. These fees were collected at the ports nearest to them. For example, throughout the Middle Ages, fees for the support of the Cordouan light were collected at Bordeaux. Similarly, a law enacted in Genoa in 1160 stated that ships entering the harbor had to pay a fee for the maintenance of the lighthouse there. A document from the 13th century confirms that the lighthouse operated by the canons near Waterford was supported by charges collected at that harbor. Even the hermit in the north of England was given permission by the king to collect tolls to support his work. And in its charter of 1514, Trinity House was authorized to collect tolls to pay for its services.

While the maintenance of lights eventually passed entirely into secular hands, the practice of levying tolls on ships passing lighthouses remained common across Europe. In fact, a large number of lighthouses after the Middle Ages were built by individuals who hoped to profit from the tolls. By the early 19th century, national governments had largely taken over building and operating lighthouses, but the costs for this service is still financed, at least in part, by users' fees assessed on ships.

Other Man-Made Landmarks

There were other man-made landmarks in addition to lighthouses. Some of the most basic were large stakes or poles driven into shoals on the edges of channels leading into harbors. Such shoals were common around ports situated on rivers that dumped silt where they met the sea. Barrels or large baskets were sometimes suspended at the top of the poles to make it easier to recognize them as guide posts. Additionally, particularly in northern waters, towers were constructed at the mouths of some rivers to mark channels leading to ports further inland which were not visible from the coast. A few of these towers were topped with lights for use at night. Members of the Hanse trade association also built towers to mark some reefs in the channels between the Baltic and North Seas, but there were no systematic efforts to flag dangers along the sea routes.

Using marker buoys was more practical than building towers and they could be used in deeper water than towers or stakes and poles. It is unclear when buoys were first used for marking hazards. The earliest descriptions of marker buoys are from the Low Countries in the 14th century. These were made of watertight barrels. They were fitted with a ring that was attached to a chain which in turn was secured to a large stone that anchored the buoy

to the sea bottom. Unfortunately, these buoys likely had a very short lifespan. Still, the use of marker buoys gradually expanded. In the 15th century, wooden buoys were used to mark the entrance to the River Elbe on the German coast.

A unique form of landmark was constructed in 11th century Norway. Large stone crosses, some possibly up to 45 feet high, were erected along the coast. The crosses appear to have been built at the mouths of fjords to mark that it was a safe anchorage or that a port lay at its further end.

Churches in coastal communities were also used as landmarks for navigation. The most common examples are along the southern coast of the Baltic Sea and the eastern coast of England. Using the profits of their maritime enterprises, merchants and mariners contributed funds to the building of these churches. In return, it seems, some of the churches were built with disproportionately tall spires. These steeples could be seen for miles out to sea and helped guide ships to safe harbors. An example of this can be found in Rostock, Germany, where St. Peter's Church was built with a spire nearly 400 feet high, which, in theory, could be seen up to 30 miles out to sea. Similar steeples were built as part of churches on the eastern coast of England.

NAVIGATIONAL INSTRUMENTS

Several tools to aid navigation were developed in the Middle Ages to supplement the navigator's own skills. These instruments became essential because they provided more accurate information that enabled the navigators to improve their determinations of their ships' locations, headings, and speed. Ultimately, they enabled navigators to safely guide their ships in more unfavorable conditions than before. With the compass, overcast days and nights no longer left them disoriented. The running glass and chart made it easier to stay on course despite unfavorable winds and currents. All these tools helped navigators to steer their ships to their destinations and to find havens when storms made sailing dangerous. These improvements made sailing safer so that it was possible to extend the sailing season and made shipping more reliable and more profitable.

The Compass

Naturally occurring magnets in the form of lodestones were known in classical antiquity but they were not developed for practical purposes until many centuries later. The Chinese developed magnets into a form of compass at some time between the 3rd century B.C. and the 3rd century A.D. The earliest compasses were spoon-shaped and were magnetized so that the handle pointed south. Later compass needles were sometimes made in the form of a small pivoting fish made of magnetized metal. Again, the Chinese interpreted these compasses as pointing south rather than north. Rather than using them for navigation, the Chinese first used compasses for divination and *feng shui*, to determine direction for laying out buildings to ensure harmony with natural forces. They do not appear to have used them for navigation aboard ships until the 11th century or later. By the 15th century at the latest, compasses were part of the standard equipment of Chinese navy vessels.

The Europeans developed the compass at the same time as the Chinese but there appears to have been no connection between the two. A Byzantine compass needle has survived from the 10th or 11th century and a writer in 12th century Paris recorded that sailors spoke of using magnetized needles to find their way at sea. The writer does not suggest that this was a new innovation but rather that to him, a landlubber, it was new information.

Early compasses were made by stroking a needle on a piece of lodestone to magnetize it. The needle was then poked through a small piece of straw and floated in a bowl of water so that it could spin freely until it pointed north. The needles were not permanently magnetized. It was necessary to have a lodestone at hand to remagnetize them.

Initially, compasses were used in cloudy weather, especially at night when the stars were obscured. A writer in 1206 recorded that sailors would place a candle or other light next to the compass so that they could read it on foggy nights. Being able to find north regardless of the weather allowed sailors to determine their approximate heading and continue on course. This use of the compass may have contributed to the increase of winter sailings during the period. Skies were overcast more often in winter than in summer. With the sun and stars partially or completely hidden from view, navigation became difficult and ships could go dangerously off course. The compass helped remedy this problem and made winter sailing safer. Over time, more advanced use was made of compasses. It was used even when the sky was clear to set the course and to plan voyages.

By the late 13th century, the compass was improved by mounting its magnetized needle on a vertical pin fixed in the center of a card instead of floating the needle in a bowl. The needle could spin freely on the pin. This "dry" compass was further improved in the 14th century by enclosing the card and needle in a box with a sealed glass lid to protect it. Early compass cards were marked with the eight primary directions (north, northeast, east, etc.) and later with 16 and then 32 directions. This greater degree of accuracy was needed as charts came into use and compass readings were matched against locations on charts.

To make reading the compass even more accurate, the magnetized needle was later attached to the card itself and the card and needle were mounted on a pin so they could spin. This eliminated any error that might have been caused by viewing the compass from different angles.

By the late 14th century, it was discovered that magnetic north deviated from true geographical north depending upon one's location. This variation could be seen by comparing the position of the Pole Star to the direction to which the compass pointed. To compensate for this, both true north and magnetic north were marked on the compass card. However, these markings were only completely accurate for the place where the compass was made since the degree of variation between true north and magnetic north depends on one's location. This means that a compass in the eastern end of the Mediterranean will show a different angle between true and magnetic north than a compass in the mid–Atlantic. Still, the variations appear to have been largely unimportant to medieval navigators in reading the compass and setting courses. Unlike modern navigators who, before the development of GPS, relied on finding true north to determine their exact latitude and longitude when sailing, medieval navigators appear to have simply set their courses based on magnetic north and confirmed their headings using the actual, uncompensated compass readings. In part, this was reasonable since the scope of the medieval maritime world was so relatively small that the variations were practically negligible. It was only with the voyages of exploration in the late 15th century that significant magnetic variations were encountered. The issue then needed to be addressed because greater accuracy was needed when sailing for long distances out of sight of land and when mapping newly discovered territory.

Aboard ships, the compasses were first mounted in the stern, near the helmsman who held the rudder and guided the ship. By the 15th century, some vessels carried two compasses. The second one was mounted in the middle of the ship near the main mast. Candles were used to illuminate the compasses so they could be read while sailing at night.

Sun Stones

In one of the Viking sagas, there is reference to a stone which enabled sailors to determine the position of the sun on cloudy days. There has been much speculation about which mineral this was and how it functioned. Some believe that the stone polarized light and that this could indicate the location of the sun.

However, such a stone has never been positively identified.

The Running Glass and Measurements of Time and Speed

Beginning in the 13th century, ships began to carry running glasses. Running glasses, now commonly referred to as hourglasses, were calibrated to measure some known length of time, typically a half-hour. With the introduction of the running glass, time was measured with more accuracy. Prior to the running glass, time was estimated by the position of the sun as it traveled across the sky, sometimes with the help of portable sundials. The glass continuously kept time through the day and night, being turned every half-hour. Eight turnings measuring a total of four hours constituted a *watch*, a term used by mariners to the present day.

The running glass was used to determine how long the ship had been traveling along a particular heading. This was important because ships' courses were measured more by time than distance. Even before the introduction of the running glass, headings were followed for a number of hours or even days instead of for a set number of miles. While measuring courses by time was practiced throughout Europe, some of the best known examples of this are found in some of the Viking sagas about travels to Iceland and Greenland which included sailing instructions in terms of days of voyaging.

Time may have been relied upon instead of distance because the passage of time could typically be better estimated or measured than the distance traveled. Skilled mariners knew approximately how long it would take to travel between two known points. They based their estimates on their prior experience and their understanding of sailing conditions and the performance of their own ships. Using this knowledge, they could also adjust their estimates as the conditions of the sea and weather changed. Further, in most instances, it was simply more relevant to know that a port was three days away rather than that it was 100 miles distant.

When it was necessary to determine the distance a ship had traveled, the navigator had to estimate the speed of his ship and the length of time that his ship had been moving at that speed. By measuring time and speed, the navigator could then estimate the distance the ship had traveled and find its current position. How the navigator estimated speed was a matter of individual skill since, as with distance, there was no accurate mechanical means of gauging speed. The speed of the ship could only be roughly estimated by watching foam slip by the hull or by observing the characteristics of the ship's wake. These qualities included whether the wake was narrow or wide, deep or shallow, and whether the ship moved away from it quickly or slowly. When the ship was traveling at its fastest, the wake was narrow, deep, and moved fast. How fast the wind was blowing as evidenced by the fullness of the sails provided another clue to the ship's speed. In a late 13th century poem, a truly skilled navigator was described as simply having a "feel" for his ship and its performance. More prosaically, if he had made the voyage before, a navigator could use that experience to estimate how fast his ship was moving. However, it is unclear whether he then calculated the distance to reach landmarks or other reference points along the ship's course or the time it would take. With the advent of sea charts, distance had to be used, but it does not appear to have entirely displaced time in sailing instructions.

While the methods medieval navigators used for measuring speed and distance were crude, they were the only ones available until the development of the log method sometime in the 15th century. With the log method, a piece of wood or "log" was dropped off one side of the ship's bow and the amount of time it took for it to travel the length of the ship was then measured. The ship's speed was extrapolated from the distance and time the log traveled. However, it is not known how commonly this technique was used. This method was improved in the 16th century by tying the log to a rope which had knots tied at regular intervals. The log was thrown off the ship's stern and allowed to freely pull its attached rope as the ship sailed away from it. A sandglass measuring a minute or other short amount of time was turned over at the moment the log hit the water. When the sand ran out, the rope was stopped. The length of rope that had been pulled out was measured using the knots, then divided by the time measured by the sandglass to calculate the ship's speed.

While lacking a precise means of measuring speed and distance may seem a grave gap in navigational methods, medieval mariners were still able to sail long distances, even out of sight of land, and arrive safely at their destinations. Even the voyages of discovery to the Americas and around the world were successfully accomplished by the Spanish and Portuguese using these methods to arrive at surprisingly accurate estimates of their vessels' speeds and the distances they had traveled.

The Cross-staff, Quadrant, and Astrolabe

The cross-staff, quadrant, and astrolabe were all instruments for measuring the angle between the horizon and the position of the sun, the Pole Star, or other stars. From these measurements, it is possible to determine one's relative position on a north-south axis. This is done by comparing these readings with known ones for ports or landmarks. They can also be converted into true readings of latitude by applying mathematical formulas.

All three instruments performed the same basic function of measuring the angle between the horizon and the sun or star but each was constructed differently.

- The cross-staff was a long wooden staff which had one or more sliding crosspieces mounted perpendicularly on it so that the crosspiece and staff formed the shape of a cross. To take a reading, the navigator placed one end of the staff just below his eye. He held the staff so that the crosspiece was vertical and then slid the crosspiece until its bottom aligned with the horizon and its top with the center of sun or star being used as the reference point. The angle was then measured using trigonometric markings on the staff. Over time, a brass sighting tube was added to the end of the staff. This could either be fitted with a pinhole aperture or disks of colored glass to provide some relief for the navigator when taking readings of the sun's elevation.

• The quadrant was a development of the cross-staff. It was a shorter staff with an arc forming one quarter of a circle mounted on the underside of the staff at the end away from the sighting end. The arc was marked with degrees of elevation. A plumb-bob on a string was attached to the center of the arc so that as the navigator lifted the staff and sighted the sun or star, the plumb-bob swung down and indicated the degree of elevation. The quadrant was also fitted with a pinhole to protect the navigator's eyes.

• The astrolabe was made of a metal disk marked with the degrees of elevation. An *alidade* was attached to the disk. The alidade was shaped like a double-headed arrow with its center attached to the center of the disk. The alidade rotated on the disk's central hub. There was a pinhole sight at each end of the alidade. To take a reading, the navigator held the astrolabe up by a string tied to a ring at its top and sighted through the pinholes at the sun or star. The arrow tips at the end of alidade then pointed to the appropriate degree inscribed on the disk.

The dates at which the cross-staff, quadrant, and astrolabe were first used aboard ship are debatable. The cross-staff and quadrant had been developed, respectively, in the 3rd and 2nd centuries B.C. The principles of the astrolabe were also developed in antiquity but the first one does not appear to have been constructed until the 5th century A.D. All these instruments were used for astronomical studies and not for navigational purposes. They fell out of use in Europe with the collapse of the Roman Empire and do not appear to have been rediscovered until the 11th or early 12th century. They were first used for astronomy and astrology. The earliest description of the use of the astrolabe by sailors dates to 1140. However, there is no other evidence of the astrolabe being used for navigation at such an early date. The next mention of navigational instruments, presumably including the astrolabe and quadrant, being used aboard ships was in a description of how sailors find their way. This was in a collection of scientific information written ca. 1270 by Raymond Llull, a noted mathematician and philosopher from the Catalan region of northeast Spain. Despite these early references, these instruments do not appear to have been generally applied to navigation until sometime in the mid– to late–15th century. Even then, it took some time for them to become standard equipment, in part because of the special training required for their use. This problem is reflected in an account of a Mediterranean voyage in the 1480s which mentions that the ship's company aboard a large galley included an astronomer to read the instruments as well as a navigator who, in turn, used the readings to pilot the ship.

The astrolabe and other instruments significantly improved navigation and provided a more sophisticated method of determining the distance a ship had traveled as well as its position. The best example of this comes from the late medieval voyages of the Portuguese. When exploring the waters down the west coast of Africa, Portuguese mariners in the 15th and later centuries relied on calculations of distance in their navigation and mapping instead of on measures of time. To determine distances traveled during their voyages down the coast of Africa in the 15th century, Portuguese navigators used the astrolabe to find their latitude. As they proceeded south, they repeatedly took readings of latitude. They took these while ashore since this would yield more accurate results than on a moving ship. By comparing these readings, they could determine how far they had traveled in terms of degrees of latitude. Using this information along with estimates of speed, the Portuguese were able to accurately map the west coast of Africa and create sailing directions for reaching points on the coast as well. In fact, later Portuguese astrolabes used aboard ships sailing around Africa were marked to indicate the latitudes of ports, capes, and mouths of rivers on the continent's coast. This enabled the Portuguese to more easily find havens for resupplying even if they had been sailing out of sight of land.

The Lead and Line

Dating back to the Romans, the lead and line was used to determine the depth of the water and to check location. The line was made of a very long rope with knots or pieces of cloth or leather tied at regular points along its length. The spaces between the knots came to be set at a standard length of six feet and were called fathoms. Completing the line, one end of it was tied to a cylindrical lead weight. The tip of the weight was hollow and was filled with tallow. The weighted end of the line was thrown overboard. The depth was read by counting the knots that were pulled under before the line stopped when the weight hit the sea bottom. When it hit the sea floor, the tallow in the tip of the lead weight stuck to the material covering the sea floor. The line was then pulled back up and the sample was analyzed and compared to known sea bottom materials. Based on personal experience and on information gained from other mariners, navigators could confirm their approximate locations based on the depth of the sea and matches between the sample and known sea bottoms. For example, courses could include directions such as "go north until the sand at 72 fathoms is fair, gray sand and then set a course north-east."

Taking soundings with a lead line was best suited to shallow waters and use of the lead line was most common in the North and Baltic Seas and along the Atlantic coast where the waters were relatively shallow. However, to some degree, the lead line could also be used to establish great depths. This was most obvious along the Atlantic coast, where the lead line, since it could no longer reach bottom, could establish that a ship had sailed so far west into the Atlantic that it was beyond the continental shelf. In the Mediterranean, the lead was used less frequently because of the sea's great depth, which averages nearly 5,000 feet. Still, the lead line was of some value when close to shore or when trying to detect submerged hazards.

The use of the lead line in relatively shallow waters is reflected in surviving sets of written sailing instructions. For example, in one set of instructions for a route from Scandinavia to England, the course is described entirely in depth soundings and sea floor samples. Even longer routes were sometimes described in these same terms. A set of 15th century sailing instructions covered a route all the way from England to Gibraltar and included soundings up to 100 fathoms (600 feet) deep, which was the maximum depth for lead lines. However, such depths were extreme and shorter lead lines appear to have been more common. Some ships likely carried both a long and short lead line. Eventually, the depths and composition of the sea floor were written down in books of sailing instructions and these continued to be used by northern mariners even after the development of sea charts.

In addition to aiding in determining location, the lead line was used to detect shoals, reefs, and other submerged dangers. By repeatedly taking soundings at short intervals, the lead line could also provide warning that the ship was approaching the shore or other dangerous shallows. These measures could help save the ship from running aground.

Portolan Charts

The Greeks and Romans did not create practical maps of the seas. They created maps of the lands and waters of the Mediterranean world and sometimes beyond but these were not drawn as usable charts and did not contain sufficient detail to make them of any practical value. The Greeks did produce sailing guides called *periploi*. These will be discussed later in this section.

Detailed, practical sea charts, typically referred to as portolan charts by most modern scholars, were a medieval innovation. Portolan charts were developed by the 13th century and the earliest surviving chart dates to around 1275. This map is called the Carte Pisane since it was believed to have been drawn in Pisa, although later research indicates that it was most likely created in Genoa.

The Carte Pisane covers the entire Mediterranean Sea along with the Black Sea and the Atlantic coast from Gibraltar to England. The outlines of the coast were drawn clearly along with the names of ports. While the Mediterranean is shown with far more detail than the waters of the Atlantic, the breadth and general accuracy of the Carte Pisane indicates that there must have been some charts before 1275. In fact, in 1270, during the sailing of Louis IX of France's crusade to North Africa, the captain of Louis' vessel reassured the king of their safety during a storm by showing him their position on some form of map. Thus, the Carte was likely the result of combining many earlier maps that covered parts of the Mediterranean, Black Sea, and Atlantic coast. Unfortunately, there are no earlier surviving charts or references to them. This may indicate that charts were actually an innovation of the mid–13th century but it is also possible that there were earlier charts which have disappeared because they were used and handed down until they were worn out. Since charts were constantly being improved as better information was gathered, old charts may have also been thrown away when they were outdated. Even in the later centuries, charts which appear to have been actually used aboard ships are extremely scarce. Most of the surviving charts are luxury editions created for kings and popes. Some of the wear and tear

on charts comes from the way they were stored. Charts were typically drawn on a large sheet of vellum made from a single sheep's hide and rolling it up was the most common means of storage. Some appear to have been wound around long wooden dowels that were attached to one edge of the chart. The repeated rolling and unrolling likely caused some damage, as did the exposure to the damp salt air and sprays of sea water. Another method of keeping a chart ready for use was to mount it on a wooden board or piece of cardboard. This helped minimize shrinkage and distortion of the chart. This was also well suited for maps pieced together from several sheets of vellum instead of the large single sheet. Mounted charts were sometimes collected and bound together to form the first atlases.

The Making of Portolans

The value of charts was well recognized. In the same law on maritime safety that required ships to carry a spare rudder, the king of Aragon also stated that ships should carry two sets of charts in case one was lost or damaged. In practice, surviving inventories of ships reveal that carrying multiple copies of charts was often done. For example, one ship was recorded as having four charts while another had three.

The production of charts appears to have begun in Genoa and Venice. Majorca and the Catalan region of northeast Spain were noted later as significant chart-making centers. The Spanish and Portuguese became more noted for their cartographic skills as the Middle Ages was ending. Spain and Portugal became important centers for map production based on the discoveries made by da Gama, Columbus, Magellan, and the others who followed them. Surviving examples show that portolans were constantly updated as new information was brought in by mariners.

Just as charts were valuable products, the men who made them were highly valued. Chart makers were sometimes granted tax exemptions from the cities in which they lived. Some cities and nations even persuaded noted cartographers to take up residence by offering them annuities or prestigious positions that came with high salaries. These perquisites were in addition to any money they made selling the charts they produced.

The craft of making charts was learned through apprenticeship but was often passed down through families without formal apprenticeships. While a few chart makers had actual experience as navigators, most were scribes and illustrators and not mariners. They gathered the information needed for their maps from interviewing navigators and looking at maps and notations they had drawn during their voyages. In the late Middle Ages and early Renaissance, there was sometimes mention of cartographers awaiting ships returning from long voyages around Africa to India and later to the Americas so they could get fresh information from the navigators and masters of these vessels.

Interestingly, outside the Mediterranean basin, the development and use of charts appears to have grown at a much slower pace as northern mariners continued to rely heavily on sandglasses, lead soundings, and dead reckoning instead of on maps and the compass.

Wind Roses and Compass Roses

To use a portolan chart, a navigator had to have a compass so that he could take a reading at one of the reference points marked on the portolan. He would then locate his position on the chart and, using the compass reading, determine his direction relative to that point. Once he had determined his heading, he could adjust his course as needed.

To make it easier to more accurately match the compass readings to the locations marked on the portolan, compass roses were drawn on these maps. The compass rose was labeled with same points as the ones on the compass card. Both the charts and the compass roses were oriented so that north was at the top of the map.

The form of the compass rose was based on the earlier *wind rose*. The wind rose was developed in the Mediterranean. Wind roses were diagrams marked with eight points showing the direction of eight principal winds of the Mediterranean basin. The points were labeled with the names of the eight principal winds. As mentioned previously, sailors could sometimes determine their direction based on which wind was blowing. Wind roses were drawn on charts covering the regions outside the Mediterranean as well. While the winds and their characteristics did not match those of the Mediterranean, prevailing winds existed on the North and Baltic Seas as well as on the Atlantic Ocean. Again, experienced sailors could tell their approximate course based on the direction from which the wind was blowing, adding in such factors as the time of year and the weather accompanying the wind. Unlike Mediterranean ones, wind roses on maps of the Atlantic and the northern seas were marked with the cardinal directions instead of the names of the winds.

Over time, charts were improved by the substitution of compass roses for the wind roses. Charts were also improved by the addition of loxodromes or rhumb lines. These lines radiated from the wind roses and, later, the compass roses. Rhumb lines showed the course a ship would travel if it followed a constant heading. Navigators used rhumb lines as references in charting their courses and for correcting their courses when underway. The rhumb lines were completely unrelated to lines of longitude and latitude. These did not begin to appear on sea charts until sometime after the Middle Ages. Similarly, the first globe made in medieval Europe did not have lines of latitude and longitude but it was marked with the equator, the tropics, and the polar circles.

There were additional tools which went along with charts. One of these was the divider. Dividers are shaped like the compasses used to draw circles except that both arms end in metal points. Dividers were in use by the 15th century at the latest. Along with ruler-like straight edges, they were used to mark off distances on the charts and to find locations for setting courses.

Mathematical Tables

Mathematical tables were another tool used by medieval mariners. Mathematics is not a skill commonly associated with people in the Middle Ages, particularly among those who weren't scholars. But navigators by the end of the 13th century were using trigonometry to determine the distance and angle that they had been forced off course by contrary winds or currents. Using the result of these calculations, they could correct their direction and get back on course. In 1275, Ramon Llull was the first to write down these calculations. In his book, *The Tree of Science*, he explained the system and created a table of trigonometric ratios for certain angles and distances to assist in making these calculations. This table was called, in Spanish, the *toleta de marteloio*. The tables were made separately from the charts but they had to be used together so that the correction of the course could be plotted out.

Books of Sailing Instructions

As mentioned previously, most scholars use the term "portolan" to refer to charts, but it also appears to have referred to a book of sailing instructions which may or may not have included some maps. For the sake of clarity, I will continue to use "portolan" to mean only charts. In the Germanic countries, the books were called *Seebuch*, meaning a "book of the sea." In English, these books came to be called *rutters*, which, in turn, was derived from the French *routier*. This reflects that the books originally addressed specific routes between certain destinations. Over time, many different routes were compiled so that these books sometimes covered quite large areas just like the portolan charts. In the late Middle Ages, sailing instructions were increasingly incorporated into atlases along with portolan charts to form more complete and useful guides.

The books of sailing instructions contained a variety of information for navigating various routes across the seas. This included descriptions of a route's hazards, landmarks, anchorages, and ports. Distances between ports as well as other reference points were also included, though some books continued to include sailing times as well. By the late Middle Ages, compass readings for ports and points along the routes were given as well. Some books contained sketches of significant features of the coastline as viewed from a ship at sea to supplement the written descriptions. These drawings typically exaggerated the features depicted, presumably to make them easier to identify from a distance. Books covering the Atlantic and the Baltic and North Seas included the depths of the sea and the composition of the material covering the sea floor to provide references for soundings taken with the lead and line.

The ancient Greeks had writings somewhat similar to books of sailing instructions called *periploi*. However, these were more like travel guides or the itineraries written for land travel than practical directions for sailing. They contained descriptions of the sights to be seen en route and accounts of history and myths related to them. The only surviving *periploi* describes some coasts with names of ports and distances between them but does not give any directions for traveling from one to another. Further, the Greeks appear to have ceased to produce *periploi* before the advent of the Christian era. The one mentioned survives in a 10th century copy of a 3rd century original. There is no evidence that the medieval books of sailing instructions developed from this or any other *periploi*. These books were a new creation.

As with portolan charts, the first surviving books date to the late 13th century. The oldest has been dated to 1296. But, again, like the maps, the depth and detail of the information in them reflects generations of accumulated navigational experience. This lore had previously been passed down orally from one generation of mariners to the next. The conversion of this knowledge into written form along with the notation of town names and other features on the contemporary portolans indicates that navigators were increasingly expected to be literate. This appears to confirm that navigators were primarily drawn from the sons of ship owners, ship masters, and navigators, all of whom were in the higher and more prosperous ranks of medieval society. Their sons had the opportunity to gain some education in reading and writing as well as in math, which would have aided in using the trigonometric tables.

Globes

Globes were the last form of maps of the Earth developed in the Middle Ages although terrestrial globes appear to have been first created in classical antiquity. A writer in the 1st century B.C. credited the Greek Crates of Mallos with the creation of a globe ten feet in diameter around the year 150 B.C. but there is no evidence of any other globes depicting the Earth until the end of the 15th century A.D. There were classical sculptures of the titan Atlas supporting a globe but this was the globe of the heavens, not the Earth. Atlas' job was to hold up the heavens and keep them from crushing the Earth.

In 1474, Paolo del Pozzo Toscanelli, a noted mathematician, described how a globe, rather than a map, would best show that the distance between the west coast of Europe and the east coast of Asia was relatively narrow. His point was to demonstrate the practicality of sailing west across the Atlantic to reach Asia. However, there is no evidence that he actually constructed such a globe. The first surviving globe was created by Martin Behaim of Nuremburg between 1487 and 1492. He called it the *erd-apfel*, which, in German, meant earth-apple, an allusion to its shape. (In Germany today, a globe is called an *erd-kugel*, an earth ball.) Behaim's globe showed the known world from Europe and Africa east to Asia. North and South America were of course absent so that India, China, and Japan were shown as lying just across the Atlantic from Europe. The globe was also flawed by the exaggerated width of Eurasia in relation to the circumference of the Earth. This was the result of using traditional faulty estimates of the size of the continents. As a result, the Atlantic was depicted as being much narrower than it really is. Coupled with the absence of the Americas, this made the distance from Europe to China and Japan seem relatively small, just as Toscanelli had proposed.

Using Toscanelli's distorted view of the circumference of the Earth along with similar information from other sources, Christopher Columbus proposed that sailing west from Europe to reach India and Asia would be shorter, quicker, and cheaper than the existing route around Africa and across the Indian Ocean. He never proposed that such a voyage would prove that the world was round. This was completely unnecessary since the vast majority of medieval Europeans, especially the educated classes, had long known that the Earth was a sphere. As for the myth that Columbus' crews were afraid of falling off the edge of the Earth, this is nonsense. Instead, they feared that the voyage was much longer than estimated and that they would run out of food and water before reaching Asia. They also feared that there would be unknown hazards out in the vast and unexplored Atlantic. One such possible hazard was the wind pattern which blew them west across the sea. If this was the prevailing wind for that part of the world, they questioned whether they would be able to sail back home against such a strong, adverse wind. In short, their fears were grounded primarily in practical concerns, not in superstitions.

ROUND VERSUS FLAT EARTH

The development of the terrestrial globe was a great advance in mapmaking but Behaim's depiction of the Earth as a sphere was not revolutionary. Even long before Crates constructed his globe, Aristotle and other philosopher-scientists of ancient Greece had reasoned that the earth was a globe and this view came to be commonly accepted. Everyday occurrences such as the gradual appearance of a ship as it came into view over the horizon, with the top of its mast visible first and then gradually the whole mast followed last by the hull of the ship, provided easily seen and understood evidence that the Earth's surface was curved. The round shadow cast by the Earth on the Moon provided more evidence that the Earth was a sphere. And all these proofs remained as visible to medieval Europeans as they had been to the ancient Greeks.

In the early Christian period, there were a few minor theologians who argued that the Bible had to be taken literally and so the Earth had to be flat like the floor of a tent and covered by a vault-like heaven. However, many important theologians, often referred to as the Fathers of the Church, accepted that the Earth was a sphere. Most of these men were generally acquainted with Greek philosophy and understood the reasoning behind the conclusion that the Earth was round. They further recognized that not all biblical passages were intended to be read literally. Some also appear to have reasoned that there were many aspects of the material world, such as its shape, which were simply irrelevant to the practice of the Christian religion. Thus, whether the Earth was round or not was not an article of faith for Christians and so was not really an issue for the Church. But, to the extent that the matter was of general concern to clerics and laity alike, some Fathers of the early Church who wrote about the issue confirmed that the evidence proved that the Earth was a sphere and that this presented no conflict between religious faith and the rational investigation of the world created by God. Throughout the Middle Ages, the Church's finest minds, including the Venerable Bede, Hildegard of Bingen, Albertus Magnus, Roger Bacon, Thomas Aquinas and many others, supported this approach and held that the earth was a globe.

While there continued to be a few dissenters, many if not most Europeans agreed the Earth was ball-shaped well before the end of the Middle Ages. The general acceptance of the round Earth was reflected in art. For example, in many cathedrals, sculptures of kings and emperors throughout the period frequently show them holding orbs. Many of these orbs have a T-shaped mark on them that mirrors the T-shape formed by the principal rivers and seas on contemporary *mappa mundi*. Others simply have a cross on them. Still, regardless of the mark, these balls are symbols of authority over the secular, the earthly world, and are models of the Earth. These statues were seen by congregations throughout medieval Europe so that even the illiterate could see an image of the Earth as a globe. Additionally, for the literate, illuminations in books also depicted orbs, including some depictions of the Last Judgment in which Christ was shown standing on a ball-shaped Earth. That the orb was Earth is confirmed by the graves on it from which people are emerging to face the judgment.

So how did the myth that all medieval Europeans thought that the Earth was flat get started? As with so many of such myths, this came from the post-medieval view of the period as a time of profound ignorance and superstition. Some people in later generations put forward these as demonstrations of how far they had advanced from their primitive ancestors. Others, particularly proponents of the Age of Enlightenment in 18th century Europe, seized every opportunity to portray the Church as being an enemy of reason and a bastion of superstition. Thus, they took the writings of the few, unimportant theologians who wrote of the flat earth and made it seem that these were the official position of the medieval Church when, in fact, these documents were virtually unknown in the Middle Ages and were certainly not representative of the majority of theologians. Later generations of writers uncritically accepted these portrayals of medieval Europeans and the Church and so believing in a flat earth became another hallmark of the depths the European culture had fallen to in the "Dark Ages."

Admittedly, as the case of Galileo and his support for the Copernican theory shows, there is merit to the view that the Church sometimes opposed scientific conclusions about the material world. It is somewhat difficult to understand why the Church could accept that the Earth was round but not the Copernican theory that the Earth revolved around the Sun rather than the Earth being the fixed center of the universe. The Church saw the position of the Earth within the heavens as a religious matter because displacing the Earth from its position as the center of the universe upset the fundamental concept that the Earth was the focus of God's creation.

Antipodes

While the shape of the Earth was generally agreed upon, there was a theological conundrum that stemmed from the teaching of the ancient Greeks themselves. Following the ancient Greeks, it was believed that the Earth was divided into five climate zones: two frigid regions with one at the north pole and another at the south, two temperate zones between the polar circles and the lines of tropics with one in the northern hemisphere and the other in the southern, and a region of unbearable heat extending from the equator out toward the two tropics. The equatorial zone was thought to be of such burning heat that it was impassable. The southern temperate zone was thought to be like the one in the northern hemisphere and could possibly be inhabited. Some theologians questioned how, if this southern zone was inhabited but the equatorial zone could not be crossed, these people could have descended from same original parents of the human race, Adam and Eve, as specified in the Bible. This led to the awkward proposition that the Earth was round and that there were unknown landmasses in the southern hemisphere, but that these lands were devoid of people. While the belief in a group of people who were not part of the common stock of humanity was heretical in theory, this issue was of little concern outside the realm of theology and those who held that there were people in the southern hemisphere do not appear to have been subjected to any significant perse-

cution by the Church. Interestingly, the whole issue seems to have simply faded away as the Portuguese and other explorers proved that the equator was not a zone of impassable heat.

The Hazards of Sea Travel

Most people in the Middle Ages dreaded sea voyages and undertook them only when there was no alternative. The threats of storms and pirates made them fear for their lives. Adverse winds could drive their ships far off course, making even the shortest of trips risky. Even without these dangers, ships seemed small and fragile on the open sea.

STORMS

Storms were, perhaps, feared even more than attacks by pirates since they could strike without mercy anywhere at any time. Even on short voyages, storms could suddenly appear with disastrous results. Untold thousands of mariners and passengers, including merchants, pilgrims, crusaders, and even nobility, died at sea as storms tore their ships apart, wrecked them on reefs and rocks, or smashed them against the shore. Hundreds or even thousands of people could die from ships being sunk by a single storm. These figures may sound like exaggerations but a large sailing ship in the late Middle Ages could carry several hundred people. Further, virtually an entire convoy of ships could be lost at the same time. Such a disaster struck a fleet of ships carrying French crusaders back from North Africa in 1270.

Sailors did their best to save their ships when storms struck. Sails were trimmed or lowered as the conditions dictated and cargo jettisoned to make the ship more buoyant. This also prevented dangerous shifting of cargo that could occur as the ship was tossed around. Whenever possible, ships' masters sought out ports or sheltered anchorages in which to ride out the tempests. However, mariners knew the risks of having their ships driven onto the shore by storms, so simply bringing a vessel close to land was not a safe maneuver. Trying to ride the storm out in open water was often the only option.

Even if a ship anchored, it was not safe from a storm. Heavy seas could tear a ship loose from its moorings. This was such a common problem that one government, that of the Byzantine Empire, issued safety regulations specifying the number and sizes of anchors that ships had to carry. The numbers specified included spares to ensure that the vessel could replace anchors lost when the anchor cables tore apart. Additionally, several anchors were sometimes needed at the same time. In 1254, a ship carrying King Louis IX of France had to use five anchors to keep from being pushed onto shore by strong winds.

Storms could also damage or snap off a ship's rudder, leaving it to drift out of control. Losing a rudder could be as catastrophic as losing a mast. As mentioned previously, in 1354, the king of Aragon addressed this danger by dictating that every ship of his country had to carry a spare rudder.

In addition to regulations to help ships cope with storms, there were rules designed to minimize losses from storms by limiting the sailing season. While severe storms could strike at any time of the year, the worst storms in the waters around Europe were in the winter, so, by tradition, most sailing was halted from late fall through the end of winter. Over time, some jurisdictions made this a formal prohibition. For example, in Pisa, any ship arriving after November 1st could not put to sea again until March 1st. As late as the 15th century, the cities of the German Hanse on the North and Baltic Seas had similar regulations. Any ship, local or foreign, that was in a Hanse port on Martinmas, November 11th, was confined to port until St. Peter's Day, February 22nd. (The choice of these dates reflects the common medieval practice of using days of religious significance as reference points.) The Hanse made limited exceptions for some of its own ships making short runs carrying beer and herring, but even this traffic had to be suspended from December through January.

Still, throughout the seas of medieval Europe, sailing did not come to a complete halt in the winter. Cargos and passengers continued to be moved. Winter sailing was usually on a smaller scale than during the rest of the year, but not in all cases. For example, in the 15th century, a quarter of London's supply of salt was brought in by ships in the winter months. Ships' masters and crews knew the risks but bowed to needs of trade and their own profit. Ultimately, formal restrictions on the sailing season gradually lapsed. Some historians speculate that improvements in navigation, such as the development of the portolan chart and the improvement of compasses, made sailing safer even in bad weather. With charts, the nearest havens could be located more easily, even when sailing out of sight of land. However, the loss of ships appears to still have been higher during the winter than in the milder seasons and as late as the 16th century the English government imposed laws attempting to restrict winter sailing to protect ships and their crews.

Restricting the sailing seasons was also often ineffective. Ships were lost at all times of the year to dangerous storms and heavy seas. For example, in the spring of 1191, a fleet carrying King Richard the Lionheart from Sicily to the Holy Land was hit by winds and storms and the ships were scattered. Richard's ship was lucky and safely reached Crete. Others of his group were less fortunate. One ship sank at sea and three were driven off course. These three reached Cyprus but only one made it safely into port. The other two were wrecked on the shore there. Events like this were far from unique and storms took a steady toll on ships, crews, and passengers throughout the period.

Adverse Winds and Calms

While strong winds and tempests were a danger, the lack of wind or wind which was simply blowing from the wrong direction was also a problem. Ships frequently had to wait for favorable winds for leaving port. At times, the wait extended to several weeks. Even a voyage which should have been short, such as from Dover to Boulogne straight across the English Channel, could take a month because of delays. The delay was likely even more maddening because the crew and ship had to be kept ready so they could set sail as soon as the right wind came up.

For sailing ships at sea, being becalmed halted all progress and even made it impossible to simply reach any port. Adverse winds caused similar problems by driving ships off course into the empty wastes of the sea. Because ships carried limited supplies of food and water, being stranded in open water was disastrous. When a voyage that was thought to take four to six days took three weeks instead, thirst and hunger became insurmountable problems if a ship could not reach a port or other place where fresh water and food could be obtained. As previously mentioned, in the Mediterranean, good ships' masters and navigators were expected to know which islands and coastal spots had fresh water and food available. They were even expected to know these places in a wide area, not just along their intended routes, so that they could find these vital resources even when blown off course. Still, in extreme cases, ships were reduced to landing at small, uninhabited islands where the passengers and crew gathered snails, crabs, and bird eggs for food.

Because of the fickleness of the winds, galleys remained popular in the Mediterranean throughout the Middle Ages. As discussed previously, galleys had masts and sails and sailed for much of the time they were at sea, but their oarsmen provided a reliable source of propulsion when needed. While both sailing ships and galleys carried pilgrims from Europe to the Holy Land, galleys were preferred because they provided the most dependable service.

SHIPWRECKS

Shipwrecks were most often caused by bad storms that destroyed a ship's masts and

sails and possibly its rudder as well, leaving it at the mercy of the driving winds and waves. Waves breaking over the ship could flood it and force it under or shatter its hull. If the damage did not result in the sinking of the ship at sea, the winds and waves could drive it onto rocks and shoals or onto the shore. Again, the ship could be broken up, spilling its crew, passengers, and cargo into the churning sea. Even today, ships with damaged or malfunctioning steering gear or engines can end up cast onto the rocks. In the 1970s, this happened to two tankers in separate instances at the entrance of the English Channel. The sea forced them onto the rocks surrounding the French island of Ushant, the same place where many medieval vessels had run aground.

Poor navigation must have caused some wrecks as well. Navigators were held to a high standard. In some countries, a navigator whose incompetence caused the loss of a ship was subject to execution, assuming he had survived the wreck. Still, many reefs, submerged rocks, and shoals were difficult hazards to avoid. Many remained killers of ships for centuries after the Middle Ages. Even today, some of these rocks and reefs claim ships despite modern navigational instruments and aids. For example, as recently 1967, the tanker *Torrey Canyon* struck the rocks around the Isles of Scilly off the southwest coast of England even though it was broad daylight and the ship's instruments were fully functional.

Once a ship had been wrecked, whether at sea or on or near the shore, the ship and any of its cargo or other contents which washed ashore were subject to the traditional right of wreckage. This custom dated back to at least the time of the ancient Greeks and Romans although the practice is likely as old as shipping itself. Under the right of wreckage, local inhabitants had the right to take any wreckage that found its way to their shore. In the Middle Ages, kings claimed the right for themselves. In turn, they granted it to those landowners, both noble and clerical, who owned seafront property. Only they had a legal right to whatever washed ashore from wrecks. However, it was difficult to prevent local people from continuing to plunder wrecks. They were usually the first ones on the scene, arriving well before any deputies of the landowners. They took whatever they could before anyone could stop them. This practice continued for centuries after the Middle Ages, with government officials rarely able to halt the "wreckers."

Even though they may not have been able to intervene when the wreck was being looted, landowners and even owners of the cargo occasionally took legal action against wreckers. For example, in 1314, a ship carrying wine wrecked at St. Catherine's Point on the Isle of Wight off the south coast of England. The wine belonged to a monastery in France. Local people, including some leading citizens, took the wine. The monastery sued Walter de Godyton, one of the men who had taken the wine, for restitution. After nine years, the lawsuit was finally decided by the papal court. De Godyton was ordered to build a lighthouse and adjoining chapel on St. Catherine's Point as an act of penance.

In antiquity and into the early Middle Ages, crews and passengers were included as part of the wreck and were subject to being enslaved and sold. In most of medieval Europe, this practice stopped as Christianity spread and the enslavement of fellow Christians became unacceptable. On rare occasions in the early Middle Ages, wealthy or noble wreck survivors were sometimes held for ransom. This happened to Earl Harold Godwinson of England in 1064. While en route to Normandy, the earl's ships were driven off course and ran aground on the lands of the Count of Ponthieu. The count took the earl hostage and planned to ransom him. However, the count was forced to release him on the orders of his overlord, William, the Duke of Normandy. (As part of gaining his freedom, Harold had to swear allegiance to William and promise to support his claim to the throne of England. Ultimately, Harold and William had some disagreements over these matters and, in 1066, settled them at a place called Hastings.) People of other faiths, primarily Moslems,

were taken hostage and either ransomed or enslaved. For their part, Moslems did the same to any Christian survivors of wrecks who washed up on their shores.

Even with the ending of slavery in Europe, the lot of wreck survivors did not always improve. Based on accounts up through the 19th century in England, local inhabitants did help save survivors sometimes. At times, they even sent out rescue boats at the risk of their own lives. But in some instances survivors appear to have been allowed to drown or even killed to avoid any challenges to the local residents' looting of the wreck and its cargo. It is impossible to confirm how widespread such heinous practices were but it is likely that they did occur in medieval Europe, as they did in later centuries.

Shipwrecks could change the course of history. For example, in 877, a Viking fleet en route to England was destroyed by a storm, preventing additional troops from reinforcing the army there. This aided the English in the war against the invading Vikings. In another instance, William, son of King Henry I of England and heir to the throne, was killed when sailing from France to England in 1120. His ship, the *Blanche Nef* or *White Ship*, ran onto rocks and broke apart. Rescuers did put out to sea in a boat and reached the wreck, but the rescue boat foundered as too many survivors tried to climb aboard it. Only one person survived. William was lost and the succession of English kings was forever changed.

NIGHT SAILING

Sailing at night could be dangerous. Darkness concealed reefs and other hazards that were treacherous even in daylight. There were some lighthouses but, as previously discussed, these provided little aid for nighttime navigation since they marked entrances to harbors rather than dangerous rocks. When sailing in waters which were known to have numerous reefs and shoals, the best option was often to anchor for the night and continue the voyage the next day.

To avoid having to anchor on the open sea for the night, ships often put into shore before dark, either by going into a port or by anchoring in the shelter of land. Both of these actions could be most safely accomplished while there was still daylight. For ports, even where their entrances were marked by lighthouses, the lack of other lights and the difficulty of safely negotiating their channels even in daylight meant that ships could not enter most harbors at night. In fact, some harbors chained their entrances shut to prevent it. Thus, lighthouses provided a signal that the ship was near shore and could drop anchor to await entering the harbor the next day.

The practice of stopping for the night appears to have been most common for galleys in the Mediterranean, especially for those galleys that carried pilgrims. As previously mentioned, carrying sufficient food and water was a problem for these ships, with their large crews and large numbers of passengers, and they needed to stop often to replenish their supplies. Stops for reprovisioning were typically combined with overnight stays. This way the ships avoided sailing at night while also serving the needs of the crew and passengers. These stops caused some delay but fresh food and water were always welcomed.

Despite the risks, many ships did not stop at night. In some instances, this may have been because the ship was simply too far from a safe anchorage, but in most cases sailing by night was a standard practice. This is reflected in the fact that navigating by the stars was common. Some ships' masters and navigators actually preferred night sailing because the stars provided reliable reference points for both direction and latitude. Over the course of the Middle Ages, night sailing was made safer by improvements such as the development of the compass and sea charts and the increasing use of the quadrant and astrolabe at sea. While these improvements also benefited ships sailing by day, some historians have concluded that these improvements made night sailing even more common.

OVERLOADING

The owners of cargo vessels made their incomes from the freight charges paid by merchants on the goods being shipped. This gave the owners an incentive to load as much merchandise as possible into the holds of their ships. Even ships' masters were willing to risk the dangers of overloading their ships if it meant more profit. To prevent the loss of lives, ships, and their cargos, some governments intervened to curb overloading. In the 13th century, Venice imposed safety measures that included mounting iron rods on the sides of galleys. The rods were marked to indicate the ship's waterline when carrying its maximum safe load. The rods were also marked in inches and fines were levied for each inch the safe waterline was submerged by excess cargo. On Venetian sailing ships, small crosses were painted on the sides of the vessels. These functioned like the rods on the galleys and marked the waterline for the ship's heaviest safe load. The crosses likely had inch marks as well for measuring how far above or below the safe waterline a ship was loaded.

The weight of the cargo was not always the cause of overloading. Cotton, a valuable commodity in medieval Europe, was a relatively light but very bulky cargo. Since it was a costly item, the Italians usually shipped cotton from the Middle East to Italy in the safety of their galleys. A load of cotton would fill a galley but would not weigh it down to its maximum safe carrying capacity. In order to carry as much cotton as possible, the bales were compressed using large boards as levers to squeeze more bales into the galley's hold. Wool being transported from England to Italy was sometimes loaded this way as well. Compressing the bales caused several problems. Merchants complained that the squeezing damaged the cotton or wool fibers and sued the ship's master and its owners for restitution. More importantly, the pressure from the compacted bales pressed out against the galley's frame and hull. This could force the planks and beams of the galley apart and cause leaks which could sink the ship. In response to these problems, the Venetian government limited the amount of force that could be used to compress the bales. But this problem did not end there. As late as the 19th century, overloading of cotton bales was still a danger for ships.

PIRACY

As with storms and shipwrecks, piracy was a constant threat to shipping. As far back as at least the Bronze Age, pirates attacked merchant ships in the Mediterranean. Piracy plagued the northern waters and the Atlantic too. The Roman Empire largely suppressed piracy in the Mediterranean but the collapse of the Empire in western Europe opened up the seas to piracy since there was no longer an effective navy to combat the problem. Only in the eastern end of the Mediterranean where the Byzantine navy still sailed was there a significant measure of security for trading ships. The general lack of protection led to a contraction of sea-borne trade in the earliest centuries of the Middle Ages. As commerce recovered throughout Europe, shipping did as well. With the gradual development of effective governments, some order was restored in their surrounding waters and efforts were made to protect their citizens' ships and combat piracy.

Pirates and Privateers

In the Middle Ages, pirates could be found in all waters. Piracy was endemic in the Mediterranean. Throughout the period, there were frequent attacks between the various Italian city-states on their rivals' shipping. Beginning in the 8th century, piracy was further increased by the introduction of Moslem pirates who sailed the Mediterranean, attacking targets both on land and sea. Elsewhere, Basque pirates attacked ships sailing the Atlantic. Scandinavian pirates plied the North, Baltic, and Irish Seas. Basques and Vikings even conducted raids in the Mediterranean. English and French pirates attacked shipping in the Atlantic Ocean, the English Channel, and the North Sea. Spanish pirates were active on both the Atlantic and the Mediterranean. Basically, every seagoing country had pirates. Some were professionals, but even merchant and fishing ships engaged in piracy when the opportunity presented itself.

Some acts of piracy were conducted under color of law. When at war, countries would call upon their mariners to attack and take enemy ships, both men-of-war and merchant vessels. Ship owners, both common and noble, responded and outfitted their ships for combat. These men came to be called privateers and were sometimes issued formal papers authorizing their actions. In many instances, privateers carried out their attacks without any formal approval. For example, even when they were not at war, the Italian city-states were often in conflict and their merchant vessels would attack those of rivals when the opportunity arose. Further, some privateers were simply pirates who were able to use wars to legitimize their activities for a time. As with piracy, there were merchants and fishermen who engaged in privateering along with their other occupations.

There was little if any difference to the victims between acts of piracy and acts of privateering. The victims' ships and their cargos would be seized. They risked being killed when their ships were attacked. They might even be executed after the battle was over. Privateers were expected to follow the rules of war and take them into port along with the captured ship but this was not done in all cases. Like pirates, privateers sometimes killed their prisoners. The Shipman in *The Canterbury Tales* may have been such a privateer or part-time pirate. Chaucer describes him as ignoring the "nicer rules of conscience" and sending his prisoners "home" by making them walk the plank. Thus, whether attacked by a pirate or a privateer, the consequences were usually the same. And for the purposes of this section, both pirates and privateers will be referred to as "pirates."

While European pirates were feared by mariners and passengers, the most feared pirates were the Moslems. European pirates would kill sailors and others when taking a ship that offered resistance. In the early Middle Ages, some pirates enslaved captured crewmen and passengers and sold them off. But, with decline of enslaving fellow Christians, they may have let some captives go, although most, especially valuable ones, were likely held for ransom. Moslem pirates, on the other hand, executed, ransomed, or enslaved all Christians they captured throughout the period.

As with Europeans, there were some Moslem merchants and other mariners who took advantage of opportunities to make a little profit from piracy, but the vast majority of Moslem pirates were full-time professionals. These corsairs were sometimes part of organized fleets and operated openly from ports that served as their bases. There were several reasons why they were able to carry out their attacks with the support and approval of rulers of the ports from which they sailed. First, their targets were usually Christian. They appear to have rarely attacked Moslem shipping. The focus on attacking Christians was tacitly, if not openly, approved of because it was in accord with the militancy of medieval Islam and its hostility towards those of other faiths. Second, as with European pirates, they sometimes served as the navies of Moslem states. The large, heavily armed crews of their galleys were ideal warships to use against European fleets. Third, piracy was simply good for business. The cargos and slaves taken by the pirates enriched the cities and towns in which the pirates were based.

Acts of Piracy

Mentioning piracy usually conjures up images of sea battles, and ship-to-ship combat was a common part of piracy in the Middle Ages. However, medieval piracy also involved attacks on ports and other coastal settlements. These were typically quick raids. The pirates landed, looted, and then swiftly withdrew before any strong defense could be organized. The Vikings commonly practiced this tactic. Beginning in the 9th century, Moslem pirates conducted such raids along the west coast of Italy. They even established bases in Italy and along the French Riviera. As discussed previously, several states in the surrounding regions attacked these bases and drove the Moslems out in the late 10th century. But they reestablished themselves in North Africa and continued raids on coastal communities across Europe into the 19th century. Besides attacking Moslem pirate strongholds, Italian city-states, such as Pisa and Genoa, carried out attacks against each other's coastal holdings. In the 14th century, as part of the Hundred Years' War, both the French and English raided each other's coasts. The French were especially adept at this and inflicted terrible destruction on a number of ports along the south coast of England.

Apart from the late examples of the French and English raids, attacks on coastal cities and towns decreased as land defenses improved and pirates increasingly targeted ships on the open sea. In large part, this was due to the revival and expansion of trade. It became more profitable to take ships than raid towns. It was also generally less risky. Pirate ships usually carried as many men as possible and could overwhelm the smaller crews of most ships. The pirate ships came prepared for battle and their men were heavily armed and experienced in using weapons. Merchant sailors often had some experience with weapons too, but most ships carried few weapons and little armor. Finally, if a ship put up an effective defense or if other ships came to assist the victims, the pirates could easily sail away.

Any vessel could fall victim to pirates. Shared nationality offered no protection. Pirates would attack ships from their own country except, possibly, during time of war. Religion was also not a barrier. Ships carrying pilgrims from England to the shrine of Saint James in Compostela in northwest Spain were even subject to attack by fellow Christians. However, in the Mediterranean, pilgrims vessels usually sailed unmolested by Christian pirates but were preyed upon by Moslem pirates.

Slavery

Besides the risks of losing their ship or cargo, crews and passengers were also in danger of losing their freedom when attacked by pirates. As with enslavement of shipwreck survivors, enslavement of men and women captured by pirates had been a problem from the earliest years of sailing. And it remained a problem through the Middle Ages and up into the 19th century for Christians captured by Moslem pirates.

As mentioned previously, within Europe, enslavement was most common in the early centuries of the Middle Ages but, by the 11th century, most of Europe was Christianized and taking fellow Christians as slaves largely ceased. In the Mediterranean, enslavement by pirates remained common throughout the Middle Ages when the victims were of a different religion than the pirates. That is, when one was Christian and the other Moslem. Both sides engaged in such slavery. Enslavement of captured Moslems by Christian pirates or navies persisted through the 16th century and gradually disappeared, but Moslems continued to engage in this practice until the early 19th century. As mentioned previously, Moslem pirates conducted raids on coasts around Europe as well as on the open seas specifically to take captives for their slave trade. Italy was hardest hit by these raids. By some estimates, the pirates of the Barbary Coast of North Africa enslaved hundreds of thousands of Christians between the 16th and 19th centuries. These depredations were finally stopped in the 19th century when the forces of the United States and some European nations destroyed the Barbary pirates. The numbers of people taken as slaves may seem high but contemporary records of losses of ships and of raids on coastal communities support these figures. Comparable documentation from the Middle Ages is sparse but there are accounts of pilgrim ships being taken by Moslem pirates, with hundreds of passengers captured in a single foray. There are also descriptions of desolate coastlines in Italy that were abandoned after repeated pirate raids. Moslem accounts also suggest that large numbers of Europeans were sometimes captured. A description of one North African city in which pirates were based speaks of the streets ringing with the sound of the chains on the feet of newly captured slaves as they were marched through the city. While limited, this information suggests that significant numbers of Europeans were taken as slaves in the Middle Ages. Although far fewer were enslaved than in the centuries afterwards, tens of thousands of medieval Europeans likely suffered this fate.

The slave trade was very lucrative. Most slaves were sold as common laborers, but skilled craftsmen, such as ships' carpenters, were always in demand and brought higher prices. Enslaved nobles and others from privileged backgrounds also sold for high prices because of the large ransoms they were expected to yield. Particularly valuable captives were sometimes claimed by the rulers of the North African ports as their share of the spoils. The most unfortunate were the ordinary sailors and peasants who were enslaved. They were pressed into service aboard the galleys and for hard manual labor, such as hauling stones for building construction.

Like their Moslem counterparts, Christian pirates did not hesitate to sell any captured person from a different religion into slavery. However, because of the nature of their shipping, Moslem vessels rarely offered prize catches for Christian pirates. There were no large Moslem passenger vessels in the Mediterranean comparable to the Christian pilgrim galleys. Only their pirate and navy galleys carried significant numbers of men. Further, shore raids by Christian pirates to capture slaves were far rarer than those conducted by the Moslems. However, in some land battles, numbers of Moslem soldiers were taken prisoner. These men, along with any crewmen of captured galleys, were forced to serve aboard European galleys.

Fighting Piracy

Countries and individuals developed tactics and strategies to fight piracy. There were a number of measures taken to combat coastal raiding. In Italy, fortifications were added or improved at some port cities and towns. In the Byzantine Empire, the government operated a coast guard fleet. In France, bridges were built to block Vikings from reaching targets upriver. Protecting coastal settlements was also a problem in Scandinavia, the home of the Vikings. A seagoing version of militias, the *ledung*, developed. Local inhabitants were required to turn out to man ships to defend against coastal raiders. In 14th century England, individual landowners near the south coast were licensed to build castles or improve their current defenses to act as strong-points in case of French raids.

At sea, the expansion of trade made piracy more attractive but this growth in trade was fostered, in part, by efforts to combat piracy. Several measures were taken to fight pirates on the open sea including carrying more men-at-arms, traveling in convoys, and being accompanied by armed ships. These measures deterred piracy but did not eliminate it.

The most common means of combating piracy was to carry armed men aboard ships. As previously mentioned, the government of Venice required merchant and passenger ships to carry arms for the crews and sometimes numbers of marines as well to fight off pirates. These regulations specified the number of marines and the arms and armor they were to have. Along with being armed with swords and javelins, a set number had to be armed with crossbows, a weapon well-suited to combat at sea. Venice encouraged men to train at using the crossbow by sponsoring competitions. The best crossbowmen were selected to serve as marines aboard the galleys. Here, they occupied a privileged position, dining with ship's officers instead of with the ordinary sailors and being authorized to take a small amount of goods, free of any charges, to trade on their own to make extra money.

Galleys, such as those of Venice, were especially well suited for fending off pirates since, in addition to the marines, their scores of oarsmen could also fight. It must be remembered that, until the end of the Middle Ages, the oarsmen were free men, not slaves, and had every interest in fighting off pirates.

Individual ships' masters sometimes added armed men to their crews even without being required to do so. A wine convoy in French waters in the late 15th century carried over 500 armed men aboard its five ships and two smaller vessels. At the very least, some masters had their crews outfitted with arms and armor so they could offer some resistance to attackers. Javelins found aboard the wrecks of some merchant ships provide physical evidence of this practice.

Guns, usually in the form of small cannons, were added to ship defenses beginning in the 14th century. One of the earliest references to guns aboard ships dates to 1350 when some Spanish ships carrying cloth from Flanders were armed with guns. They gradually became a common shipboard weapon. Like crossbows and javelins, guns enabled vessels to engage in combat before they closed for hand-to-hand combat. Effective use of projectile weapons could repel an attacking ship.

Another means for deterring or repelling attacks, whether from pirates or warships of hostile nations, was to sail in convoy. This tactic was used throughout the seas of medieval Europe. One of the earliest mentions of convoys was by Frisian merchant ships in northern Europe in the 8th century. Later in the period, Venice often used convoys to protect its merchant ships during wars. Venetian sailing ships as well as galleys would sometimes sail in convoys. The Venetian convoy system was so effective that merchants did not take out any insurance on their cargoes aboard these ships. The Hanse used convoys as well for its fleets of ships making the annual trip to the Bay of Bourgneuf to pick up salt. Groups of 50 or more ships were recorded. While it offered safety from attacks, ships' masters did not like the convoy system since it wasted time as vessels had to wait until all the ships arrived and were ready to sail. This could create days or even weeks of delay. Any delay was expensive since the crews had to be fed and paid while they were waiting. When the convoy was finally ready, it could then proceed but could travel no faster than the slowest ship. Sailing in convoy also increased the risk of collision as the ships moved in relatively close formation. A sudden adverse wind or heavy seas could drive ships into one another. Such an accident befell the same flotilla of ships carrying French crusaders home from North Africa mentioned previously. In addition to being hammered by waves and wind, ships in the storm-battered fleet were rammed by one of their own vessels that had broken its moorings. Finally, not all convoys were effective and individual ships or even large numbers of vessels could still fall prey to pirates. In 1449, this latter disaster befell a convoy of 110 ships from Hanse cities and the Low Countries. The ships were headed home from the Bay of Bourgneuf and were fully laden with salt. English pirates captured the entire fleet in a single attack. A smaller convoy of 50 ships of the Hanse had suffered the same fate in 1405.

Convoys were sometimes supplemented with armed vessels carrying men-at-arms. At times, Venice prohibited cogs and other sailing ships from traveling without armed escorts. Galleys did not usually need escorts but, as mentioned before, sailing ships had smaller crews than galleys and so were more vulnerable to attack. Examples of the use of escorts can be found in areas outside the Mediterranean too. In the 14th century, the duke of Brittany arranged for an armed ship to accompany a fleet carrying wine from Bordeaux to Brittany. The escort was paid for with funds collected from merchants who owned the wine.

There were also counter-piracy operations both at sea and against pirate bases. The Byzantine Empire, which had the only effective navy in early medieval Europe, patrolled its waters and engaged pirate ships when found. As mentioned before, the city-

states of Italy successfully pushed Moslem pirates out of their bases in Italy and the islands of the Mediterranean, although the Moslems regrouped and fell back to bases in North Africa. In the late Middle Ages and later centuries, one of the strongest anti-piracy forces was the Knights of the Order of the Hospital of St. John of Jerusalem. With the loss of the Holy Land, the Hospitallers were driven into exile in 1291 and retired to their holdings in Cyprus. In the early 14th century, the Knights captured the island of Rhodes and established their headquarters there. For the next two centuries, their fleet fought Moslem pirates throughout the eastern Mediterranean. They also attacked pirate bases on the coast of Asia Minor. In 1523, the Order was forced from Rhodes after a prolonged siege by the massive army of Sultan Suleiman the Magnificent. The Knights moved to Malta and continued their operations against pirates. They are still headquartered there today but they have long since stopped conducting military activities. Their mission now focuses on humanitarian relief.

WAR

As on land, traveling by ship during wartime was dangerous. As mentioned earlier, pirates acting as privateers were common since most countries' travelers lacked standing navies. In addition to authorizing privateers, governments typically impressed merchant ships into service to serve as combat ships and as transports and landing craft when invasions by sea were planned.

When sailing during a war, some passengers obtained safe conducts before venturing out. These could provide protection, as in one instance in which a ship and its passengers were seized by an English ship during the Hundred Years' War. A passenger produced his group's safe conduct document and the English released the ship and even provided advice on setting its course for the next part of its journey.

REPRISALS AND COMPENSATION

Merchants and ship owners did not take the loss of their goods or vessels lightly. They sought compensation whenever possible. Some examples of this can be found during the Hundred Years' War. Shipping vessels in the North Sea and Atlantic were subject to attack by both France and England and by their allies. Occasionally, the governments attempted to make amends to victims when it was politically expedient. For example, in one instance, France indemnified the losses of one of its allies caused by English pirates. Compensation was also sometimes paid to merchants and ship owners whose vessels had been attacked by pirates from an allied nation. Victims from neutral countries were only rarely compensated.

Countries sometimes provided compensation for their own citizens when the origin of the pirates could be identified. For example, in 1304, a ship carrying an English merchant's goods was taken by Zeelanders (Zeeland is now part of the Netherlands). In reprisal, English authorities seized ships and merchandise belonging to any Zeelanders who happened to be in London and other English ports. The merchant received compensation for his loss from the property seized. This form of economic revenge and restitution was used by many countries over the course of the Middle Ages. Like compensation during wartime, this form of collecting restitution was subject to foreign policy considerations. If the pirates came from a country that was weak or as hostile, it was more likely that reprisal would be carried out. It was far less likely if the country was a valued ally or was strong enough to make it dangerous to antagonize them.

PRAYERS AND PILGRIMAGES

During a disaster at sea, sailors and passengers prayed for deliverance. Many promised to undertake pilgrimages if they safely reached land. Some promised to make offerings to the Church if they lived. On occasion, prayers, pleading, and bargaining worked and ships were miraculously saved from danger.

There were many different saints whom sailors and ships' passengers invoked in hopes that they would intercede with God and save their lives. Some of the most popular saints for mariners and passengers were Saint Nicholas, Saint Clement, Saint Elmo, and the Virgin Mary.

There were two saints named Nicholas that sailors venerated. One was Saint Nicholas of Tolentino, whose miracles included resurrecting drowned children and saving a ship in a storm. The more famous Saint Nicholas was Saint Nicholas of Bari, who was a bishop of Myra in Asia Minor in the 4th century. His connection with the sea stems from calming a storm on a voyage to the Holy Land. He was originally buried in Myra but, in 1087, Italian sailors and merchants from the maritime town of Bari stole his body. The theft was motivated in part by the recent capture of Myra and other parts of Asia Minor by the Turks. The mariners of Bari and others feared that the saint's shrine might be destroyed by the Turks or, at the very least, that they would make it more difficult to make pilgrimages to the shrine. Incidentally, this is the same Saint Nicholas who is associated with Christmas as Santa Claus.

Another saint popular among mariners was Saint Clement. According to apocryphal accounts, he was martyred by order of the Emperor Trajan by being tied to an anchor and cast into the sea. Saint Erasmus, better known as Saint Elmo, was also a patron saint of sailors. He had no special connection to the sea but sailors attributed the appearances of pale blue balls of static electricity around masts and rigging before and during storms as a sign that they were under the protection of the saint. The sailors referred to the ghostly balls as "Saint Elmo's Fire." Confusingly, there was another person sometimes referred to as "Saint Elmo." This was Peter Gonzalez, a 13th century Dominican preacher, who was treated as a patron saint by sailors of Portugal and Spain even though he was never canonized. Gonzalez had specialized in preaching to the sailors in waterfront towns along the Spanish coast. How he came to be called "Saint Elmo" is unclear but Iberian mariners appear to have merged Gonzalez with Erasmus since both were affiliated with the sea.

Saint Mary, the mother of Jesus, was a popular saint for prayers during disasters at sea. She has no particular association with the sea but was seen as a particularly merciful figure and so was invoked in many crises.

In addition to petitioning help from saints, there were also instances when the desperate sought protection from a holy object, as in the 7th century when holy oil thrown onto a stormy sea instantly caused calm. Religious relics could also deliver ships from danger. In one case, a ship transporting a relic was saved from a storm. In another, a relic was credited with the ship's escape from pirates.

Prayers were often accompanied by promises of donations to the Church. These offerings were most often money or other valuables, but models of ships were sometimes left at shrines as votive gifts. Ship's crews and passengers also promised to go on pilgrimages to various shrines if they survived the catastrophe confronting them. Under the regulations of the Hanse trade federation, if a ship's master vowed to God that he would go on a pilgrimage if he and his ship were saved, the cost of the pilgrimage was to be divided between the master and the merchants whose cargo had been aboard his ship. The theory was that the master's pilgrimage vow had benefited them as well and so they too should pay their fair share.

Besides prayers and promises of offerings and pilgrimages, another practice intended to draw divine protection was to give ships religious names. Ship owners throughout Europe gave their vessels names such as *Holy Ghost*, *Trinity* (a reference to the divine trinity of the Father, Son, and Holy Ghost), *Saint Mary*, *Notre Dame*, and *Ave Maria* as well as the names of other saints in the hope that God would look favorably on them. Despite their godly names, some of these ships turn up in records of piracy, such as the *Holy Gost* (sic) of Newcastle which seized a Hanseatic cog in 1435.

Harbors and Ports

The facilities needed for landing ships and handling cargo varied widely over the course of the Middle Ages. There were some regional differences as well. Early in the period, around the Atlantic coast, open beaches were adequate for all vessels, but, as ships evolved, permanent structures were needed to meet these changes. Around the Mediterranean, Roman wharves and docks survived in many ports and were well suited to the types of vessels used in that sea.

BEACHES AND TIDAL LANDINGS

The most basic places for ships to land were beaches or tidal flats. To land, a vessel would be run onto the shore and then pulled further up onto the beach by its crew. It was then anchored or tied off to a mooring post to prevent it from slipping back into the sea. Most commonly, landings were made with the help of the tides. The ship would be brought in as close to shore as possible at high tide. Again, it would be anchored or tied off. As the tide receded, the ship was left grounded on the now exposed flat or beach.

With the tide out, the ship could then be loaded or unloaded. Since the flats were often very muddy, planks were laid for people to walk to and from the ship, although this may not have been necessary where the shoreline was gravelly or a well-drained sand beach. At some frequently used landing spots, more permanent boardwalks were built. Ships were sometimes pulled in by winches or gangs of men when they arrived at high tide so that they could be brought as close to land as possible. This minimized the distance that cargo had to be carried. Still, moving cargo to and from a beached ship was cumbersome. It was easy for goods to get wet. Sledges were sometimes used to slide loads across the beach but moving heavy loads across mud or sand was still very difficult.

Once its business was concluded, the ship left with the aid of the tide. Its departure would be timed to coincide with the turning of the tide. This was the point when the high tide began to ebb. At high tide, the ship was once again afloat and the ebbing of the tide helped draw the ship back out to sea.

Landing on tidal flats and beaches was most common around the Atlantic coastline of Europe. There are significant differences in water levels at high and low tides along much of the coast so that the water depth close to shore changes, sometimes drastically, with the tides. This facilitated beaching ships. Tidal flats used for landing could be found a surprising distance inland. For as far inland as a river's level was substantially affected by the tides, it was possible to make a landing. For example, the original port of London centered on portions of the Thames foreshore that were exposed at low tide. Having seagoing cargo ships reach this far inland encouraged trade and developed markets. Later, however, on rivers throughout Europe, many of these landing places shrank or disappeared as the shoreline was pushed out by infilling and revetting that narrowed the river and left it a deep channel with a far narrower shore. Still, beaching remained possible along the seaside.

In other parts of Europe that did not border the Atlantic, landing on beaches may have been less common. In both the Mediterranean and Baltic Seas, the differences in high and low tide levels are far less than in the Atlantic. Apart from a few spots where tides can measure one to two feet, most of the shores around both of these seas have tides of only a few inches. It was still possible to land a ship by running it aground and having it pulled ashore with ropes, but this was far more difficult without the aid of the tide.

Besides the tide, ship design also affected the landing of vessels. Most ships in northern Europe in the early Middle Ages were built with shallow keels and relatively broad hulls that curved gradually up at the sides. These features allowed them to land easily and stay upright. Their hull shape was also better able to withstand the stresses of being grounded. In the Mediterranean, the two primary designs for merchant ships were the round ship and the galley. The round ship had a rounded hull and relatively high sides which grew higher over the course of the period as it evolved into other forms of ships (see illustration 16). When run ashore, these ships tended to roll over to one side. They could nearly fall completely on their sides. Putting a ship in this position was called careening. It was done to perform maintenance or repair on the ship's hull but careening the ship every time it landed would have caused excessive wear and tear to the vessel. Further, this position was unsuitable for loading or unloading cargo. Additionally, the draft of the round ship appears to have been too deep to bring the vessel close enough to shore for routine beaching. It could only be pulled ashore with great effort. As for the galley, its hull was relatively wide and similar in shape to those of northern ships and small galleys could be easily beached. However, for larger galleys, some of which could be up to 150 feet in length, it was impractical to land by beaching.

THE DEVELOPMENT OF HARBOR FACILITIES

As the Middle Ages progressed, shipping moved off the beach and into harbors. In the Mediterranean, harbors with wharves, warehouses, and other structures had been in use since the beginning of the period. They were a legacy of the Romans and other earlier civilizations. Many of these harbors went into decline after the fall of the Empire and port facilities everywhere appear to have suffered from lack of maintenance. But some continued to function. Those in the eastern Mediterranean that were protected by the Byzantine Empire maintained their Roman facilities, although the volume of shipping for all ports was reduced in the early Middle Ages with the contraction of international trade. Northern Europe, too, had its early harbors. A few ports, such as in London, had some wharves and other structures built by the Romans but these fell into disuse and virtually disappeared after the withdrawal of Roman forces. Until the end of the 10th century, most harbors in northern Europe appear to have had very rudimentary facilities, often just bare beaches with a few buildings such as stalls for selling the cargo brought ashore. Still, with the general decline in the volume of shipping and the differences in the designs of the local vessels and those of the Romans, these simpler, more primitive ports were adequate for the shipping of the time.

WHARVES AND DOCKS

Ports around the Mediterranean typically had docks and wharves. Wharves are also called "quays." Wharves had been a feature of these harbors since classical antiquity. These structures were built so that the vessels could pull right alongside and tie up. This obviously made loading and unloading much easier than carrying or sliding cargos across a tidal flat. Additionally, with the absence of significant tides, it was easier and more practical for ships in the Mediterranean to tie up to a wharf or dock than to be hauled up onto a beach.

As mentioned above, the Romans had constructed wharves in their port cities outside the Mediterranean as well but these were largely abandoned. Wharves began appearing again in major ports along the coasts of the North and Baltic Seas in the late 10th century. They were also likely built at high-traffic ports along the Atlantic. This improvement was driven by the increasing volume of trade and growing sophistication of ships and shipping. As trade grew again, larger ships were built to carry bigger amounts of goods. These ships increasingly required better landing facilities than open beaches. Many vessels became too big for routine beaching. They were also built with increasingly deeper drafts that made it difficult and dangerous to bring them close enough to shore to unload. This problem was solved, in part, by building wharves and docks that projected out into deeper water. Besides

simply making it possible for ships to land, these facilities made it quicker and more efficient to load and unload vessels. In turn, it was possible to make more efficient use of the ships. With speedier cargo handling, they could spend more time hauling goods rather than waiting in harbors. This may have increased the number of voyages vessels could make during the sailing season and provided another stimulus to trade.

Wharves and docks were first constructed in wood at most ports, although some harbors around the Mediterranean still had stone ones from the days of the Romans and constructed new ones in stone as well. Beginning in the early 13th century, stone construction of docks and wharves began in northern Europe, but most continued to be built of wood, which remained the standard practice well after the Middle Ages. In the 20th century, docks and wharves in major harbors were still being built of wood. Many small docks and wharves are still being constructed of wood today.

It took centuries for wharves and docks to become a standard feature in most harbors. There was a long transitional period in which ports kept beaches open for landing while wharves and docks slowly became more common. Keeping some beaches open was necessary since ships suited for beach landings continued in use and were only gradually replaced with other ships that were suited to docking. Maintaining open beaches also benefited riverborne traffic since these smaller craft remained suited to beach landings. Some smaller, shallow-draft ships used for the local coastal trade also continued to land on beaches.

LIGHTERING

Not all ships tied up at wharves or docks. For some ships, especially larger ones such as carracks, *lightering* was commonly used for loading and unloading vessels. For lightering, goods and passengers were ferried back and forth between the wharf and the ship by smaller boats. In English, these boats came to be called *lighters*. While its origin is uncertain, the term may be derived from word *lighten* since these boats lightened the load of the ship. The use of lighters became more common as the Middle Ages progressed and ship sizes increased. Lightering remained a standard practice throughout the age of sailing ships and lighters are still used today to carry a wide variety of cargos from ships into shallow-water ports.

The primary advantage of lightering is that it permits vessels to moor in deep water in the harbor or offshore and still be loaded and unloaded. The need for this may not be clear today, when ocean-going ships routinely pull right up to the wharves. But in the Middle Ages, the depth of the water at the edges of the wharves and docks was often still relatively shallow, sometimes too shallow for seagoing vessels. This problem was worse in areas with significant tides. The fluctuations in water levels could leave some ships grounded at low tide. A vessel kept out in deeper water would stay safely afloat regardless of the tide. Lighters could then ferry its cargo to and from the shore and the lighters could use the wharves and docks since they had shallow drafts. Further, lightering was generally safer for vessels since bringing a large sailing ship into dock was a painstaking and risky process. One mistake could drive the ship into the wharf or onto shallows. In later centuries, tugboats made this maneuvering easier, but the only tugboats available until the 19th century were large rowboats that were used to pull the ships in and out of harbors when the winds were unfavorable. To avoid these difficulties and dangers, it was better for the ship to stand offshore in the harbor basin.

While not as efficient as having the ship dock directly at a wharf, the docks and wharves did make it possible for the lighters to load and unload more quickly and easily than if the ship had landed on a beach. Lightering also allowed seagoing ships to serve ports that were otherwise too shallow to reach directly. But lightering took more time, effort, and expense than unloading and loading directly at a dock or wharf. Cargos had to be loaded twice: once aboard the lighter and then again from the lighter onto the ship, or in the reverse when unloading. This lengthened the loading process and required the hiring of the lighter and its crew. Loading and unloading offshore between two vessels bobbing in the water was also more difficult and risky than loading directly on the dock or wharf with the ship tied up securely. Still, lightering remained a necessity in many harbors, especially as ships grew larger and their drafts grew deeper.

While they needed to stay in deeper water, it was always preferable for ships to moor in the sheltered waters of a harbor. To make mooring easier, some harbors had wooden piles driven into the sea floor for ships to use as mooring posts. In some Italian harbors, as at Pisa, stone pillars were built for mooring. While ships did have anchors, mooring posts provided a stable point for securing a vessel.

CRANES

To further aid in moving cargo on and off ships, wharves were often fitted with some form of lifting equipment. One early device was called the hoisting spar. The spar was a long beam or pole attached to a tall, mast-like timber. The midpoint of the spar was lashed high up on the timber. The lashing allowed the ends of the spar to tip up and down like a see-saw. It also allowed the spar to be turned from side to side. To move a load, it was attached to one side of the spar and then lifted by pulling down on the opposite end. The pole was turned to swing the load around. The load was then lowered onto the desired spot on the dock or on the ship's deck.

Beginning in the 13th century, cranes began to appear on docks and wharves. These were cranes in the modern sense of the word, with a winch, ropes, pulleys, and a long arm for lifting loads. By the end of the Middle Ages, some of these cranes were quite large and lifted heavy loads such as tuns of wine. These cranes were built like those used in construction. They were powered by one or, more commonly, two large treadwheels that were attached to a horizontal axle (see illustration 10). The lifting rope of the crane was wound around the axle. The treadwheels were open-sided so that men could get into them. They would walk along the inside of the wheels, like hamsters in exercise wheels, to wind and unwind the rope to raise and lower loads. The entire structure could be rotated so that cargos could be lifted and then swung around to be placed on the wharf or ship.

WAREHOUSES AND TRADING QUARTERS

In the early Middle Ages, the relatively limited amount of trade meant that cargos brought into port could be stored in the homes of the merchants who dealt in these goods. This practice persisted through the Middle Ages. Merchants' homes often had large undercrofts. In these vaulted stone basements, merchandise could be safely stored until sold or shipped out. Over time, as the volume of trade increased and larger amounts of goods required storage, warehouses became a common feature of all European ports. Many warehouses were built to hold specific items. For example, granaries were a common storage facility at many ports. In the Hanse city of Lübeck alone, there were 22 granaries. There were also storehouses for salt and herring-houses for storing barrels of preserved herrings.

Another feature of many ports was residences and storage facilities for foreign merchants. As previously discussed, these merchants often lived in residences or compounds with others from the same country. Along with housing, the compounds also provided warehouses. The most developed trading compounds were the *kontors* belonging to the merchants of the Hanse. These German traders had kontors in the major cities that they traded with the most: London, Novgorod in Russia, Bergen in Norway, and Bruges in Flanders. They also had smaller facilities in many other port cities and towns, such as King's Lynn in England. The Hanse compounds typically had living quarters for the merchants, storage space for their goods, and an assembly hall. Those in port cities often had their own wharves and cranes as well. The kontors also had a residence for the official Hanse master who was in charge of the kontor's affairs. He served as an ambassador for the Hanse.

SHIPYARDS

With the exceptions of galleys, ship building took place on open stretches of shoreline. A sloping beach or small inlet was a typical location. The primary factor was that it had to be a spot where it was easy to get a vessel in and out of the water. Apart from this, the facilities were minimal: a shed for storing materials and tools, a few braces for holding the vessel upright, and a fence to protect the site from thieves. Some form of a slipway, a ramp for sliding the ship into the water, may have also been a feature of more permanent shipbuilding facilities. Because most medieval shipyards had so few structures, few have been found by archaeologists. Additionally, while some locations likely became well-established sites for shipbuilding, others may have been used only once. In London, possible sites of shipyards have been located based on the presence of fragments of vessels. These fragments are evidence of the common practice of breaking up old ships and recycling their wood to build new ships. The huge timbers that formed ships' keels were reused whenever possible since recycling was far easier than finding new timbers of large sizes. Wood was also sold off to builders for the construction of shops, houses, and other structures. Apart from the pieces of ships, little other evidence of shipyard sites has been found.

Over the course of the Middle Ages, improvements were made to the basic locations for ship building. In the early Middle Ages, channels were dug to make it easier to slide a land-built vessel into the water. Inlets were sometimes improved by excavating to make them deeper and to improve their access to open water. Their banks were sometimes stabilized as well with walls of timber and wattle panels. By the 14th century, man-made inlets were constructed with walls or dams built across their mouths. Water was bailed, or possibly pumped, out of the enclosure and the ship built on frames on the dry floor within. When the ship was complete, the wall or dam was broken down at low tide. The vessel floated off the frames with the rising tide and was launched out of the enclosure.

At the end of the Middle Ages, more permanent shipyards became common. At this time, dry docks, now commonly a part of shipbuilding and repair, began to be constructed. Dry docks were known in Egypt in classical antiquity but were extremely rare. They seem to have disappeared completely from the Mediterranean by the 3rd century A.D. at the latest and were only reinvented in the late 15th century. The first dry dock in Europe was built in Portsmouth, England, in 1496. Dry docks may have been built earlier in Italy but there is no clear documentation of this. Dry docks are primarily used for major repairs and maintenance of ships, but they can also be used for building ships. Dry docks, then and now, comprise a large enclosure built in a harbor and fitted with watertight gates and pumps. To operate it, the gates are opened and seawater fills the enclosure. A ship can then enter the enclosure and the gates are closed behind it. The water in the enclosure is pumped out. The ship comes to rest on frames built on the floor of the enclosure. These carefully support the vessel. The vessel can then be repaired or receive maintenance. To leave, water is gradually allowed back into the chamber and the gates are opened when the water levels inside and outside the enclosure are equal. When building a ship, the dry dock is first closed and the water pumped out. The vessel can then be constructed on the dry floor of the enclosure. Dry docks were also developed outside of the Europe and the Mediterranean. There is a record of a dry dock in 11th century China, but they do not appear to have become common until many centuries later.

GALLEY YARDS

Some galleys were constructed in ordinary shipyards. This was the case in England in the late 13th century when King Edward I ordered several port cities to build fast galleys to serve in his navy. However, in Italy and France, galleys were constructed and maintained in special galley yards. The most famed galley yard was the Arsenal of Venice, which was founded in 1104. The Arsenal's primary purpose was to build and maintain war galleys but, beginning in the 14th century, it also constructed some of the large merchant great galleys. The Arsenal had docks, warehouses, workshops, and large sheds which sheltered the galleys while under construction. Some of the docks were covered to protect the galleys that were in port. For performing maintenance on hulls, there was an area where the galleys could be pulled up onto the shore. In France, the *clos des galées* in Rouen was built in 1293 for the war galleys of King Philip the Fair. Local shipwrights and carpenters lacked the skills to build and maintain the galleys so craftsmen from Genoa were periodically brought in to perform the work.

OTHER FACILITIES

Roperies or ropewalks were a common feature of larger ports. A ropewalk was a workshop where rope was made by twisting hemp fibers together. Ropewalks were usually long but relatively narrow sheds or open spaces. They had to be long so that there was adequate space for making long lengths of rope. Ropes were essential for ships' rigging and ropewalks remained in use throughout the age of sailing ships.

Customs houses could be found in ports across Europe. Customs duties were an important source of revenue for rulers. The customs house was the administrative office for the port's chief customs official. He and his assistants kept a constant eye on all merchandise entering and leaving the harbor. Whenever a ship came into dock, a customs official went to greet it and examine its cargo so that he could assess the proper duties on it. In some ports, small, valuable cargos were sometimes taken by customs officials and secured in the customs house until the duties were paid.

Some ports had walls, towers, and other structures for their defense. In the Mediterranean, some harbors had chains that were used to block their entrances (see illustration 17). The chains were used to defend the port in time of war by preventing enemy ships from entering the harbor. They were also frequently used at night to restrict the entry and departure of ships. This was to regulate harbor traffic and ensure that all required fees were collected from vessels using the harbor. It also protected against pirates entering the harbor under cover of darkness. The chains were quite large and heavy. The one for the Porto Pisano is estimated as having weighed 2,500 pounds. The chains were usually connected to points at the mouth of the harbor, such as the seaward ends of breakwaters. In the late 12th century, the chain at Tyre in the Holy Land was stretched between two towers on opposite sides of the harbor's mouth. How the chains were put into position does not appear to have been recorded. Illustrations suggest that they were allowed to sink to the bottom when not in use and then were raised using winches to close the harbor. The chains were effective. As part of their devastating attack on the Porto Pisano in the 13th century, the Genoese had to break the chain protecting the harbor. The Genoese kept parts of the chain as souvenirs of their victory and displayed them in their city's churches.

REVETMENTS

Beginning in the late 11th century, revetments were constructed in many harbors. These were walls of wood or stone built along the shore to stabilize it. Revetments could also be extended out into the river to create more land for building near the waterfront. Additionally, they were used to extend wharves further out into deeper water, making it possible for ships with deep drafts to dock.

Most revetments were thick, heavy wooden walls. The earliest ones were constructed by driving upright timbers directly into the shore. More commonly, the uprights were set into large wooden frameworks laid out on the shore. These uprights were typically braced from either the front or back with other timbers. Planks were then laid horizontally behind the uprights to form the wall of the revetment. The planks were sometimes recycled wood taken from the hulls of old ships. The walls were built so they extended above the high-tide line. The space behind the wall was then filled in with earth, rocks, and even trash, such as old shoes. During the 14th century, revetments began being built with stone walls, but wooden walls remained common.

By enclosing the shoreline behind a wall, the revetment protected it from erosion. It also extended the usable land right up to the edge of the water. Revetments were typically built first at the low-tide line but they were frequently rebuilt and were placed further and further out into the water. This created more and more land that could be used for warehouses, market stalls, shops, and other buildings that needed to be located near the port. This need grew as trade expanded over the course of the period. Archaeological evidence has revealed that the process of extending the shore took place over centuries. Despite its slow pace, the results of this process were sometimes impressive. In London, the north shoreline was pushed 50 to 100 yards out into the Thames between the 12th and 15th centuries. The accumulated infilling was 30 feet deep in some places. The Thames' south shoreline was also extended, but to a much lesser degree.

By pushing the shoreline out, the gradual extension of revetments partially or totally eliminated any preexisting tidal flat or beach. The new edge of the shore faced directly onto water at low tide as well as at high. As the revetments were pushed out into deeper water, it was possible for ships to dock directly alongside the revetment, or rather the wharf built on top of it, and remain floating even at low tide. While tides were not a problem for ports in the Baltic and Mediterranean, revetting was still carried out to contain the shore and provide deep-water docking.

While it appears to have been a civic improvement in some cases, revetting was usually a private undertaking. Excavations in London have revealed that revetments were extended piecemeal by the owners of each waterfront land parcel. Public access to the water was preserved as narrow spaces between some private holdings. These spaces were either unimproved and still opened onto little beaches or had wooden ramps or stairs that led down into the river. These spaces allowed citizens to continue using the river for drawing water for their own use and to water their horses and other livestock.

Revetting along rivers had other negative impacts besides restricting public access to the water. As early as the mid–13th century, the narrowing of the Thames was recognized as a hazard to navigation. Further, the river's narrower channel increased the erosive force of the river was increased. Despite these problems, no actions appear to have ever been taken to limit the construction of revetments.

MOLES AND DREDGING

With the shift from landing ships on beaches to having them tie up at docks and wharves, it was necessary for a harbor to have deep water. Even for those ships that moored in the harbor and were unloaded by lighter, the harbor basin still needed to be deep enough to accommodate them. Further, as ships grew larger and their drafts became deeper, some ports were faced with the problem of needing to deepen their harbors if they were to remain seaports. The primary way to accomplish this was by dredging. Constructing moles could also help maintain the depth of a harbor.

Many harbors had problems with silt. For a harbor at the mouth of a river, the problem was especially severe as the river dumped the soil it had collected at the point where it met the sea. The accumulation of silt in the

river that led into and out of the harbor could create several problems. The most direct problem was the silting in of the harbor basin itself. Just as serious was the silting in of the river that connected the port to the sea. This could leave the river too narrow or shallow to be navigable and so cut the port's connection with the sea. In extreme cases, when it was partially or completely blocked, the river would cut a new channel. Again, if the new channel was not navigable, access to the sea would be cut off. Silt also created shallows at the river's mouth which made it difficult or impossible for ships to safely approach the harbor.

In addition to silting, drastic changes in river courses can also be triggered by severe flooding that causes rivers to break their banks and cut new channels. For example, major floods struck the coast of Flanders in 1134 and submerged parts of the land along the shore. This disaster was a great boon to the city of Bruges. The sea was now closer to the city and the flood had created a new estuary for the River Zwijn so that Bruges had a navigable channel connecting it to the port of Damme.

Not all problems with infilling were caused by rivers. Currents running along the coast can cause this as well. These currents carry sand and rocks. One expert has likened it to a conveyor belt that moves along the coast. This natural flow of materials suspended in the current can gradually block the river leading out of the harbor. Unless the river's current is strong enough to keep clearing a channel through the constant stream of sand and rocks or the topography of the sea floor prevents it, the river's mouth will become choked off. If a river has already created shallows around its mouth, the sand and rock will add to them. Having the river's exit to the sea blocked was a dire problem.

This problem was less common for harbors that opened directly onto the sea. The natural flow of the current brought materials into the mouth of the harbor but also removed it as well. However, in some locations, this movement of sand and silt could ruin ports by directly filling them in. Many ports are located in protected spots along coastlines, such as in coves or in the shelter of peninsulas, capes, or other land that projects into the sea. Coastal currents are sometimes slowed by these projections and the material they carry can settle out. This can eventually fill a harbor in such a sheltered location.

There were protective structures that helped prevent the depositing of sand and other materials by currents. These were called *groins* or *moles*. A mole was a stone jetty built at the mouth of the harbor. It was built on the side of the harbor that faced the oncoming current. The mole deflected the current from the shore and out into deeper water. It also held back the sand, silt, and rocks flowing along in the current so that they did not block the channel leading into the harbor or fill in the harbor itself. Moles were commonly built starting at the shore and extending out into the sea. Large stones were used to create a massive foundation capable of withstanding the force of the sea. Moles were sometimes built in pairs, one on either side of the harbor's mouth, to provide more protection against the sea. Depending on its placement, a mole could even enlarge a harbor by enclosing additional space that was formerly open water (see illustration 17).

Besides serving as a shield against currents and their loads of debris, moles enhanced harbors by acting as breakwaters and sheltering harbor basins from waves. In addition to moles, there were breakwaters built exclusively for this purpose. One example of this was at Venice, where a breakwater was built to protect the city and its lagoon from the open sea.

The tips of moles and breakwaters were sometimes chosen as sites for lighthouses. Additionally, windmills were occasionally built on moles. The most noted example of this was on the island of Rhodes which had a mole with a dozen mills, three of which survive today (see illustration 17). Moles were an ideal place for mills since they were an unobstructed location, fully exposed to the strong winds coming off the sea. This is also one of the reasons that some of the new electricity-generating

windmills are being placed offshore. Moles were also used to defend harbors. As mentioned previously, forts and walls were built on some and chains used to close harbor entrances often had their ends anchored on moles.

While moles could help protect a harbor from infilling, the primary way to keep harbors and the channels open, regardless of the cause, was dredging. Scooping out the muck that builds up on the floor of the harbor and its channel to the sea has always been a laborious process. Today, it requires massive machinery. How this difficult work was accomplished in the Middle Ages and before is unclear. One record of dredging operations mentions a device called a "sea harrow." While not described, its name suggests that it may have been similar to the agricultural harrow in some way. The harrow used on farms was a heavy wooden grid set with spikes that was dragged across fields to break up clods of dirt. The sea harrow may have been a simple dredge with spikes mounted at the front to loosen the seabed and a scoop at the back to catch the material as the harrow was dragged along. Hoisting the loaded harrow and dumping it out must have been hard work to say the least. How the dredges were pulled along is not specified. They may have been dragged by large rowboats.

Near the end of the Middle Ages, more complex, mechanized dredging equipment began to appear. Again, full descriptions are lacking but one seems to have operated like a conveyor belt fitted with scoops while another was a large wheel with buckets mounted along its rim. These could be mounted on barges that would also catch the dredged mud.

Dredging was always a communal effort. Part of the funds that the governments of port cities collected as duties or other fees was applied to dredging. Money was also likely collected from citizens to keep their harbor open. One example of such public funding can be found in Venice. By 1328, the city-state had a fund for dredging and drainage projects.

Dredging was often not successful and

some harbors on rivers lost their connection to the sea completely or partially as their channels filled with sediment. This happened to the city of Bruges in Flanders. This inland city was connected to the port of Damme and Sluys via the Zwijn and Reie rivers. The Zwijn became silted in over the course of the Middle Ages. Bruges made repeated attempts to cut a channel through the Zwijn but failed. Without a connection to the sea, Bruges declined as a trading center and merchants shifted their businesses to other cities which had access to the sea.

Another means of keeping a port open was to bring more water into the harbor. The force of the additional water helped keep the river channel through the harbor clear of silt. In 1239, the city of Bristol in England accomplished this by diverting a river. Bristol's harbor is located on the River Avon. Another river, the Frome, flowed into the Avon at a point downstream of the harbor. The citizens of Bristol diverted the Frome so that it joined the Avon upstream of the harbor instead. The added flow of the Frome helped flush sediment out of the harbor's channel and kept the harbor deep enough for seagoing vessels. This measure saved the harbor and Bristol's livelihood.

When dredging or other measures failed to maintain the depth of a harbor or the channel connecting it to the sea, one option for coping with this problem was to develop out-ports. Out-ports were simply harbors that were closer to the sea that could still accommodate seagoing traffic. Goods were brought to the new port and then transported to the former harbor city by lighters that could still navigate the shallower water. Examples of this can be found in various locations around Europe, as in Italy where the city of Pisa developed the town of Porto Pisano as its replacement harbor. In Flanders, Bruges had always relied on its out-ports of Damme and, later, Slvys, even before it began losing its connection to the sea. Damme was developed first and Sluys a century later since it had a deeper harbor and so could accommodate the deeper-draft ships. Ultimately, however, out-ports

slowed but did not prevent the decline of the original harbor cities as trade shifted to the new ports.

DUMPING

Nature was not the only force that filled in harbors. People did so as well. Some port cities took measures to prevent and punish the dumping of refuse in their harbors. These seem at first glance to have been early anti-pollution measures but the goal was to keep harbors navigable rather than to protect the surrounding waters from contamination. For example, in the 12th century, the port of Marseilles employed men to clean the streets around the waterfront to prevent trash from being flushed into the harbor. Crews of ships entering the harbor had to take an oath that they would keep the harbor clean. Anyone who unloaded a ship before the crew had taken the oath had to remove a boatload of mud from the harbor or pay to have it done. Anyone caught dumping garbage in the harbor was subject to the same penalty, at the rate of one boatload per basket of garbage that had been dumped. Cleaning the hulls of boats was also regulated since the barnacles and other matter scraped off would drop into the harbor. Similar regulations were enacted in many harbors across Europe. Besides throwing refuse overboard while in the harbor, the dumping of ballast was also often prohibited. Since large ships could carry several tons of stone or sand as ballast, this was a serious problem.

RUNOFF

In some instances, human activities worsened the natural process of silting. An example of this can be found in Italy. Having been built on pilings in a lagoon, the city of Venice was uniquely vulnerable to silting. Water running off the lands around the lagoon carried silt into the city's harbor. A significant part of the runoff problem was caused by the cutting of trees around the lagoon and along the streams and rivers that fed into it. With less ground covered by trees, more soil was carried off by rainwater and deposited into the streams and rivers that emptied into the lagoon. (The causes and attempted solutions for this deforestation will be discussed further in the section on wood as a trade good.) Dredging was the only means of trying to keep the lagoon clear for ships.

TOLLS AND CHARGES

Maintaining and operating a harbor cost money. Additionally, the local rulers saw port traffic as another source of income. As a consequence, a wide variety of tolls, customs, and other charges were levied on the ships and merchants who used the ports.

Even in the days when a port was no more than a stretch of beach or a tidal flat, tolls were still collected for the privilege of landing ships. If a ship did not land but was moored offshore, it could still be subject to tolls. Examples of these beaching and mooring charges can be found as early as the 7th and 8th centuries. When other facilities were added to harbors, additional fees were invented. Docking fees and charges for using public wharves were added to the beaching and mooring tolls. If a cargo had to be lifted off a ship, there was a cranage charge for using

the public crane. There was a fee charged for the use of the public scales as well. As part of selling many goods, they had to be weighed first using one of the public scales. Some merchandise also had to be weighed to determine the amount of customs to be levied on it. Above all, merchants had to pay customs taxes on the value of the goods they brought into the port. While customs were usually assessed in cash, they were sometimes calculated and collected as part of the ship's cargo. In England, the king had the right to a few of the barrels of wine aboard each ship carrying wine into London. Ships carrying preserved fish were similarly assessed. Even such mundane items as wooden boards were subject to having the king's share collected. The money paid as customs duties far exceeded the value of duties collected in kind. It was such a valuable source of income that the kings of England sometimes used it to secure large loans from private citizens, such as wealthy merchants.

Some of the money collected was actually applied to the maintenance and improvement of the port. Large public works such as moles and lighthouses were built and operated under the authority of the local government from funds collected from citizens and port users. As previously discussed, dredging was also paid for out of these funds.

IV

TRADE

The mention of trade in the Middle Ages typically evokes two images. One is subsistence-level bartering for basic necessities, such as foodstuffs, carried on by the peasants who formed the majority of medieval society. This form of trade is often pictured as transactions such as one person trading some eggs for a few turnips, or a farmer giving a potter a chicken in exchange for new cooking pots. The other image is of long-distance trade in exotic luxury goods in which merchants travel to the bazaars of the Middle East buying silks and spices to satisfy the wants of the nobility and wealthy.

While there is some truth to these perceptions, commerce in the Middle Ages was far more varied and complex. For example, in large parts of Europe, obtaining such basic but vital foods as salt and wheat frequently involved international trade, with the products being shipped hundreds of miles by seagoing vessels. The web of trade to meet these needs covered all of medieval Europe. For luxury goods, more was involved than simply trading with ports on the coast of the Middle East. Trade networks in Asia and Africa were tied into the European channels so that spices from as far as away as Indonesia were brought to the households of royalty as distant as England and Scandinavia. Arranging the movement of all of these goods were the merchants. These included adventurous and tough businessmen who trekked to the trading stations of Russia to obtain the best furs or who journeyed to the cities of Central Asia to buy silks. Others limited their enterprises to Europe and bought and sold wine, preserved fish, luxurious wool cloth, and a wide variety of other items produced within the Continent and on the British Isles.

In this section, we will examine the scope of trade and the trade networks, the merchants, and many other aspects of trade in medieval Europe. Trade by Italian merchants will come up in many of these areas. The commerce of the Italians is especially noteworthy for several reasons. Italian city-states, primarily Venice and Genoa, dominated trade within the Mediterranean region, including the importing of spices and other exotic items that were produced in or channeled through the Middle East. The Italians were also extensively involved in trade throughout the Continent and England. This led them to develop means of coping with the difficulties of long-distance transactions. The large scale of businesses built by the Italians, along with their extensive involvement in international trade, encouraged them to innovate and create various methods of financing their operations. While many of these innovations were only gradually adopted by the rest of Europe, the various forms of loans and insurance developed by the Italians formed the groundwork for modern finance.

Trade Patterns

Many transactions did take place directly between consumers and suppliers. Farmers brought their produce to villages and towns to sell at weekly markets. Craftsmen sold their wares at booths in these markets and out of their homes too. But it was not always this easy for producers to get their goods to their customers. It was one thing to take a few bushels of wheat a mile or two to the nearest village, but it was quite another to get that wheat to a market in a city that was 50 miles away or even across the sea. It was not practical or efficient for the farmer to spend days on the road to bring a cart load of wheat to market. Instead of wasting his time and money on moving and selling the wheat himself, he could sell his wheat to a merchant. The merchant typically would buy as much wheat as he could within an area and then ship it to the market where he could get the best price. For example, in England, wheat for London came from farms far to the west of the city. At regional market towns, wheat from many farms was gathered together and shipped by barge down the River Thames to London and sold by grain vendors there.

In addition to saving the farmer the time and expense of selling the wheat himself, the merchant, rather than the farmer, incurred the costs of transporting the wheat and took on the risks of the wheat being damaged or lost in transit. He also ran the risk that he would not be able to find a buyer willing to pay enough for the wheat for him to recoup his expenses and make a profit. For all these factors, the merchant charged a price higher than that which he had paid the farmer. As this illustrates, commerce in the Middle Ages involved the same expenses and risks as business today and was often more complicated than just bartering or even paying a craftsman a few pennies for his wares.

The long-distance trade in grain also reveals some of the complexities of commerce in the Middle Ages. It was not always as straightforward as the preceding example might suggest. The closest sources may not have always been the cheapest sources or have been sufficient to meet demand. For example, Paris, with its large population, had an enor-

mous demand for wheat and imported it from the surrounding lands. By some accounts, grain was shipped in from distances as far as 100 miles. One of the regions that exported grain to feed the metropolis was Artois, which was on the border with Flanders. Artois was closer to Ghent and other Flemish cities than to Paris. These cities also needed grain but the grain from Artois was primarily shipped west and sold in Paris. In part, the reason for this was economic. To meet their needs, the Parisians were likely willing to pay a higher price for the grain than it would have sold for in Flanders. Even with the added transportation costs, the merchants who sold the grain from Artois must have been able to sell it in Paris at profit. And this profit was likely greater than if they had sold it in Flanders. As an alternative, the Flemish cities imported grain from Poland and northeast Germany, which, despite the costs of being shipped in by sea, was sold at a reasonable price. Besides economic forces, politics sometimes interfered with the logical flow of trade as well. As discussed later in this section, the movement of grain and other goods between one land and another could be restricted or even blocked for political ends.

The spice trade was even more complex and involved many more merchants in the chain between the producer and consumer. For example, a farmer who harvested nutmeg in Indonesia would sell his crop to a local merchant who in turn would sell it to a merchant from India who would ship the spice to a market in India. Once there, a Moslem merchant would buy it and transport it overseas, via the Persian Gulf, to what is now Kuwait and then overland to Baghdad. The nutmeg would be sold in a market there to another trader who would bring it to a Middle Eastern port on the Mediterranean. Here, it would be sold to an Italian merchant who would bring it back to Genoa and sell it to another Italian trader who would carry it over the Alps to the trade fair at Champagne in France. He would sell the nutmeg to a merchant from London who would then take it back to England and sell it to a nobleman's servant in London. The servant would take the nutmeg home to his master's manor in Lincolnshire, where his master would enjoy a cup of wine spiced with the nutmeg. In the end, the nutmeg had traveled halfway around the world and passed through the hands of seven merchants between the producer and the consumer.

The merchants, while often characterized as mere middlemen, contributed to the process of moving goods such as the nutmeg to their customers. Each of these merchants paid for part of the shipping of the nutmeg and ran the risk that it would be lost while in transit. They each added these expenses onto the price they had paid for the spice when calculating how much they should charge when reselling it. The merchants also took into account the demand for the nutmeg in the market and bargained for as high a price as possible to recoup their expenses and obtain the highest profit. With this process of reselling happening multiple times, it becomes understandable why spices were so expensive by the time they reached the consumers in Europe.

The distance the spices traveled, as shown in the example, is also part of the reason why such goods were relayed to Europe through middlemen rather than being brought by a single merchant traveling all the way from Indonesia to England and back. The cost and time required to make the round-trip would have been great. Even if the merchant defrayed some of his expenses by bringing along merchandise to trade along the way, he would have likely had to charge an extremely high price for the spices to recoup his expenses and make a profit. By having merchants specialize in particular segments of the spice's journey, risks and possibly the costs of transport were reduced since' these merchants were knowledgeable of the conditions in their particular areas. Merchants native to the region would know which routes were currently the safest, whom to bribe to avoid excessive duty charges, and other vital information. It would have been extremely difficult, if not impossible, for a single man to accumulate this knowledge and keep up-to-date on any changes. There was

also the more pressing problem that the residents of the Middle East and Egypt tried to keep a monopoly on the spice trade by blocking European merchants from reaching the sources of the spices. This policy was generally successful since the spice routes led directly across their lands. A few European merchants did reach India but did not establish any regular trade with the subcontinent. It was only with Vasco da Gama's voyage around Africa at the end of the 15th century that the monopoly was broken and it became practical and economical to travel directly from Europe to India and beyond.

While some trading voyages proceeded directly from the home port to the market, in the Mediterranean, it was common for such voyages to involve several stops along the way. These were necessary, in part, for resupplying food and water. As previously discussed, galleys in particular required frequent stops. At these stops, it was common for the merchants aboard, and even some of the crew, to engage in trade. Some of the goods onboard were sold and other goods bought. In fact, merchants typically planned ahead and brought goods specifically for such trading. Some ships made a circuit of the Mediterranean by sailing west from Italy, around the north shore of the sea, around the western end, and turning back east and cruising along the North African coast before reaching Egypt and the Middle East. This enabled merchants to accumulate goods that were more saleable in the Middle East than the goods they started out with in Italy. For example, there was little market for fine woolens in the Middle East so the merchants would carry other goods, such as linen, some woolen cloth, and olive oil as well as supplies of silver. When the ship called in at Aigues Mortes on the south coast of France, merchants could trade the olive oil and woolen cloth for salt. At ports on the north coast of Africa, the merchants could trade more olive oil along with some of the linen cloth and the salt. In return, they would get gold and slaves that had been brought up from West Africa. They would then proceed to Egypt and the Middle East, where they could trade the slaves, the remaining linen, and some of the gold for spices, cotton, and other goods. However, the value of the goods they bought was usually greater than the value of the goods they sold. They had to make up the difference with payments in silver. This trade imbalance led to a drain of silver from Europe to the East. Trade imbalances are discussed further at the end of this section.

While some trade goods were carried over land or inland waterways, commerce requiring sea voyages was common and grew over the course of the Middle Ages. Shipping and access to the sea were important to any nation's long-distance commerce. For example, Genoa conquered Pisa in 1284. The Genoese did this, in part, to eliminate Pisa from the grain trade and gain control of the importing of grain for all of Tuscany. In turn, in the early 15th century, Florence fought Genoa for control over Pisa and its port. Florence ultimately bought the Porto Pisano from Genoa in 1421. By securing direct access to the Mediterranean, Florence could have the wool shipments that were vital to the city's wool industry go directly to its own port and not be at the mercy of Genoa.

PEDDLERS, MERCHANTS, PARTNERS, INVESTORS, AND AGENTS

There were several different types of merchants. At the lowest end were the peddlers who made the rounds of towns and villages or of city neighborhoods to sell small quantities of merchandise directly to consumers. Their goods appear to have typically been small household items such as needles, ribbons, and, perhaps, some fabric. Peddlers operated throughout the Middle Ages and for centuries afterward.

Like peddlers, merchants originally traveled with their goods. They did not have agents to whom they could delegate the jobs of bargaining for the purchase or sale of their merchandise. They had to go in person to where the items were being sold, whether in a market or directly from a producer. They bargained with sellers over the price for the goods, transported them to a market, and then haggled with buyers over the sales price. The merchants who traveled abroad sometimes took great risks. Attack on the roads or a storm at sea could mean the loss of not just the merchandise but the merchant's life as well. Just by venturing into jurisdictions outside their homeland, merchants placed themselves at risk. Particularly in the early Middle Ages, foreigners, including merchants, were not given the same protection as local residents under the laws of the lands they were visiting. This improved over time as more rulers came to appreciate the financial advantages of encouraging trade by protecting merchants. Commerce, through the taxation of sales transactions and the assessing of import and export duties, brought money into the ruler's treasury.

While merchants trading alone could be found throughout the period, it was common for merchants to be carrying on a family business which they would pass on to their sons. A father would take his son along on business trips so that he could learn the trade in an informal apprenticeship. Other family members participated as well. Wives often helped run the business, especially during their husbands' absences. Daughters also learned something about trading as well and took these skills along when they were married. This may have made them more attractive brides for marriage within merchant communities. Some family businesses included members of the extended family as well. Uncles, cousins, in-laws, and nephews were sometimes partners in the business. Some invested their money while others were active merchants. All received a share of the profits in proportion to their contributions.

There were many family-based businesses across Europe that engaged in international trade. They often grew to include outside investors and non-family members as well. A few succeeded in becoming major companies that had significant commercial power. Many of these large businesses were Italian. By having more personnel and money, merchants could expand their businesses and branch out into trading in many different types of goods. Some grew so large and successful that they employed agents and placed them in commercial centers around Europe. The agents were sometimes younger family members or employees. In either case, they had been with the company for some time, worked their way up through the business, and proven that they were competent. Leading merchants stayed at their central offices and directed all their enterprises from there. Additionally, many successful merchants engaged in other commercial pursuits such as trading in commodities, manufacturing, and lending and banking. Through their branches, they financed the ventures of other merchants and made loans to governments.

The next most common form of business after family-run ones were partnerships. As with taking in family members, partnerships were a way to obtain the capital and human resources needed to operate a business larger than that of a lone merchant. For example, an individual merchant might have the resources to buy several barrels of wine but purchasing an entire shipload of wine required more money. As these larger deals yielded larger profits, there was a great incentive for merchants to amass as much money as possible to finance and expand their operations. Partnerships were the most basic means of pooling funds to finance trade. Partners could include other businessmen or, as discussed, family members of the merchant. Some partnerships involved only two people while others had multiple members. In some partnerships, all partners actively participated in the business. This appears to have been common in the early Middle Ages. In others, some partners ran the business while others just provided financing. The active partners would make all the business decisions and conduct all the necessary transactions, including going out and buying merchandise and then selling it. The profits

from the venture were again divided among the partners based on their contributions to the business. Typically, this meant that each received a share in proportion to the money they had put into the business. However, the active partners were sometimes given a larger share of the profits in recognition that their skills in selecting quality merchandise and in shrewdly bargaining for purchase and sale prices were clearly valuable contributions. However, not all partnerships made a profit and all partners shared equally in the loss as well. As for their duration, some partnerships lasted only for one business deal. Others were more permanent and continued for years, sometimes surviving the addition or loss of partners.

In Italy, partnerships in which some partners contributed only money while one partner carried out all the activities of the business were used as early as the 10th century. They became so common that they came to be standardized. They were first called *colleganza* and were later called *commendas*. The commenda was a contract between two or more persons. One contributed no money but carried out all the business, including traveling, selecting and bargaining a price for the merchandise, transporting it, and finally selling it. The others contributed all the financing for the venture. At the end, the financing partners typically received three-quarters of any profits and the active partner received one-quarter. The active partner was usually a man who was just starting his career as a merchant and lacked the resources to finance his new business. Under the commenda, he could begin accumulating the capital needed to trade on his own. Commendas did not benefit just the young merchant. Surviving contracts reveal that people from all classes of Italian society, from craftsmen and merchants to patricians, participated in financing commendas. Women, including widows, invested independently in them too. Additionally, some people invested in several different ones simultaneously. As with many partnerships, commendas were undertaken for only a single venture and then dissolved.

The Italian *societas maris*, society of the sea, was a business arrangement similar to the commenda. Two-thirds of the money for the venture was provided by financiers while the active partner put up one-third. Again, the financial backers could include anyone who had money to invest. At the conclusion of the enterprise, the financing partners received half of the profits and the merchant was given the other half. This appears to have been an intermediate step for merchants on their way to gaining sufficient resources to trade independently.

Over the centuries, growing numbers of merchants opted to stay in their home cities and send out partners or agents to various commercial centers to do business for them. This became a common practice. However, many Hanse merchants continued to travel with their merchandise. Additionally, some merchants, even if they had partners, continued to take to the road or the sea and do business themselves, especially when the stakes were high. Even in the later Middle Ages, there were many examples of merchants personally pursuing rare and highly lucrative goods. In this way, they could bargain for the merchandise themselves and take charge of its security. For example, to trade for silks and other luxuries from East Asia, merchants traveled to Central Asia and even to China itself to buy the choicest goods. A few ventured to India to buy incredibly valuable gemstones and personally bring them back to Europe. Using agents over such long distances would have been completely impractical. Even within Europe, some merchants continued to accompany their merchandise when it was an expensive item such as saffron.

THE HANSE

The Hanse was unique trade organization. It was a federation of cities and towns in northern Europe, primarily located in what is now Germany. They were united by their common interest of protecting their trade. The Hanse had 80 principal towns and cities as members and grew to include between 180 and 200 at its peak. They were located along the south coasts of the North and Baltic Seas as well as further inland. Initially, these cities acted independently but by the early 13th century, they were beginning to band together.

The Hanse dominated trade in the Baltic and North Seas. They monopolized the shipment of salt into Scandinavia and around the south coast of the Baltic. Without the salt, the herring fisheries could not preserve their catch and the industry would be devastated. From their trading station at Novgorod, they also controlled most of the trade with Russia and so virtually cornered the fur and beeswax market. Just as important, they were able to push other countries out of the carrying trade in the northern waters. Using their economic power, they were able to block Swedish ships and merchants from sailing out of the Baltic Sea. From the other direction, English, Flemish, and other traders from the west were barred from entering the Baltic. They were even able to take over shipping between England and Norway. The Hanse did not operate actual blockades to enforce their limits on traffic in and out of the Baltic. Rather, the Hanse used the threat of economic sanctions against any transgressors. Additionally, the Hanse's control over trade within the Baltic meant that foreign merchants would have had difficulty finding any port that would trade with them.

Because of their dominance, the Hanse cities were frequently able to extract commercial privileges in the countries where they traded. As early as the early 12th century, the kings of England had extended special rights to merchants from cities that would later form the Hanse and they continued to extend such rights through the 14th century. These privileges included such benefits as exemption from all taxes and from any increases in customs dues as well as the right to trade freely throughout the entire country. The counts and countesses of Flanders also gave Hansards special privileges such as reducing customs duties on their merchandise.

The Hanse was able to have such control because of its economic power. If a country attempted to deprive the Hanse of its privileges there, it risked a boycott by the Hanse cities which could cause significant harm. For example, in 1284, the king of Norway attempted to prune back the privileges that the Hansards enjoyed in his country. The Hanse quickly responded by imposing an embargo on all grain, flour, vegetables, and beer to Norway. The Hanse went so far as to station ships on the Danish strait to catch any smugglers from the Baltic who attempted to break the embargo. The blockade worked. Since Norway was unable to find other sources for grain, the embargo was causing a famine. The king capitulated and was forced to grant the Hansards even more privileges than they had had before.

In the 14th century, the Hanse cities even fielded navies and armies to fight for their trade rights. While a war against Denmark in 1358 ended in defeat, a second war with Denmark in 1367 was successful. The Hansards destroyed Copenhagen and forced the Danes to confirm their commercial rights and surrender four key fortresses that guard the principal strait connecting the Baltic and the North Seas.

Ultimately, the Hanse went into decline in the 15th century. Dutch and English merchants and shippers began to compete in the markets previously monopolized by the Hansards in the North Sea and Baltic. At the same time, southern Germans entered into trade with the Russians and bypassed the Hanse's trading station at Novgorod. Many governments also moved to curtail Hanse privileges and favor their own merchants instead. There was discord among the Hanse members as well, as individual towns and cities acted more in their own interests than in support of Hanse policies. This had always been a problem but it became chronic and severe over the course of the 15th century. These and other problems led to the collapse of the Hanse in the 16th century, although it continued to exist until the 17th century.

Finance

As we have seen, commerce in the Middle Ages was more than just swapping a bushel of barley for a sack of turnips. While there were periodic shortages of coins, cash transactions were common even in the early centuries of the period. Producers sometimes brought their goods to markets and sold them directly to consumers, but, in all but the most basic transactions, merchants played an ever-increasing role in moving goods from suppliers to consumers. As trade became increasingly complex and varied, more sophisticated means were needed to assist with various aspects of business. These included creating business entities to provide adequate financial resources, taking measures to lessen the impact of losses resulting from catastrophes, making capital available to merchants through loans, and developing the means to facilitate large, long-distance transactions.

COPING WITH RISK

Every honest business deal has an element of risk. Wise businessmen today typically take all reasonable measures to minimize that risk, but it cannot be eliminated entirely. There is always the chance that one party will default on their obligations, that a natural disaster will destroy merchandise, that consumers won't buy the product, or any of a number of other scenarios. Medieval merchants were subject to many of these same risks and sought to hedge against economic ruin befalling their businesses. They used a variety of methods, some of which are still used today.

Sharing Risk

For merchants who dealt with goods that were shipped by sea, such as spices from the East or wine from France, one means of limiting risk was to divide the shipment between several vessels whenever possible. If the whole cargo was placed on a single ship which was lost in a storm or taken by pirates, the entire venture was lost. If the shipment was split between four ships, there was much less chance of losing all the merchandise. Of course, there were exceptions, such as when entire convoys were captured or when groups of ships were lost in severe storms. Still it was far more common for most, if not all, of the ships to make it through.

Another method of limiting risk was to invest or become a partner in a number of different enterprises. For example, ships from the Hanse cities and from the Italian city-states were most frequently owned by groups of partners. This helped in financing shipbuilding, especially for large ships, but it was done primarily to reduce potential losses if a ship was lost. By owning shares in several different ships, a partner or investor could reap the profits of owning a ship while limiting the economic damage if any one ship was lost. Shipments of merchandise were sometimes similarly divided by partnerships or investors. A single cargo could have dozens of owners. As with ships, by being a part-owner of several different cargoes, a merchant could potentially profit as much as if he owned a single cargo of the same value. Again, while it would reduce his profit if one or more of those cargoes was lost, it would not cause complete bankruptcy.

Fractional shares in ships could be bought, sold, and inherited. And the share in a ship brought more than just the profit or loss from its voyages. Liability went with it as well. All shareholders owed proportionally for repairs to the ship. Failure to pay up led to forfeit of an investor's share.

Diversification was also used as a hedge against some catastrophes in the market as well as natural ones. For example, some goods, such as furs and some types of cloth, had to be purchased, transported, and processed before they could be sold. By the time they reached the market, consumers' tastes might have changed and a particular type of fur or shade of cloth could no longer be popular. (Such changes in demand for clothing occurred far less frequently than in the present

but they are known to have been an issue for high-end customers such as nobility and royalty.) Selling the undesirable furs or cloth could take months and might require selling at a loss. If a merchant had invested his entire fortune in this merchandise, he could have been ruined. To avoid this fate, a merchant could buy a wider variety of merchandise because it would be unlikely for all the merchandise to drop in value before it reached the market. Thus, instead of buying only squirrel fur, a merchant might buy ermine fur as well. Along with luxury velvets suitable for the wealthy, a merchant might buy some cheaper cloth for which there was a larger market. Even such a slight expansion of the range of merchandise could help the merchant avoid total ruin. In some cases, a greater degree of diversification was advisable. For example, a merchant might buy a shipment of pepper in the Middle East to sell in one of the Italian cities. His ship could reach port just after another large cargo of pepper had arrived. By the time his cargo was sold, the market would have already been flooded with pepper and he would be forced to accept a low price. Had he bought other spices or goods, such as cotton, he could have minimized his loss.

In both of these examples, the merchant suffered losses from unforeseeable problems in the market. To reduce this risk, some merchants invested or partnered in several different ventures. This diversification could yield lower profits than if all the money was put into one business that proved successful. But if that one business failed, the merchant could be bankrupted. By investing in several different commodities, a merchant was far less likely to be wiped out financially by a loss in any one particular enterprise. It was highly unlikely that all goods would go down in value. Diversification could be as limited as trading in wider varieties of furs or cloths or as broad as investing in importing timber from the south coast of the Baltic and exporting German wine. Some merchants even branched out beyond directly engaging in trade and lent money to other merchants to finance their ventures.

Marine Insurance

The most common way to protect against financial loss from disasters now is to take out insurance. In exchange for the payment of a premium, the insurance company agrees to pay in the event of a loss covered by the insurance policy. The amount of the premium is based on the company's calculation of the value of the item to be insured and the likelihood of an event causing the loss. This is all very straightforward. However, it took some time for insurance to evolve to this point.

By the late 14th century, marine insurance for ships and cargoes was developed in Genoa. This insurance was the direct ancestor of modern marine insurance. Premiums were based on a number of risk factors, such as time of the year (sailing in the winter was usually more risky than sailing at other times of the year), levels of pirate activities in the waters to be crossed, and whether the merchant and his ship were from a country currently at war or would be entering a war zone.Other factors included the value of the cargo, the length of the voyage, and the type of vessel. Galleys were considered very safe and their large crews deterred pirate attacks. Sailing ships were expected to have marines as part of their crews since these ships had much smaller crews than the galleys.

Taking all this into account, insurers would set a premium for accepting the risk of the loss of the ship or cargo on that particular voyage. Insurers were usually groups of merchants who shared the premium and the liability for paying out the settlement if the ship was lost. Having groups as insurers was better than having a single merchant be the insurer. If the ship was lost, a single insurer might lack the funds to pay out the complete settlement or have sufficient funds but still be bankrupted by such a drain of his wealth. But by dividing the risk among several merchants, there was less chance of any one merchant being completely ruined. Each would still suffer a loss but would not be wiped out. This benefited the insured as well since it increased the like-

lihood that he would be fully compensated for his loss.

Initially, premiums were sometimes 20 percent or more of the value of the ship or goods to be insured. Such high premiums deterred the purchase of insurance and many merchants continued to rely on the methods outlined above to lessen the risk of total loss. However, by the mid–15th century premiums had dropped to 3 to 15 percent and so were more affordable.

Also at this time, insurance for shipments by land and by river developed. While such transportation was generally not as risky as shipping by sea, the availability of this insurance similarly lessened the likelihood of ruin for merchants who used inland shipping.

LOANS

The need for loans to conduct business increased drastically over the course of the Middle Ages as enterprises grew in size and scope. Loans ranged from simple extensions of credit by sellers to buyers to the supply of massive amounts of money to finance the wars of princes and kings. Yet, despite their utility, loans in any form ran afoul of the Church's prohibition on usury and placed the lender's soul at risk of eternal damnation. However, even such dire punishment was not sufficient to stop determined businessmen from making loans.

Loans were often needed for conducting even the most basic transactions. Before a merchant could sell merchandise, he had to buy it. A common form of loan was for the seller to finance the purchase by not requiring the buyer to pay for goods immediately. Instead, the seller would extend the buyer credit by agreeing that the buyer could pay at some future date, presumably allowing sufficient time for the buyer to resell the goods. In exchange for extra time given to pay for the goods, the seller/lender often charged the buyer/borrower a higher price than if the buyer had paid for the merchandise at the time of the purchase. This higher price covered both the cost of the goods and interest charges covering the period between the date of sale and the date of payment.

If a buyer did not have sufficient funds to pay for goods and the seller would not extend credit to him, he had to borrow the money to purchase the merchandise from someone willing to loan it to him. This could be a professional lender or another merchant who had extra capital and was looking for a profitable investment. Regardless of who was loaning the money, they expected a return on the loans they made. As today, this return was in the form of interest. The interest was a fixed amount payable on a set date. The interest charge was based on the amount loaned and the duration of the loan.

But extending credit or taking out a loan was often condemned by the Church. The Church viewed any lending of money subject to interest charges, regardless of the interest rates, as a sinful act of usury because the lender had not earned the interest paid by the borrower. All he had done was temporarily provided money to the borrower. The lender was not actively involved in the business and took no risks himself. (The Church ignored the fact that he ran the risk that the borrower would default on the loan.) The principal and interest were due whether the business succeeded or failed. In the Church's opinion, the lender had not worked for the money and was simply charging for the time that the borrower was using his money. The Church held that time belonged to God and that a man could not charge another man just for the passage of time. Alternatively, Thomas Aquinas, famed 13th century theologian, stated that lenders were selling something that did not exist. Regardless of the exact theory, the Church condemned all loans as usury throughout most of the Middle Ages, and usurers were at risk of eternal damnation for their lending. In the 13th century, the Church slightly softened its position to permit lending at fair rates. It appears that the Church came to accept that interest compensated the lender for the profits he could have made from other uses of his

money had he not used it for the loan. However, at times, the Church returned to a harder position against loans. Even at best, the Church continued to view lending with suspicion and it was still advisable for lenders to make acts of charity, such as suitable donations to the Church, to offset the stain of usury on their souls. Moreover, as late as 1274, a Church council stated that usurers who had not made amends to their borrowers were to be denied Christian burials.

Secular rulers sometimes condemned usury as well. In 806, Charlemagne outlawed lending in which a borrower was required to pay back more than the amount he borrowed. Others, such as Louis VII and Louis IX of France, recognized the utility of loans and simply capped interest rates to prevent predatory lending.

Regardless of the prohibitions, loans of various forms were still needed for conducting many commercial transactions, particularly the increasingly complex business transactions of the later Middle Ages. To meet this need, lenders and borrowers found ways around the Church's ban. One way was to find a lender to whom the prohibition did not apply. This contributed to the rise of Jews as moneylenders. As Jews were not subject the Church's laws, they were free to make loans and charge interest. Unfortunately, this contributed to hatred towards the Jews since they were perceived as unfairly growing rich on the work of Christians. This problem was exacerbated when Jewish lenders had to take action to enforce loans against defaulting borrowers. Resentment of the Jews over debts provided fuel for attacks on individual Jews and even entire Jewish communities. Kings and other nobility, however, sometimes intervened to protect Jews in their domains. But this was not done for moral reasons. Rather, Jews provided loans to kings and other nobles. They also paid special taxes and other payments, effectively payoffs for their protection, to the royal and noble treasuries. Kings and other nobles did not want to lose these sources of funds. This changed, however, in the latter half of the period, when kings began expelling all Jews from their realms.

Another option was to find Christians who were willing to risk their souls and make loans. Such lenders were scattered across Europe but a few cities were noted for having relatively large numbers of lenders. One of the most famed was the city of Cahors in France. Cahorsin lenders operated primarily in England and were so successful that "Cahorsin" became a synonym for usurer. Another group of noted lenders was called "Lombards," although they were actually from the Piedmont region of Italy. Lombards were active in France and the Low Countries. As with "Cahorsin," "Lombard" became a byword for usurer. Like the Jews, the lenders of Cahors and Lombardy became despised for their activities and were sometimes attacked.

Other solutions were developed that did not involve stigmatizing groups of lenders. For example, even before the Church modified its position on the point, the government of the city-state of Venice deemed loans made at the fair market rate as not being usury and so declared that there was no usury in their jurisdiction. The Italians pioneered other, more complex methods of sidestepping the Church's prohibitions as well so that ordinary lenders, such as merchants with extra capital, could make loans. As explained previously, Italian businesses and banks were the most sophisticated commercial enterprises of the Middle Ages and so they developed these techniques to extend credit and make the loans required.

Some methods involved creating contracts and other transactions that hid the interest charges. Some disguised the interest as increases in prices of merchandise as part of fictitious sales. In such a case, a buyer needing money to buy some goods would buy them using a loan. He would pretend to sell the goods to the lender and agree to buy them back later for a higher price. The difference between the sale price and repurchase price was actually the interest. Another way in which interest was disguised was to stipulate

in the contract for the fake sale that the repurchase of the goods was to be made in a currency different from that used to buy the goods in the first place. For example, the first sale would be paid for in Florentine florins and the repurchase price would be in Venetian ducats. The interest would be disguised in the currency exchange rate. The borrower and lender would have agreed to a conversion rate higher than the fair market rate. The difference between the two rates was the interest.

Despite their usefulness, not all businessmen saw loans as beneficial. As early as the late 13th century, German merchants learned how to use credit from seeing Italian practices at trade fairs. But in the late 14th and early 15th centuries, the Hanse as a whole began discouraging its merchants from using credit and taking out loans and later attempted to abolish their use. Apparently, too many Hansards had fallen into financial ruin by buying too many goods on credit and then finding themselves unable to pay off their loans. Some may have simply run up too much debt or taken out loans with truly usurious interest rates. Others may have reasonably borrowed money to buy merchandise but then suffered some disaster such as the loss of the shipment or a drop in the value of the goods which left the borrower without enough money to pay off the loan. Additionally, loans were not useful in the important Hanse trading center in Novgorod. The Russians had no use for promises that they would be paid later for their furs. Further, collecting debts from the Russians was difficult. The Russians also would not accept coins because they believed that coins carried diseases such as the bubonic plague. As a consequence, trade was done primarily by bartering, with the merchandise due at the time of the deal was made. Finally, the Hansards appear to have seen the loans as primarily benefiting the lender and not the borrower. Since most large-scale lenders were Italians, the members of the Hanse did not want to put money in the pockets of their competitors.

Merchants were not the only borrowers. Peasants and craftsmen also borrowed money from local lenders or pawnbrokers when in need. Nobility and even royalty and the Church borrowed as well.

Pawning was a common practice. The poorest members of medieval society were sometimes reduced to pawning their clothes. Nobles pledged large pieces of silverware from their households. This was actually fairly routine and silver platters and other serving pieces were viewed as financial assets rather than just tableware. Royalty sometimes pawned even their crowns and other jewelry to secure loans. In one instance, the crown of King Charles VI of France was actually broken up and the pieces distributed among several lenders who held shares of the king's debt. One pope even hocked the papal mitre, the ornate, jeweled headdress that was part of his ceremonial vestments.

While loans to ordinary individuals were purely local matters, loans to royalty and the Church impacted international trade. In exchange for loans, rulers frequently bestowed commercial privileges on the foreign businesses that made such contributions to the royal treasury. These privileges typically included the right to trade freely as local merchants rather than under the restrictions typically imposed on foreign merchants. Exemptions from import and export duties were sometimes granted as well. In other instances, lenders were given monopolies in some commercial areas. For example, one pope gave a lender the exclusive right to sell luxury goods at the papal court in Avignon. Given the wealth of the cardinals and others who formed the court, this was a significant coup for the lender. In some instances, loans to kings were secured by promises of repayment from reliable sources of revenues such as customs duties. Edward I of England made such a promise to the Ricciardi company of Lucca, which served as his banker. The Church made similar pledges. One pope secured a loan by promising the lender a share in the tithes collected by the Church. Such high-level ending was not without risk. King or pope could revoke trading privileges or take back sources of

revenue at any time. This was sometimes done when they needed a new loan and the favors were transferred to the new lender. Additionally, like any other borrower, a king could default on his loans. In the 14th century, several major Italian banks were bankrupted when Edward III of England defaulted on a number of very large loans he had taken out to finance the war against France.

Foreign merchants who enjoyed special trading privileges also risked physical harm. In England, resentment over the privileges granted to Italians and other foreigners occasionally boiled over and gangs of men, often including apprentices, attacked any foreign merchants they found.

FINANCING LONG DISTANCE TRADE

Partnerships, companies, insurance, and loans all served to encourage commerce, both locally and internationally. But, as trade expanded and more goods were shipped long distances from suppliers to consumers, more challenges developed. Besides the growth of long-distance trade, improvements were needed because of the medieval monetary system. While some trade was conducted by bartering, most transactions were paid for in coins. Silver coins were the primary currency for most of the Middle Ages. Gold coins went out of circulation in the early centuries of the period and were not reintroduced until the 14th century. Whether gold or silver, large-scale transactions, such as those involving international trade, required shifting huge amounts of coins between the buyer and seller. Shipping the coins was burdensome, costly, and risky. Alternative means were needed to make payments without actually moving coins. In response, merchants and bankers developed more complex forms of commercial transactions to facilitate trade.

Beginning in the early 13th century, the merchants and bankers of Italy pioneered methods that eliminated the need for shipping coins. Their increasing role in international trade and the general expansion of commerce drove them to develop contracts called letters of credit and bills of exchange. These contracts relied on the network of banks and business offices that Italian companies established across Europe.

Letters of Credit

Merchants, as well as governments and individuals, frequently needed to move cash from one location to another. As previously mentioned, shipping coins was always risky. Even government shipments were not safe. They required large, heavily armed escorts and, even then, were still sometimes waylaid. The Italian banks created the letter of credit to lessen the need for such shipments. With a letter of credit, a merchant or anyone else could deposit money at one bank branch and withdraw it at another. For example, a merchant could deposit ten French *gros turnois* at a bank's office in Paris. The bank would issue him a letter of credit as a receipt for the money. He could then travel to Bruges, present the letter at the bank's branch there, and withdraw Flemish *groots*. Today, depositing money at one branch of a bank and withdrawing at another is a very basic banking function but it was a major development back then.

The letter of credit had another advantage. Not only did it save the merchant from having to carry the money, but he also avoided having to go to a moneychanger and exchanging the French money for Flemish. However, the banks did charge a fee for their services. The fee was typically concealed in the exchange rate. The exchange rate given by the bank was lower than the market rate so that the merchant received fewer groots than he would have had he changed his gros tournois on the open market. Still, the convenience outweighed the cost.

Even the Church used letters of credit. In the 14th century, rather than carting tons of silver coins paid as tithes to the papal court in Avignon, the pope contracted with one of the large Italian banks to have them send their representatives out to major cities across throughout Europe, from Poland to Portugal, and collect the donations that had been brought there by local Church officials. The bankers would total up the donations and issue letters crediting the Church for the amounts of the donations. The letters were redeemable in Avignon so the pope could use the funds there without having to incur the incredible expense and logistical nightmare of moving all those coins. The bankers, for their part, then had large amounts of money cached in all the main commercial cities as well as many others. They could then loan the money out to merchants or use it for investments of their own. And they again collected a fee for their service by setting exchange rates so that the Church paid more than the market rate.

Individual travelers, including pilgrims, university students, clergy, and diplomats, were sometimes able to use versions of letters of credit as traveler's checks. For example, in 1203, a cleric traveling from Wales to Rome stopped at one of the fairs in Champagne and bought a letter of credit from Italian merchants. In Italy, he cashed the letter to pay for his expenses. This was much safer and easier than carrying a purse full of coins. The only drawback was that a traveler had to find a bank or merchant that would honor the check, which were usually found only at major trade fairs and in a number of cities.

Over time, letters of credit were accepted by banks other than the ones that had originally issued them. Companies also came to accept the letters as payments for merchandise purchased. By accepting letters of credit, these companies encouraged the letter's holder to do business with them. However, Italian banks and companies long remained the only institutions that issued and redeemed letters of credit. Merchants from other countries were slow to adopt the use of the letters. Some appear to have been suspicious of such transactions, perhaps fearing that the letter would not be honored when presented. As a consequence, they did not begin to use the letters until the end of the period.

Bills of Exchange

Besides being difficult to move, coins were poorly suited for carrying out large business transactions. Using silver pennies to pay for a year's worth of wool produced by a large monastery or for a boatload of alum was burdensome, if not impossible. As early as the 12th century, Italian businessmen began developing a solution for this problem. They created a form of contract that came to be called a *bill of exchange*. Bills of exchange were used both as a means of transferring credit from one place to another and as a form of loan.

The bill of exchange recorded the transaction, the amount of money to be paid by the buyer to the seller, the date that payment was due, and the place where the payment was to be made. But, instead of requiring the expensive and risky transfer of bags and bags full of small silver coins for payment, the bill established a credit for the seller with the buyer. Additionally, the bill of exchange could serve as a form of loan and help the buyer finance the transaction. Here is how a bill of exchange worked:

1. A sells B 200 sacks of wool in London for 20 English pounds.
2. Instead of paying cash for the wool, B gives A a bill of exchange stating that an agent of B will pay the money owed to A in one month in Bruges. The payment will be 24 Flemish gros.
3. At the end of one month, A presents the bill to B's agent in Bruges and is paid the money owed to him.

(Note: For the sake of example, the fair market exchange rate is one pound to one gros. The price and exchange rate do not reflect actual prices and rates of the period.)

Twenty pounds would not seem to be a huge amount of coins. However, pound coins did not exist in the Middle Ages. The value of a pound was used only for accounting purposes. Instead, the pound of silver, for which the "pound" was named, was minted into 240 silver pennies. Thus, paying 20 pounds would have required 4,800 silver pennies.

Besides avoiding the burden of paying with coins, A gave B time to resell the wool so that he would have enough money to pay back A. In this respect, the bill of exchange was also used as loan by the seller to finance the buyer's purchase. In this example, by giving B a month in which to pay for the wool, A has loaned B the price of the wool for one month. Like the transaction fee for a letter of credit, the interest is hidden in the exchange rate. Here, A has charged B four gros as interest by setting the exchange rate rather than using the fair market rate. Concealing the interest charges was necessary to avoid prohibitions against usury, but it was not without risk. Exchange rates could rise or drop before the payment was due and reduce or increase the profit.

Ultimately, bills of exchange became transferable so that someone could buy a bill from the original creditor and become the new creditor. A merchant would sell a bill because he did not need credit where the bill was payable. Another merchant would buy the bill because he did need the credit in that particular city. However, the market for bills depended on where they were payable. Those payable in major commercial centers such as Bruges or Venice were relatively easy to buy or sell because many merchants had need of credit there. On the other hand, bills that provided credit in smaller cities that had less business activity were not as desirable and might have been difficult or impossible to sell to other merchants.

Like letters of credit, bills of exchange were initially used only by Italian merchants. Merchants from France, England, and Germany were more cautious about using them and generally did not accept until the 15th century. As the letter of credit and bill of exchange show, Italian businessmen developed sophisticated and sometimes complex methods of financing their long-distance trading. These gave them a significant advantage in conducting large-scale international trade and contributed to the dominance of Italian merchants in much of Europe. Merchants from other nations only gradually came to accept the Italian practices and some did not do so until after the Middle Ages.

Despite their advantages, bills of exchange did not solve all the needs for shipping large amounts of coins or bullion. Wages for armies, dowry payments for noble and royal weddings, bribes to allies, and ransom payments for kings and other nobility all required delivery of huge cash payments. These shipments were often quite risky. One payroll shipment to an army in Italy was escorted by 150 mounted men-at-arms but was still successfully ambushed and robbed. Some trade continued to require large payments in coins or bullion as well. At the fringes of Europe and beyond, bills of exchange had no value. A Russian fur trapper or a Moslem spice merchant would not accept the bills since credit in some European city was worthless to him.

Money Changing

Exchanging money has been mentioned several times already in this section. It was a common part of trade because Europe was fragmented into dozens of independent and semi-independent jurisdictions and many minted their own money. At times, even individual cities minted their own money. Since they typically had to make their purchases in local currency, merchants and other travelers had to exchange money as they crossed from one land to the next.

It was extremely difficult to keep track of exchange rates. With each jurisdiction issuing its own money, there was a bewildering variety of coins in Europe over the course of the Middle Ages. These included Bohemian groschen, English pennies, Florentine florins, Venetian ducats, Provinois deniers, and many more. In the late 15th century, there were over 70 different varieties of coins in circulation, both gold and silver.

Another complication was that the weight and metal content of the coins were not standardized. They varied widely in weight and purity from one jurisdiction to the next. Some coins might weigh an ounce and be only 75 percent pure precious metal while others could weigh half an ounce and be 95 percent pure. Determining the relative value between coins required careful weighing and a knowledge of the standard of purity for the country that issued them. But to further confuse matters, some rulers attempted to increase their money supplies by issuing coins with lower precious metal content and a higher content of base metals. Thus, a silver écu issued in one year might contain far less silver than an écu issued the previous year, leading to distinctions such as "old écus" and "new écus." It was essential to know the silver or gold content of coins because that was what determined their real worth. Unlike today, when coins are made of cheap metal alloys that have little or no value, a medieval coin had intrinsic value that was based on the fair market value of the silver or gold it contained. In a few instances, some merchants found coins so unreliable that they specified that payments had to be made in ounces of silver rather than in a certain number of coins. This was a standard practice for trade in Central Asia and further east.

Weighing coins was also needed to detect counterfeiting and coin clipping. Poorly made counterfeit coins could be heavier or lighter than genuine ones or contain flaws in their designs. Clipped coins would be lighter than the standard weight. In coin clipping, unscrupulous individuals discreetly trimmed off part of the edges of coins to steal the silver or gold and then passed off the coin on some unsuspecting person. Fighting coin clipping was one of the primary reasons that coins came to be designed with a raised or patterned rim. Any clipping of the coin's edge would be readily apparent. Even though most modern coins contain little or no precious metals, coins today are still minted with ridged edges, raised rims, and other features which originated to combat coin clipping.

Exchanging coins sometimes required a knowledge of the value of both silver and gold.

Most medieval coins were silver. Gold coins went out of circulation in the early Middle Ages and did not reappear until the late 13th century. When both gold and silver were in use, it was necessary to know their relative value when converting from coins of one metal into the other.

As the above suggests, changing money required some expertise. The most experienced merchants kept themselves informed of the relative value of the principal currencies. They kept track of the current values of silver and gold and the metal content of coins new and old. They watched out for counterfeits and clipped coins. Some were such experts that they changed money for other merchants. There were also professional money changers. They could be found in cities, towns, and fairs across Europe. In cities, their shops or stalls were often located just inside the city gates so travelers could change their money and be prepared to make purchases with local money. They could also be found in other key locations in cities, such as near marketplaces or on bridges. Bridges were important traffic centers in medieval cities so shops on bridges were well located and easy to find. Shops on bridges were also more secure from break-ins. Some money lenders served as bankers. Using their secure shops, they would store coins and bullion for customers. They also made loans using the capital they accumulated from their trade. This came from the fees they charged for exchanging money as well as profits derived from their expertise in trading silver and gold. As might be expected, money changers, including merchants who changed money as a side business, often became wealthy. Over time, the number of money changers shrank as banks became more common. Banks issued and redeemed letters of credit and other financial instruments, which greatly reduced the need for merchants to change money to conduct business.

Couriers

Rapid transmission of orders as well as guidance to business agents and information about distant market and political conditions were all needed as part of the growing international trade. Knowledge of a sudden drop or increase in demand or supply for a particular good could mean the difference between great profit and bankruptcy. But it was very difficult to send messages so that they would arrive in a timely manner. Today, we can make telephone calls or send messages by e-mail and communicate instantaneously with others around the world. In the Middle Ages, the only option was to send a written message via courier.

Initially, messages were sent via travelers who happened to be going to the right destination. Sending messages this way was usually slow and unreliable. For important communications, merchants sometimes sent the same message with several different travelers who were using several different routes in hopes that at least one of them would get to the destination in time for the information to still be useful. In other cases, merchants hired men to quickly carry the message to their partners or agents. Over time, this practice evolved into regular courier services. One of the earliest was established in the 1260s between the Champagne fairs and cities in Tuscany, primarily Florence. Beginning in the mid–14th century and continuing through the end of the Middle Ages, a number of services ran from Milan, Florence, and Genoa and other cities in northern Italy to commercial centers around the Continent. Bruges, Cologne, Barcelona, Avignon, and many other cities were linked to the central hub in Italy. The services were all financed by consortiums of the various companies that used them. Courier systems were not cheap to operate. The greatest expense was maintaining the relays of horses across Europe. Companies that were not part of the group that established the service were sometimes allowed to use it as well but their mail was delivered last.

Not all businessmen appreciated the regular service. In late 14th century Avignon, an agent of Francesco Datini, a successful merchant who left behind extensive records of his business, complained that reading and replying to all the letters sent by Datini took up half his time. It appears that micromanagement is not a new phenomenon.

Markets and Fairs

From the early Middle Ages, there were two different venues for trade: markets and fairs. These terms appear to have been used interchangeably at times. From actual practice, the general distinction between them was that fairs were regional or even international events and were held annually on the date of a Christian holy day while markets were usually more local in scope and held more frequently.

Some markets and fairs developed on their own, while many were established by charters issued by the ruler of the region. Having a fair or market was very beneficial to a town or city and those that had traditional fairs and markets guarded their rights carefully. At times, however, rulers succeeded in requiring a town or city to pay for a charter to confirm their existing fair or market and all new fairs or markets had to be chartered. For the many new towns established over the course of the Middle Ages, rulers sometimes granted market charters for free to encourage settlement in their lands.

Regardless of how frequently they were held, markets and fairs served the same purpose of bringing producers, consumers, and merchants together so that they could buy and sell goods. The small weekly markets gave people the opportunity to buy and sell basic items that were produced locally, such as fresh vegetables, wooden dishes, or ceramic ware if there was a pottery in the area. There were also some goods brought in by outside traders. These could include cloth, metalwork, and other necessities which were not available from local sources. These markets continued to be held through the Middle Ages and can still be found in towns and cities in many parts of Europe.

Regional markets appear to have been held less often than local ones. They may have been held fortnightly or monthly. Some cities and large towns always possessed regional markets as well as smaller local ones. The size of these urban centers provided a large customer base that attracted merchants from outside of the immediate area. Some regional markets developed from smaller ones held in towns that grew in size or even developed into cities. Regional markets had greater selections of merchandise which were brought in from a wider area than served the local ones. Along with goods produced within the region, even more items from further away were available. Spices and other expensive and rare products could be found at some of the larger markets.

As with markets, fairs varied in size, but they were likely at least regional in scope. Many fairs attracted more buyers and sellers as they became reliable places for them to rendezvous. It became more practical and profitable for merchants to travel greater distances to buy and sell goods at these fairs since they could count on reaching more customers. The risks and expense of traveling to a fair were offset by the greater certainty of gain. Circuits of fairs developed in some areas, with merchants traveling from one fair to the next. One fair might be held in one town in March and then in another in April. The towns would be far enough apart so that merchants would have a new group of customers at every stop. The opening and closing dates of fairs often provided merchants with adequate time to travel between the fairs.

Dates of fairs were typically tied to religious holy days. It may seem odd to connect commerce with religion but, during the Middle Ages, people gauged time in accordance with Christian observances. Hours of the day were set by the ringing of church bells and dates within the year were typically referred to by their religious significance. For example, the Lendit Fair in Paris was held from St. Barnabas' Day until St. John's Day. This was more meaningful to a medieval European than saying that it was from 11 to 24 June. In addition, a few of the holy days on which markets were held were celebrated with festivals. These celebrations drew people together and so provided crowds of potential customers for the fairs.

THE CHAMPAGNE FAIRS

Some regional fairs developed into marketplaces for specific goods while a few had always been best noted for a particular product. Some fairs came to specialize in spices and other exotic imports while some dealt in herring. The fairs were sometimes located near the primary place that the goods were produced or consumed. Others were located at a town or city that was a convenient rendezvous point between the consumer and supplier. From the 12th century through the 13th century, the most successful of these meeting points were towns in the county of Champagne. Champagne lay along the principle north-south route between Italy and Flanders, which were the two primary commercial centers in Europe for much of the Middle Ages. Being located near the mid-point of the most direct route between the two, Champagne provided a convenient spot for merchants from both regions to meet. Along with Flemish and Italian merchants, the fairs drew attendees from around Germany, France, and elsewhere. The Champagne fairs were the first to have large-scale international participation.

While its location was ideal, the counts and countesses of Champagne took further measures to make the county appealing to commerce. As discussed previously in the section on travel aids, the counts and countesses encouraged merchants to attend fairs by guaranteeing them safe passage within the county. They were able to expand the safety zone by obtaining similar guarantees from neighboring rulers, which further attracted merchants. Ultimately, they persuaded the king of France to issue a royal guarantee of safe conduct within all his lands. By expanding the circle of protection and adding higher levels of nobility right up to the king, they greatly increased the

deterrent value of the safe conducts. Lesser nobility felt pressure to provide protection for merchants crossing their lands since they knew that their overlords would be displeased if the flow of trade was impeded.

The counts and countesses also maintained order within the fairs. County officials policed the fairs and oversaw their operations. Initially, complaints between merchants over business transactions appear to have been decided by county officials on the spot but merchant courts gradually developed to hear the cases. Unlike most other courts, the fair courts ruled quickly. Rapid decisions were an absolute necessity given the limited length of the fairs and the transient nature of the merchants. The court also had the important power to order the settlement of debts contracted at the fairs. Merchants who failed to obey the rulings were excluded from the fairs. This was a powerful incentive to comply, given that the fairs were often an essential part of a merchant's business. The courts' enforcement of contracts and debts also gave merchants confidence in the deals that were made at the fairs.

The counts and countesses also took steps to reduce the likelihood of disputes. Official scales were operated at each fair and used the standard weights of the county. Other measures, such as units for measuring the length of cloths, were also set by the county. While the provision of standard weights and measures was common in most major market towns and cities, it was unusual for official scales to be used at fairs. This was another indication of the importance of the Champagne fairs and their commitment to fair dealing.

The rulers of Champagne did not do all these things simply because they thought that the promotion of trade was a good thing to do. The fairs were the major source of revenue for the counts and countesses. While they levied relatively low taxes on the goods sold at the fairs (which further encouraged business), the total taxes collected were substantial. The money spent by the merchants themselves for accommodations, food, drink, and other necessities also pumped money into the local economy. With all this money at stake, it is quite understandable why the counts and countesses were so active in protecting merchants and took it as a personal offense when any were attacked en route to the fairs. The money to be made from the merchants and their trade also explains why other rulers were willing to extend their protection to the merchants as well.

There were six fairs in Champagne. The first began in mid–September and the last started during the first two weeks of July. Each fair lasted for about six weeks, with intervals of one to two weeks between them, except for the longer gap between the July and September fairs. During the first week of the fairs, sales were not taxed. Each of the fairs was actually made up of a number of smaller fairs held sequentially. Cloths were the first items to be presented for sale. The leather fair followed and then the fair for goods sold by weight. These last items included spices, beeswax, and other expensive merchandise. When sales by weight were concluded, the final days of the fair were the time for settling debts for the purchases made at the fair.

Ultimately, the Champagne fairs began to decline in the late 13th century. There were several reasons for their demise. The court of the counts of Champagne greatly declined when the heiress to the county married the heir to the French throne and moved away to Paris. This eliminated the local demand for luxury goods. Wars and the taxes imposed to finance them further weakened the fairs by reducing attendance and dampening trade. The rise of large and permanent, rather than periodic, markets in major cities also removed one of the fundamental reasons that the fairs existed. Buyers and sellers could meet at any time rather than wait for the cycle of fairs. It also eliminated the need for them to travel around to the different fairs. Additionally, sellers no longer had to bring their merchandise to a fair and risk not finding a buyer willing to pay a reasonable price. Instead, sellers could meet with one or more buyers in one of the market cities and arrange a sale. The goods could then be shipped directly to the buyer without having to be relayed through the fair. Along with these changes, large businesses were setting up offices and stationing employees in key commercial cities such as London and Bruges. This was most common for the Italians, who had always been important participants in the trade fairs. The companies' agents could buy and sell goods, arrange transportation, make loans, and engage in any other necessary business transactions. Finally, shipments of goods between Bruges and the Italian city-states were increasingly moved by sea. This was cheaper than most land travel and avoided crossing war zones in France created by the onset of the Hundred Years' War. These last two developments largely eliminated the value of Champagne's position on the land route between the two economic centers, which had first brought the fairs to the county.

Still, some fairs continued to be held. These were primarily specialty fairs that featured specific products or goods from particular regions. For example, a fair selling salted herring and cod was held annually in the Skania in Denmark. Hanse merchants were the primary buyers and they resold the herring to England and across northern Europe. Salt from Lüneberg was also sold there to Norwegian merchants and others who would resell it to fishermen for salting down the next big catch. Other specialty fairs included the Leipzig fair that dealt primarily in furs from Russia and Poland and the fairs at Nuremberg and Frankfort that specialized in German products such as Rhine wines and metalwork.

Government Regulations on International Trade

Apart from purely commercial factors, trade was affected by international politics as well. All trade involving import and export was affected when military conquests temporarily or permanently disrupted access to supplies or markets. Merchants, whether on land or water, were at risk of attack and even death, especially when crossing war zones. They were also subject to the whims of the rulers of the lands where they traded. For example, Vasily II, the grand duke of Moscow, had all the German merchants at the trading station in Novgorod imprisoned in 1424. Thirty-six of the merchants died while in captivity. Less violent, but still devastating to merchants, were measures by governments to use trade to carry out foreign policy or raise funds for their treasuries. In some instances, restrictions on exports of goods were used as an early form of economic warfare. Such embargoes on exports were intended to cripple a hostile country's economy by denying them materials that were vital to their important businesses. The most common material used in this way was wool. Producing woolen cloth was of such importance to Flanders that any English restrictions of the export of wool had an immediate negative impact on its economy. During the Hundred Years' War and the years leading up to it, the English used embargoes and other measures against Flanders since parts of it were ruled by the French.

Restrictions on the export of raw materials were also used to encourage the development of domestic industries and weaken foreign competitors. In England, less wool being taken out of the country meant that more was available for local production of cloth. The increased availability of locally made cloth was intended to lessen demand for foreign-made cloth. The cloth could also be sold abroad in competition with foreign businesses. Reducing or eliminating export duties on the cloth made it cheaper and easier to sell in foreign markets. A further step was to increase import duties to protect domestic industries. Duties drove up the costs of foreign goods and deterred consumers from buying them. Theoretically, the consumers would turn to the cheaper, locally made goods as a substitute. Higher import duties had the added benefit of taking more money in from those imports that did

sell and so raising revenue for the royal treasury. In fact, most duties were imposed solely for the purpose of collecting revenue.

Another form of control was the use of *staples*. A staple was a city designated as the exclusive point of sale for a commodity. By requiring that all sales take place in only one city, designated merchants of that city were given the valuable position of being the only authorized middlemen for sales of that particular product. At the same time, the king or other ruler who dictated the location of the staple could usually expect payments from these merchants for the privilege they received. Bribes were always welcome. Additionally, staples were not always located within the country that produced the good being traded. They could be placed abroad. This was sometimes done as a political move to win the favor of the area where the staple was located. Again, the best examples of all these practices can be found in England, where the kings manipulated the wool trade to achieve political ends and generate revenue for their treasuries during the Hundred Years' War. Ultimately, however, these machinations, combined with high export taxes, damaged the market for English wool in Flanders. In the 15th century, the Flemish began to import most of their raw wool from Spain, where the recently introduced merino sheep were producing high-quality wool. Additionally, the Spanish were stable and reliable suppliers since their government did not use wool as an economic weapon.

Besides the added expense of having to sell through local middlemen or *staplers*, staples were a great inconvenience for both the producers and the buyers. Stapling required producers to transport all of their goods to the staple city to sell it. This often resulted in spending additional time and expense on transportation since staples did not always lie on the most direct routes between sellers and buyers. For example, when London was the wool staple for England, all the wool in the country had to be brought there. Thus, wool produced in Yorkshire in the north of England had to be brought the length of the country before it could be sold. In an open market, the wool could have been sold at York or another nearby city or town. This problem was even worse when the staple was located in Antwerp in Belgium or the English-held city of Calais in France. For buyers, having a single place to buy a good was somewhat convenient but there were the extra costs added by the staplers.

There were also import staples. As with export staples, all import staples benefited local merchants by forcing passing merchants to use them as middlemen. At an import staple, foreign merchants were forced to sell their goods to the local merchants or staplers. These forced sales were presumably at lower prices than the foreign merchants would have been able to obtain on the open market. Instead, the staplers bought the goods and resold them at the market price. By doing this, the staplers effectively took a share of the profits that would have otherwise gone to the foreign merchants. Import staples existed in a number of cities. For example, the duke of Austria gave Vienna the right to force all merchants shipping goods on the Danube River to stop at the city and sell their merchandise only to the Viennese. Only items that went unsold were allowed to be shipped out. Merchants on the major road that passed by the city were subject to the staple as well. Some cities on the Elbe River in Germany had a similar right called *stapfelrecht*. Under the stapfelrecht, all river boats had to stop at particular ports and offer their goods for sale to local merchants for three days before being permitted to reload the unsold merchandise and travel on. Some cities in the Low Countries located on the Rhine and other major rivers as well as the city-state of Venice had versions of import staples as well. Merchants did try to fight against these staples. For example, the Bohemians and Hungarians boycotted Vienna and rerouted their trade routes to bypass it. Unfortunately, the boycott did little good and Vienna continued to be a major hub of international trade. Similarly, river traffic could not avoid the staple

in the Low Countries and Venice was such a major trade center that it was not practical to bypass it for most merchants trading in the area.

There were also controls on sales and exports which applied to items that had military value. These export controls date back to the early centuries of the Middle Ages. They carried out the defense policy of denying weapons or other matériel to an enemy or potential enemy. The problem of arming one's enemies was apparent as early as the 8th century. In 781, Charlemagne, the king of the Franks and, later, Holy Roman emperor, banned the export of any weapons, stallions, or female slaves. The stallions were those used for horse-breeding warhorses. (The strategic value of female slaves is less clear.) In 864, Charles the Bald, king of the western Franks, prohibited selling armor, weapons, or any horses to the Vikings. Even giving them to Vikings as a ransom payment was forbidden. Anyone who violated these bans was to be considered a traitor and executed. In 972, the doge (the ruler) of Venice forbade Venetian merchants from selling arms or wood for ship building to the Moslems. The Church also issued prohibitions on trade with the Moslems several times over the course of the Middle Ages. Those that violated the bans were subject to the ultimate punishment of excommunication. To get around the ban, some merchants rerouted trade from the Middle East through Armenia, a Christian country, and many merchants appear to have just ignored it. Even after warfare between Moslem and European countries intensified in the 15th century, some merchants still traded at Moslem-held ports around the Mediterranean.

Other Trade Regulations

Besides export controls, there were regulations to protect economic interests. Some of these addressed problems still faced today.

In 13th century Venice, the *consoli dei mercanti*, the council of merchants, was established to deal with commercial practices that were held to be detrimental to Venetian merchants as a group, such as contracts that restrained trade by creating monopolies. A monopoly could be created by agreements between a Venetian merchant and foreign suppliers that gave the merchant exclusive rights to import the suppliers' product. With this monopoly, the Venetian could then take over the entire market for that product, artificially control its price, and reap all the profits. This anti-competitive practice harmed other Venetian merchants and the *consoli* was empowered to nullify the contracts and break the monopoly.

Another common government practice was to regulate the price of essential foods, most importantly grain. Attempts were also made to prevent individuals or groups from conspiring to artificially raise the prices for foodstuffs. The three methods for doing this were forestalling, regrating, and engrossing. Forestallers bought up a commodity before it reached the legitimate market or deterred others from taking the commodity to market. By doing this, they attempted to cause a shortage and drive up the price of the goods. Regrating was the purchasing of all or most of a commodity available at a market to cause a shortage and then reselling the goods at a higher price in the same market or one nearby. Engrossing was much the same practice. Engrossers bought large quantities of a commodity with the intent of cornering the market so that they could resell the commodity at higher prices. All these activities were held to be contrary to the public good and were generally forbidden.

Trade Imbalances

Importing and exporting was rarely an equal exchange. It was common for one area to export more than it imported or vice-versa. England provides one example. Despite its exports of wool and cloth, the value of the goods imported to England often exceeded the value of the country's exports. As a consequence, money, in the form of silver coins, was gradually drained out of England. This flow of money out of the country damaged the economy. Part of the harm was that it reduced the supply of money within the country and caused or worsened shortages of coins. To address this problem, the kings of England forbade the export of bullion and coins. This even applied to the tithes to the Church which were to be sent to the pope. Denying foreign merchants the easiest means for taking their profits out of England forced them to buy more English goods or invest their gains in English enterprises. It also contributed to the drafting and transfer of bills of exchange. Merchants with profits tied up in England could transfer them to another merchant who wanted to do business in England in exchange for credit usable in some city on the Continent. The restriction also likely had the impact of deterring some foreign merchants from importing goods to England, since they could not readily take their profits out of the country. This would have actually had a negative impact on the economy if it interfered with the production of goods within England but, from the government's point of view, it would be positive if it deterred the import of consumer goods, especially costly luxury goods. Limiting the import of consumer goods was also achieved by imposing high tariffs on these items. If this did not deter these imports, the duties at least provided additional revenue to the royal government, which was an acceptable outcome for the king.

Another more serious imbalance existed between Europe as a whole and the Middle East, Asia Minor, and the lands around the Black Sea and beyond. With the high value of the spices, silks, cotton, and other goods imported from these lands, Europe, as a whole, was rarely able to export sufficient merchandise to equal the cost of the imports. There was little demand for most European merchandise in the East. The fine woolens and furs which were so valued throughout Europe were of little interest to merchants in the warm climes of the Middle East. The difference in value between the exports and the imports had to be made up in silver. This was so common that small ingots of very pure silver were cast in Genoa and Venice especially for use in trade at ports around the Black Sea and at markets further east into Asia. All trade such as this led to a drain of silver from Europe and into the coffers of the other countries. Historians differ on how severe this problem was. Many believe that as much as half or more of the items purchased from the East were paid for with silver. Others hold that that figure is an exaggeration. In either case, significant amounts of silver were shipped out of Europe every year to pay for imports from the East. Further, unlike the situation in England, bills of exchange were useless for reducing this flow of silver. Asian and Moslem merchants had no use for credit valid only in the cities of Europe. Only merchandise or silver, in coin or bullion, were acceptable forms of payment.

This imbalance was only gradually resolved. There were a number of developments that lessened the imbalance. One was the spread of cotton and sugar growing across the islands along the southern edge of Europe. This greatly lessened the need to import these products. Similarly, European glass and paper manufacturing developed to the point that the quality and quantity of the goods produced met or exceeded those that could be imported from the Middle East. In fact, some European paper and glass was exported to the Middle East in the late Middle Ages.

The trade imbalance was also reduced by the decline of trade with the East in the final centuries of the Middle Ages. As mentioned previously, during this time, hostilities increased between Moslems and Christians. In the 14th century, the Ottoman Turks advanced out of Asia Minor, into Greece, and on into the Balkans. They conquered most of the lands formerly held by the Byzantine Empire. By 1453, all that remained of Byzantium was its capital of Constantinople and some surrounding lands. The Ottoman Turks took Constantinople that year and consolidated their foothold in Europe. They also gained control of the entrance to the Black Sea. By 1475, they had pushed the Genoese and Venetians out of their trading posts around the Black Sea and crippled European trade with Central Asia. European access to ports in Egypt and the Middle East was also severely limited. Throughout this period, European ships were increasingly at risk of attack by Moslem warships or pirates. There was open warfare in the Mediterranean as the navies of Italian city-states fought those of the Turks. Elsewhere in the world, the need for trade with the Middle East was greatly diminished by the establishment of direct trade with India by the Portuguese. This ended the Moslem control of the spice trade. Additionally, the discovery of the New World brought new sources of silver and gold under Spanish control and provided an ample supply of precious metals for currency. Despite all these changes, trade between European and Moslem nations did persist, but on a greatly reduced scale which no longer required the transfer of tons of silver every year.

V

TRADE GOODS AND THEIR SOURCES

The variety of goods traded within medieval Europe was nothing short of amazing. From Iceland to Crete, and Spain to Russia, Europeans created a vast array of products, from basic foodstuffs and clothing to luxury fabrics and artworks. There were also goods imported from outside Europe, such as gold, silk, and spices. All these items circulated within the trade network and ultimately reached consumers across the continent. While some of these items had been traded for millennia before the Middle Ages, the volume and scope of trade during the period far exceeded those of earlier times.

Food

Throughout the Middle Ages, 80 percent or more of the population of Europe was engaged in agriculture. Communities strove to grow and produce as much of their own grains, fruits, vegetables, meats, and dairy products as possible. Despite such catastrophes as blights and bad weather that damaged and destroyed crops and murrains that killed livestock, surpluses of food were regularly produced, even in the early Middle Ages. The surplus went to feed those not engaged in producing food. Traditionally, rents and fees owed to the nobility and tithes and other contributions to the Church were paid in the form of food. After all the local needs and obligations

were satisfied, farmers and stockbreeders brought their surplus to market. Most was sold to city and town residents. As previously discussed, these sales could either be made directly by the farmer or herdsman or by merchants who had bought the surplus food for resale. Over time, as agricultural production grew, more was available to sell to townspeople and city dwellers. This contributed to urban growth.

Some areas were naturally suited to produce certain crops or livestock and therefore specialized in their cultivation or husbandry. By using their natural resources and specializing in production of one particular crop or animal, many such regions routinely produced surpluses which consumers came to rely on. In turn, areas that were great producers of one foodstuff sometimes lacked other important foods. For example, in Gascony in southeastern France, so much land was used for growing grapes to produce wine that the Gascons no longer had enough land on which to grow wheat. As a result, while they exported great quantities of wine, the Gascons had to use some of the revenues from the sale of their wine to buy wheat. As all this suggests, trading foodstuffs was essential for all parts of Europe since it was extremely rare for any single area to produce all the different foods its citizens needed.

Food was exported over varying distances from producers to customers. Some items, such as grain and wine, could be shipped scores of miles overland or via inland waterways or even hundreds of miles across the sea as part of their trip to reach their consumer. Others, including fresh fruit and vegetables, could be transported from farms that were at most a few days distant from their customers. Still other products, most notably milk, were highly perishable and could be sold only a few miles from the site of their production.

GRAIN

Grains, including wheat, rye, barley, and oats, were the basis of the medieval diet. They were grown across Europe, but some regions had the soils and weather to produce grain, primarily wheat, in vast quantities. Noted wheat-growing areas included Poland, northeastern Germany, Sicily, and some of the lands surrounding the west and northwest coasts of the Black Sea, including what are now Romania, Moldova, and Ukraine. While these areas produced far more wheat than was needed for local consumption, there were other lands which could not grow enough to feed their people. Among these were the city-states of Italy, the cities along the southern coast of the Baltic and North Seas, and Norway. Importing large amounts of grain to feed its populace was nothing new to Italy. In the days of the Roman Empire, Sicily and Egypt served as the "granaries" of the Empire. In the Middle Ages, while exports from Sicily continued, grain was rarely imported from Egypt. Instead, the Italians found new sources around the Black Sea. For the Low Countries and northern Germany, importing grain was not necessary until the populations of their primary cities grew so large that local grain supplies were inadequate and grain had to be imported from the vast wheat fields of Poland and northeastern Germany. The scale of this trade was immense. For example, in the summer of 1481, 1,100 ships of various sizes brought wheat and rye from the Hanse port of Danzig (Gdansk in Poland) to ports in the Low Countries. Merchants of the Hanse trade federation made fortunes from the grain trade in the

north. Similarly, Genoa and Venice profited by controlling most of the grain imports to Italy and the Dalmatian coast.

Famines led to importing grain from even further away. During the crop failures that afflicted northern Europe in the early 14th centuries, grain was shipped in from the Mediterranean, despite the astronomical transportation costs. The massive grain shipments of 1481 appear to have been driven by famines in France and Germany that year. Again, grain prices reached record levels.

SALT

Salt was as vital as wheat. The human body requires small amounts of salt daily to remain healthy. Additionally, in an age before refrigeration, canning, and other modern food preservation methods, salting was the primary means of preserving meats. Thousands of tons were used across Europe every year to salt down beef, pork, and fish. Even smoking and other drying techniques typically used some salt to help desiccate the flesh and prevent the development of bacteria. Salt was used for preserving fish and was essential to the North Sea and North Atlantic fishing industry. Hundreds of thousands of herring, cod, and other fish were caught every year and pickled in brine or dried and salted down. One barrel of salt was required for preserving every four barrels of herring. Without salt, most fish would have spoiled long before they reached consumers. Finally, salt was also the most commonly used flavoring for food.

Some salt was obtained from natural brine wells at locations such as Droitwich in England. The water in the brine was boiled off, leaving the salt crystals. Rock salt was mined, as at the Wieliczka mine near Krakow in Poland. But the majority of salt was produced in pans along the shores of the Atlantic Ocean and the Mediterranean Sea. On the Atlantic coast, the French coast along the Bay of Bourgneuf was the major production center for sea salt. Salt from this source was commonly referred to as "bay salt." In the Mediterranean, the pans of the islands of the western half of the sea, such as Sardinia, along with the pans on the coast of Provence, including some at Aigues Mortes, produced huge quantities of salt. Venice and other spots around the Adriatic Sea also had pans.

The salt pans were vast shallow enclosures which were flooded with seawater and then shut so that the trapped seawater gradually evaporated, leaving the sea salt behind. These pans were set up in many locations, especially in warmer climates where the water evaporated more quickly. When the pan was dried out, the salt crystals were raked off. This type of salt often had grit in it from sand and silt in the bottom of the pans. But it was produced on a far larger scale than brine salt or rock salt and was cheaper. And it was still suitable for use in food preservation. However, the brine and rock salts were preferred for cooking and flavoring foods.

Regardless of which method of production was used, salt was guaranteed to make money. The original wealth of Venice was based on the salt pans built in the city's lagoons. Salt was so valuable that the Hanse cities sent fleets of ships annually all the way to the Bay of Bourgneuf on France's Atlantic coast to bring back "bay salt" to sell in the Scandinavian countries and to Russia and other consumers around the coasts of the North and Baltic Seas. The value of salt is also reflected in some trade regulations. At Droitwich in England, salt was sold by the man-load, pack animal-load, and cart-load. To prevent buyers from abusing this system for selling salt, there were fines for overloading. A pack animal was deemed overloaded if its back broke under the weight of the load. Similarly, loading a cart so heavily that its axle broke was a finable offense. There appears to have been no penalty for overloading a man.

MEAT

Raw meat was a highly perishable food, but, when kept in the form of livestock, it could be traded over long distances. Live cattle

and sheep were even transported by sea when necessary, but herding, or *droving*, them was the most common means for moving them to markets in towns and cities. While cattle drives conjure up images of the American West, they occurred in Europe centuries before, although the drovers were herdsmen on foot rather than cowboys on horseback. Along with cows and sheep, herdsmen or drovers herded pigs and even geese to market. Pigs and geese could be driven only short distances between their farms and markets in towns and cities, but cattle and sheep were sometimes herded long distances. Markets in southern Germany and northern Italy were supplied with cattle driven from Hungary. The Hungarians drove cattle to Germany over the same open plains that their ancestors had crossed to invade the German lands centuries earlier. To reach the northern Italian markets, cows were driven around the east end of the Alps and then put out to pasture in the countryside in northeast Italy to recover and fatten up before proceeding on to market. In the early 14th century, Florence and other Tuscan cities and towns were also fed on tens of thousands of sheep driven up from southern Italy. Shorter drives were even more common. Paris was fed on cattle herded in from lands to the northwest of the city.

Droving had many advantages over slaughtering the animals on the farms and sending the meat to market. Pieces of meat required preservation, such as by smoking, salting, or drying, to prevent spoilage before they reached the market. Sausages, hams, and other preserved meats were widely produced but they constituted only a fraction of the total volume of meat production. In addition, the preserved meat would then have had to be carried by cart or wagon to market. All this would have entailed additional time and expense. However, with livestock, the meat was kept fresh until the animal was slaughtered in the city or town. In addition to keeping the meat fresh, transportation costs were minimized since the animal carried itself to the consumer. No cartage was needed. Further, after slaughter, the animal's hide could be sold directly to tanners in the town or city.

There was one rare exception to the practice of slaughtering animals only immediately before the sale of their meat. In 15th century Moscow, markets in the winter were on the city's frozen river. Skinned cows and pigs, some of which were positioned on their feet, were sold up to three months after slaughter.

FISH

Fish were a common part of the medieval diet wherever fresh fish could be found. Every coastal region engaged in fishing, ranging from setting up weirs to catch fish as the tide ebbed to sailing far out into open waters and casting nets. Fish from the sea were sent as far inland as was practical. For example, fresh fish were sold in London, which is about 45 miles upstream from the mouth of the Thames. People further inland who were fortunate enough to live near a fish-bearing river could sometimes get fresh fish such as salmon or eels. In addition, some of the rich as well as some monasteries maintained fish ponds to provide a steady supply of fish. Some nobles could even afford to have live fish, packed in damp grass and placed in a basket, shipped to them from the sea or river. However, fish were not always in season. Further, most of the population lived too far away from the sources of fish to have fresh fish shipped to them. The only way for them to obtain fish was to buy preserved ones. As mentioned before, these fish were usually preserved by salting either in brine or with salt crystals, although some were preserved by smoking.

Preserved fish were not that popular. One form of preserved fish was called stockfish. It had to be soaked and beaten repeatedly to render it edible. Other fish typically required less drastic treatment but their flavor and texture appears to have been generally unappealing. Besides the fact that fresh fish were not always available, the main reason that medieval Europeans consumed preserved fish by the barrelful was for religious reasons. The precepts of the medieval Christian Church prohibited the consumption of meat on certain days of the week and for entire months during certain times of year. But fish were permitted as a substitute for meat during these times of fasting and so the demand for fish was enormous.

The main area that produced fish for northern Europe was the North Sea. Fishermen from England, the Low Countries, and Scandinavia fished the North Sea primarily for herring. Norwegians and Icelanders fished for cod in the North Atlantic as well, but herring was the most common. Great shoals of herring appeared at certain times of the year and were caught by the thousands. To keep such large catches from going to waste, the fish had to be preserved as quickly as possible. Besides keeping the huge catches from spoiling, preserving the fish changed it into a form which was far less perishable and could be shipped to distant consumers. Merchants from Cologne sold stockfish as far away as markets in Austria while other Hanse traders brought herring to northern Spain. Stockpiling preserved fish was also the best way to meet the seasonal demand for fish. Fish was eaten year-round on fast days during the week, including every Friday, and so there was a constant demand for preserved fish. But the main time that fish were eaten was during Lent. Lent is the period of 40 days before Easter. it was observed by medieval Christians by fasting, so no meat could be eaten during this time. Instead, preserved fish, primarily herring, that was either white with salt or red from smoking, were consumed by the hundreds of thousands across much of Europe. Merchants from the port cities in the east of England and the south coast of the North Sea made fortunes on this trade by buying up the preserved fish and reselling them at markets. In the Mediterranean basin, it was possible to obtain fresh fish throughout the year and, especially in Italy, many areas were relatively near the coasts so that preservation was less necessary. In fact, apart from tuna and sardines packed in olive oil, preserved fish do not appear to have been a significant trade good in this region.

Fresh Fruits and Vegetables

Despite the common perception that medieval Europeans generally shunned fresh fruits and vegetables, they were actually quite popular. There were orchards with apple, pear, or cherry trees. Gardens, including some on lots in cities, were filled with beans, cabbage, lettuce, carrots, parsnips, onions, celery, beets, and other vegetables, and fruits such as strawberries and melons. These were brought to markets in towns and cities as quickly as possible after harvest. This could include transporting them in a cart and loading them onto small barges and ferrying them to market. Commercial gardens in the cities sold them directly to residents. Because of their perishable nature, the supply chain had to have been relatively short. Since they could be sold only relatively near where they were produced, it was sometimes practical for the farmer or gardener to take them to market himself. Still, in cities at least, it appears that there were middlemen who bought produce from the farmers and resold it in the markets.

Wine and Beer

As today, the most common beverage in the medieval world was water. Admittedly, in some areas, such as in and around cities, well water and even river water were sometimes contaminated with dangerous bacteria, but cool water was always a popular thirst quencher. The alcohol produced as part of fermentation made wine and beer more hygienic beverages than water and they were consumed in huge quantities across Europe.

Wine

Thanks to the Romans, the cultivation of grapes and production of wine was spread to most parts of western Europe that had suitable soil and climates. They also traded in wine. Amphorae, and later barrels, of wine were shipped around the Empire. As with other trade, the collapse of the Empire diminished the wine trade, but wine production continued and wine was sold on a regional basis. For example, wines produced in the Rhine valley continued to be shipped to towns and cities in the vicinity. As international trade gradually resumed, wine was again exported across Europe. Except for Scandinavia, wine was produced locally in most of Europe but certain areas came to be noted for their wine and some became major exporters.

The region of Gascony in southwestern France was a major wine producer and exporter. Gascony was located in the Duchy of Aquitaine, which was held by the kings of England in their capacity as dukes of Aquitaine. Because of this connection, England was the primary market for Gascon wine. During the first half of the 14th century, Gascony is estimated to have exported up to 18 million gallons of wine to England annually. The wine was given favorable customs rates and provided the English with a vast supply of cheap wine. Large numbers of English ships sailed every year to Bordeaux and other Gascon ports to bring back huge barrels of wine. However, this trade was curtailed in the late 14th century as the area was devastated in the course of the Hundred Years' War. Ultimately, England lost Gascony entirely and turned to other sources of wine in Spain, Portugal, and the Rhineland. Wines from these regions had been imported before but they now constituted the majority of England's wine imports. These wines were generally more expensive than the Gascon wines and, while wine remained popular with those who could afford it, beer grew greatly in popularity as a consequence.

Within France, wines from the Loire valley and Burgundy circulated widely but were rarely exported any further. Similarly, most wine produced in Italy was consumed there so the trade in it was limited. In fact, Italian wine production did not satisfy the demand so wines were imported from Spain and southern France. German Rhine wines were traded internationally and were shipped to England, the Low Countries, and lands to the east, including the German cities on the Baltic coast. The most sought-after wines were those produced on the mainland and isles of Greece. These were sweet wines. Although their sweetness may not suit modern tastes, the elite of medieval society across Europe considered these wines to be the finest and enjoyed them mixed with spices. The high demand and the relatively small amounts produced contributed to these being the most expensive wines in the Middle Ages. They were exported with other luxury goods from the Mediterranean to noble courts around Europe.

The medieval wine trade left its mark on history. As mentioned previously, the largest barrels of wine were called *tuns*. A tun held about 252 gallons and weighed around 2,240 pounds when completely filled with wine. Tuns of wine were such a common cargo that the capacity of ships came to be measured in tuns. Over the years, the tun became a standard throughout Europe and the modern long ton is 2,240 pounds.

Beer

Beer has been brewed from various cereals such as wheat and barley for millennia. In the Middle Ages, it was made and consumed primarily in the north — England, Scandinavia, the Low Countries, and the German-speaking lands — but it was also produced in northern France and Bohemia. In the early Middle Ages, millions of gallons were brewed every year but production was on a small scale. In England, for example, part of a wife's weekly chores often included brewing a few gallons of beer for her family. Some women came to specialize in brewing and produced enough to sell to their neighbors. By the late 11th century, commercial breweries began to appear. But regardless of whether it was brewed in a brewery or in the house next door, the beer had to be consumed within a few days of its brewing because its quality deteriorated quickly. To use modern terms, it had a short shelf life. Because it was so perishable, there was little trade in beer apart from local sales.

It was not until the wide-scale use of hops that beer became durable enough to be produced in large quantities and shipped significant distances to consumers. (In fact, the use of hops is what makes it beer. Technically, beer without hops is ale. Hops are the flower clusters from a type of herbaceous plant.) Besides altering the flavor, hops inhibited the growth of harmful bacteria and made the beer more stable and slowed spoilage. Hopped beer had been produced as early as the 9th century but it was not until around the year 1200 that the use of hops began to be common. Brewers in the Hanse cities of Bremen, Hamburg, and Wismar were the first to produce hopped beer on a large scale and they were exporting beer by the mid–13th century. By the 14th century, Hamburg alone is estimated to have produced approximately six million gallons of beer and shipped over two and a half million of those gallons to Amsterdam and other cities, primarily in the Low Countries. Besides the trade in beer itself, brewing promoted other commerce as well. It led to a marked increase in the demand for grains, especially barley. This meant that even more grain had to be imported from Poland and northeast Germany to the cities that produced beer. Additionally, while hops were grown near, and even in, these cities, hops from Poland were also imported to meet the growing demand for beer.

DAIRY PRODUCTS

Milk in fresh liquid form had to come from the immediate vicinity. It was very difficult to transport milk fast enough to sell it before it spoiled. Some residents of cities and towns kept their own cows to guarantee a fresh supply. It was also common to convert milk into more durable forms, such as cheese and butter, so that they would last longer. In these forms, they could even be shipped over surprising distances. For example, while most butter came from farms surrounding a city or town, butter from the dairy herds of Denmark was shipped to markets in Norway and other parts of Scandinavia as well as in northern

Germany and England. Typical of medieval butter, Danish butter was heavily salted to preserve it so it could be shipped long distances and remain edible. (To cope with the saltiness of butter, clarifying butter to remove salt was a common part of cooking in the Middle Ages.)

LUXURY FOODS AND GOODS

The foods discussed so far were the staples of the diet of medieval Europeans. There were also luxury foods that were consumed only by those wealthy enough to afford them. These foods were generally referred to as *spices*. The term "spice" covered a wide variety of edible and inedible items. Spices included sugar, dates, figs, raisins, frankincense, musk, borax, aloes, alum, cloves, ginger, grains of paradise, galingale, cumin, rhubarb, cinnamon, cardamom, gemstones, pearls, pepper, and many other things. Their common link was that they were expensive, relatively rare, and usually imported from outside Europe. Many originated in India, Ceylon (modern day Sri Lanka), Southeast Asia, and the Indonesian archipelago. Some were from the Middle East. There were also luxury foods, including almonds, citrus fruits, pomegranates, and olive oil, from the Mediterranean basin that were exported to the rest of Europe.

Cloth

After agriculture, the production of cloth was the major industry of medieval Europe. At any one time, it employed tens of thousand of weavers, dyers, and fullers in lands from England to Italy. In 14th century Florence alone, one contemporary chronicler estimated that 30,000 residents were involved in some aspect of cloth manufacturing. To support this massive enterprise, merchants traded in fibers and dyestuffs as well as finished cloth across Europe and beyond. It was the equivalent of

a modern multi-billion-dollar international industry. The importing and exporting of the raw materials as well as the finished cloth involved some of the most complex trade in the Middle Ages. In part, this was a result of the shifting of production centers as one region vied with another to take control of some aspect, or all, of the production of a certain type of fabric. For example, Bruges was the major importer of English wool and Flanders was the primary producer of woolen cloths for much of the Middle Ages. Wool cloths from the Low Countries were exported throughout Europe. This dominance brought rich rewards to the Flemish but it also attracted the interest of the Italians. The Italians became competitors with Bruges for raw wool from England and succeeded in increasingly diverting the wool to Italy, where the cloth production industries grew dramatically. The Flemish and Italians then competed in producing various types and qualities of wool cloth to capture segments of the market. This competition had consequences outside of Italy, Flanders and England. At times, particularly when English wool was in short supply, the Italians used more domestically grown wool and wool from Spain, which was generally of lower quality than the English wool. This wool was used to produce cheaper grades of cloth but even this limited demand spurred the growth of wool production in Spain and, in the 15th century, led the Spanish to introduce the merino sheep from North Africa to develop wool to rival that of England. The Flemish began importing most of their wool from Spain. As all of this suggests, the cloth trade was very dynamic. It was not simply a matter of buying some wool and weaving it into cloth.

In the remainder of this section, we will look briefly at the different materials that were traded as part of the cloth industry, including their principal markets.

WOOL

Sheep were raised across Europe but certain regions developed major centers for wool production. These areas had the conditions necessary for grazing large herds and the sheep with the right genetic stock for producing high-quality fibers. As mentioned above, England, especially the Cotswolds and Welsh marches regions, was the primary land to possess these resources and large parts of the country came to specialize in sheep husbandry. It is estimated that, in a typical year in the mid–14th century, England produced six million fleeces or more. Wool production was clearly vital to England and its economy. In recognition of this, in the 15th century, a wool sack (a large bale of raw wool) was made the seat of the Lord Chancellor in the House of Lords in Parliament. It is still used by the Lord Speaker today. The English initially used their wool to produce cloth locally but, as early as the 12th century, large quantities of raw wool were sold and shipped to markets in the Low Countries for sale to their cloth industry. During the 13th century, Italian merchants became the primary purchasers of English wool. To secure a steady supply of high-quality wool, Italians sometimes contracted with major sheep-raising concerns to buy their wool clips a year in advance.

Unfinished woolen cloth was also traded. Before the Italians began to dominate the wool trade with England in the late 13th century, the Flemish sold unfinished, high-quality cloth made of English wool to Italian merchants for dyeing and finishing of surfaces. This finishing was very specialized work and was needed to produce the highest quality and most expensive fabrics such as crimson velvet. The cloth finishing trade dwindled as the Italians increasingly bought the raw English wool themselves and used it in their own weaving industry.

Not all wool cloth was luxurious velvets. While England produced high-quality wool, sheep, even within the prime sheep-raising areas, did not all yield the best wool. Additionally, the wool from sheep in other parts of England as well as in Flanders, Italy, and many other parts of Europe varied in quality, but all wool was put to use in making cloth. All the woolen cloth weaving centers produced cheaper cloths made from the lower-quality wool. As with the luxury fabrics, these cloths were sold all around Europe.

LINEN

Linen, as with wool, was produced throughout Europe. It was made anywhere flax could be grown but, like wool, certain areas came to specialize in flax and turn it into linen. However, unlike wool, raw flax was rarely shipped long distances to be made into cloth. All stages of linen production, from retting (soaking the flax and separating its fibers) to dying and weaving, were usually performed within a relatively small radius of where the flax was grown. Processing flax and weaving linen remained a cottage industry.

Noted areas for linen production were southern Germany, Switzerland, and northern Italy, while the finest linens were made in Reims in the county of Champagne. Linen was used to make underclothes and lightweight clothing as well as sailcloth. Linen was also woven with cotton and with wool. The linen-cotton material was called *fustian* and was durable but soft. There was a large market for linen within Europe yet, apart from the finest linen, it remained relatively cheap and was generally not as popular as wool. However, linen was one European cloth which found a ready market in Asia, including China. It was also exported to the Middle East and North Africa. Its light weight made it suitable for warm climates. Further, linen was not produced within Asia so Europeans were virtually the sole source for it. Linen had been produced in Egypt for millennia but it does not seem to have been widely exported. In fact, linen cloth from Europe appears to have been cheaper than the Egyptian fabric and the finest linens, such as those from Reims, were superior to it. European linen was even exported to Egypt.

The finest linen was used to produce one of the most expensive fabrics made in Europe. This was *opus anglicanum*, or English work.

Opus anglicanum was fine embroidery worked on the highest-quality linen. Only the richest people could afford it. Most surviving pieces are religious vestments made for the highest levels of the clergy. Nobility and royalty are known to have owned some as well, but most have disappeared.

COTTON

While flax was grown in Europe, cotton was imported for most of the Middle Ages. Italian merchants bought raw cotton that was grown in Iran and Iraq and brought to markets in Armenia, the Middle East, and Egypt. They also bought it from Sicily and Spain, where the Moslems had introduced it in the 9th century. Cotton farming was eventually introduced to southern Italy and southern France.

Cotton cloth production was centered in Lombardy, with Florence as the leading cotton producer. In the late 14th century, cotton was also imported to southern Germany where it was used to weave fustian. Like linen, cotton was used in combination with other fibers to created blended cloths. Besides fustian, these included silk, wool, and hemp blends. Cotton cloth was exported across Europe and became especially popular for making lightweight underclothes.

SILK

Silk was the single most expensive commodity in medieval trade. By weight, it was worth far more than gold. The best-quality silk cloths were woven in China and were imported to Europe via the Silk Road across Asia as they had been in the days of the Roman Empire. In the Middle Ages, sericulture had been introduced in Syria and silk cloth was woven there and in Asia Minor. These cloths were still valuable but did not command the astronomical prices paid for the best Chinese silks. Silk was imported both as finished cloth and as raw fibers. The raw fibers were processed into fabric and ribbons in Lucca in Italy, although Paris also developed production of silk ribbons.

Silk cloth was such a valuable product that Europeans went to great lengths to develop domestic sources of silk. By the late 13th century, the Italians had brought silkworms to their lands and were planting mulberry trees to feed them. By the 14th century, Lucca was using raw silk grown in Sicily and the southern tip of Italy. The silk-weaving industry spread across the north of Italy. In 1441, Florence ordered the planting of more mulberry trees. Other Italian city-states tried similar campaigns to create domestic silk production but sericulture flourished only in southern Italy and the supply was still not meeting the demand. Silk cloth and raw silk continued to be imported but it was increasingly difficult to obtain them. By the late 15th century, the Moslem Ottoman Turks controlled Asia Minor as well as the lands around the Black Sea. This cut Europe's direct trade with Central Asia, where most of the Chinese silks had been bought.

Dyestuffs, Soap, Alum, and Oil

Virtually all of the cloths produced in medieval Europe, from the cheapest cloths to the most luxurious velvets, were dyed. Dyestuffs produced colors from the palest blues to the richest reds. But more than dyes were required to color fabrics. Most fabrics, especially wool, had to be processed to enable the dyes to permanently color them. Some dyestuffs and other materials were produced within Europe while others were imported. Even within Europe, these materials were often shipped long distances from producers to consumers.

DYESTUFFS

A great variety of materials were used to produce the different colors of cloth. Except for a few metal- and mineral-based dyes, these dyestuffs were from plants. They included nuts, barks, berries, flowers, roots, and leaves. The three most common dyes were derived from the madder, weld, and woad plants. Madder roots produced a red dye and the leaves, seeds, and flowers of weld yielded a yellow dye. Madder and weld were cultivated across Europe. They were cheap, easy to obtain, and do not appear to have been traded to any significant extent. Woad leaves were used to produce a blue dye. Also, when combined with weld, it dyed fabrics green. Like madder and weld, woad was grown in many places in Europe but the south of France and Lombardy came to dominate its production. From there, it was shipped to dyers in Italy, Bruges, London, and other cloth centers. The other principal blue dye was indigo. It was imported from India through the Middle East. It appeared in the Middle Ages as early as the 12th century but did not become common until after the period.

While weld, madder, woad, and other plants produced many different hues, the nobility and other wealthy consumers often wanted shades that were out of the ordinary. Very deep, rich reds were particularly desirable. One dyestuff imported to produce darker reds was brazilwood. The dye was made from the brazilwood tree's dark red heartwood. This tree was grown in Java and Sri Lanka. The brazilwood was sold to merchants from China and India, and shipped through India to the Middle East, where it was bought by the European merchants. Despite the distance and cost of shipping, it was widely used. Brazilwood-dyed wool velvets were especially prized. Incidentally, in the 16th century, European explorers in South America found trees related to the Asian brazilwood trees and named the region "Brazil" after them.

The most luxurious red was produced from insects native only to the Mediterranean. Called "grain" or kermes, this dye was made from the eggs of a parasitic insect that grows only on one species of evergreen shrub-like oak tree. In turn, this oak tree only grows in Portugal and around the coast of the Mediterranean. The limited production of the dyestuff

and the quality of the dye it produced made it expensive. It was used exclusively for dying the highest-quality wool cloth, creating deep, beautiful reds. The exclusivity of the dye and the color it produced, along with the expense of the cloth itself, made kermes dyed cloth one of the most expensive fabrics.

SOAPS, ALUM, AND OIL

The production of woolen cloth required more materials than just dyestuffs. Wool fleeces were very dirty when they were fresh off the sheep. They were coated in lanolin. Lanolin is the rich, waxy oil that the sheep secretes to keep its fleece waterproof. The fleeces also contained all the dirt, plant matter, and other material that had gotten caught in the wool. As a consequence, the first step in processing a fleece was to wash it to remove the filth and most of the lanolin. This required lots of soap. Soap was produced from animal fat and ashes on a small scale everywhere in Europe but much of the soap for washing fleeces was produced in Spain. It was called "black soap" because it was rich in ashes.

Soap alone was not sufficient to degrease the wool. The mineral alum was used to further clean the wool and, more importantly, leave it in a condition to absorb and hold dyes. Alum was vital to the production of woolen cloth. For most of the Middle Ages, the only source was at Phocea in Asia Minor. The Venetians had a monopoly on the alum trade for most of the Middle Ages. They shipped the alum to markets in Italy as well as in England and Flanders. Huge quantities of alum were shipped and this drove the development of larger cargo ships to carry the alum in bulk. In the late 14th century the Genoans succeeded in taking the monopoly away from the Venetians but, with the conquest of Asia Minor by the Ottoman Turks, all Italians were ejected from Phocea. The Turks cut off the alum supply in 1463. Fortunately, a new source of alum had been discovered in Italy in 1460. The Medici family, which dominated renaissance Florence, made part of their fortune from controlling the concession for mining and distributing the alum.

While it was necessary to remove the natural oily lanolin from the fleece, it was also necessary to oil the wool during some stages of its processing to restore its flexibility. In England and Flanders, rancid butter or fat from pigs was sometimes used for this purpose, especially in the early Middle Ages. In later centuries, old olive oil, presumably of a low grade, was imported from Spain and southern Italy for this task.

Furs

Furs were used to line and trim the clothing of royalty, nobility, and wealthy commoners. Furs included *vair* (squirrel), marten, beaver, otter, and even wolf. Most furs came from lands now in Finland and northeastern Russia. Trappers ranged as far north as the Arctic Circle in pursuit of their quarry. Winter was the primary time for trapping fur-bearing animals. Their coats were at their thickest and most luxurious then. For some animals, this was also the season when their coats were the most desirable color. For example, the ermine's coat was a lustrous white so that it could blend in the snow. White ermine fur was used only by royalty and the high nobility. Animals were trapped by the tens of thousands or more every year. The small vair skins were so numerous that they were packed and transported in barrels. A hundred or more vair skins were required for lining a single gown. Larger skins were stacked and secured in bales. The value of furs was so great that some German merchants traveled to the trading station at Novgorod in the fall and stayed the winter so that they could obtain the best furs and ship them out the following spring. The fur trade was a key part of the Hanse federation's economy.

The skins of sable or marten were so valuable and so well recognized that they were sometimes accepted as currency. They were called "leather money." They originated in Novgorod, where they were traded with Hanse merchants for various goods. Surprisingly, they were also accepted as money in places as distant as Venice and Barcelona.

Wood, Metal, and Stone

In addition to food and clothing, wood, stone, and metal were essential materials in medieval Europe. They were widely traded and used for an array of purposes.

Wood

Wood in many different forms was in constant demand. Most buildings, such as houses, shops, and barns, were made of wood. Even some castles were made entirely of wood. Stone buildings also needed wood both during construction and when completed to make roof beams, interior walls, and doors. Additionally, while some use was made of peat, coal, and oils, wood was the primary fuel for the entire period.

Firewood

The largest demand for wood was for fuel. Homes were heated with wood. Wood, both as logs and in the form of charcoal, was also consumed in huge quantities by a number of industries (see illustration 3). For example, at the salt works at Salins in France, 11,000 tons of firewood was burned in a single year to boil brine to produce salt crystals. The wood came from the surrounding area but some areas exhausted their resources and supplies of firewood and charcoal were sometimes shipped in from long distances, even from overseas. Venice was one example of this. Besides needing fuel for its many residents to heat and cook with, Venice's famed glassworks consumed huge amounts of charcoal. The Venetian mainland near the city was gradually stripped of trees. Some were taken for ship building but most were cut down so they could be made into charcoal to feed the glassmakers' furnaces. By the mid–15th century, the deforestation was so severe that the formerly treed lands were eroding and the silt was running off into the lagoon and filling it in. More importantly, in the eyes of the Venetians, the supply of oak for ships, including the city's famed galleys, was running out. To deal with these problems, the government established a reforestation program in 1470. The program met with little success. Shipwrights had to go to woods far inland to find suitable timbers. As for glassmaking, the Venetians began importing wood from the east coast of the Adriatic Sea in Dalmatia. Vast numbers of trees were cut, reduced to charcoal, and shipped across the sea. This trade led to clear-cutting of Dalmatian forests with the same destructive consequences of erosion of the newly barren lands.

Venice was not alone in having a shortage of wood. For example, the industries and homes of the highly urbanized Low Countries required large amounts of firewood but local wood supplies were extremely limited. To meet the demand, firewood was imported from southeastern England. Even though it had to be shipped across the English Channel, it was still the most economical source available to the Low Countries.

Wood for Buildings

Besides firewood, forests produced the timbers and boards needed to construct buildings. For major works such as castles and cathedrals, very large timbers were needed for the rafters and framing of their roofs. Even by the 12th century, it was becoming difficult to find trees large enough for this use. One abbot in France credited his success in finding trees of suitable size for his abbey to divine guidance. Ultimately, increasing amounts of wood for building were shipped into England and elsewhere in northern Europe from Scandinavia and Poland.

Wood for Ships and the Military

Having an adequate supply of wood was essential for ship building. In much of Europe, trees suitable for use in ship building, especially for use as masts, became increasing difficult to find over the course of the Middle Ages. Forests closest to the coastlines were used first and, as these became depleted, sources further inland were sought out. There were also a few areas, such as in the Low Countries, which had always lacked significant forests. Regardless of the reason for the lack of trees for large timbers, many countries came to import wood from those regions that were still well-forested, primarily in Norway, Poland, and parts of northeast Germany. Commercial records such as customs accounts of duties levied on imports, along with archaeological finds, have confirmed that timbers from these regions were used in many ports around the North and Baltic Seas.

Having to import wood or have it transported from distant, inland forests increased the costs and potentially impeded ship building. This was a matter of concern not just to merchants but to governments as well. For many nations, an active commercial fleet was vital to their economies. Having large numbers of merchant ships was also a military matter. Only a few ships in the Middle Ages, such as the Viking long ship and the Italian war galley, were constructed especially for naval action. Instead, ships used for combat and for troop transport were merchant vessels that were pressed into naval service whenever needed. As mentioned previously, some countries did attempt to reforest areas and some did eventually build up an adequate reserve of trees after the Middle Ages but the importing of wood continued. Surprisingly, despite their shortages of wood, some Italian city-states continued to export wood. The most notable exporter was Venice, some of whose merchants continued to ship timbers to Moslem countries despite papal prohibitions. The Moslems used these timbers to build their fleets, which they then used in their wars against the Christian nations of the Mediterranean.

The military forces of England had a unique need for wood. The longbow, which became a key weapon of English forces in the late Middle Ages, was made primarily from yew. Domestic yew was preferred but there was too little to meet the demand so it was necessary to import the wood from Italy. Yew grown in Italy made superior bows. To ensure adequate supplies of yew, English merchants importing goods from Italy were encouraged and eventually required to include pieces of yew suitable for making bows in their cargos.

Pitch and Resin

Pitch and resin from pine trees were also imported along with wood for ships. They were used for caulking and waterproofing vessels.

Ashes

As well as timbers, firewood, and charcoal, wood was also traded as ashes. Ashes were imported from Poland and Russia. These ashes were from burning trees and other plants. They were processed to yield alkali in the form of lye, which could be used to produce soap for bleaching and cleaning cloth. Lye soap was also used for general cleaning, including for personal hygiene. Ashes were also imported from Syria to supply the Venetian glass industry. These ashes were made from burning shrubs unique to Syria and were used in the production of high-quality glass. Through the end of the Middle Ages, Venice controlled the trade in Syrian ashes to maintain its dominance in glass production.

METALS AND METALWORK

While the Middle Ages are often depicted as a primitive time, craftsmen throughout the period worked a variety of metals to create a vast array of items from pewter spoons and copper cooking pots to golden reliquaries and steel armor. Many production centers grew up near the mines where the metal ores were extracted but huge quantities of metal were transported, sometimes great distances, to reach the forges and foundries where they were made into objects.

Gold

Gold deposits are scarce in Europe. The Roman Empire had obtained its gold from mines in Wales, Spain, and parts of what are now Bulgaria and Romania. The rest was imported from Africa via Egypt. With the decline of the Roman Empire, the mines ceased production. The primary source of gold within medieval Europe was Hungary, which at that time included parts of what is now Slovakia. The Hungarian mines were recorded as producing gold as early as the 12th century but it was not until the early 14th century that a major lode was discovered in the mines near Kremnica in modern day Slovakia.

The supply of gold within Europe was extremely limited for most of the Middle Ages, and so it was imported throughout the period. Some of it was in the form of gold coins issued by Islamic countries while some came as nuggets, flakes, dust, or even finer powder in tightly sealed leather pouches from North Africa. But none of this gold was produced where the Europeans obtained it. Rather, it all originated in West Africa. In the early Middle Ages, the Ghana Empire controlled the gold-producing lands. Gold was transported north, across the Sahara Desert, and traded primarily for salt with the natives of North Africa. In the 13th century, the Mali Empire replaced the Ghana Empire but the trade continued, centered on the Malian capital of Timbuktu, and salt continued to be the primary trade good.

Europeans sought to cut out all the middlemen and trade directly with the West Africans for their gold. A Florentine adventurer allegedly reached Timbuktu at the end of the 15th century. However, the first documented European traveler to reach Timbuktu achieved his goal in 1826. Even if a medieval European trader did reach Timbuktu, it did not result in any lasting trade contacts. Portuguese explorations down the west coast of Africa began in the late 15th century but the Portuguese did not venture inland and did not reach the gold-producing regions. Thus, all trade for gold was conducted in cities along the North African coast, Egypt, and the Middle East. A variety of European products were traded for gold but one of the primary goods was silver. The Moslem lands lacked silver mines and needed silver for minting coins. Silver was so sought after that its value to the Moslems was frequently higher than its value in Europe, that is, a silver coin bought relatively more in the Middle East than it did in Europe. Moslem traders were often willing to exchange gold for silver at rates favorable to the European merchants. Unfortunately, this led to a constant drain of silver out of Europe. The full reason for this and its impact on trade are discussed in the section on trade imbalances.

Silver

Silver was mined in many locations around Europe. Like gold production, the collapse of the Roman Empire disrupted most silver-mining operations. However, unlike the gold mines, they went back into service relatively quickly and silver coinage never went out of circulation. Besides the reopening of the Roman mines, silver was found in several new locations such as in the Harz Mountains of central Germany in the late 10th century. Silver was the primary metal used for coins. It was also made into a wide variety of goods such as spoons, serving platters, and objects for churches.

Other Metals

Many other metals besides gold and silver were mined. While not "precious" metals, they were vital to the production of tools, armor, cookware, nails, and all the other metal goods that were essential to medieval society.

Iron

Iron was used throughout Europe although it was only mined in a limited number of locations during the Middle Ages. Northern Spain was one of the primary producers and exporters of iron. Merchants from across northern Europe imported Spanish iron. As well as bars of iron, the Spanish also produced and exported some iron goods, including anchors, nails, and the spiked combs that were essential for processing wool. Iron was also exported from lands near the Rhine River in Germany. These exports included finished iron or steel products such as tools, locks, wire, nails, needles, and weapons. Iron was also produced in Lombardy in northern Italy and in Austria. It was this iron that supplied the famed armor production centers in Milan and Brescia. Armor from these two cities came to dominate the armor trade and was sold throughout Europe. Milan alone was capable of producing thousands of complete suits of armor as well as helmets and breastplates every year. Some of the armor was carefully crafted for elite customers while many others were mass-produced plain armor made for ordinary men-at-arms. There were other production centers in Germany at Cologne, and later Passau, Regensburg, Landshut, Augsburg, and Nuremberg, that also forged armor that was widely exported. Swords were made in Toledo using iron from the nearby mines of northwestern Spain. Sölingen in Germany was another producer of high-quality blades. Even today, Sölingen is a source for high-quality knives.

Tin

Tin was a surprisingly important metal. It was required for producing bronze and pewter. It was also used to plate iron objects to make them rustproof. In classical antiquity, Cornwall was the sole source of tin in Europe and the tin it exported fueled the creation of bronze in the Mediterranean basin. Cornwall remained the sole significant source of tin in medieval Europe. Throughout the period,

Cornish tin was exported to every part of Europe.

Zinc

Zinc was another essential base metal. Combined with copper, it produced brass. Sources of zinc were rare and large quantities were needed for making brass. The primary site of zinc mining was in Flanders and northwest Germany and several cities in the region produced brass. Being close to the supply of zinc was so important that brass forges and foundries were established there rather than at the sources of copper. Despite the expense and inconvenience, the heavy bars of copper were shipped in from mines near Goslar, Germany, over 200 miles away. The Flemish city of Dinant became synonymous with the industry and *Dinanderie* became a byword for brassware. Brass goods from Dinant and the other cities were exported across Europe. During the 13th century, brass pans, pots, and cauldrons began to replace pottery cookware. Brass was also used to make plates and other tableware as well as candlesticks and many other household items.

STONE

Stone was another heavy commodity that was traded both locally and internationally. As previously discussed, building stone was often shipped from quarries to construction sites. At times, the distance between the two was surprisingly far. For example, marble from Caen in France was exported to England and used in the construction of cathedrals and other prestigious buildings. In Italy, marble from the famed Carrara quarries was used throughout the northern and central parts of the country. In Denmark, some of the stones used to build the cathedral at Ribe were imported from Andernach in Germany. This required moving the stone more than 200 miles down the Rhine River and then several hundred miles more across the North Sea. More mundanely, millstones cut from volcanic rock in western Germany in the Middle Ages have

been found at locations around northern Europe, even as far away as England.

Luxury Goods

Royalty, nobility, and the highest ranks of the clergy also bought a wide selection of other luxuries in addition to expensive food, cloth, and furs. These people had the wealth to afford these items. There was also an element of conspicuous consumption. They wanted to display their wealth and importance by having things that ordinary people could not have. These included jewelry and works of art.

Paris was a noted center of jewelry production. Jewelry was sometimes set with semiprecious stones from within Europe, including amber from the eastern shores of the Baltic. For the wealthier, diamonds, emeralds, sapphires, or rubies from Sri Lanka and southern India and pearls from the coast of Sri Lanka or from the Strait of Hormuz at the mouth of the Persian Gulf were used. Pearls were also sewn onto women's clothing to create expensive and beautiful garments.

Works of art were created using a variety of mediums. Carved ivory objects made from elephant tusks were popular. These items were of both secular and sacred subjects. Workshops in Paris produced statuettes of Saint Mary and miniatures depicting the life of Christ along with small caskets carved with scenes of courtly love.

In the late Middle Ages, the wealthy sometimes commissioned paintings. These were always of religious subjects. Many were of saints or events in the life of Christ and the patrons were often depicted kneeling in prayer in the foreground of the scene. Painters from Italy and, later, from the Low Countries became the primary producers of this type of art. For those who did not want or could not afford such personalized pieces of art, portraits of Christ, Saint Mary, and other saints and religious subjects were produced in many cities in Italy, particularly in the north in Siena and Florence. While not mass produced, these works were painted in numerous studios and yielded a steady supply for the art market. The mercenary nature of this trade is reflected in directions from an Italian merchant in France to his agent back in Italy. The merchant needed paintings to sell and told his agent to look for painters and studios that were in financial trouble and buy up all their work at low prices.

Tapestries and painted cloths were other popular decorative artworks. The main production center for tapestries was around Arras in Flanders. The tapestries were woven from fine wools by expert craftsmen. They were sold throughout Europe to adorn the walls of palaces and castles. Painted cloths were a substitute for tapestries. As their name suggests, these were large cloths that were painted with scenes similar to those found on tapestries. They appear to have generally been cheaper than tapestries and some were listed as being used as curtains, but many were still works of art in their own right and were suitable for the halls of dukes and other ranking nobles. As with tapestries, most painted cloths appear to have been created in Flanders and both were widely exported.

HYGIENE ITEMS

The elite of medieval society also bought goods for their personal hygiene. One such item was mastic from the Greek island of Chios. Mastic is a resin collected from a shrub that is unique to the Mediterranean basin. It was chewed like modern chewing gum and was believed to freshen breath and whiten teeth. Modern research has found that it may have value for dental care. Mastic was exported from Chios by Italian merchants and sold to wealthy people concerned with good oral hygiene. While mastic was very expensive because of its limited sources, soap was cheaper and more plentiful. White soap made with olive oil in Castile in northern Spain was used by nobility throughout Europe as early as the 13th century. Italian cities copied the Castilian soap and sold it as well. It was milder than the ordinary soap made with tallow and wood ashes that was produced locally throughout Europe.

EXOTIC ANIMALS

There was traffic in a number of exotic animals during the period. Falconry was a popular pastime for the elite of society and birds were captured and sometimes shipped long distances from their native habitats to noble customers. The most extreme example is the trafficking in gyrfalcons. These large birds of prey were captured in Iceland and shipped to Norway. Merchants bought them there and sent them to Bruges. From there, they were sold in London, Paris, Avignon and cities in Italy. They were owned only by the elite. They were suitable as gifts to Moslem rulers and were brought to places as distant as Baghdad.

Animals from Africa were imported to Europe as well. Some of the most noted were apes, often Barbary apes from North Africa. A tract written in England in 1430 that complained about the state of the English economy and the decline of its shipping industry mentions apes among the useless and expensive imports that were, in the opinion of the tract's author, hurting the nation's economy.

BIBLIOGRAPHY

Abrahams, Israel. *Jewish Life in the Middle Ages.* Philadelphia: Jewish Publication Society, 1896 (1993 reprint).

Adler, Elkan Nathan. *Jewish Travellers in the Middle Ages.* New York: Dover Publications, 1987.

Ayton, Andrew. "Arms, Armour, and Horses." In *Medieval Warfare: A History*, edited by Maurice Keen. New York: Oxford University Press, 1999.

Backhouse, Janet. *The Luttrell Psalter.* London: The British Library, 1989.

Barker, Juliet. *Agincourt— Henry V and the Battle That Made England.* New York: Little, Brown, 2005.

Basing, Patricia. *Trades and Crafts in Medieval Manuscripts.* New York: New Amsterdam Books, 1990.

Bautier, Robert-Henri. *The Economic Development of Medieval Europe.* Translated by Heather Karolyi from the French. London: Thames and Hudson, 1971.

Beaver, Patrick. *A History of Lighthouses.* Secaucus, NJ: Citadel, 1973.

Belke, K. "Roads and Travel in Macedonia and Thrace in the Middle and Late Byzantine Period." In *Travel in the Byzantine World*, edited by Ruth Macrides. Aldershot, UK: Ashgate/Society for the Promotion of Byzantine Studies, 2002.

Berggren, Lars, Nils Hybel, and Annette Landen, eds. *Cogs, Cargoes, and Commerce.* Toronto: Pontifical Institute of Mediaeval Studies, 2002.

Binski, Paul. *Medieval Death.* Ithaca, NY: Cornell University Press, 1996.

Blair, John, ed. *Waterways and Canal-Building in Medieval England.* Oxford: Oxford University Press, 2007.

Blair, John, and Nigel Ramsey, eds. *English Medieval Industries.* London: Hambledon and London, 2001.

Campbell, I. C. "The Lateen Sail in World History." *Journal of World History* 6, no. 1 (1995): 1–23.

Campbell, Tony. "Portolan Charts from the Late Thirteenth Century to 1500." In *The History of Cartography, Volume 1*, edited by J. B. Harley and David Woodward. Chicago: University of Chicago Press, 1987.

Casson, Lionel. *Illustrated History of Ships & Boats.* Garden City, NY: Doubleday, 1964.

Clark, John, ed. *Medieval Finds from Excavations in London. 5: The Medieval Horse and Its Equipment,* c.1150–c.1450. Woodbridge, UK: Boydell Press, 2004.

Clutton-Brock, Juliet. *Horsepower.* London: Natural History Museum Publications, 1992.

Collins, Marie, and Virginia Davis. *A Medieval Book of Seasons.* New York: Harper Collins, 1992.

Contamine, Philippe. *War in the Middle Ages.* Translated by Michael Jones from the French. Oxford: Basil Blackwell, 1990.

Cook, Martin. *Medieval Bridges.* Princes Risborough, Buckinghamshire: Shire Publications, 1998.

Cummins, John. *The Hound and the Hawk: The Art of Medieval Hunting.* New York: St. Martin's Press, 1988.

Dalché, P. Gautier. "Portulans and the Byzantine World." In *Travel in the Byzantine World*, edited by Ruth Macrides. Aldershot, UK: Ashgate/Society for the Promotion of Byzantine Studies, 2002.

Daniell, Christopher. *Death and Burial in Medieval England.* London: Routledge, 1997.

Daumas, Maurice. *A History of Technology and Invention, Volume I.* Translated by Eileen B. Hennessy from the French. New York: Crown Publishers, 1969.

Davies, Hugh. *Roads in Roman Britain.* Stroud, Gloucestershire: Tempus, 2002.

Davis, R. H. C. *The Medieval Warhorse.* London: Thames and Hudson, 1989.

Davis, Robert C. *Christian Slaves, Muslim Masters.* New York: Palgrave Macmillan, 2003.

Delbruck, Hans. *History of the Art of War, Volume III: Medieval Warfare.* Translated by Walter J. Renfroe from the German. Lincoln: University of Nebraska Press, 1990.

Dilke, O. A. W. "Cartography in the Ancient World: An Introduction." In *The History of Cartography, Volume 1*, edited by J. B. Harley and David Woodward. Chicago: University of Chicago Press, 1987.

_____. *Greek and Roman Maps.* Ithaca, NY: Cornell University Press, 1985.

Dollinger, Philippe. *The German Hansa.* Translated from the French and edited by D. S. Ault and S. H. Steinberg. Stanford, CA: Stanford University Press, 1970.

Dyer, Christopher. *Standards of Living in the Later Middle Ages: Social Change in England c. 1270–1520.* Cambridge: Cambridge University Press, 1990.

Eckold, Martin. *Fluesse und Kanaele, Die Geschichte der deutschen Wasserstrassen.* Hamburg, Germany: DSV Verlag, 1998.

Egan, Geoff. *Medieval Finds from Excavation. 6: The Medieval Household, Daily Living c.1150–c.1450.* London: HMSO, 1998.

Egbert, Virginia Wylie. *On the Bridges of Mediaeval Paris.* Princeton, NJ: Princeton University Press, 1974.

Ellmers, Detlev. "The Cog of Bremen and Related Boats." In *The Archaeology of Medieval Ships and Harbours in Northern Europe,* edited by Sean McGrail. Greenwich, UK. National Maritime Museum, 1979.

Fabri, Felix. *The Book of the Wanderings of Felix Fabri (circa 1480–1483 A.D.).* Translated by Aubrey Stewart from the Latin. London: Palestine Pilgrims' Text Society, 1896.

Favier, Jean. *Gold and Spices: The Rise of Commerce in the Middle Ages.* Translated by Caroline Higgitt from the French. New York: Holmes & Meier, 1998.

Firebaugh, W. C. *The Inns of Greece and Rome.* Chicago: Pascal Covici, 1928.

Fitz Stephen, William. *Norman London.* New York: Italica Press, 1990.

Flower, Raymond. *The History of Skiing and Other Winter Sports.* New York: Methuen, 1976.

Forbes, R. J., and E. J. Dijksterhuis. *A History of Science and Technology.* Baltimore, MD: Pelican Books, 1963.

Forey, Alan. *The Military Orders from the Twelfth to the Early Fourteenth Centuries.* Toronto: University of Toronto Press, 1992.

Galloway, James A., Derek Keene, and Margaret Murphy. "Fuelling the City: Production and Distribution of Firewood and Fuel in London's Region, 1290–1400." *Economic History Review* 49, no. 3 (1996): 447–472.

Gans, Paul J. "The Medieval Horse Harness: Revolution or Evolution?" In *Villard's Legacy,* edited by M.-T. Zenner. Aldershot, UK: Ashgate, 2004.

Gardiner, Mark. "Hythes, Small Ports, and Other Landing Places in Later Medieval England." In *Waterways and Canal-Building in Medieval England,* edited by John Blair. Oxford: Oxford University Press, 2007.

Gardiner, Robert, and John Morrison, eds. *The Age of the Galley.* Annapolis, MD: Naval Institute Press, 1995.

Gardiner, Robert, and Richard W. Unger, eds. *Cogs, Caravels and Galleons.* Edison, NJ: Chartwell Books, 2000.

Graham-Campbell, James, ed. *The Viking World.* New Haven, CT: Ticknor and Fields, 1980.

Grew, Francis, and Margrethe de Neergaard. *Medieval Finds from Excavation. 2: Shoes and Pattens.* London: HMSO, 1988.

Gurney, Alan. *Compass.* New York: Norton, 2004.

Hagen, Ann. *A Second Handbook of Anglo-Saxon Food: Production and Distribution.* Frithgarth, Norfolk: Anglo-Saxon Books, 2002.

Hammel-Kiesow, Rolf. "Lübeck and the Baltic Trade in Bulk Goods for the North Sea Region, 1150–1400." In *Cogs, Cargoes, and Commerce,* edited by Lars Berggren, Nils Hybel, and Annette Landen. Toronto: Pontifical Institute of Mediaeval Studies, 2002.

Harley, J. B., and David Woodward, eds. *The History of Cartography, Volume 1.* Chicago: University of Chicago Press, 1987.

Harvey, P. D. A. "Local and Regional Cartography in Medieval Europe." In *The History of Cartography, Volume 1,* edited by J. B. Harley and David Woodward. Chicago: University of Chicago Press, 1987.

_____. "Medieval Maps: An Introduction." In *The History of Cartography, Volume 1,* edited by J. B. Harley and David Woodward. Chicago: University of Chicago Press, 1987.

Harris, Susan E. *Horse Gaits, Balance and Movement.* New York: Howell Book House, 1993.

Harrison, David. *The Bridges of Medieval England.* New York: Oxford University Press, 2007.

Hendrick, Bonnie L. *International Encyclopedia of Horse Breeds.* Norman: University of Oklahoma Press, 1995.

Herlihy, David. *Pisa in the Early Renaissance.* New Haven, CT: Yale University Press, 1958

Historisches Museum der Pfalz. *The Jews of Europe in the Middle Ages.* Speyer, 2005.

Hooke, Della. "Use of Waterways in Anglo-Saxon England." In *The Archaeology of Medieval Ships and Harbours in Northern Europe,* edited by Sean McGrail. Greenwich, UK: National Maritime Museum, 1979.

Hunt, Edwin, and James Murray. *A History of Business in Medieval Europe 1200–1550.* Cambridge: Cambridge University Press, 1999.

Hutchinson, Gillian. *Medieval Ships and Shipping.* London: Leicester University Press, 1994.

Icher, Françoise. *Building the Great Cathedrals.* Translated by Anthony Zielonka from the French. New York: Harry N. Abrams, 1998.

Keen, Maurice, ed. *Medieval Warfare: A History.* New York: Oxford University Press, 1999.

Kerr, Nigel, and Mary Kerr. *A Guide to Medieval Sites in Britain.* London: Grafton Books, 1988.

Lane, Frederic C. *Venetian Ships and Shipbuilders of the Renaissance.* Baltimore, MD: Johns Hopkins Press, 1934.

_____. *Venice and History.* Baltimore, MD: Johns Hopkins Press, 1966.

Langdon, John. "The Efficiency of Inland Water Transport in Medieval England." In *Waterways and Canal-Building in Medieval England,* edited by John Blair. Oxford: Oxford University Press, 2007.

_____. *Horses, Oxen and Technological Innovation.* New York: Cambridge University Press, 1986.

Leighton, Albert C. *Transportation and Communication in Early Medieval Europe, A.D. 500–1100.* Newton Abbot: David & Charles, 1972.

Macrides, Ruth, ed. *Travel in the Byzantine World.* Aldershot, UK: Ashgate/Society for the Promotion of Byzantine Studies, 2002.

McGrail, Sean, ed. *The Archaeology of Medieval Ships and Harbours in Northern Europe.* Greenwich, UK: National Maritime Museum, 1979.

McGrail, Sean, and Roy Switsur. "Medieval Logboats of the River Mersey." In *The Archaeology of Medieval Ships and Harbours in Northern Europe*, edited by Sean McGrail. Greenwich, UK: National Maritime Museum, 1979.

Milne, Gustav. *The Port of Medieval London.* Stroud, Gloucestershire: Tempus, 2003.

Newman, Paul B. *Daily Life in the Middle Ages.* Jefferson, NC: McFarland, 2001.

Olsen, Sandra L., ed. *Horses through Time.* Boulder, CO: Roberts Rinehart Publishers for Carnegie Museum of Natural History, 1996.

Peters, Tom F. *Transitions in Engineering.* Basel: Birkhäuser Verlag, 1987.

Pognon, Edmond. *Les Trés Riches Heures du Duc De Berry.* Translated by David Macrae from the French. Geneva: Productions Liber S.A., 1987.

Pryor, J. H. "Types of Ships and Their Performance Capabilities." In *Travel in the Byzantine World*, edited by Ruth Macrides. Aldershot, UK: Ashgate/Society for the Promotion of Byzantine Studies, 2002.

Riche, Pierre. *Daily Life in the World of Charlemagne.* Translated by Jo Ann McNamara from the French. Philadelphia: University of Pennsylvania Press, 1978.

Roesdahl, Else, and David Wilson, gen. eds. *From Viking to Crusader.* New York: Rizzoli, 1992.

Rogers, Clifford J. *War Cruel and Sharp: English Strategy Under Edward III, 1327–1360.* Woodbridge, Suffolk: Boydell, 2000.

Russell, Jeffrey Burton. *Inventing the Flat Earth: Columbus and Modern Historians.* New York: Praeger, 1991.

Saunders, Frances. *The Devil's Broker: Seeking Gold, God, and Glory in Fourteenth Century Italy.* New York: Harper Collins, 2005.

Silverberg, Robert. *Bridges* (1966). In *History of Technology*, edited by Charles Singer et al. Oxford: Clarendon Press, 1956.

Spufford, Peter. *Power and Profit: The Merchant in Medieval Europe.* New York: Thames & Hudson, 2002.

Staccioli, Romolo Augusto. *The Roads of the Romans.* Los Angeles: Getty Publications, 2003.

Swanick, Lois Ann. "An Analysis of Navigational Instruments in the Age of Exploration: 15th Century to Mid–17th Century." Masters thesis, Texas A&M University, 2005.

Sweeney, Del, ed. *Agriculture in the Middle Ages.* Philadelphia: University of Pennsylvania Press, 1995.

Thomas, Christopher. *The Archaeology of Medieval London.* Stroud, Gloucestershire: Sutton, 2002.

Trow-Smith, Robert. *A History of British Livestock Husbandry to 1700.* London: Routledge and Kegan Paul, 1957.

Tunis, Edwin. *Colonial Craftsmen.* Cleveland, OH: World Publishing, 1965.

Tyler, J. E. *The Alpine Passes: The Middle Ages (962–1250).* Oxford: Basil Blackwell, 1930.

Unger, Richard. *Beer in the Middle Ages and Renaissance.* Philadelphia: University of Pennsylvania Press, 2004.
_____. *The Ship in the Medieval Economy, 600–1600.* Montreal: McGill-Queen's University Press, 1980.

van Doornick, F., Jr. "The Byzantine Ship at Serce Limani." In *Travel in the Byzantine World*, edited by Ruth Macrides. Aldershot, UK: Ashgate/Society for the Promotion of Byzantine Studies, 2002.

van Tilburg, Cornelis. *Traffic and Congestion in the Roman Empire.* New York: Routledge, 2007.

Verdon, Jean. *Travel in the Middle Ages.* Translated by George Holoch from the French. Notre Dame, IN: University of Notre Dame Press, 2003.

Vernet, Joan. "The Scientific World of the Crown of Aragon Under James I." *Quaderns de la Mediterrania*, no. 12, 2009.

Warner, Philip. *Sieges of the Middle Ages.* New York: Barnes & Noble, 1994.

Webb, Diana. *Medieval European Pilgrimage.* Basingstoke, Hampshire: Palgrave, 2002.

Willan, T. S. *River Navigation in England, 1600–1750.* London: Frank Cass, 1964.

Wolfegg, Christoph. *Venus and Mars: The World of the Medieval Housebook.* Translated by Almuth Seebohm from the German. Munich: Prestel Verlag, 1998.

Woodward, David. "Medieval Mappaemundi." In *The History of Cartography, Volume 1*, edited by J. B. Harley and David Woodward. Chicago: University of Chicago Press, 1987.

Websites

Utrecht Psalter, electronic facsimile — http://psalter.library. uu.nl/
Horse breeds — www.ansi.okstate.edu/breeds/horses/
Shire horses — www.shire-horse.org.uk/
London Bridge — www.oldlondonbridge.com

INDEX

Numbers in **_bold italic_** indicate pages with illustrations.